POLICE AND COMMUNITY IN CHICAGO

Recent Titles
STUDIES IN CRIME AND PUBLIC POLICY
Michael Tonry and Norval Morris, *General Editors*

Can Gun Control Work?
James B. Jacobs

Penal Populism and Public Opinion: Lessons from Five Countries
Julian V. Roberts, Loretta J. Stalans, David Indermaur, and Mike Hough

Mafia Brotherhoods: Organized Crime, Italian Style
Letizia Paoli

When Prisoners Come Home: Parole and Prisoner Reentry
Joan Petersilia

The Contradictions of American Capital Punishment
Franklin E. Zimring

*Thinking about Crime: Sense and Sensibility
in American Penal Culture*
Michael Tonry

Juvenile Justice in the Making
David S. Tanenhaus

Fallen Blue Knights: Controlling Police Corruption
Sanja Kutnjak Ivković

Changing the Guard: Developing Democratic Police Abroad
David H. Bayley

Locked Out: Felon Disenfranchisement and American Democracy
Jeff Manza and Christopher Uggen

Street Gang Patterns and Policies
Malcolm W. Klein and Cheryl L. Maxson

Police and Community in Chicago: A Tale of Three Cities
Wesley G. Skogan

POLICE AND COMMUNITY IN CHICAGO

A Tale of Three Cities

Wesley G. Skogan

UNIVERSITY PRESS

2006

OXFORD
UNIVERSITY PRESS

Oxford University Press, Inc., publishes works that further
Oxford University's objective of excellence
in research, scholarship, and education.

Oxford   New York
Auckland   Cape Town   Dar es Salaam   Hong Kong   Karachi
Kuala Lumpur   Madrid   Melbourne   Mexico City   Nairobi
New Delhi   Shanghai   Taipei   Toronto

With offices in
Argentina   Austria   Brazil   Chile   Czech Republic   France   Greece
Guatemala   Hungary   Italy   Japan   Poland   Portugal   Singapore
South Korea   Switzerland   Thailand   Turkey   Ukraine   Vietnam

Published by Oxford University Press, Inc.
198 Madison Avenue, New York, New York 10016

www.oup.com

Oxford is a registered trademark of Oxford University Press

Library of Congress Cataloging-in-Publication Data
Skogan, Wesley G.
Police and community in Chicago : a tale of three cities/by Wesley G. Skogan.
    p. cm. — (Studies in crime and public policy)
ISBN-13 978-0-19-515458-0
ISBN 0-19-515458-4
1. Community policing—Illinois—Chicago. 2. Crime prevention—Illinois—
Chicago—Citizen participation. 3. Chicago (Ill.). Police Dept. I. Title. II. Series.
HV7936.C83S564   2006
363.2'30977311—dc22   2005032359

9 8 7 6 5 4 3 2 1

Printed in the United States of America
on acid-free paper

Acknowledgments

This book reports the findings of a study that took more than a decade to complete. It took that long because the Chicago police kept inventing new and interesting things to do, and it never seemed opportune to call the project to a halt. Most of the financial support for the evaluation came from the National Institute of Justice and the Illinois Criminal Justice Information Authority. Their directors—Jeremy Travis, Candice Kane, and Dennis Nowicki—were remarkably patient, as was our NIJ grant monitor Lois Mock. The evaluation twice received timely funding—when we were broke— from the John D. and Catherine T. MacArthur Foundation, which has a special interest in its hometown. Susan Lloyd was responsible for keeping us afloat. The independence of the research from the politics of the city and the police department was ultimately assured because we could secure our own long-term funding for the project.

Just as remarkable is the endorsement the evaluation received from the City of Chicago. From the mayor on down, the city supported the concept of an independent review, and the police department made that commitment a reality. We were able to interview anyone we wanted and attend any meeting or event that seemed relevant. We had easy access to department databases and facilities. Three chiefs of police served during our time, and they were all supporters of the evaluation: Matt Rodriguez, Terry Hillard, and Phillip Cline. I would like to identify others in city government and the police department who were important in this effort, but the list is too long and half of them have already retired—a liability of our having remained "in the field" for so long.

Over the years almost eighty people worked on various aspects of the study. They ranged from summer undergraduates to professional researchers who were with us full time. The two most important were there from the beginning to the end: Susan Hartnett and Jill DuBois. There is nothing in this book that they did not contribute to. Jill DuBois was the study team's editorial director, and she polished many sections of this book. The other full-time staff members were

Jennifer Comey, Aimee Fagan, Erik Gudell, Marianne Kaiser, Justine Lovig, Lynn Steiner, and Karla Twedt-Ball. The evaluation was conducted from Northwestern University's Institute for Policy Research. The Institute had two directors over this period, Burton Weisbrod and Fay Lomax Cook, and they both gave us a great deal of encouragement and support.

Contents

List of Illustrations   ix

1   Community Policing   3

2   Crime, Police, and the Three Chicagos   21

3   Reengineering the Police   53

4   Involving the Community   101

5   Representing the Community   139

6   Tackling Neighborhood Problems   177

7   Trends in Neighborhood Problems   211

8   Trends in Crime and Fear   235

9   Police and the Public   271

10   How Did Chicago Do?   305

Notes   327

Bibliography   331

Index   343

List of Illustrations

Figures

Figure 2.1   Trends in Population by Race, 1950–2004   22

Figure 2.2   Race and Residence in Chicago, 1990   24

Figure 2.3   Trends in Crime in Chicago, 1980–1991   34

Figure 2.4   Crime Rates by Race, 1991   37

Figure 2.5   Crime, Disorder, and Decay Problems by Race, 1994   40

Figure 2.6   Confidence in the Police by Race, 1994   46

Figure 2.7   Police Views of Their Role in Community Policing, 1993   49

Figure 3.1   Chicago's Problem-Solving Model   71

Figure 3.2   CAPS Service Request Form   78

Figure 4.1   Sources of CAPS Awareness, 1996–2003   109

Figure 4.2   Trends in Beat Meeting Attendance, 1995–2003   113

Figure 4.3   Community Engagement and CAPS Involvement, 1998   121

Figure 4.4   Frequent Beat Meeting Participants, 2003   126

Figure 5.1   Demographic Representation at Beat Meetings, 1998   151

Figure 5.2   Perceptions of Problems among Matched Meeting Participants and the General Public, 1998   157

Figure 5.3   Interest Representation at Beat Meetings, 1998   158

Figure 5.4   Police and Participant Priorities   164

Figure 5.5   Neighborhood Capacity and Crime, 2001–2003   171

Figure 6.1   Beat Needs and Service Delivery, 1997–1998   195

Figure 6.2   Correlates of CAPS Activism   205

Figure 6.3   Citizens' Priorities and Service Delivery Patterns   206

Figure 7.1   Trends in Physical Decay by Race, 1994–2003   213

Figure 7.2   Trends in Social Disorder by Race, 1994–2003   220

Figure 7.3   Areas of Latino Concentration, 2003   227

Figure 7.4   Language, Latino Concentration, and Neighborhood Problems, 1994–2003   228

Figure 7.5   Trends in Survey and Predicted Disorder and Decay, Latinos, 1994–2003   232

Figure 8.1   Trends in Recorded Crime, 1991–2003   240

Figure 8.2   Trends in Crime by Race, 1991–2003   243

Figure 8.3   High-Rate Robbery Beats, 1991–1992 and 2001–2002   245

Figure 8.4   Crime Problem Trends by Race, 1994–2003   249

Figure 8.5   Language, Latino Concentration, Poverty, and Crime Problems, 1994–2003   252

Figure 8.6   Trends in Fear by Age, Gender, Home Ownership, and Income   259

Figure 8.7   Trends in Fear by Race and Language   261

Figure 8.8   Trends in Survey and Predicted Fear   266

Figure 8.9   Chicago and Big-City Trends in Crime, 1991–2003   269

Figure 9.1   Trends in Confidence in the Police by Race,
              1993–2003   280

Figure 9.2   Personal Factors and Confidence in the Police,
              2001–2003   285

Figure 9.3   Trends in Confidence by Age, Affluence, and
              Language, 1994–2003   286

Figure 9.4   Age-Race-Sex Distribution of Stops by Police,
              2001–2003   295

Figure 9.5   Survey and Predicted Trends in Confidence in
              Police   302

Figure 10.1   Cumulative Beat Meeting Turnout Rates by
              Race, 1995–2003   312

Figure 10.2   Trends in Crime and Fear by Race,
              1994–2003   315

Figure 10.3   Trends in Disorder and Decay by Race,
              1994–2003   318

Figure 10.4   Trends in Confidence in the Police by Race,
              1994–2003   321

Figure 10.5   Trends in Latino Representation, 1998 and
              2002   323

Tables

Table 4.1   Personal Background and Awareness of CAPS,
             1996–2003   105

Table 4.2   Social and Economic Correlates of Beat Meeting
             Turnout, 2002   116

Table 4.3   Topics Discussed at Beat Meetings, 1998   129

Table 5.1   Agenda Setting, Monitoring the Police,
             and Mobilizing the Public, 1995, 1998,
             and 2002   143

Table 6.1   Beat Meeting Participant Activism   202

Table 6.2   Correlates of Beat Service Delivery Rates   207

Table 7.1   Hierarchical Models of Physical Decay and
             Social Disorder, Latinos 1994–2003   230

Table 8.1   Fear, Personal Factors, Neighborhood
             Conditions, and Confidence in the Police,
             1994–2003   263

Table 9.1   Hierarchical Models of Confidence in the
             Police   290

POLICE AND COMMUNITY
IN CHICAGO

ONE

Community Policing

Community policing is the most important development in law enforcement in the past quarter century. Cities across the country report that they are moving toward this new model, which supplements traditional crime fighting with problem-solving and prevention-oriented approaches that emphasize the role of the public in helping set police priorities. So popular is the concept with politicians, city managers, and the general public that few police chiefs want to be caught without an initiative they can point to. One of those cities moving toward this new model is Chicago, which developed the most prominent big-city neighborhood-oriented program in the nation. It features extensive resident involvement, a problem-solving approach toward tackling chronic crime and disorder problems, and coordination between police and a wide range of partner agencies. Police and civic leaders come from around the world to see it in operation. It is a political program, conceived in the mayor's office as a response to mounting crime in the early 1990s, when violence reached the highest point in the city's history. But despite these origins, the city's response was to turn toward the community rather than make a hard right turn in the direction of tougher enforcement. Embracing the "broken windows" theory of neighborhood decline, it deploys a network of volunteers, community organizations, and city service agencies to help fix the windows, not just arrest people. In the neighborhoods, thousands of residents meet monthly with the police who work in their area to review the status of ongoing problems and identify new priorities for police and community action. Politicians running for local offices know that putting "community-policing activist" on their resumes is an important credential. Unlike many places, in Chicago, community policing is not the police department's program; it is the city's program.

This book uses Chicago as a laboratory to address several fundamental questions about the reality of the community-policing movement. First, can police departments—and especially *big* departments—

really change? Dorothy Guyot (1991) once described changing police departments as "bending granite," and she did not think it could be done. The forces resisting change are strong at all levels of policing. Community policing runs counter to police culture and the self-image of many officers. The sergeants, who supervise officers in the field, never practiced it themselves. Union-organized resistance among the rank and file, and the unwillingness of top managers schooled in a command-and-control tradition to give up that control conspire against its implementation. Community-policing opponents can count on friendly politicians to stir up fear that the community is being put at risk by venturing into this "social experiment." Yet Chicago, with the nation's second-largest police department, committed itself to changing the entire organization and even the rest of city government in order to support community policing.

The second question is can it work? The book reports the findings of a twelve-year evaluation of the city's program that addressed this issue. Assessing the effectiveness of a program involves examining all of its fundamental goals, and Chicago had several. The city chose to tackle a broad range of neighborhood problems, not just crime, and it aimed to do so by mobilizing neighborhood activists and building their capacity for self-help. The mayor wanted to improve the effectiveness with which his service agencies met neighborhood needs, and linking it service delivery to community policing advanced that agenda. Police hoped that along the way they could heal the breach that had opened between them and residents of the city's poorest neighborhoods, for the number of white residents in the city was dropping fast and the city's remaining taxpayers had less affection for the police. But could breaching the divide between police and community be accomplished equally well in the city's white, black, and brown communities? In light of the huge disparities in the life chances of the city's residents, there was ample reason to be skeptical that this program would be any more effective than others in the past. Chicago is a particularly suitable site for addressing racial disparities. African Americans constitute the largest group in Chicago, and it is also home to one of the country's largest and fastest-growing Mexican American populations. Latinos are the nation's biggest immigrant group, and the research described here found ample reason to fear for how well police can reach out and serve their interests. As ensuing chapters will document, this was the greatest shortcoming of Chicago's community-policing effort.

What Is Community Policing?

Whatever it is, community policing is certainly popular. In a 1997 survey of police departments conducted by the Police Foundation, 85 percent reported they had adopted community policing or were in the process of doing so (Skogan 2004). Bigger cities that were included in the survey (those with populations greater than one hundred thousand) all claimed in the survey to have adopted community policing—half by 1991 and the other half since. This group included both urban giants and less populous places like Akron, Richmond, Mobile, and Jersey City. By 2000, a federal survey with a much larger sample found that more than 90 percent of departments in cities with more than 250,000 in population reported having full-time, trained community-policing officers in the field (Bureau of Justice Statistics 2003).

What do cities that claim they are "doing community policing" actually do? In some places community policing is in the hands of special neighborhood officers, whereas in other cities it involves the transformation of the entire police department. In some communities, residents participate in aggressive Neighborhood Watch patrols as part of their city's program, though in many more communities, public involvement is limited to asking citizens to call 911 quickly when they see something suspicious. Departments also point to a long list of activities they have underway. Under the rubric of community policing, officers patrol on foot (in the 1997 survey, 75 percent listed this) and on horses, bicycles, or even Segways. Departments train civilians in police procedures, open small neighborhood storefront offices, conduct surveys to measure community satisfaction, canvass door-to-door to identify local problems, publish newsletters, conduct drug education projects, and work with municipal agencies to enforce health and safety regulations.

However, community policing is not defined by these kinds of activities. Projects and operational tactics come and go, and they should, as conditions change. Communities with distinctive problems and different resources to bring to bear against them should try various things. Community policing is not a set of specific projects; rather, it involves changing decision-making processes and creating new cultures within police departments. It is an organizational strategy that leaves setting priorities and the means of achieving them largely to residents and the police who serve in their neighborhoods. Community policing is a process rather than a product.

Across the nation it has proved to have three core strategic components: decentralization, citizen involvement, and problem solving. In practice these three dimensions are densely interrelated. Departments that shortchange even one of them will not field a very effective program.

The first common feature, administrative decentralization, is closely linked to the implementation of community policing. More responsibility for identifying and responding to chronic crime and disorder problems can be delegated to midlevel district commanders. Departments have experimented with how to structure and manage a decentralization plan that gives midlevel managers real responsibility while holding them accountable for their success. Here community policing intersects with another movement in law enforcement, that of a culture of systematic performance measurement and managerial accountability. Like many cities, Chicago adopted its own version of New York City's CompStat, a management accountability process that scrutinizes unit effectiveness. Unlike New York, however, Chicago's version explicitly supported community policing as well as crime fighting. In addition, more responsibility for identifying and responding to community problems may be delegated to individual patrol officers and their sergeants, who are, in turn, encouraged to take the initiative in finding ways to deal with a broad range of problems specific to the communities where they work. Sometimes there are also moves to flatten the structure of departments by compressing the rank structure in order to shed layers of bureaucracy and speed communication and decision making within the organization. Decentralization is adopted not only so police can become more proactive and more preventive but also so that they can respond efficiently to problems of different magnitudes and complexities. Under the old model, marching orders for the police traditionally came from two sources: calls from the public concerning individual incidents, and citywide initiatives or programs originating at police headquarters or even city hall. Departments were not organized to respond systematically to the organized groups and community institutions that constitute "civil society." They were also uncomfortable with having one priority in one part of town, and another somewhere else. Decentralization, paired with a commitment to consultation and engagement with local communities, allows the police to respond appropriately to problems that are important to particular communities.

The second common feature of departments that are adopting this

new model of policing is community engagement. Community policing encourages agencies to develop partnerships with community
groups, to facilitate "listening" to the community and constructively
sharing information. To this end, departments hold community
meetings and form advisory committees, survey the public, and create informative Web sites. In some places, police share information
with residents through educational programs or by enrolling them in
citizen-police academies that give them in-depth knowledge of law
enforcement. Engagement usually extends to involving the public in
some way in efforts to enhance community safety. Residents are
asked to assist the police by reporting crimes promptly when they
occur and cooperating as witnesses. Community policing often
promises to strengthen the capacity of communities to fight and prevent crime on their own. Residents get involved in coordinated or
collaborative projects when they participate in youth-oriented crime
prevention projects or walk in officially sanctioned neighborhood
patrol groups. Even where these are old ideas, moving them to center
stage as part of a larger strategic plan can showcase the commitment
of police departments to resident involvement.

The third common feature, community policing, usually involves
broad-ranging problem solving. Problem solving is an approach to
developing crime prevention strategies. As a police strategy, problem
solving represents a departure from the traditional approach to policing, which too often was reduced to driving fast to crime scenes in
order to fill out reports describing what happened. Traditionally, the
police equated crime prevention with arresting lots of people. To do
so, they organized themselves to patrol the streets looking for crimes
(random and directed patrol), to respond to emergency crime calls
from witnesses and victims (rapid response to 911 calls), and to find
the guilty parties (follow-up investigation by detectives). Concerned
residents, on the other hand, do not want the crime that initiates
these efforts to happen in the first place, and their instinct is to press
for true prevention. Problem solving has brought crime prevention
theories to the table, leading police to tackle the routine activities of
victims and the crucial roles placed by "place managers" such as
landlords or shopkeepers, and not just offenders. Rookies now learn
about how victims, offenders, and places form a "crime triangle" that
needs to be broken in several places to shut problems down. An emphasis on "target hardening" has gotten them involved in conducting
home security surveys and teaching self-defense classes.

Community-policing problem solving stresses involving the pub-

lic in identifying and prioritizing a broad range of chronic neighborhood conditions. One of the consequences of police opening themselves up to the public is that police inevitably get involved in more
and different issues than they did in the past. At community meetings, residents complain about bad buildings, noise, and people fixing their cars at the curb, not just about burglary. If police reply
"that's not our responsibility" and try to move on, no one will come
to the next meeting. Of course, the police are not very good at solving
all of the problems of distressed neighborhoods, so they need to form
partnerships with other government agencies. Officers can learn at a
public meeting that loose garbage and rats in an alley are big issues
for residents, but some other agency is going to have to deliver the
solution to that problem. Police partners frequently include the bureaucracies responsible for health, housing, and even street lighting.
And community policing also involves the public in solving problems. Neighborhood residents can paint over graffiti, walk their dogs
in areas frequented by prostitutes, and hold prayer vigils in the midst
of street drug markets.

Police have also gotten into the "fear reduction" business. Reducing fear is now being seen as important in its own right, but promoting
the reclamation of public spaces and the exercise of effective informal
social control, and fostering public cooperation in crime reporting
(stepping forward as witnesses) may also enhance the crime control
effectiveness of the police. This focus has important implications for
police priorities and operations. It leads departments to pay more
attention to social disorder, a category that includes public drinking,
panhandling, teen loitering, and other problems that police traditionally found unpalatable. The "broken windows" agenda highlights demoralizing neighborhood problems that fall in the physical decay
category, including abandoned buildings and graffiti. While there is
academic controversy over whether or not these issues contribute to
serious predatory and property crime (I'm in the "yes" camp), there is
universal agreement that these are powerful generators of fear and
neighborhood decline.

What do claims about adopting community policing mean in actual practice? As I noted at the outset, police departments everywhere claim that they are doing community policing because no city
wants to seem out of step with the times. They all have a list of activities to point to when they are asked if they practice community
policing. For example, based on the 2000 federal survey, 96 percent
of Americans lived in places where police reported meeting regularly

with neighborhood residents (Bureau of Justice Statistics 2003). However, skeptics might claim that there is a lot of window dressing hanging around community policing, and that programs frequently fall short of what is described in their press releases. It is certainly the case that agencies have mounted sophisticated public relations campaigns to sell their programs, and they compete hotly for national awards for innovation. Assistant chiefs get promoted, and chiefs move to more visible prominent cities because they are said to have made a success out of community policing. But is there real substance to what they have accomplished?

An issue is that a serious program can be expensive. Some of the expansion of community-oriented policing reported in agency surveys has been financed by the federal government. In 1994, the U.S. Congress approved the Violent Crime Control and Law Enforcement Act, which included an allotment of nine billion dollars to hire as many as one hundred thousand new police officers. The Act specified that one of the roles of these new officers should be "to foster problem solving and interaction with communities by police officers." The Act created a national Office of Community Oriented Policing Services in the Justice Department to coordinate spending these funds. The office also provided training in community policing, paid for new computers and other technological assistance for police departments, and assisted them in setting up community-policing programs.

However, within the first five years of the twenty-first century, federal support for community policing was on the wane. The 1994 Act had achieved at least one of its intended effects: major police groups endorsed the presidential candidate who sponsored it. But a decade later, crime was down, a new team was in the White House, and federal largess toward local law enforcement was being redirected to post-9/11 security concerns. Even where commitment to community policing is strong, maintaining an effective program can be difficult in the face of competing demands for resources. For example, *The New York Times* reported that between 1995 and 2003 the City of Cleveland received thirty-four million dollars in federal assistance for hiring police officers, but the 2004 figure shrank to $489,000, and the city expected to receive even less in 2005. To handle the shortfall the City cut 250 officers from the payroll and closed the neighborhood mini-stations that were opened as part of the city's community-policing effort (Butterfield 2004). An important test of the staying power of community policing will come when cities have to pay all of its costs. There is also pressure from the federal government to in-volve local police extensively in enforcing immigration laws. This ef-fort is being stoutly resisted by many chiefs of police, who claim that it would be a great setback to their community-involvement and trust-building projects. We shall see if they can continue to resist.

While the popular interest in law enforcement policy sparked by community policing is certainly a good thing, its popularity is also a reason for caution. Adopting community policing in a serious way is hard work that entails considerable political risks. Translating its fundamental principles into actual practice is difficult. Abstract con-cepts need to be turned into lists of practical, day-to-day activities and then enshrined in enforceable orders to officers in the field. The troops out there have to actually go along with those orders, and the emphasis should always be on the "para" in these paramilitary or-ganizations. Surveys and ethnographic studies find that officer buy in is both critical and difficult to achieve, and that problem solving does not come naturally to many police officers. Predictably, it can also be hard to get other city bureaucracies to take ownership of problems raised in police-community meetings; they consider them to be the police department's problems. It can be surprisingly diffi-cult to get the community involved in community policing. Resi-dents have to be motivated to get involved, and to keep them coming back requires evidence of accomplishment.

So, the overarching question that is addressed in this book is Can community policing live up to its promises? Like many new pro-grams, its adoption in many instances preceded careful evaluation of its consequences. The effectiveness of community policing has been the subject of some research, ranging from its impact on crime to how openly it is embraced by the officers charged with carrying it out. Public opinion surveys have plumbed its popularity, and sur-veys have been used to assess the perceived quality of service deliv-ered by programs in various cities. There has not been enough re-search to definitively address the question of how effective it has been, and not much at all on how it really has been implemented. Some have concluded that there is no evidence that community policing reduces the crime rate (Weisburd and Eck 2004). My reading of the research is that the issue of its effectiveness derives from the absence of evidence rather than evidence of the absence of its effec-tiveness. Other reviewers are more optimistic (Zhao, Scheider, and Thurman 2002), but they would admit that the quality of many of the studies to date has not been very good. But is this important? I do not know a single police department that adopted community policing just because they thought it was a direct route to getting the crime rate down. Chiefs do so because it is popular with the taxpayers, because they are pressed to do so by their mayors and city council members, and because they want to reestablish their legitimacy in poor minority communities. Efforts to evaluate community policing need to focus as well on the important community and governance processes that it is intended to set in motion, because they represent potentially important "wins" on their own. In the case of Chicago, increased confidence in the police, neighborhood revitalization, and a renewed capacity of city bureaucracies to respond effectively to a broad range of problems were very much on the minds of the city's leaders when they launched their new program.

The question raised by the subtitle of this book is whether community policing's promises can be delivered to all Americans. What we know about police operations and police-community relations does not augur well in this regard. Police and residents of disadvantaged neighborhoods have a long record of not getting along. The decade during which community policing was to flower began with the Rodney King episode in Los Angeles (he was the victim of a brutal attack by Los Angeles–area police), and eventually a higher number of Americans (98 percent) reported seeing the videotape of that encounter than those who actually knew the name of the president. Soon after came complaints about what quickly became known as "racial profiling." These complaints began to surface in the national media at about the time Chicago's community-policing initiative was becoming a citywide program. In a 1995 article, Lewis Henry Gates Jr. chronicled the anguish expressed by prominent, law-abiding African Americans who nevertheless had been stopped by police and subjected at times to humiliating treatment. He concluded that "there's a moving violation that many blacks know as 'DWB'—Driving While Black" (Gates 1995). Surveys document a profound gulf between the races in their views of the legitimacy of the police. African Americans are more likely to think that police racism is common and that police treat them more harshly than they do whites (Weitzer 2000). African Americans and Hispanics stand far from whites on questions about how police respect and help people and treat them fairly, are more likely to report that police have been discourteous to them (Roberts and Stalans 1997), and are more likely to have observed police wrongdoing (Flanagan and Vaughn 1996). Community policing promises to rebridge this gulf by helping police come to the aid of "the good people" of the community, to focus on issues that concern them, and even to involve them as partners in problem-solving projects, although the reality of this remains to be seen. In Chicago, no one doubted that allying with the police would be popular in white, home-owning neighborhoods. In other places this coalition seemed more problematic. Cities have a history of not following through very well on promises made in poor and disenfranchised communities, and residents there may need to be convinced that "this time it is for real."

Making It Work in the Three Chicagos

This book examines how effectively community policing lived up to its promises in one American city. Chicago provides an important test of community policing because, as is apparent to any observer of the local scene, there are actually three Chicagos: one white, one African American, and one Latino. Chapter 2 describes the dimensions of the three Chicagos, and details the problems they were facing as the story presented here began to unfold. The description of what happened during the 1990s and early in the twenty-first century is based on an evaluation of Chicago's initiative. The study began in late 1992, when the department's plan for community policing was still on the drawing board. Because of this early start, the evaluation team could gather some baseline information before the program began, a luxury that many studies of real-world, politically driven programs do not enjoy. During 1993 and 1994, Chicago police developed a working program by experimenting in five of its police districts, while business as usual reigned in the other twenty districts. As detailed in chapter 3, the department first decentralized by forming teams of officers with new, long-term assignments to small police beats. Finding ways to involve the public came next. Police soon began holding regular meetings with residents of each of the fifty-four small beats that made up the experimental areas, and every district formed an advisory committee to work with the local commander. Officers working in the experimental districts were trained in their new duties and got some rudimentary instruction in problem solving. During 1994, the city first struggled, and then succeeded, in linking community policing to the timely delivery of services by city agencies. The neighborhoods that were involved represented most of the city's diversity.

The phased implementation of the program enabled us to contrast changes in the test districts with matched parts of the city, drawing on data collected before the program began and again about eighteen months later. Some of the strongest conclusions about whether the program itself caused changes in quality of life, fear of crime, and confidence in the police in these neighborhoods come from this period. The findings of this evaluation are summarized in the chapters that follow. More details can be found in Wesley G. Skogan and Susan M. Hartnett (1997), which covers this period.

By early 1995, Chicago's version of the community-policing program was in place. Chapter 3 describes the main elements of the program and some of the agony involved in keeping it alive until it could become part of the routine work of the police department. Teams of officers were assigned to work specific beats, and the 911 dispatching system was revamped to keep them there. Beat team sergeants were appointed to coordinate their efforts. Officers all over the city were trained in problem solving. By the autumn of 1995, community organizing and problem-solving training sessions were being held for the general public, and eventually about twelve thousand residents were trained. Coordinated attacks against bad buildings and negligent landlords began in 1996, as did the recruitment of a staff of civilian community organizers to drum up attendance at beat meetings and coordinate focused problem-solving projects. Later, city attorneys were assigned to the bad-building project and a new city department was created to address housing management issues more effectively. In 2000 a new oversight unit was created within the police department, and part of its mission was to improve the management of key components of community policing.

As the program expanded, the evaluation grew in scope as well. Early on we determined that we would try to encompass the entire city. Instead of watching the program unfold in a few selected places, the evaluation would be based on samples of residents, activists, patrol officers, and police beats representing the entire city, so that the findings could describe general trends in Chicago and what was happening in its three major communities. The citywide phase of the evaluation lasted ten years, through the summer of 2004. Over the course of the entire effort we surveyed about 48,500 residents, about two-thirds of them at home by telephone and one-third by distributing questionnaires at meetings. Several thousands of these respondents were community-policing activists and members of various committees advising the police districts, and another five thousand were problem-solving training participants. About 13,600 police officers were surveyed, either at roll call or when they gathered for training sessions or beat meetings. Over the years, members of the evaluation team conducted more than one thousand in-depth personal interviews with police and community leaders, and field observers made a detailed record of what took place at 1,079 beat meetings. The project's computers stored more than eight million crime reports and almost thirty-seven million records of 911 calls. There were in-depth field studies of more than a dozen selected communities, and an analysis of the extent of involvement by 253 community organizations. Almost eighty people worked on the project, and all of their names are listed in the final evaluation report (Skogan and Steiner 2004a).

Spreading the evaluation net broadly was important because it enabled us to speak about many of the city's important constituencies. While the city was deeply divided by race, class and culture added important complexities to the equation that needed to be considered. Certainly everyone anticipated that community policing might be a hard sell in Chicago's predominantly African American neighborhoods. Our surveys indicated that in the early 1990s white and black views of policing differed enormously, and most police shootings of civilians took place in African American areas. But blacks were, to a certain extent, divided by social class, and across the mid to far South Side of the city lived a swath of more than three hundred thousand middle-class African Americans who were excited about this new opportunity to ally themselves with the police. When police started meeting with the public there, they received a warm welcome. In 1990, Latinos constituted just 20 percent of the population, but everyone knew their numbers were growing fast. During the course of the evaluation the city's white population dropped by about 16 percent, but its burgeoning Latino barrios made up for that loss. As the number of Latino immigrants soared during the 1990s, that community cleaved apart, divided by economics, language, and culture. Understanding the consequences of this for community policing became one of the central focuses of the study. Whites faced fewer problems than anyone else, even before community policing began. Looking at the data, if the quality of life in predominantly white neighborhoods and their residents' relationship with the police had, in fact, been shared by everyone else, there would have been no particular need for a community-policing program in Chicago. But whites voted heavily and paid the most taxes, so their interests had to be accommodated as well.

Race threatened to intersect with community policing in numerous ways. First, Chicago's diverse communities faced distinctively different problems, and some were more tractable than others. This could be seen in the kinds of problems that were brought up in the thousands of neighborhood meetings held every year, and what the residents who attended told us in questionnaires that we distributed. Broadly speaking, African Americans came to the meetings concerned about street drug markets; Latinos were terrified by gang violence; and whites complained about parking and traffic. Many whites had priorities other than crime, including stabilizing their neighborhoods in the face of threatening racial transition. Chapters of this book examine trends in crime, social disorder, and physical decay— all targets of various community-policing efforts. In the field we found that drug problems were divisive. The seeming inability of police to control what residents perceived to be blatant public dealing by well-known local toughs was a major source of public frustration with the quality of policing. In our first survey, more than half of African Americans gave police very low ratings in response to a question about their effectiveness in preventing crime. The battle against gangs ran afoul of the stumbling block known as the U.S. Constitution. In Chicago, groups of troublemaking young toughs ("gangbangers") are well known to all, and residents want them off the streets. Surveys revealed that gang violence was the top-rated problem in Latino neighborhoods, but what to do in response was a tough question. The courts, and eventually the U.S. Supreme Court, did not like what the city was doing in the early 1990s, but that did not make the problem go away.

Chicago also tackled grime as well as crime, using the police and an array of city services to confront a set of challenges rooted in economics, with building dilapidation and abandonment among them. Many of city's residential buildings were in sad disrepair because keeping them in good repair was uneconomic. The people who lived there could not afford to pay very much for the roof over their heads, and the inattention of absentee landlords meant that they did not get very much for what money they had paid. This class issue translated into a race issue because class and race are hopelessly intertwined in Chicago. In fact, the city is home to relatively few poor whites; in the 1990 U.S. Census, only 5 percent of white households were receiving public assistance, in contrast to almost 30 percent of African American households.

Graffiti and abandoned cars were also targeted, for these were a source of public complaint in many neighborhoods. These issues proved somewhat more tractable than the problems of the desperately poor, illustrating that it is important to have modest expectations about the capacities of local government. One challenge to making the program work everywhere was that many of the city's neighborhoods were facing problems that were seemingly intractable.

There was also reason to fear that not every community would enjoy the undivided attention of the police. A 1993 report by the Illinois Advisory Committee to the U.S. Civil Rights Commission concluded that the city's predominantly African American police districts were understaffed relative to their white counterparts. They had fewer officers than they should have had based on the department's official allocation formulas, and many fewer officers were assigned there relative to the level of violent crime. The report intimated that the imbalance was due to police pandering to powerful white politicians. Indeed, from 1999 through 2004, intensive research was conducted within the department on how to best reallocate officers in order to rebalance workload inequities created by shifting population and crime patterns, but every plan that threatened the staffing level of politically important white wards was vetoed by city hall.

Throughout, this book keeps a watchful eye on the possible influence of race on how well community policing was carried out. This was a circumstance we prepared for. In an evaluation of one of the very first community-policing programs, in Houston, Texas, I found that white, home-owning residents garnered most of the benefits of the program. They found it easy to cooperate with the police. For example, they readily opened the doors of their homes to a community-organizing team formed by the police and found that they shared a common view of whom the troublemakers were in the community: African Americans and Latinos living in rental apartments next to the freeway. In other areas, whites and homeowners were the ones who showed up for public meetings and who walked into a store-front office set up by the police in another Houston neighborhood. Two waves of neighborhood surveys found that as crime, fear, and perceived social disorder went down, neighborhood satisfaction went up, and people were more optimistic about the police—if they were white homeowners (Skogan 1990a). African Americans and Latinos remained uninvolved in the programs and saw no visible change in their lives. As a result of this experience, every chapter of this book considers the possibility of differential outcomes by race.

Ironically, it is not just the police who are difficult to get on board with community policing. It can also be difficult to sustain community involvement, especially in areas that need it most. Research on participation in community crime-prevention programs conducted during the 1970s and 1980s found that turnout for police-sponsored events was higher in places honeycombed with block clubs and community organizations (Skogan 1988). In high-crime areas, on the other hand, people tend to be much less organized. Instead they are suspicious of their neighbors, and especially of their neighbors' children. Fear of retaliation by gangs and drug dealers can undermine public involvement as well (Grinc 1994). In Chicago, a 1998 study of hundreds of community meetings found that residents expressed concern about retaliation by gangs for attending these gatherings or working with the police in 22 percent of the city's beats, almost all of them poor (Skogan and Steiner 2004a).

In addition, police and residents may not have a history of getting along in poor neighborhoods. Residents are as likely to think of the police as one of their problems as they are to see them as a solution to their problems. It probably will not be the first instinct of organizations representing the interests of black and brown communities to cooperate with police. Instead, they are more likely to press for an end to police misconduct. There may be no particular reason for residents of the most crime-ridden neighborhoods to think that community policing will turn out to be anything but another broken promise; they are accustomed to seeing programs come and go, without much effect (Sadd and Grinc 1994). Our interviews indicate that the most elemental concern of many new immigrants is fear that contact with the police will somehow threaten their status in the United States. They flock to the new Spanish-speaking barrios that have begun to dominate several areas of the city, where they can keep a low profile. The growth of these areas is driven by conditions in Mexico, and their experiences abroad seem to color their view of the police, particularly their expectations about police brutality and corruption. Rodney King was famously reported to have asked, "Why can't we all just get along?" It is obviously not that simple, so several chapters of the book cast a careful eye on the intersection between race and community involvement in Chicago's program.

Plan of the Book

The next chapter sets the stage by describing conditions in the city at the beginning of the 1990s, as plans for community policing were being formulated. As the story unfolds it will become clear that the three great communities that make up the city began at different points early in the decade and went in different directions as the city entered the next millennium. Chapter 2 describes some of the dramatic changes that have taken place in the city's demography even in that short span of time. These include the continued numerical decline of the city's white population and the growth of the immigrant population. Then it turns to the crime, drug, and social disorder problems facing the city in the early 1990s, and what people thought about the police. There were indeed three Chicagos, each facing a different constellation of issues. The chapter concludes with a description of what the police initially thought about community policing, and what all of this augured for the city's future.

Chapter 3 describes the key elements of the program, and how they came to be. There is a description of the program development process and the product that eventually emerged after field-testing in selected districts. It then dissects the obstacles to making the plan actually work. This is an important issue in Chicago and around the nation, since actually fielding a meaningful program is the central problematic of community policing, so another section describes the police department's struggle to overcome these obstacles. Among their strategies was the inauguration of a management-accountability system resembling—on the surface—New York City's CompStat. They also added a staff of professional civilian community organizers, who were charged with boosting participation and supporting problem-solving projects.

Chapters 4 and 5 examine the effectiveness with which the public was incorporated into the program. They examine avenues for public involvement in community policing and how effectively they worked. Chapter 4 reviews the city's extensive (and expensive) campaign to market community policing, and the efforts of organizers to turn people out for marches and meetings. It examines who got involved, and what happened at the meetings. Most of chapter 5 is devoted to an analysis of the "establishment bias" that influenced who turned out, and what that meant for the effectiveness with which community interests were represented. Citizen involvement was one of the early successes of community policing in Chicago, so the chapter concludes with a discussion of what made it work, and why it was not very successful among Latinos.

Chapters 6 and 7 examine the effectiveness of community policing in addressing two of its more important targets: social disorder and physical decay. To an astonishing degree, the city's leaders and police officials believed in the "broken windows" argument that physi-cal dilapidation and low-level misconduct are precursors to more se-rious victimizing crime. Unlike some cities, Chicago's response was to fix the windows rather than just look for someone to arrest. The chapters describe the extensive coordination of city-service agencies that was required to make problem solving work, and how residents got involved in repairing their own windows when they could. Chapter 7 tracks trends in disorder and decay over time, and con-cludes with an analysis of why community policing failed to suc-cessfully address mounting problems in the city's growing Latino neighborhoods.

Chapter 8 describes the dramatic decline in crime and fear recorded by the city during the 1990s and into the early years of the new millennium. Some of that drop could be attributed to commu-nity and prevention factors, and others to policing and the changing character of crime. A comparison of official statistics and survey as-sessments of the extent of crime problems suggests that the drop was a real one in the city's worst off African American neighborhoods, but that official figures for the city's burgeoning immigrant popu-lation were deceptive. The surveys documented that concern about drugs, gangs, street crime, and burglary was mounting among the city's Latinos at the same time that everyone else was feeling better about conditions in their neighborhoods.

Chapter 9 examines Chicagoans' changing views of the police during the course of the 1990s, as community policing took root in the city. Police gained significant support during the decade, and they did so among all major groups. Much of the explanation for this lay in improving neighborhood conditions. Many—but not all—Chicagoans felt their neighborhoods were growing cleaner, safer, and more comfortable as a place to live, and official rates of crime were declining. These improvements in quality of life rebounded to the benefit of the police. Some of the remaining gaps between views of whites and African Americans can be attributed to their personal ex-periences. There continued to be a great gulf between the races in how they evaluated being stopped by the police, who heavily target young African American males.

Finally, chapter 10 reviews the challenges facing Chicago's community-policing program. It evaluates whether or not the pro-gram succeeded (or, more precisely, to what *extent* it succeeded) in meeting those challenges. The challenges including successfully im-plementing a program, engaging the public, responding more effectively to crime and fear, fixing broken windows, and healing the breech between police and the city's black and brown residents. Throughout, the evaluation criteria are whether community policing actually helped close the gap between whites, African Americans, and Latinos. Because Latinos and the city's poorest residents were *not* helped very much, there is also a review of the forces buffeting the Latino community and what this augurs for community policing.

Crime, Police, and
the Three Chicagos

This chapter describes the condition of the city and the state of police-community relations in Chicago in the early 1990s. It provides a baseline from which to assess what happened during the remainder of the decade and into the next, as community policing took hold in the city. In brief, the situation looked grim. In the early 1990s, crime hit record levels. The population of the city had been dropping for forty years, and better-off African Americans already had joined white families in the flight to the suburbs. Those who remained behind were sharply segregated by race, and the racial composition of the city's neighborhoods provided a template that described the distribution of almost every social and physical ill. The relationship between the police and the public was also bad. This was especially true in the eyes of African American and Latino residents, although our surveys demonstrated that Chicagoans of *all* races thought that in important ways police were not doing a very good job.

Race is central to this story. During the course of the 1990s, community policing played itself out differently in Chicago's white, African American, and Latino neighborhoods. The crime and disorder problems that needed solving varied from group to group. As the program developed, whites, African Americans, and Latinos adopted distinctive patterns of involvement in the program. They "got the message" in different ways, and they varied in the extent to which they took advantage of the opportunities that the program provided. Finally, their neighborhoods changed in dramatically different ways over time. In general, African Americans saw tremendous improvements. On many dimensions things got a bit better in white neighborhoods, but they did not have that many problems to start with. Among Latinos, things got worse. Because of these differences in trends over the course of the 1990s, the discussion that follows—and virtually every topic covered in this book—examines police and crime issues separately by race, the "color line" dividing the city into three distinct Chicagos.

African Americans

Figure 2.1 describes trends in the racial composition of the city between 1950, the year when Chicago's population hit its peak, and
2004. African Americans first came to Chicago in large numbers during World War I and the 1920s, to fill labor shortages in the North
and escape oppressive conditions in the South. The rigid segregation
of African Americans in the city began at that time. In the 1950s, the
bulk of the city's African Americans were concentrated in the Black
Belt, a narrow strip running south from the city center into the South
Side. But the pressure of population growth soon began to expand
the dimensions of the color line that defined the boundaries of
African American residence. Many African Americans migrated farther south and westward from their traditional core, while others
leapfrogged over the city's southern boundary and began to settle in
large numbers in close-in suburbs on the fringe of the city. By the
1970s, Chicago's African American communities had begun to bifur-
cate geographically, splitting into better-off and persistently poor
areas (Wilson 1978). In addition to the effects of black suburbaniza-
tion, the decline of industrial jobs in the city effectively sentenced
less skilled or less educated African Americans to precarious low-

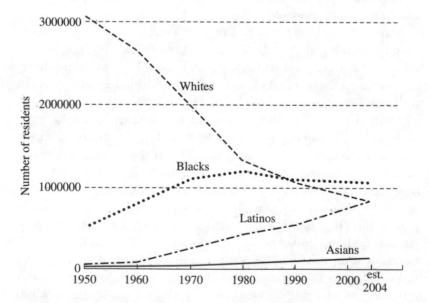

Figure 2.1. Trends in Population by Race, 1950–2004

wage, nonunion jobs and life in poverty-stricken, racially segregated inner-city neighborhoods (Wilson 1987, 1996).

The continued growth of the African American population during the 1950s and 1960s is apparent—their numbers nearly doubled during that twenty-year period. Then growth came virtually to a halt. The relatively slight increase in the size of the African American population during the 1970s was principally due to births rather than in-migration, which diminished to a trickle (Wilson 1987). The flattening African American population trend during the 1980–1990 period, and then its decline in the 1990s, reflects the movement of a significant number of better-off blacks from the city to the southern and southwestern suburbs. They were searching for what others wanted as well: better housing and schools, green space, lower crime rates, and less disruption in their daily lives. This can be seen in the growth of the suburban African American population in the Chicago area. While the number of African Americans living in the city remained essentially unchanged between 1990 and 2000, their numbers in the suburbs grew from 271,000 to 414,000 during that ten-year period. Others moved but remained in the city, pressing farther south and southwest to find better housing and creating in-city middle-class and solidly blue-collar African American neighborhoods (Pattillo-McCoy 1999).

Where did they live, and what was life like there? To analyze geographical data (such as crime rates), 1990 data on the racial composition of the city's 279 police beats were used to identify the predominant group in each area. Beats are the fundamental geographical unit in this book, because they serve as the organizing framework for police activities and they can be linked to data of all kinds from the police and other city agencies. Chicago's very high level of African American segregation made classifying the composition of many beats quite easy. Clusters of beats were formed to maximize their internal homogeneity with respect to race. The groupings are not "neighborhoods" in the conventional sense, or necessarily even physically contiguous; they are analytic units, and not named places. However, the term "community" is applicable to them because the clusters group Chicagoans who share important common interests, concerns, problems, and ways of life. Figure 2.2 depicts where everyone lived in 1990, when communities are identified just by race.

The map identifies two large, predominantly African American areas of the city: the West Side and the Near South Side, where residents were mostly poor, and the Far South Side, where both poor

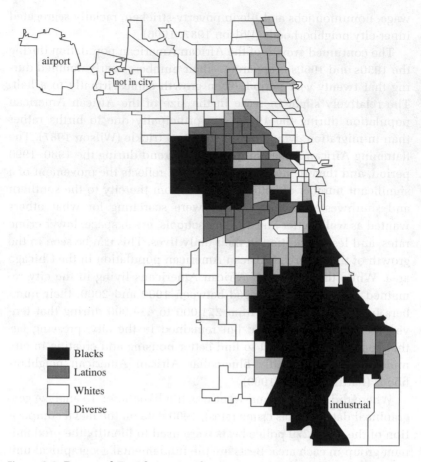

Figure 2.2. Race and Residence in Chicago, 1990

and many relatively affluent blacks lived. In the aggregate, the 1990 population of these predominantly African American beats was 95 percent black, and only 2 percent white and 3 percent Latino. About 34 percent of the city's 1990 population lived in these 121 areas. In better-off African American neighborhoods, about two-thirds of the residents owned their homes compared to only 16 percent of those in poor black areas, and more than 60 percent lived in single-family homes compared to 12 percent of their counterparts. Public housing played a significant role in concentrating poverty in Chicago, and the city's public housing projects were mostly found in poor African American beats. In 1990, major family public housing developments were found in thirty-two beats, and twenty-two of those were in poor black areas. Only one better-off African American beat had a housing project, and six diverse and Latino beats accounted for most of the remainder. Only three of the city's public housing developments were located in predominantly white areas. By the end of the 1990s this situation had begun to unravel, as Chicago aggressively used federal Project Hope VI funds to knock down the worst of the high-rises and residents scattered, looking for housing they could afford and landlords who would take them.

Latinos

As figure 2.2 depicts, in 1990 there were two large blocks of concentrated Latino residence in Chicago. One was to the Near Northwest side and one on the near southwest side of the city center, the latter serving as the home to most Latinos of Puerto Rican heritage. Another long-established Latino community could be found on the city's far southeastern border, within sight of its now-abandoned steel mills. The thirty-two beats where the city's Latinos were then concentrated were 73 percent Latino, 10 percent African American, and 15 percent white, and they were home to 14 percent of the city's population.

Latinos began to make their mark on the city during the 1980s, and by 2000 they totaled 754,000. Illinois is one of the five largest states in terms of Latino population, and Chicago is home to half of the state's total. Like African Americans in an earlier era, the Latino community is fed by an immigrant stream. That stream originates in Mexico, and sometimes drains virtually the entire young male population of a village northward to the Windy City. In 1990, as this story begins, 65 percent of the city's Latinos were of Mexican origin; by 2000 it was 70 percent. Puerto Rican migration to Chicago began later, and the proportion of Puerto Ricans in the city declined, from 22 percent to 15 percent of the Latino total between 1990 and 2000. The fraction who were of Cuban origin remained in the 1 to 2 percent range, and the remainder came from a variety of points of origin in Central and South America and the Caribbean.

Some may object to the characterization of "Latino" as a racial category, but, of course, race is a social and political construct. The U.S. Census Bureau has changed its mind about how to handle "Latinos" in almost every decennial census. In recent decades the Census Bureau has classified everyone by using questions asking about "race" that does not allow a Hispanic choice. They then ask other questions to separately identify people of any racial group who consider themselves Hispanic. In different censuses the Census Bureau has used self-identified national origin, self-reports of "mother tongue," the language spoken at home, and a long list of "Hispanic surnames" to make this second designation. Mind-numbing demographic nomenclature, including terms like "Non-Hispanic White" grew out of this process. But in 1930 the Census Bureau automatically classed all Hispanics among the "other races" in most data tables, regardless of other designations they might choose. In 1940, on the other hand, the Census Bureau automatically classed them all as white (U.S. Bureau of the Census 2000b).

Latinos themselves have been trying to send demographers a message. In surveys conducted during the 1990s, Latinos in large numbers began checking the "other race" box for the first question on their race, indicating when allowed that their race was some variant of Hispanic, not black or white or Asian. In 2000, 42 percent of those who were identified by the Census Bureau as being "of Hispanic origin" chose "other race," rather than white, black, and so forth, on their racial background question (U.S. Bureau of the Census 2000c). In Chicago, 52 percent of Latinos chose "other race," and they constituted 97 percent of those who did so (U.S. Bureau of the Census 2000d). In 1997, the federal Office of Management and Budget ruled that the terms "Hispanic" and "Latino" could be used interchangeably in government reports, but did not consider them a "race" for reporting purposes (U.S. Bureau of the Census 2000a).

But Latinos in Chicago constitute a racial grouping for many practical reasons. There are a growing number of concentrated Latino neighborhoods; they are served by Spanish-language media; they evidence a distinctive culture and days of celebration; the economic and social makeup of the group differs from that of whites and African Americans; they have distinctive patterns of voter turnout and local political preference; and their representatives in the city council and the U.S. Congress belong to a "Latino Caucus." Of course the city's Latinos are internally differentiated by national origin and many other factors. But others treat them as a racial group: in the neighborhoods, whites commonly refer to them collectively as "the Spanish," or in other terms, and this undifferentiated treatment by outsiders contributes to their definition as one of Chicago's three large racial groups.

Why are they known as "Latinos"? The term emerged in Chicago in the 1970s as an outgrowth of a deliberate effort to build a political coalition uniting Mexican Americans and Puerto Ricans. An organization dubbed The Spanish Coalition for Jobs was created to press for the application of job discrimination regulations to their demands for employment. The Coalition brought suit against the telephone company and a major grocery store chain, picketed the homes of company executives, and held mass demonstrations in front of stores. Their conscious adoption of the term "Latino" to describe the movement's constituency was a strategy for forging a group identity around which they could organize for collective purposes, against the external world (Padilla 1984). This strategy highlighted the intense competition between Latinos and African Americans for the same set of jobs. The Coalition's struggle to make affirmative action, job discrimination, and (later) minority preferences in city contracts applicable to them as well as to African Americans also helped to spike the development of any "minority group" solidarity in the city, for it threatened to cut the size of the pie available to blacks.

The effects of immigration on the composition of the Latino population can be seen in the yearly surveys. Because they come to the city without much formal education, immigrants have had the effect of pushing down average levels of education. In our 1994 survey, 71 percent of those identified as Latinos reported having a high school diploma; by 2003, that figure had dropped to 64 percent. (By contrast, in 2003 96 percent of whites and 83 percent of African Americans reported having a high school diploma.) The results can also be read in their choice of language. Using as an indicator the language in which survey respondents preferred to be interviewed, about one-third of Latinos were classed as "Spanish speakers" in the 1994 survey. In 1997 that figure was 49 percent, and in 2003 it was 54 percent. In the 1990 U.S. Census, almost a third of all Latinos in Chicago lived in what the U.S. Census Bureau dubs "linguistic isolation." This is the percentage of households in which *all* members fourteen years of age or older routinely speak a language other than English and none of them speak English (by their own assessment) "very well." Linguistic isolation was closely associated with the emergence of large, poor, Spanish-speaking immigrant neighborhoods in Chicago, and these are places in which many survey respondents who reported worsening neighborhood conditions are concentrated (Skogan and Steiner 2004b).

Finally, the surveys help point to the future composition of the population in Chicago. Immigrants tend to arrive as young adults, and Chicago's adult Latino population grew younger during the

1990s. More were of childbearing age and, in addition, marriage rates for Latinos were the highest of the city's three population groups. As a result, the 2003 survey found that 69 percent of Latino households had children at home; the comparable figure for whites was only 26 percent, and for African Americans it was 49 percent. The schools were full and sometimes running on double shifts in Chicago's Latino neighborhoods, and their youthfulness will fuel the group's future growth.

However, compared to predominantly African American areas, few Latino families were headed by females with children, and in Latino areas households were most likely to be made up of married couples. Latinos also stood slightly above whites in the percentage of respondents who had a full-time job. As a result, the percentage of families receiving public assistance in predominantly Latino areas (17 percent, based on the 1990 U.S. Census) was also relatively low, about half the African American rate. The combination of working and holding together intact families kept most Latinos out of poverty despite their many liabilities in the labor market.

At the same time, Latinos were concentrating in the oldest sections in the city; they were just the latest of successive waves of migrants to live there. Only 9 percent of the buildings in heavily Latino beats were constructed after 1949, and fully two-thirds were constructed prior to 1910. In a land use inventory conducted in the mid-1990s, buildings in Latino beats were twenty times as likely as those in predominantly white areas to be rated in bad condition. By contrast, while many African Americans were poor, by 1990 many lived farther south, in more newly developed housing areas outside of their aged port of entry, the Black Belt on the Near South Side. Housing conditions on the Far South Side were significantly better than in areas of concentrated Latino residence.[1]

Whites

The map presented in figure 2.2 identifies large concentrations of white Chicagoans in the southwestern and northwestern corners of the city and along the North Side lakeshore. The city's white residents report diverse backgrounds. A 1992 survey conducted by the Metro Chicago Information Center questioned 1,250 Chicagoans about their ethnic origins. The analysis of their data presented here is my own. Respondents could give multiple responses (a few named six nationalities), but based on their first response to the question, the largest group (25 percent) was of German extraction. They were followed by the Irish (16 percent), Polish (15 percent), and those originating in England or Wales (8 percent). In the survey, almost 50 percent of whites reported they were Roman Catholics, and only 23 percent were Protestants. At the time of the 1990 U.S. Census, almost half of all children in white neighborhoods were enrolled in private, primarily Catholic schools. Survey figures on religion were reversed among the city's African Americans, 66 percent of whom were Protestant and only 10 percent Roman Catholic. Almost all of the survey's self-identified Republicans were white, but that still was not many: only 18 percent of whites admitted they supported the GOP.

The most dramatic trend traced in figure 2.1 was the precipitous drop in Chicago's white population. During a half-century it dropped from more than three million to less than one million, a decline that in sheer numbers was larger than the total population of Houston in 2000, by then the nation's fourth largest city. Where did they go? Some retired and moved south, but most fled to the suburbs. During this period, other groups grew in size, including the still-small number of Asians, but the growth of all other groups combined did not match the magnitude of the white exodus. As a result, between 1950 and 2000 the city's population dropped by 725,000. By comparison, just the drop in Chicago's total population was more than the total number living in Columbus, Ohio, in the year 2000. By then the city had become more "diverse" (i.e., almost evenly divided among its often contending groups), but more by subtraction than by addition. This decline in the size of the white population is contrasted with the growth in the number of Latinos by the population projections that are presented in figure 2.1. Based on past trends, the two groups were almost identical in size by 2004, with Latinos projected to become the larger group in 2005.

As there were both poor and better-off African American beats, there was also some differentiation within the white community. While African Americans broke along economic lines, white areas were differentiated by lifestyle. On several measures, residents of white "bungalow-belt" beats on the Far Northwest and Southwest sides of the city looked very much like those in better-off African American areas. They were the only groups likely to live in single-family homes, 64 percent in the white bungalow belt and 62 percent in better-off African American areas. Like residents of better-off

African American beats, bungalow belt residents sported relatively high household incomes and home ownership rates by maintaining the city's highest proportion of two-adult, two-earner families. The blue-collar character of both the bungalow belt and better-off black areas was signaled by a high percentage of high school graduates (71 percent and 70 percent) and a low proportion of college graduates living there (15 percent and 13 percent, respectively). Home owner-ship was relatively low (39 percent) in white areas close to the lakeshore. Few residents near the lake (only 16 percent) lived in single-family homes, despite their high incomes and levels of educa-tion; more lived in condominiums, townhouses, and high-rise apart-ment towers.

Diversity within the white community did not extend to including other racial groups in their neighborhoods, however. Chicago has long been portrayed as the nation's most segregated large city, com-posed of enclaves protecting the city's whites and hemming in its blacks. Beginning in the 1950s, the color line separating whites and African Americans begin to shift, sequentially breeching barriers erected along the major north-south arterials—first Halsted Avenue, then Ashland Avenue, then Western Avenue and beyond. Supported by community organizations and even churches, white residents manned the barricades. Ostracism of those selling to blacks and at-tacks on real estate offices helped maintain white solidarity in the face of pressure on their real estate. An occasional firebomb warned newcomers that they were unwelcome. Substantial collective disor-der broke out in Englewood in 1949, along Cicero Avenue in 1951, in Trumbull Park in 1953, Calumet Park in 1957, and Marquette Park and Gage Park in the mid-1960s (Skogan 1976b appendix A). But African Americans moved in anyway, whites moved out, and it ap-peared that the city's only integrated communities were those caught in the midst of transition. Even in the more relaxed 1990s, the beat-level correlation between percent black and percent white was −.82, and few beats were home to anything resembling an even balance of the two groups. The burgeoning Latino population constitutes a bit of a "wild card" in the race and real estate game. While many lived in the new barrios of the Northwest and Southwest sides, others were scattered more widely, buying small homes and two-flats in many parts of the city. The 1990 correlation between beat percent white and percent Latino was mildly positive, reflecting the development of white-Latino population mixes on the Northwest and Southwest sides of the city.

Other Groups

Figure 2.1 also describes the growth of the city's Asian population. Percentage-wise, they were growing the fastest during the 1990s, up by 25 percent between 1990 and 2000 alone. It will be difficult to say much about them in this book, however. Their numbers are still relatively small, and as a result, they are not well enough represented in surveys to track trends for this group with any confidence.

They are also not really a "group" in any social, economic, or political sense. In 2000, people from South Asia (Indians, plus Pakistanis and others) constituted 25 percent of all Asians identified by the U.S. Census. The East Asian population includes both long-established descendants of Chinese immigrants (another quarter of all Asians) and refugees from the region including Vietnam and Cambodia (8 percent of the total). Koreans (10 percent of the total, and including many Protestants) and Catholic Filipinos (23 percent of all Asians) are the other large components of the Asian population. In general, Asian groups do not live or work in close proximity to one another. Outside of the city's Chinatown, Asians are spread throughout the North Side of the city. Only a few of the beats designated "diverse" in figure 2.2 were home to substantial numbers of poorer Asians. In short, Chicago's Asian groups do not have much in common except that they are not white, black, or brown. In addition, there are now a noticeable number of people who voluntarily identify themselves in surveys as "Middle Eastern" when they are asked about their race, and they are another group we cannot track with any confidence.[2] Together, all of these "others" made up almost 10 percent of our survey respondents, but it is not clear what it would mean to say anything about them.

The three big Chicagos that we can consider formed separate arenas in which Chicago's experiment in community policing would be carried out. Using a combination of census data, city administrative records, police crime files, field observations, and yearly surveys of city residents, the chapters that follow will track trends in conditions in these areas during the course of the 1990s, and into the twenty-first century.

A Note on Surveys

Many sections of this book report findings from nine citywide surveys that were conducted between 1993 and 2003.[3] All were conducted by telephone, by professional academic interviewing organizations. The surveyors contacted households using random-digit-dialing procedures in order to ensure that new households, those who recently had moved and changed their telephone numbers, and persons who chose to be unlisted (which is more than 50 percent of Chicagoans) would be included in the sample. Only household members eighteen years of age and older were eligible for interviewing, and when more than one adult lived there, one was chosen at random to represent the family. Because of these procedures, the results of the interviews were weighted in order to correct for the overrepresentation of households with multiple telephone numbers (they had more chances to fall into the sample), and for the underrepresentation of individuals living in multiple-adult households (they each had a smaller chance of being selected for interviewing). Unweighted data were used to calculate tests of significance and in multivariate analyses.

The first survey in 1993 was quite small, involving only 540 respondents, and it was conducted exclusively in English, so it did not present a very accurate portrait of the city's Latinos. In the first year, more of our resources were poured into surveys in the department's experimental areas and our matched comparison areas. As a result, the results of the 1993 survey will be discussed very infrequently. During 1994 through 1996 the surveys included thirteen hundred to eighteen hundred respondents. During 1997 through 1999 they involved twenty-eight hundred to three thousand respondents, and in 2001 about twenty-five hundred people were interviewed. The last survey, conducted in 2003, included 3,124 Chicagoans. Response rates for the surveys ranged between 40 to 60 percent, declining somewhat over time. While the respondents remained anonymous, they were asked to identify the general location of their home by giving the name of their street and the nearest cross street, or, failing that, to indicate the name of their neighborhood. Responses to these questions enabled most of them (92 percent) to be identified by their police district and beat. Some of the analyses presented here combine the responses of people living in the same area to produce geographical data from the surveys.

Crime in Chicago

Planning for the city's new community-policing program began in 1991, the year in which crime hit new heights in Chicago. The number of assaults and robberies stood at an all-time high, and other crimes were not far behind. In August 1991 a full-scale drug war broke out between warring gangs on the city's South Side, and that was the worst month for murder in the city's history (Skogan and Hartnett 1997). Except for a one-year upward spike in 1974, 1992 was the peak homicide year in Chicago's history. Based on Chicago police classifications, 1991 had the largest number of gang-motivated homicides in the city's post WWII history (the Al Capone–era was another story). There was a shift in the firepower deployed on the street, as automatic and semiautomatic weapons began to replace revolvers, and the "stopping power" of the bullets being employed took a sharp jump upward. Many forms of homicide were still going down, not up, including intimate partner violence and killings fueled by alcohol. What was up was gang- and drug-related murders, which were the outcome of conflicts over drugs and businesslike decisions to kill off the competition (Block, Jacob, Christakos, and Przybylski 1996; Illinois Criminal Justice Information Authority 1995).

Some of these ominous trends are depicted in figure 2.3. It presents rates of burglary, auto theft, aggravated assault, and robbery between 1980 and 1991, as presented in yearly reports by city police and the FBI's annual crime tabulations. The use of population-based rates (here, per ten thousand residents) accounts for the gradually shrinking size of the city over the period. In raw numbers, police reported 16,300 robberies in 1980, and 43,800 in 1991, a more than 250 percent rise. The number of aggravated assaults (roughly speaking, the serious ones) rose even more, by 550 percent between their low in 1981 and their high in 1991. In 1992, the overall city homicide rate for black males was 128 per 100,000, more than twice the group's national figure. For the city's black males age 15 to 19 it was 274 in 1992 (Illinois Criminal Justice Information Authority 1995). These were frightening numbers, and pressure on the city to "do something" was one factor that pushed city hall into searching for something new that could be sold as responding more effectively to crime (Skogan and Hartnett 1997).

Of course, it is important to examine crime statistics with care. They are affected by a number of factors in addition to the true rate of crime. Many victims do not report their experiences to the police. A national rule of thumb is that only about 50 percent of crimes are reported, and it is less than that for some large-volume offenses like property theft (Hart and Rennison 2003). In chapter 8 we will see

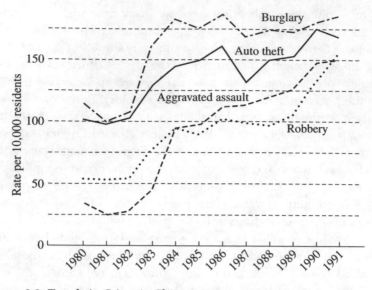

Figure 2.3. Trends in Crime in Chicago, 1980–1991

that Chicago's Spanish-speaking Latinos are probably underreporting to the police in large numbers, and official crime figures do not adequately reflect conditions in places where they are concentrated. In addition, the police do not always properly record crimes when they are reported. In many cities it is the practice of police to accommodate politicians who want lower crime rates during the run-up to elections, and area commanders find ways to placate their superiors when the word comes down that "crime is getting out of hand" (Skogan 1976b; Seidman and Couzens 1974). Of course, police also screen complaints to ensure that they meet legal and bureaucratic requirements before they file an official record, and this also reduces the count. As a result, the falloff between crime as measured by victimization surveys and by department records can be substantial.

In Chicago, the earliest data presented here were particularly notorious for their inaccuracy. As revealed by an investigative television reporter, detectives were "killing crime" in a big way during the early 1980s, and probably before. Rather than properly investigating rapes, robberies, assaults, and burglaries, they sat comfortably in coffee shops and made up report narratives out of thin air. Then, so that their fictional accounts would not be investigated any further, they "unfounded" them by checking a box indicating that no legal offense had taken place. In this way they conveniently disposed of as much as half of all the work that came their way in a given month. This also increased their apparent effectiveness, because they kept cases alive if they thought they would be able to catch someone. This practice went officially unrecognized, for no one wanted to challenge the detective bureau, but it was so widely known within the department that police headquarters actually worked with two sets of crime data. They used informal, but more accurate, counts that were compiled and relayed each night from the station houses while blithely announcing the official, lower, crime counts to the outside world, including to the FBI for publication in their yearly crime report.

When all of this became public, the FBI flagged Chicago's entries in its yearly report. It noted in various footnotes that the "figures are not comparable with previous years," and that they were "not in accord with national UCR guidelines." The wording of these brief notations was negotiated between the department and a representative of the FBI's crime reporting division. The state of Illinois responded by segregating Chicago's figures into a separate section of the state's yearly crime report. Andrew Gordon and I wrote a long analysis of the situation that was printed in the state's 1982 crime report. It detailed how the department had been cheating and why its numbers should be taken with a grain of salt (Skogan and Gordon 1982). In response to the furor, the police department instituted an internal auditing process, beginning in 1983. They began by selecting tape recordings of 911 center operations on random days, and then tracked each call to its final disposition to make sure it was handled properly. Figure 2.3 surely reflects the salutary effects of having the agency's internal inspectors checking on things. Jumps in crime during 1983 and 1984 that probably reflected improvements in the crime-recording process accounted for most of the increase in property crime over the entire period. The 1984 total of fifty-five thousand reported burglaries was scarcely bested for the remainder of the decade. Violent crime continued to go up even after the scandal, and because this paralleled national trends it is plausible that this reflected real and continuing increases in violent crime in Chicago during the last half of the 1980s.

All of these are reasons for using surveys as well as official figures to chart trends and evaluate programs. Surveys get around problems with citizens not reporting and police not recording complaints. Survey measures of crime bypass these barriers by going directly to the public, who are in a position to report on crime as it is experienced rather than as it is counted. This experience can include not just their own victimization but, in addition, what they hear from their friends and neighbors. Survey respondents can factor in what they see with their own eyes, even if they are lucky enough not to be involved personally. Surveys are also not bound by the technical categories that define official statistics, and can put things in terms that make sense to the general public. Surveys can measure the seriousness of problems as well, for not all are of equal import to neighborhood residents. This book uses both police and survey evidence about crime, in this section to identify crime patterns in Chicago during the early 1990s, and in chapter 8 to examine subsequent trends as community policing took hold in the city.

Race and Recorded Crime

At the beginning of the 1990s, the city's communities varied greatly in levels of victimization, especially by violent crime. Figure 2.4 is based on an analysis of approximately 630,000 incident reports of all kinds completed by the Chicago police during 1991. Figure 2.4 presents recorded crime rates for the city's geographical racial clusters in 1991, the beginning point for the analyses of crime trends. Because they vary in size (with the most residents found in African American beats), each cluster's crime totals were divided by the total population for the area.

Figure 2.4 distinguishes between two general categories of crime: personal offenses and property crime. In every case, residents of largely African American areas came off worse, but the gap varied by type of crime. Figure 2.4 examines three types of violent crime: robbery, rape, and murder. Robbery rates are scaled at the left side of the figure, while rapes and murders—which are much less frequent—are scaled on the right. The immense concentration of the city's violent crime in African American areas is apparent. Robbery and rape rates there were both almost six times as high as in predominantly white areas, and almost three times as high as in Latino and racially diverse areas. In 1991, 64 percent of all reported robberies and 66 percent of all rapes were committed in the city's 121 predominantly African American beats, which were home to 35 percent of the population. Murder, which was much less frequent, was just as concentrated; two-thirds of all of the city's homicides took place in African American beats. The murder rate there was ten times that in white areas, and more than twice the rate in Latino and racially diverse beats.

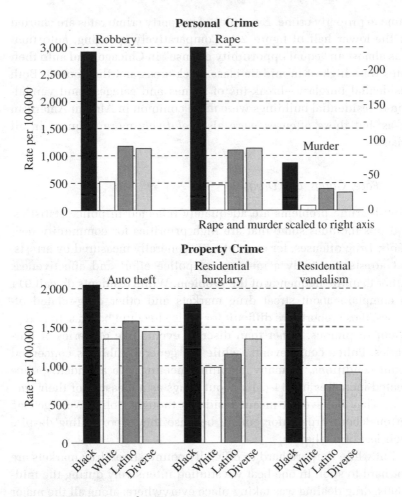

Figure 2.4. Crime Rates by Race, 1991

As we have seen, these communities were themselves highly varied, and so were crime patterns. Class made a great deal of differ nce
in the risks facing the city's African Americans. Homicide and ob-
bery rates were more than twice as high in poor black areas as iey
were in better-off African American neighborhoods, but they were
still the second most victimized cluster of beats. Homicide rates were
twenty-seven times higher in poor black beats than they were in
white homeowner areas, where the murder rate was only three per
one hundred thousand residents.

Differences between the areas were somewhat smaller when it

came to property crime. Examples of property crime rates are charted in the lower half of figure 2.4. Comparatively speaking, auto theft was almost an "equal opportunity offense" in Chicago, and auto theft rates were highest in middle-class black areas, not the poorest. Both residential burglary—break-ins of homes and garages—and vandalism to residential buildings were more common in African American areas, but those offenses were also *relatively* more frequent in all areas.

Race, Gangs, and Drugs

Not all crime problems are adequately reflected in police statistics, and this includes some that are high priorities for community residents. Drug offenses, for example, are generally measured by arrests, but arrests are really a measure of police effort and effectiveness rather than the frequency of the problem. While residents do call 911 to complain about street drug markets and other drug-related offenses, these reports are difficult for police to count because they represent suspicions, rather than discrete events like robberies or burglaries. Police count events, while the general public is concerned about conditions. In many planning meetings we attended, police treated increases in 911 calls about drugs as a measure of their *success*. They believed it meant residents thought police were getting serious about drug enforcement, because they were calling despite their fear of retaliation.

But while they are hard to officially count, street drug markets are not hard to spot. In one beat we studied intensively during the mid-1990s, drug dealing was taking place everywhere: along all the major arterial and shopping streets, in front of liquor stores, in the front yards of houses and apartment buildings, along side streets, and on many street corners. Scores of men and teens loitered in the vicinity, some yelling "Rock!" and "Blow!" at passing cars to advertise their wares. Buyers pulled over, exchanged a few words and a handshake, and then moved on. As police approached, cries of "Five-O" warned everyone, and they slowly scattered. As I like to note in lectures to fellow academics, only a sociologist needs a research grant in order to locate a street drug market.

The disjuncture between concerns and counts is also apparent in another problem of public interest: gangs. Concern about gangs is concern about "whodunit" as well as what they did. In Chicago, the best measure produced by police is the gang homicide rate; another is a count of gang-related criminal offenses. While these measures are carefully done, they only partly capture the reality of the city: circa 1990, there were forty serious street gangs with thirty-six thousand members; nineteen thousand of them belonged to the four biggest gangs (Block et al. 1996; Block and Block 1993). Much of the city had been carved up into recognizable gang turfs. Gangs monopolized the recruitment of new members and the sale of drugs and guns in their zones. Their "enforcers" maintained discipline there through the studied application of violence. Many gangs are well-known: organizations like the Black Gangster Disciples, the Vice Lords, and the Imperial Insane Vice Lords dominate African American areas, while the Latin Kings, Spanish Cobras, Latin Disciples, Familia Stones, and others are active in Latino neighborhoods. Far from lying low, gangs flaunt their presence through their dress, demeanor, and turf-demarcating graffiti. Despite this, organized white gangs are hard to find; when one appeared briefly in the mid-1990s, sociology students at the University of Chicago ran to study them (for a book that came out of this see Carr 2005).

As an alternative to official measures of drug and gang problems, the yearly surveys questioned city residents about what was going on in their neighborhood. Many of the findings will be discussed in detail in chapters 7 and 8. Here the findings of the spring 1994 survey—the first year in which questions were asked about a broad range of neighborhood problems—are presented separately for white, African American, and Latino respondents. The survey described gang problems as "shootings and violence by gangs," and respondents were questioned separately about "drug dealing on the streets." In each case they were asked how they rated each in their neighborhood. The response options ranged from "no problem" to "some problem" to "a big problem." The topmost panels in figure 2.5 chart the percentage of Chicagoans who rated these as big problems in their area.

The concentration of gang problems in Latino and African American areas is apparent in figure 2.5. About 40 percent of African Americans and more than 30 percent of Latinos rated gang violence a big problem, compared to only 10 percent of whites. Street gangs were one of the most commonly cited problems among Latino survey respondents. Chicago's Latino community was home to fighting gangs as well as those plying the drug trade. There was intercommunal warfare between gangs of Mexican and Puerto Rican origin, and between them and African American gangs along the periphery of their home turf. In contrast, drugs funded the operation of the large and

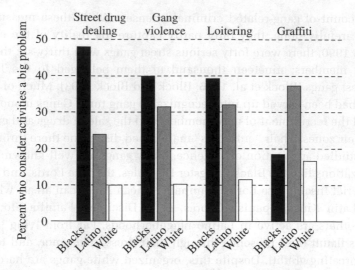

Figure 2.5. Crime, Disorder, and Decay Problems by Race, 1994

powerful gangs dominating the city's African American beats. Outbursts of gang violence there were frequently tied to conflict over
control of street drug markets and illegal arms sales. Turf wars easily
escalated into shootouts with semiautomatic weapons that put everyone in the neighborhood at risk. Residents spoke at meetings with
police about sleeping on the floor and away from the windows to
avoid stray bullets. Many knew families who had lost members to
drug-related gang violence. The high level of concern about street
drug markets among African Americans and Latinos can also be seen
in figure 2.5. Almost half of all African Americans interviewed reported that drugs were a big problem in their area, compared to
"only" 23 percent of Latinos. In both instances, levels of concern
were quite low among whites.

Drug markets were also a source of dissatisfaction and even suspicion of the police. At community meetings residents rose to name
names and street numbers, and to complain that they had been
telling police repeatedly about these problems and trying to supply
them with information about specific dealers, but to no avail. We observed one resident complain that he had been calling "for several
years" with information about a dealer living down the street, but
still no arrest had been made. Some grumbled that the apparent unwillingness of police to deal with such visible and widely known
crime must signal corruption, for they could observe street-savvy of-

ficers bantering with known dealers on a regular basis. At a meeting in one South Side beat, our observer reported:

> The most widely discussed issues were drug sales and drug use in the street; "thugs" hanging out in the street; and most of all, criticism of police responsiveness and their ability to resolve neighborhood problems. Many of the residents stood up or yelled, and many seemed to be at the end of their ropes, not knowing where to turn for a solution. One man in particular stood to talk many times. He announced the license plate number and description of a man who had been continually selling and using drugs on his block, at times in front of his kids. He repeated many times, "If I give specifics, when do I get results?!" The officers dealt with the criticisms in a professional manner and tried to answer the residents' questions to the best of their ability. Several residents went so far as to say they were ready to take on the offenders in the street in a violent manner rather than letting them take over the neighborhood.

In situations like this, officers often protested that their hands were tied by the courts; police frequently find refuge in this claim when the going gets tough in public meetings. They point out that they needed legal grounds to search people, and that street dealers had become very sophisticated about guarding their operations. At these meetings—and there were many of them—drugs are a divisive issue, for all the agreement by those in attendance that "something" had to be done.

Later chapters will document what happened to crime in Chicago, and how those changes were linked to other forces that were at work in the city during the 1990s. Both personal crime and property crime rates dropped dramatically over that period, and the greatest declines were reserved for African American beats where crime was initially so high. In parallel, yearly surveys documented a drop in concern about gang and drug problems, and African Americans enjoyed most of the benefits of that decline as well.

Disorder and Decay

Crime is not the only problem that disturbs city residents, and the city's new program was designed to accommodate that. Police knew that when they met with the public to discuss neighborhood priorities, a great deal of what would come up would not fall into the categories of problems that they were organized to respond to. This book considers two general classes of "nontraditional" policing problems: social disorder and physical decay. I have described social disorder as "signaled by bands of teenagers deserting school and congregating on street corners, prostitutes and panhandlers soliciting for attention, public drinking, . . . verbal harassment of women on the street, street violence, and open gambling and drug use" (Skogan 1990a). Others have added fare beating in subways (Kelling and Coles 1996), recreational violence in clubs and pubs, threatening phone calls (Leigh, Read, and Tilley 1998), homeless squatters, and "dumpster divers" searching for food (Finn 1988). Physical decay is another aspect of disorder. It encompasses visible neglect, abandonment, and the ravages of purposeful vandalism. It also includes the widespread appearance of junk and trash in vacant lots, graffiti, stripped and burned-out cars, collapsing garages, and boarded up buildings. Some of these activities and conditions are clearly illegal, others probably are but can be hard to get police interested in them, and some are the responsibility of city code enforcement agencies. Albert Reiss (1985) captured the essence of many forms of disorder when he described them as "soft crimes," lying on the boundaries of traditional definitions of crime and the priorities of police.

Later chapters will examine the city's success at addressing social disorder problems and fixing broken windows. To lay a baseline for establishing this, the 1994 survey included questions about a broad range of disorder and decay problems. Like the questions about gang and drug problems described above, answers were assessed by asking survey respondents how big a problem each activity was in their neighborhood. Figure 2.5 also charts the proportion of whites, African Americans, and Latinos who reported that selected issues were a big problem in their area, the most serious rating.

Figure 2.5 depicts the frequency of concern about one aspect of the physical decay of the city's neighborhoods: graffiti. Concern about graffiti was heavily concentrated among Latinos. Almost 40 percent of Latino respondents thought graffiti was a big problem in their neighborhoods, about twice the rate for whites and African Americans. Chicagoans study graffiti carefully, and ponder its significance for the neighborhood. It can be a sign that gangs are moving into their area, or growing more confident of their control of the neighborhood, and discussions of specific instances of graffiti take place at numerous police-community meetings. The following dialogue was described by one of our observers attending such a meeting in a heavily Latino area on the city's Near North Side. Note the detailed knowledge of the beat officer.

> A resident said there is a problem with graffiti and drug use in a nearby alley. The officer replied that the person painting the graffiti is an "I-Quest." He said the graffiti is signed "AOM," which stands for "another outrageous mind." He said he has been to the kid's house and told him that if he sees anymore graffiti, he will return. The officer noted that other graffiti is the work of peewee Maniac Latin Disciples. A resident said that residents must paint over graffiti immediately; he said they "cannot let it go." The officer added that there had been a big problem earlier, because of the anniversary of the death of a gang member. He reported that this graffiti was painted over quickly, and that arrests have been made.

Figure 2.5 also presents comparable data on public concern about one form of social disorder: loitering. In the surveys, loitering was described as "groups of people hanging out on corners or in the streets." In 1994, loitering was the most highly rated social disorder problem in the city. Among African Americans, 39 percent reported that loitering was a big problem in their neighborhood, and among Latinos the figure was 32 percent. Chicagoans associate loitering with a host of related problems, including gang activity, violence, street gambling, public harassment, drug sales, public drinking, and other activities. When asked about his neighborhood's biggest problem, one respondent to a neighborhood survey replied: "Drugs. How the guys stand on the corners, you can't even walk down the street because they are selling the drugs. They stand in the middle of the block." Another was concerned because, "the guys are always on the corners saying 'rock,' 'hot,' and 'weed'." A third observed that, "gangs get together on the weekend. They hang out in the streets. They have problems with other gang members and gangs start shooting each other." Another identified his beat's biggest problem as: "Teenagers. No respect. There is no curfew. You hear them cursing, hanging on the corners." Others pointed to problems like: "People on the corners in the liquor stores cause fear to other people," "Guys hanging on the corners all night long," and "Younger kids hanging out on the corners and on the next block. It has become a party street because the teenagers hang out on the weekends, and I have called the police because they were so loud around two in the morning."

Social disorder and physical decay were among the primary targets of community policing, once public complaints began to help steer the program's priorities. Chapter 6 details some of the strategies that were employed to deal with them, including police partnerships with city-service agencies, more intensive enforcement of city codes, and campaigns against bad landlords and liquor outlets. Chapter 7 examines how Chicago fared during the 1990s and early 2000s.

Confidence in the Police

Another challenge facing the city as it moved toward community policing was whether the public—and especially those who needed help the most—would be interested. The community side is critical as the police side for sustaining an effective community-policing program, but many cities have experienced difficulty in getting residents involved. One multi-city study found that "all eight . . . sites experienced extreme difficulty in establishing a solid community infrastructure on which to build their community policing programs." It concluded that, of all the implementation problems these programs faced, "the most perplexing . . . was the inability of the police departments to organize and maintain active community involvement in their projects."[4]

The problem for American cities is that residents of poor and minority neighborhoods with serious crime problems often have antagonistic relationships with the police. The police are another of their problems. Police frequently are perceived to be arrogant, brutal, racist, and corrupt. African American families worry about being "profiled" on the way to work, and how it will go when their sons are stopped and frisked while they are out with their friends. It could be a stretch for the poor and disenfranchised to think of police as potential partners rather than as adversaries. In our first survey, Chicagoans were divided along class lines, with homeowners and better-off residents sharing more positive views of the police than their counterparts. They also split sharply along age lines, with city residents under age thirty being dramatically less enamored with police service than were those in older categories. But the most significant cleavage over policing was along racial lines. In the original prototype police districts where the program was developed, African Americans and Latinos were two-and-a-half to three times more likely than whites to report that the police were unfair, impolite, unconcerned, and unhelpful (Skogan and Hartnett 1997).

Groups representing these neighborhoods will not automatically look to the police for legitimacy and guidance either. Rather, they are likely to be involved in monitoring misconduct and pressing for police accountability. In the 1960s, African American communities could be found organizing to protect themselves *from* the police (Marx and Archer 1971). More intensive policing today in the areas they represent could seem as likely to generate new complaints about harassment, indiscriminate searches, and conflicts between police and area youths as it would to solve serious crime problems. Groups in these areas are more likely to point with alarm to "the root causes of crime," and to press for jobs, better housing, and health care. There may be no reason for them to think anything about community policing except, "here today, gone tomorrow." Too often their past is strewn with broken promises and programs that flowered but then wilted when the funding dried up or the newspapers lost interest. They are rightly skeptical that it will be any different this time, especially when they discern that the police officers they deal with are not fully committed to the program.

Chapter 9 traces a bit of the history of police-community relations in Chicago. The litany of public concerns is a sad one, ranging from discrimination in police recruitment, promotions, and assignments, to the apparent misallocation of police resources in ways that favored predominantly white districts. African Americans and Latinos were much more likely than whites to feel badly treated during routine encounters with police, and they were much more likely to be shot by the police. These, along with recurring episodes of corruption and nagging evidence of organizational ineptitude that bothered everyone, undermined public confidence in Chicago's police in a noticeable way.

To illustrate divisions over policing by race, figure 2.6 examines the depth of racial division around policing at the outset. It is based on responses from the 1994 survey, the first that was conducted in Spanish as well as English and was large enough (with more than thirteen hundred respondents) to reliably examine the views of whites, African Americans, and Latinos separately. Figure 2.6 presents the percentage of respondents giving police a favorable rating on three selected questions about the quality of police service in their neighborhoods. The questions represent three general dimensions of

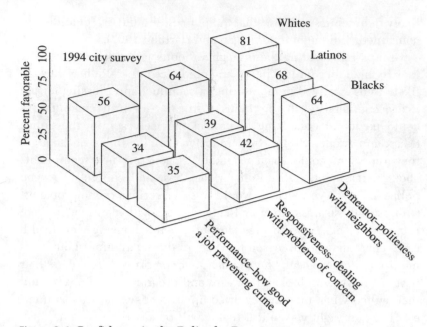

Figure 2.6. Confidence in the Police by Race, 1994

public opinion that will be described in detail in chapter 9: police demeanor, responsiveness, and performance. The height of each bar represents the percentage of respondents who were either "very" or "somewhat" satisfied; that percentage is also reported at the top of each bar. Racial differences in opinion were quite large. Everyone was most satisfied with how politely police treated people in their neighborhoods. Even among African Americans, two-thirds reported that police were very or somewhat polite, rather than somewhat or very impolite. However, the *gap* between whites and others was still 17 percentage points for African Americans and 13 points for Latinos. In terms of police responsiveness to the problems that concern neighborhood residents, whites were substantially more likely than either African Americans or Latinos to give police a favorable rating, and the gap was not much smaller when people were questioned about police effectiveness at preventing crime. And, unlike the question about police demeanor, far less than a majority of African Americans and Latinos were willing to give police a positive rating on their responsiveness to neighborhood concerns, and only about one-third of both African Americans and Latinos thought they were effective at preventing crime.

Of course, within these groups, Chicagoans were not of one mind about their police. The divisions varied, and they were often considerable. In 1994, the most consistent factor was age: younger people of all races were less positive about the police. For example, among African Americans under age thirty, only about 15 percent believed that police were responsive to the community, while among those over age fifty the comparable figure was 50 percent. Among whites, homeowners were more positive than renters, dividing 52 percent to 42 percent on the same measure. Among Latinos, education was also important: only 16 percent of Latinos without a high school diploma believed police were responsive, while among high school graduates the comparable figure was 34 percent.

But race was the paramount factor dividing Chicagoans. It was clear to everyone that community policing could be a hard sell in many sections of town. The white population was continuing to decline, further draining the city of the police's greatest supporters. Latinos, who were arriving in large numbers, were more dubious in their outlook, perhaps reflecting their experience with police in their native countries. African Americans—who were holding their own in terms of numbers—did not look to be strongly in the police camp, either.

Police Support for Community Policing

Finally, a key part of the backdrop for the events that ensued in Chicago during the 1990s and the first decade of the twenty-first century was the readiness of police officers themselves to get involved in community policing. Across the country, efforts to implement community policing have sometimes failed in the face of resistance by ordinary officers. Enthusiasm by public officials and community activists for neighborhood-oriented policing encourages its detractors within the police to dismiss it as "just politics." They see it as a passing fad, and something dreamed up by civilians for the police to do. Police are also very protective of their autonomy. They are often skeptical about programs invented by civilians. Policing is dominated by a "we versus they" or "insider versus outsider" culture that assumes that the academics, politicians, and community activists who plan community-policing programs cannot possibly understand their job. They do not like civilians influencing their operational priorities or evaluating if they are effective. Officers who serve in community-policing units also are at risk of being seen as not being "real policemen." Police officers prefer to stick to crime fighting (for a case study of how this happens in New York City, see Pate and Shtull [1994]).

Evidence of some of this could be seen in our earliest surveys of police officers. In 1993, a round of questionnaires was completed by officers who served in districts that had been selected for the experiment. They were questioned before anyone at their level in the organization knew anything in particular about the new program. The questionnaires were administered to 1,470 officers at the beginning of orientation sessions that were held at the police training academy. The results provide some insight into potential impediments to organizational change, and a baseline for evaluating subsequent changes in officer's attitudes. The officers who were to serve in the experimental districts were typical of the department as a whole: almost 80 percent were male, nearly two-thirds were white, 26 percent were African American, and almost 10 percent were Latinos.

The results were not encouraging to the program's promoters when we fed them the results. Officers were certainly concerned about outsiders intruding into their business. They were asked whether the new program would make a list of outcomes "more likely," versus "less likely" or "no change." They thought the following would be more likely: "greater citizen demand on police resources" (72 percent more likely); "more unreasonable demands on police by community groups" (71 percent); "greater burdens on police to solve all community problems" (65 percent); and "blurred boundaries between police and citizen authority" (51 percent).

Their views of their roles on the street also were not very congruent with the demands that community policing was going to make of them. They were asked whether they agreed or disagreed with a list of statements "about police work and law enforcement in this city," and they did not express much enthusiasm for community-oriented work. Figure 2.7 charts the percentage of African American, Latino, and white officers who agreed "strongly" with three statements that encapsulated the role they were about to be trained to take. In response, almost 20 percent of African American officers, but only 7 percent of white officers, were enthusiastic about the view that "police officers should work with citizens to try and solve problems in their beat." About the same low proportion strongly supported the view that they should make frequent informal contact with beat residents. Police can easily find ways to justify their aloofness from the

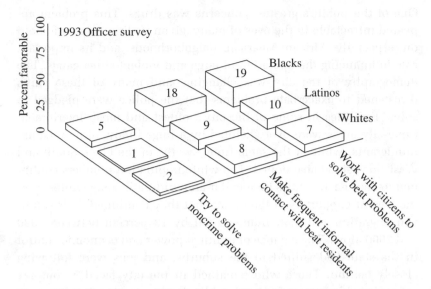

Figure 2.7. Police Views of Their Role in Community Policing, 1993

community; as one officer told me at the time, "You can't be the friend of the people and do your job." On this and many other measures there were some racial cleavages within the patrol force over community policing. One reading of figure 2.7 is that African American officers were more than twice as supportive of community-oriented work as were white officers. Another view is that hardly anyone saw community-oriented work as their job.

Finally, many Chicago police officers were unconvinced that they had much support from the community. They were asked if they agreed or disagreed with statements concerning this point, including: "most people have no idea how difficult a police officer's job is" (85 percent agreed); and "citizens do not understand the problems of the police in this city" (78 percent agreed). Most tellingly, when asked if "the relationship between the police and the people in this city is very good," only 13 percent said yes.

The City's Prospects

This was the situation the city found itself in in the early 1990s. Crime, and especially violence, stood at a high level. In fact it peaked in 1991, but no one yet knew that crime was taking a long-term slide.

One of the public's greatest concerns was drugs. This problem appeared intractable in the eyes of many, given its firm economic hold on, especially, African American neighborhoods, and its important role in financing the operation of large and violent street gangs. The demography of the city was changing, and many of these shifts threatened to exacerbate problems that the police were pledged to solve. Facilities in some of the city's oldest and most deteriorated inner-city areas were overwhelmed by a huge inflow of new Latino immigrants, while at the same time, swaths of the black South and West sides stood abandoned. The white population numbers continued to decline; the city's blue-collar and middle-income whites were the biggest supporters of the police, but they continued their suburban migration and their numbers fell by 13 percent between 1990 and 2000 alone. The balance of political power and economic control in the state had shifted to the suburbs, and jobs were following closely behind. Those who remained in the city faced a complex array of problems, ranging from public drinking and gang loitering to rampant gang graffiti and streets and alleys choked with abandoned cars.

The solution to all of this could not just be to just arrest more people. During the early 1990s, some cities were turning to policies like "zero tolerance" to solve their problems. Arresting massive numbers of people for "quality of life" offenses and stopping many more on the street for name checks and pat-downs was their path to reducing crime. But Chicago had a larger vision. While arresting people who broke the law remained a valued goal of policing, it was not clear how that responded to many problems that analysts thought were central to the viability of the city and that residents swore were driving them crazy. In 1993 the chief of police released the department's first strategic plan, and in it he described the underpinnings of the new community policing initiative he was about to launch. He noted in his rationale that "Chicago police are identifying and apprehending more offenders than ever before." But, he concluded, "the primary result of all this arrest activity has been backlogs in the courts and severe overcrowding in the jail and prison systems, not a reduction in crime or in citizen fear of crime."[5] On the next page he stated:

> There is a growing realization that enforcement of the law, long the primary source of legitimacy and direction for police agencies, is just one of several means for the police to get their job done. A strong and efficient criminal justice system remains

an important element of crime control. . . . But the role of police in society is larger than simply enforcing the law. Other
approaches—order maintenance, conflict resolution, problem
solving, coordination of government services that impact crime—
must be developed in the future. The quality of life in Chicago's
neighborhoods will be improved not only by removing hard-
core criminals from the streets, but also by addressing those
conditions that contribute to unacceptable levels of fear and disorder.[6]

So, Chicago crafted a program that spoke to complex problems as
well as simple ones, and involved residents and other city agencies
in addressing them. It was not going to be easy, and change had to
begin with the police department itself.

THREE

Reengineering the Police

Chicago's community-policing initiative was formally inaugurated in April 1993. Dubbed "CAPS" (for Chicago Alternative Policing Strategy), the program plan was not devised on a desk at police headquarters. Rather, a rough outline of a program was developed and then tested and refined over a fifteen-month period in five experimental districts. There it sometimes succeeded and sometimes failed, and senior department managers used this experience to reformulate its structure. Following this development period, community policing expanded to encompass all twenty-five police districts and to involve almost every city agency.

However, as time passed, it became apparent that many elements of the program were still not working, and that the reasons for this were deeply rooted in the organizational structure and culture of the police department. By 1998, community policing in Chicago was dead in the water. Police were just going through the motions. But just as things were looking bleak for CAPS, a new generation of leaders within the department seized on this organizational drift, seeing it as an opportunity to implement new management initiatives aimed at revitalizing CAPS and other important aspects of the department. Among their solutions was the inauguration of a management accountability system resembling—on the surface—New York City's famous CompStat process. Over the long haul this last move may or may not have proved to be good for community policing, but it was part of a package that promised to bring the management of the department into the twentieth century, just as it was ending.

This chapter describes the program-development process and the product that eventually emerged. It dissects the obstacles to making it work, and describes the police department's struggle to overcome them. There is an analysis of how well selected aspects of the program operated, but the evaluation's findings about what happened in the community are reserved for the chapters that follow. This description of the program development and implementation process is based on observations of meetings and interviews with hundreds of police managers and civilian department employees, conducted over the twelve-year period of 1993 through 2004. It also incorporates findings from surveys of police officers, observations of public meetings, and an analysis of administrative records of the police department.

Inventing Community Policing

Chicago's community-policing plan proposed to redefine the department's mission, reorganize its operations, and forge a new relationship between police and residents of the city.[1] While CAPS was to be implemented by the Chicago Police Department, its genesis was in city hall. Community policing was the mayor's response to his city's many ailments. These included racial division, crime, and dissatisfaction with police service. Such issues had the potential to derail his upcoming 1995 bid for reelection. He would be challenged by an African American candidate, and in order to win he needed to gain support within the city's growing Latino population. Unlike his white constituents, Latino neighborhoods were plagued by gangs, drugs, disorder, and decay. Latinos also were skeptical about many aspects of police performance. Surveys conducted in 1993 in the experimental districts documented that Latinos were even more likely than African Americans to report that police in their neighborhood were unhelpful and seemingly unconcerned about their problems (Skogan and Hartnett 1997). Alleviating the conditions contributing to crime and actually resolving racial conflict may have seemed beyond his reach, but the mayor could prod his police to become more effective and popular in the neighborhoods. He also hoped to extract more value out of the nearly one billion dollars that his police department cost each year.

A management consulting firm was hired to help set the course for the overhaul of the Chicago Police Department. Its report proposed a sketchy plan for using the people and money saved by its recommendations to begin a community-policing program. Actual responsibility for devising and implementing a neighborhood-oriented policing program was placed in the hands of a manager who sat four layers down in the department's organizational hierarchy. He found leadership and staff support in the department's research and development unit. However, the unit did not sit in the chain of command with direct authority over actual police operations. Everything it wanted done in the field had to be approved by separate layers of administrators, and many of them thought that the turn toward community policing was a bad idea. Progress was halting, but pressure from city hall to get something into the field did not go away. So instead of developing an elaborate, citywide plan for community policing, a bare bones experiment was conducted in selected districts. The idea was that the prototype districts would provide test-beds for refining a program that eventually would be implemented citywide. The prototypes generally represented the diversity of Chicago's neighborhoods, and the experiment was conducted using the district managers and street officers who were already in place, in order to test if community policing could work in the real world.

The general direction in which the department was supposed to move was outlined in its strategic plan, *Together We Can.* This thirty-page document set forth the department's rationale for adopting community policing, describing it as going "back to the grass roots." A section on "the components of change" described some of the steps that were to follow, ranging from the introduction of new technology to changes in performance evaluation. It included a new mission statement calling for quality service and a partnership with the community that would empower both police and residents. In an introductory statement printed next to his picture, the mayor announced that "community policing means reinventing the Chicago Police Department."[2] In his message, the chief noted that the mayor "has made this a top priority for all municipal agencies, not just the police."[3] *Together We Can* was widely distributed and mailed directly to every member of the police department. Just as important, it was included on the official list of documents that were fair game for inclusion on the department's promotion exams.

While it highlighted some of the key steps necessary to implement community policing, the department's strategic plan was not a "how-to" manual. It provided a fairly coherent vision that a small group of research and development staff members, consultants, experienced district commanders, and a few senior department managers could pursue. They, in turn, developed an operational plan and eventually drove the process of expanding CAPS to encompass the entire city. The mayor made it clear to the heads of his agencies that cooperation with the police in this joint venture was to be their highest priority, and they sent high-level administrators to planning and coordinating meetings. One of those was a monthly summit conference held by the mayor in his outer office. These "CAPS oversight meetings" brought together the most senior police and agency managers and the

CAPS development team. There the mayor announced his solutions to seeming impasses and pounded the table demanding that those attending pick up the pace of change.

The first round of training for community policing involved all of the officers serving in the five experimental districts. To put the scale of the experiment in context, they constituted a force that was larger than the entire police department in cities like Cleveland and Atlanta. They went through a one-day orientation session that introduced CAPS and the inevitable paperwork it would entail, and then a three-day program aimed at developing their decision-making and interpersonal skills. Next, every department supervisor and manager attended training sessions—two days for captains and lieutenants, and four days for sergeants. Finally, in 1995 the entire patrol division—more than nine thousand officers—received two days of training in problem solving. Since each training module was the first of its kind, developing and delivering all of this training was an expensive and exhausting effort. In 1995, training sessions ran twenty-four hours a day, six days a week, at three different sites, and it still took months to move the patrol division through the process. However, without training, officers would inevitably fall back on the tried-and-true, regardless of what the department's plan called for.

Taking CAPS Citywide

Following this development period, CAPS expanded to encompass the remainder of the city. The coordinated delivery of city services was phased in five districts at a time, beginning in January 1994, and was operational in all twenty-five districts by July of that year. During autumn 1994 the twenty nonprototype districts began to divide their officers into rapid response units and beat teams. During this period, the department's outmoded 911 system struggled to accommodate distinctions between beat teams and rapid response units, and to follow dispatching procedures that would keep the new beat teams in their assigned area. The districts all began to hold community meetings on a regular basis by May 1995. By autumn 1995, teams of civilians and police officers were conducting problem-solving training sessions for the general public all across the city. In addition, the city trained municipal workers serving the twenty new CAPS districts on how to respond to CAPS service request forms identifying problems that included abandoned buildings, car tows, potholes, and broken lights.

As it expanded to encompass the entire city, CAPS acquired a new operating unit. Chicago made a significant political and financial investment in the community side of community policing by establishing the CAPS Implementation Office. Civilians were hired to push resident involvement in community policing and coordinate problem-solving projects. The CAPS Implementation Office eventually expanded to a staff of eighty-eight. Each police district had several community organizers and a service coordinator. Some organizers were supplied by about a dozen nonprofit community organizations that were contracted to hire and supervise them. All of the organizers had four goals: to create new block-level organizations where they were needed; to involve existing organizations in CAPS and problem solving; to teach community members to work together to solve problems; and to identify the extra resources needed to solve the most serious problems and support specific police problem-solving projects in their neighborhoods. The Implementation Office also coordinated a CAPS marketing campaign, which is described in chapter 4. Youth services coordinators worked on school safety initiatives, and building services coordinators identified problem buildings and worked with their owners to improve the properties. By 1999, the Implementation Office had a budget of about nine million dollars. Its budget was carried as a line in the police department's overall budget in order to protect it from hungry city council members, who otherwise would try to capture control of the jobs.

Organizational Design for Community Policing

The central elements of the community-policing plan for Chicago that evolved out of the prototyping experience can quickly be summarized under four subheadings: turf orientation, community involvement, problem solving, and interagency partnerships. But CAPS was a complicated effort, and coordinating the many activities that fell in those simple categories was not easy. Patrol activities had to be reorganized in a fundamental way, and with more than nine thousand officers, the patrol division was the largest unit in the department. Some goals of the program potentially conflicted with provisions of the union contract. Another challenge was that only some elements of the program were in the hands of the police. To make problem solving work, CAPS required the close support of other agencies of city government. These agencies—all large bureaucracies with firm ideas about how to do their job—had to adjust their priorities to accommodate unpredictable service requests by the police. Residents and the community organizations that represented them had important new roles to play as well: in helping set police priorities, identifying service problems, and undertaking their own problem-solving projects. On their side, police had to develop participatory structures that involved residents in these activities.

Turf Orientation

The city first decided that community policing in Chicago was to be a neighborhood-oriented, turf-based program. What problems did this solve for the department? In a remarkable section of *Together We Can,* the chief of police described the lessons of what he described as "national research" that "exposed, and for the first time quantified, many of the limitations of the traditional policing model, in particular its ability to impact levels of crime."[4] One lesson he drew was:

> The demise of foot patrols and beat integrity in favor of directed patrol over a large geographic area prevented officers from becoming knowledgeable about specific problems and individual people on their beats. And as police officers' time became managed almost entirely by 911 calls, their ability to engage in meaningful proactive law enforcement activities nearly evaporated. The very technology that O. W. Wilson and others introduced to help professionalize law enforcement—squad cars, radios, 911 systems, and the like—ended up isolating officers from the citizens they were sworn to serve and protect. Ironically, this isolation from the community cut police off from a critical source of information and support they needed to succeed under the traditional model.[5]

The solution, what the chief of police called "a smarter way of policing," was to reestablish the connection between individual officers and geographical areas small enough that they could practically serve them. Some cities (one example is Fort Worth, Texas) tried to do this by assigning a "community service officer" to each neighborhood, leaving the remainder of the department comfortably uninvolved in community policing. In some cities, only poor and minority areas get a community officer. Other cities have created roving teams of specialized "problem solvers" who respond to the crisis of the week. In Chicago, beat work and local problem solving is not a specialized task. Rather, all patrol work was reorganized around small geographical areas, the city's 279 police beats. Teams of officers were assigned to handle all of the regular 911 work that originated in their beat, and the dispatching system was reorganized to help them handle that load *plus* have some time free for other community-oriented duties. There are either nine or ten officers on each team (in safer areas a day watch officer may patrol alone rather than with a partner), and about 2,700 officers are dedicated to this scheme. Before, the central radio dispatch system sent patrol officers from place to place across their entire district in response to 911 calls. District officers knew a lot about the area's regular troublemakers, but after that their knowledge of the neighborhoods and the many problems there was very uneven. In particular, they had little contact with what officers like to call "the good people" of the community; they only talked to residents when they were in trouble or making trouble. Under CAPS, officers are tied to specific areas to enable them to learn more about the problems there, and so that residents can get to know them. This kind of contact is fundamental to adopting a problem-solving approach to policing, and for working with residents on those problems.

As in all cities, the traditional work of district officers in Chicago consists primarily of driving around, looking out the window while waiting for a call. Because of this, the department's fundamental work unit had been an eight-hour duty tour by a pair of officers in a car. But shifting the center of gravity from cars to places made it natural to think of teams of officers, because places need to be guarded twenty-four hours a day, seven days a week, all year around. So, the officers who were needed to regularly work in a beat "24-7-365" were assigned a sergeant and turned into a beat team. Procedures were created to encourage information sharing and coordinated activity across watches among members of the team. Early on these included small huddles (known as "face-to-face relief") between incoming and departing beat officers at roll call, and paperwork that remained in the front seat of their dedicated beat car. Beat cars prominently display their beat numbers on the roof and have become quite familiar to residents. The department also strove for continuity of assignment. The idea was that beat team officers would keep their assignment for at least a year, as opposed to switching jobs every few months or even weeks, as they had in the past.

At this time the department also shifted from the practice of rotating officers' shifts every twenty-eight days, so that in about three months they had worked their way around the clock, to one in which everyone worked the same shift on a regular basis. Rotating shifts had proved to be a real impediment to establishing personalized police-community linkages in other cities. For example, Minneapolis had tried to establish a "cop on the block" program, but the same officers could not be counted on to be available for more than a few weeks at a time (cf. Skogan 1990a). In 1993, Chicago moved to a system of fixed tours of duty on one of three daily watches. This was done independent of CAPS, as part of negotiations with the police union, but the stability that it created played a major role in ensuring that the same police faces would turn up on a regular basis at meetings with the public. More training could be concentrated on the day and early evening officers, who have many opportunities to deal with the general public, and less on the men and women coming to work at midnight.

The department's dispatching process was reorganized to ensure that most of the calls that officers answered originated in their assigned beat, and that they spent most of their time on that beat. This is known in police parlance as "maintaining beat integrity," and you may recall that in the quote above, the chief of police lamented having lost it. Priority was given to responding to calls for which officers' knowledge of local conditions could make a difference. Other kinds of calls (such as "cold" burglaries for which victims just needed a report for their insurance companies) were routinely assigned to other units. Keeping teams on their beats necessitated creating another group of officers—district rapid response teams—who picked up calls that beat officers could not handle. Rapid response units did drive from place to place in order to backstop beat teams that were overloaded. Because assigning beat cars off of their beat was supposed to be a last resort, the dispatching rules even specified that plainclothes tactical officers and sergeants were supposed to answer calls rather than send a beat team out of their area. However, tactical officers (who often dress like pirates and lurk in alleys) usually stay off the radio when they think a regular beat job might come their way, and they are too wily for dispatchers to find them.

Finally, not very much would have been gained if beat teams just continued to drive from call to call, for they still would not have time to work on problems or meet with residents of the area. The management consultant's original calculations included some "unassigned" time when it recommended an increase in the size of the patrol force to support community policing. To make this possible, changes were made in the dispatching system that freed beat officers' time for community-oriented work. In particular, they attend public meetings that are being held in every beat, virtually every month.

While committed in principle to keeping beat units in place, implementing the concept was difficult. Chicago traditionally responds to a high percentage of 911 calls—about two-thirds of them—from a total of about five million calls each year. Senior managers routinely grumble about this and lament that they have been unable to force through alternative procedures that could handle the large number of calls that actually do not require that a car be sent to the scene. However, that is the local custom, and as a political matter the department could not risk backing off from this commitment in order to staff an untried community-policing program. Grumpy politicians and the media, fed by the program's opponents within the department, would crucify them the first time a call did not get answered fast enough. The consultant who had drawn up the original CAPS plan warned that the charge that police were unable to respond to 911 calls because officers had been diverted to community work had sunk community policing in Houston at the end of the 1980s. The consultant's staffing calculations made it clear that the city had to hire more officers to deal with the unrelenting pressure of calls and maintain beat integrity at the same time. Their analysis indicated that this would take as much as a 15 percent increase in the number of district patrol officers, and the mayor took on the task of finding the money. In addition, for several years the department's antiquated 911 and radio system made hard to ration the assignment of beat teams and rapid response units. Field sergeants were supposed to intervene on the radio to correct misassignments in order to maintain beat integrity, but it was highly variable whether or not they did so. In 1998 we conducted a 3 p.m. and 4 p.m. roll call survey of more than eight hundred officers in all twenty-five police districts. Officers with beat assignments were asked if their supervisors corrected dispatchers when they heard misassignments. Just over half (54 percent) reported that their supervisors intervened "rarely" or "not at all."

However, this aspect of the program gradually became a success. The department's initial goal was to keep beat teams on their turf for 70 percent of their dispatches. For a few years it was virtually impossible to get any useful data on how well they were doing in this regard. On one occasion the research and development unit had tabulated a sample of several thousand handwritten forms in order to calculate a rough measure of how well dispatching was going. The opening of a new computerized dispatch center eventually solved this problem. The first complete numbers, which were not available until 1998, indicated that the average team stayed on its beat for 66 percent of the calls they handled.

The data were silent, on the other hand, about what officers did when they were *not* hurrying to respond to calls. That was supposed to be their CAPS time, but apart from data from the 911 operations center on dispatches, it was hard for headquarters to pin down what officers were doing with that time. To be sure, officers had packets of forms in the front seat of their cars that they were supposed to fill out documenting how they spent their "free" time, but little of this information was keyed and analyzed. The only way downtown managers could check on what officers were doing was to pull a sample of paper watch assignment forms and read down the lines of entries, a very labor-intensive task. When it came to CAPS, not much of the information on the forms was relevant to community policing anyway. On their part, officers were dismissive of paperwork, for they had joined the force to be "doers" rather than "pencil pushers." Perhaps they were doing much more than they recorded, but perhaps not.

To make use of the data they did have, in 2000 the city commissioned a university-based consulting group (not us) to restructure patrol work and reallocate resources so that beat teams could both stay on their beat and deal with most of the calls there. It was apparent that the one-team-per-beat model could only work if beats were frequently resized to balance workloads. However, being flexible ran in the face of other program goals. CAPS also required geographic stability, so that both officers and residents could identify with their beat and get to know one another. Before CAPS, beats were record-keeping units of minor importance to the police department and unknown to the public. By 2000, when the reallocation process was set in motion, CAPS had succeeded in making beat boundaries a highly salient way that Chicagoans thought about their neighborhoods. The districts distributed maps that outlined the boundaries of the area's beats and told people when and where they could find "their" beat meeting. Many beats were holding successful meetings and fielding problem-solving projects, and they were hesitant to give up what they had won. Many community organizations were at first hesitant about CAPS. They sensed that beat meetings and other activities associated with the program would compete for their members and their members' time. However, by 2000 they too had accommodated the current system, for being "against CAPS" was not a winning posture in most communities.

There were also conflicting views—almost a philosophical debate—of how the boundaries *should* be redrawn. Should beats be homogeneous with respect to race and class, so that residents shared mutual interests and concerns? This might help them deliberate and decide on community priorities and speak with one voice about what they wanted from their local police. It might also minimize community infighting, something that the police feared would dominate redrawn beats. Or, should the goal be to ensure diversity in the composition of beats, to give residents an opportunity (and the challenge) to build communication and trust across race and class lines? In an attempt to turn a set of highly political questions into an administrative matter, the consultant was charged with figuring out how to reconcile these contending agendas while improving the capacity of beat officers to get their work done.

But a fatal blow struck the process. It turned out that politicians also wanted a voice. They wanted, at a minimum, to influence how beat lines intersected their ward boundaries. More important, they wanted to shape the remapping process so that they could keep what they already had, and get more too. Everyone developed a formula demonstrating that they were underpoliced, and needed more officers in their constituency. Politicians representing poor and African American areas pointed to their high violent crime totals and claimed that this required more police officers. A report of the Midwest office of the U.S. Civil Rights Commission presented data supporting this position, as part of a detailed description of the racial politics of the department (Illinois Advisory Committee to the United States Commission on Civil Rights 1993). Politicians in areas with less crime preferred per capita calculations, arguing that "equal protection" meant that everyone had the right to the same level of policing. In the end it came down to racial politics. In truth, any crime-based or workload formula would document that predominantly white parts of town had more than their share of officers. However, their representatives were not going to give them up, and they had the most clout in city hall on this matter. Internally, the police department prepared elaborate scenarios that would support any direction that the mayor wanted to move, but he was immobilized by the conflict that would break out over any change to the current beat map. Four years after the planning process began, no officer reallocation had taken place.

In addition to beat integrity, continuity of assignment for individual officers also proved difficult to arrange. An important aspect of the CAPS plan was that working officers—members of the beat team—would be the ones who met with residents on a regular basis, not the public relations specialists who previously gave speeches at community events. Several beat officers who were not on duty at the time would also attend community meetings in order to represent other shifts, and they would be paid overtime. Shortly, this would cost the department more than one million dollars a year. Officers who worked in the district's neighborhood relations units also came along. They were trained in how to deal with the public, but they were instructed not to take leadership roles at the meetings because they were not actually working there. An anticipated feature of the meetings was that residents would come to know the officers who regularly attended, and the officers would also be the ones who answered calls and could be seen around the neighborhood. On their part, beat team officers needed to stay in one place long enough for residents to meet them and learn to trust them. Time would also help officers develop a personal sense of "ownership" of their turf and develop an ethos of teamwork.

However, police in Chicago regularly bid for their district and shift assignment by seniority, so officers could be held to a specific beat assignment for no more than one year. Managers had no choice when it came to which officers they had on hand to do which jobs. In addition, personnel transfers, vacations, relief duties, court appearances, and compensatory time off made it hard to maintain staffing stability. The resulting turnover of officers from public meeting to public meeting did not go unnoticed, and both regular attendees and community organizations periodically complained about it. To assess the department's ability to stabalize beat meeting attendance by police officers, we examined department reports that were filed about each beat meeting and recorded the employee identification number of each officer listed as present. During 1998, an average of seven police officers attended each beat meeting, and during the course of the year 4,650 different officers showed up for at least one meeting. Beats meet an average of ten times per year, so officers were classified as "regular participants" if they attended at least five meetings in a beat during that period, a generous standard. In total, 14 percent of all beats did not have *any* regular officers, and another 22 percent had only one or two. About one-quarter had three or four regular officers. Overall, we judged that 36 percent of beats had adequate personnel stability, with at least five officers (remember that the count includes neighborhood relations specialists) attending meetings regularly. Continuity of officer participation in beat meetings was far from random. In particular, poor African American areas least often had a full compliment of regular participants; only 26 percent of those beats had five regularly attending officers. Beats in Latino areas did not do much better (28 percent). Better-off African American beats did better still; 42 percent of those beats saw a large compliment of officers on a regular basis. On the other hand, more than 60 percent of the predominantly white, middle-income beats in the bungalow belt ringing the far edges of the city had five or more police officers attending meetings there on a regular basis.

But all in all, the department's reorganization effort was a success. In an extensive report issued in 2004 (Skogan and Steiner 2004a) the evaluation team issued grades to various aspects of CAPS. Our analysis of the effectiveness with which Chicago reorganized to support community policing received an "A." While many departments announce that they are doing community policing and then rely on the commitment of their officers to make something happen, Chicago fundamentally reorganized their daily work and how it was assigned and managed.

Community Involvement

Chicago's strategic plan envisioned a significant role for the community in its new policing program. *Together We Can* noted that: "the police are part of, not separate from, the larger community; and . . . a partnership of shared responsibility with the rest of the community is critical to effective public safety. . . . The partnership should be based on open, ongoing, and constructive communication between Department members and the rest of the community, including residents, business owners, and their customers. All Department members . . . must develop an intimate understanding of the communities they serve—their cultures and customs, their problems, their hopes, and their needs."[6] In terms of involvement, the strategic plan stated: "Beyond opening up lines of communication, the Department and the rest of the community must establish new ways of actually working together. New methods must be put in place to jointly identify problems, propose solutions, and implement changes. The Department's ultimate goal should be community empowerment"[7]

As the department's plan evolved, four distinct roles emerged for community residents in the new program. Citizens could: (1) provide information and identify local problems, (2) help police set priorities, (3) take actions on their own—and in conjunction with the police—to solve neighborhood problems, and (4) use the meeting to hold police accountable for their efforts. The success with which CAPS involved residents in all of these roles is examined in detail in chapters 4 and 5.

Why did the department take this turn toward community involvement? Several factors were pushing them in this direction. The first was city politics. As noted above, it was widely understood that there was deep dissatisfaction among Chicagoans concerning both crime (which peaked in 1991) and policing (which did not do well in the polls). Adopting community policing, which was a hot buzzword at the moment, played well as a response, especially with the media and sophisticated community organizations that were aware of what was already going on in other cities. At another level it was about regaining legitimacy among the most disaffected Chicagoans, who were black and brown. As we saw in chapter 2, the city's white population was shrinking, and leaders with an eye toward the long term understood that finding ways to capture the loyalty of African Americans and Latinos was essential for the long-run stability of the city. In any event, Chicago did have a long tradition of organizing communities around neighborhood problems, and this was just a new take on an established way of doing business in the city.

In part because of this tradition, many Chicagoans—especially community activists pushing for reform through community policing—also believed that empowered community members could be effective agents for crime prevention. We will see in chapter 5 that few outside neighborhood activist circles were really interested in sharing very much power, despite the chief's declaration that his "ultimate goal" was community empowerment. However, this was an effective way to sell community policing to groups that had the potential to make trouble. In *Together We Can,* the chief noted: "The Department will be most effective when it is able to create conditions under which communities can improve themselves up front, instead of always relying on the Department and other government agencies for after-the-fact responses."[8] By the mid-1990s the city found ways to funnel grants and contracts to a number of city hall friendly community organizations that paid them to turn out residents for beat meetings and problem-solving projects. This was a Chicago-style tradition of community empowerment that everyone was fairly comfortable with.

Finally, the mayor had agendas besides community policing. Another was to improve the effectiveness with which his service agencies responded to the concerns of the voters and taxpayers. The next section of this chapter reviews the problem-solving aspects of CAPS, but public involvement in setting priorities for his agencies was one of his strategies for imposing more discipline on them. During the first eighteen months of CAPS, during the program development stage in the five prototype districts, the mayor invested his own time, effort, and staff to seeing to it that the city services component of the program worked effectively.

Two organizational structures were developed to give community involvement a chance to emerge: beat meetings and district advisory committees. Beginning in mid-1993, police began holding neighborhood meetings in every beat in the prototype districts. They were regular—usually monthly—gatherings of small groups of residents and officers working in the area. By the spring of 1995 these meetings were being held in church basements and park buildings all over the city. In the CAPS plan, beat meetings were to be the principal mechanism for building and sustaining closer relationships between police and the general public. The meetings were to provide a forum for exchanging information, and a venue for identifying, analyzing, and prioritizing problems in an area. They were a very convenient place to distribute announcements about upcoming community events, circulate petitions, and call for volunteers to participate in action projects. The meetings also provided occasions for police and residents to meet face to face and get acquainted, a feature that was facilitated by the formation of fairly stable beat teams. As they evolved, beat meetings also became a venue for regular reports by police to the community on what they had done since the last meeting about the problems that had been discussed.

Beat meetings are public gatherings open to all and are generally attended by beat officers on duty at the time, a few team members from other shifts, and the sergeant who supervises the beat team. Officers serving in specialized units, such as gang officers or detectives, are often present as well, along with a representative of the district's neighborhood relations unit. The meetings are sometimes attended by representatives of the city's service departments, local aldermanic staff, and organizers from the CAPS Implementation Office, as well as by people working for area community organizations. School principals and local business operators come as well. Almost all beats meet monthly and the sessions are well publicized. Surveys in the late 1990s and early years of the new millennium indicate that more than 60 percent of Chicagoans were aware that beat meetings were being held. Chicagoans attended beat meetings 59,200 times during 1995 and on about 67,000 occasions during 1999. In 2003, a total of 60,000 Chicagoans showed up, and by the end of that year the cumulative turnout since 1995 totaled more than 582,000.

Over time, the variety of meetings involving police and the public grew. A few large and diverse beats were subdivided and regularly hold separate meetings. Beginning in 2002, meetings in a few beats plagued by low turnout were merged with those held in adjacent beats in order to boost attendance. The department also began to experiment with holding meetings at new times and days, including—for the first time—on Saturdays. Beats in the downtown area meet less often, and many who attend there represent businesses and building security units. Heavily commercial police districts have a specialized business liaison officer to handle these kinds of events. Civilian facilitators are recruited and trained by the police to assist them in running beat meetings. Police districts and individual beats sponsor other kinds of assemblies as well, including marches, rallies, and block parties; smaller meetings between police and neighborhood activists or ministers; and neighborhood watch and cell-phone patrol groups. District officers are assigned to attend meetings held by the subcommittees of the advisory committee for their district.

Beat meetings are one of the most remarkable features of CAPS. Cities that adopt community policing typically form a few citizen advisory committees, and the chief of police can be counted on to deliver a few speeches each year at large city assemblies. Only Chicago sustains anything resembling this turnout. Nobody else's community meetings have Chicago's explicit representation and action components. Police agencies from around the world send representatives to see beat meetings in operation. Most go away shaking their heads, however, for few nations other than the United States have a tradition of autonomous, voluntary citizen action in the public safety domain.

It should be clear that beat meetings and the other participatory structures developed for CAPS are not a "grassroots" movement, for all their popularity. They are creatures of city government. The meetings have heavy support from district officers, who identify places where the meetings can be held, publicize them, largely run them, and are paid for attending. Police who are there generally have been trained in how to run a good meeting, although this is not their strong suit. The meetings are an example of an emerging governance strategy that Archon Fung (2004) dubbed "empowered participation." For reasons that suit the city and the police, they have granted participants the ability to influence the actions of the police, by expressing their priorities, voicing complaints (and praise) about police effectiveness, and choosing to lend a hand in this or that project. While they meet in church basements and park district buildings all over the city, there are limits on what they can do. They only have what Fung (2001) labeled "accountable autonomy," for the police officers who are in charge are held responsible for what goes on there by their sergeants and lieutenants. Residents who attend are free to deliberate and express their preferences, but the meetings do not take votes to decide things, and the only residents involved in running these meetings are chosen and trained by beat sergeants. Chapter 4 explains the political dynamics that lay behind this tightly constrained role, for there were other visions of the role that the public could play in community policing.

Chapters 4 and 5 present a detailed examination of the involvement of the public in beat meetings. There were problems in making them work. Attendance proved to be highly seasonal, and Chicago has a long, bad winter. Early on, the meetings were dominated by public relations specialists from district neighborhood relations offices, while officers who worked the street sat as a group in the back with their arms folded. It took awhile for a clear linkage to develop between discussion at the meetings and action on the street. Not enough meetings had effective Spanish-language translation, and Latinos, in particular, were very underrepresented at the meetings. But, as chapter 5 documents, the meetings improved substantially over time, and the sustained turnout at beat meetings signals that residents think they are getting something for their time and effort. Beat meetings were most popular in African American neighborhoods. Rates of attendance were higher in the poor, deteriorating, high-crime areas that needed help the most.

The police officers who attended beat meetings were also quite satisfied with what happened at them. In 2002 observers attended multiple meetings in a sample of 130 beats, in order to observe what happened and to survey those who were present. The 640 officers who were surveyed reported that the residents who attended adequately represented the beat (85 percent agreed), relations between police and residents at the meeting were good (92 percent reported they were "congenial"), the problems discussed concerned the beat rather than just individual concerns (80 percent), and that they were satisfied with the level of community attendance at the meetings (70 percent). More than 80 percent reported that they made personal contacts with people who live in the beat when they were not involved in answering calls.

In addition to beat meetings, committees were formed to advise commanders of each district. District Advisory Committees (DACs) are composed of community leaders, school council members, ministers, business operators, and representatives of organizations and institutions of significance in the district. They were supposed to help police managers identify and prioritize problems for the district as a whole. However, the DACs were not a success. Few followed through on their responsibilities and they played a very limited role in planning and priority setting. They were not very successful in representing all segments of their communities, or at independently representing residents' views (Skogan and Steiner 2004a). Beat meetings, on the other hand, have been a big hit. Residents turn out steadily and in large numbers. As described in chapter 4, surveys of those who attend find they are generally very satisfied with what goes on at the meetings and feel that things are changing in their neighborhood as a result. Chapter 6 presents evidence that beat meeting activism helps steer the distribution of city services. Finally, the marketing program orchestrated by the CAPS Implementation Office succeeded in driving awareness of the program to high levels. We gave Chicago a "B" for public involvement. Beat meetings deserved an "A" but rudderless drifting of the DACs and some shortcomings in resident representation and their involvement in problem solving (see below and chapter 5) pulled down the final grade.

Problem Solving

In the plan for CAPS, officers were to move beyond responding in traditional fashion to individual 911 crime calls, and to adopt instead—or more accurately, in addition—a proactive, prevention-oriented stance toward a wide range of chronic crime and disorder problems.

In Chicago's model for policing, a "problem" is defined as a group of related incidents or an ongoing situation that concerns a significant portion of those who live or work in a particular area. The links between incidents can arise from common victims, offenders, or locations. Together these three elements are known as "the crime triangle," and part of problem-solving training is to learn how to tackle these components of a crime problem. The general rule taught at training is that at least two sides of the crime triangle need to be "brought down" (this is police training) in order to successfully eradicate a problem. Figure 3.1 presents a graphical depiction of the crime triangle that is used by the police for training purposes. Problems are also defined by their persistence; the CAPS plan describes targeting *chronic* crime and disorder problems. These are problems that are unlikely to go away without an intervention of some magnitude, because they typically have already survived routine attempts to resolve them. Because problems are persistent, the repeated incidents probably share causes, so dealing with underlying conditions may help prevent future problems. This is the basis for claiming that CAPS is "prevention oriented." It is also important that problems potentially can be solved using the resources that police and the community can bring to bear on them; not everything is in their power.

Finally, problems need not be serious criminal matters. While dealing with crime remains at the heart of the police mission, it was envisioned from the beginning that the responsibilities of the Chicago police would expand to cover a much broader range of community concerns. These include minor social disorders, municipal service problems, and a broad range of code enforcement matters that are handled by civil courts and administrative hearing officers. Problems frequently are not serious criminal offenses; they range from noise to people draining their car radiators at the curb to the dilapidated condition of many of the city's older rental buildings. A very important feature of Chicago's model for problem solving is that it involves a significant expansion of the police mandate.

Another feature of the plan is that it offers problem-solving roles for the general public. Citizen involvement intersects the activities of

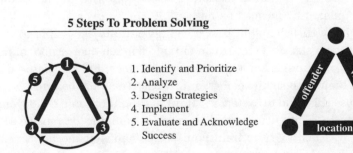

5 Steps To Problem Solving

1. Identify and Prioritize
2. Analyze
3. Design Strategies
4. Implement
5. Evaluate and Acknowledge Success

Figure 3.1. Chicago's Problem-Solving Model

the police on the action side of the program as well as on the problem identification and prioritization front. As chapter 6 describes in
more detail, residents get involved in a variety of ways. They can be
seen painting out graffiti with city-supplied materials, clearing vacant lots, and pasting street address numbers on garages so police
can find their way to problems through the alleys. They also can sign
up for more assertive forms of neighborhood vigilance—for example,
picketing a troublemaking business and getting in the way of customers in order to encourage the owner to clean up his act. Beats can
use their meetings to plan these activities and sign up participants.

Police and neighborhood residents were trained to tackle neighborhood problems using a five-step process. Figure 3.1 also presents
the chart used in department training programs to describe it to officers and members of the public. The first step is to *identify* problems
and prioritize them, and in Chicago this features a great deal of community input. Next, officers and residents are to *analyze* problems
following the "crime triangle." The process calls for them to gather
information about offenders, victims, and locations of crimes. Subsequently, they are to *design strategies* that might deal with the chronic
character of priority problems. They are asked to think "outside the
box" of traditional police enforcement tactics, and to use new tools
that were developed to support their problem-solving efforts. Chicago's model also recognizes a stage during which the community,
police, and other city departments *implement* strategies. This highlights the special skill and effort required to actually put plans in
motion. Finally, police and residents are to *evaluate* their own effectiveness by assessing how well they carried out their plan and how
much good they accomplished. Technology was developed to encourage this kind of thinking when addressing crime problems. An
easy-to-use crime mapping system was developed that runs on familiar personal computers at each district station, using data constantly updated by means of a network. Crime maps and arrest data
are routinely distributed at beat meetings and are accessible to the
public at each station. Officers can tap into a much deeper pool of information, including color pictures of arrestees and databases describing their tattoos, nicknames, and "MOs" (*modus operandi*).

Because this kind of systematic thinking about chronic conditions
was alien to a city accustomed to reactive policing driven by 911
calls, it was necessary to train both police and neighborhood residents on how to implement the model. Without training, both groups
could have fallen back on their old expectations and habits. Between

1995 and 1997, most patrol officers and more than twelve thousand civilians were taught to analyze how offenders and victims collide at particular locations to create crime hot spots.[9] Both police and residents were also given new tools for solving problems, ranging from computerized crime analysis to the expedited delivery of city services, and without training they might not have made very effective use of the new resources that were created for the program.

Another aspect of the department's new turf orientation was that officers were supposed to be able to "step down" from the radio. Officers assigned to beat teams were expected to engage in identifying and addressing a broad range of neighborhood problems in partnership with neighborhood residents and organizations, and to attend community meetings. In order to get involved in community-oriented work, they needed time away from dispatches. During problem-solving training sessions conducted in 1995, police we interviewed were particularly skeptical that they would get this kind of time. There was only mixed success in turning the unassigned time created by the new dispatching system to proactive beat problem solving. An officer survey conducted at beat meetings in 1998 (there were 1,030 respondents) included questions about what they did with their "free time" on patrol. In the survey, only 30 percent of the officers indicated they often had time for preventive work, rather than reactive work assigned to them through radio dispatches. Fewer still (22 percent) said they easily could request and be granted down time to work on beat problems. Officers working the critical 4 to 12 p.m. shift, who were in the best position to be involved with community organizations and beat meetings, were also the busiest and least likely to have the time to do so.

Part of the problem was that breaking away from the radio ran contrary to the organization's informal culture. Officers who did so were accused of "dogging it," or not picking up their share of the workload. From their vantage point, supervisors reported they rarely heard officers requesting specific CAPS problem-solving downtime. One beat sergeant noted: "[Officers] don't [ask for downtime] enough. I tell them to. Maybe they're afraid. Sometimes when officers request dispatch to go down to do problem solving, other officers 'cat call' [a sharp whistle on the radio to show displeasure]." There was some success in the department's effort to foster cross-shift teamwork among beat team members. Before the advent of beat team meetings, officers serving on different watches rarely had an opportunity even to exchange information about conditions in their beat. With CAPS, beat teams began to hold some regular cross-shift meetings that served two purposes: to foster team planning and strategizing about problems, and to exchange information across shifts. The meetings were led by their beat team sergeant, who was to monitor officers' priority-setting and problem-solving activities.

Why did Chicago adopt this complex plan? In *Together We Can* the chief of police argued that policing in urban American was broken and needed fixing.

> Like other metropolitan police agencies, the Chicago Police Department's ability to address these conditions is presently limited. Chicago police are identifying and apprehending more offenders than ever before: in the last ten years, the number of arrests for index crimes [a traditional measure of police effectiveness] has increased 20 percent. But the primary result of all this arrest activity has been backlogs in the courts and severe overcrowding in the jail and prison systems, not a reduction in crime or in citizen fear of crime. . . . These conditions suggest that the police must find new ways of enhancing their crime-fighting capacity beyond the traditional law enforcement techniques they have come to master over the years.[10]

The report reviewed more of those "lessons of national research" that exposed the limitations of the traditional policing model. Among them were that police have to address fear of crime and not just index crimes measured in their statistics; there are limitations in the effectiveness of preventive patrol by automobile; rapid response to 911 calls is reactive rather than truly preventive; and "continually arresting and incarcerating offenders has little deterrent effect in the long run."[11] One conclusion the chief of police drew from all of this was that the time was past when he could just demand that the city hire more police officers so they could "get the job done." And besides, the city could not afford that. "Chicago is faced with a widening gap between citizen demands and government resources. The resulting strains on the budgets of not only the Police Department, but also schools, parks, streets and sanitation, and other city services, only exacerbate the already dangerous conditions that are contributing to high levels of crime, disorder, and fear in so many of our neighborhoods."[12] He went on to describe the integrated nature of the new program: "This new strategy must go beyond the limitations of traditional policing. It must expand the Police Department's capacity to control and prevent crime. It must emphasize the results of our work, instead of just the activities we perform. And it must mobilize the resources of City government and the community in a united effort to make a real difference in the lives of all Chicagoans."[13]

In the text, *Together We Can* referred to "problem solving" or "solving problems" nineteen times.

There were other reasons for adopting a very broad problem-solving orientation as part of CAPS. As I pointed out in chapter 1, by the early 1990s the city had bought into what is known as the "broken windows" theory of neighborhood crime, and this was another force pushing the expansion of the police mandate. In Chicago it is widely believed that crime is rooted in a broad range of neighborhood conditions and events, and that it is necessary to address both criminal and criminogenic problems to take the mission of preventing crime seriously. In addition, in the early 1990s the mayor had another item on his agenda: cleaning up the city and making it greener. In no small measure, community policing in Chicago is linked to painting out graffiti, towing abandoned cars, cleaning up alleys, boarding up abandoned buildings, and clearing and mowing vacant lots, because the mayor wants his city to look better and feel safer. Through CAPS service requests and agency partnerships—considered in the next section—he was able to harness this agenda to community policing.

Making problem solving work was probably the most difficult challenge the department's new program presented, and CAPS got its lowest grade for it. To be fair, every police department has trouble making problem solving work: it requires a great deal of training, close supervision, strong analytic capacity, and organization-wide commitment. For all the rhetoric about gathering and analyzing data, thinking outside the box for solutions to problems, and involving tactics in addition to trying to make more arrests, a close examination of problem solving in practice can find it wanting. In San Diego, the most problem-oriented police department in the country, officers use their personal experience to figure out ways to arrest someone that they have identified as an offender, and that's about it (Cordner and Biebel 2005).

We concluded that many efforts to solve local priority problems had not been very effective. District-level priorities get more sustained attention, but the same problems, in about the same locations, persist year after year. As we shall see in chapter 5, the effectiveness of beat meetings in setting problem-solving agendas for the public declined a bit over time. Officers received no refresher training in problem solving, and more than a decade has passed since resident activists were offered any training opportunities. Like police everywhere, Chicago officers traditionally work with a very limited "toolbox" of strategies. During the 1990s, the solutions they proposed to the priority problem they identified for their beats could be summarized as drive by more frequently and make more arrests. Analysis of hundreds of beat-level plans (the study was detailed in our January 2003 report) found that efforts to solve local priority problems had not been very effective. District-level priorities got more sustained attention, but the same problems, in about the same locations, persisted year after year. Over time the effectiveness of beat meetings in setting problem-solving agendas for the public declined. After their initial exposure to problem solving in the classroom, officers received no refresher training, and the department gave up offering resident activists any training opportunities. Refocusing on problem solving could provide an opportunity to re-engage the community in the active partnership promised by CAPS

Agency Partnerships

Having accepted responsibility for a broad-ranging problem-solving orientation, CAPS planners knew that the police department could not go it alone. Many of the issues that vex neighborhood residents—abandoned buildings and cars, garbage-strewn vacant lots, rats in the alley—cannot be solved by traditional police methods, nor usually by the police at all. Yet they anticipated that when police began to meet with the public these kinds of concerns would surface frequently, and it would be important to have in place a way to respond to them.

Just as important, the mayor understood this as well. In his preface to *Together We Can,* the mayor served up a warning to his service agencies. "As Mayor, I recognize that the police can't do it alone. If community policing means reinventing the way the Chicago Police Department works, it also means reinventing the way all City agencies, community members, and the police work with each other. Everyone must share the responsibility for the safety and well-being of our neighborhoods"[14] From the beginning Chicago planned that coordinating the delivery of the full range of city services would be an integral part of community policing, and that service requests routed through the police would receive priority attention. The process is initiated when police officers complete a CAPS service request form. These forms capture information about the service being requested and the location. They include space for a brief narrative description of the problem. Most service needs can be described on the form with only minimal effort, reducing the paperwork burden that police officers dread. Completed forms are funneled through the districts, with some noted as emergency cases when appropriate, and then entered into a case-tracking system that sends them to the proper city agency. Problems can be identified by officers on routine patrol, but many surface at beat meetings or in informal contacts between beat officers and residents. Figure 3.2 presents a sample service request form.

Making this process function smoothly was difficult. The service agencies are large, entrenched bureaucracies with their own ideas about neighborhood priorities and the pace at which their workers can respond to "outside" complaints. They are used to responding to politicians' demands, but at first they thought that community policing was the police department's program. Soon, however, the mayor made his commitment to interagency cooperation clear in a very forceful way. He called a meeting of his agency heads and announced that they would either make service coordination with the police department work or lose their jobs. They toed the line (cf. Skogan et al. 1999). An interagency task force worked on the logistics of coordinating efforts against problems, while programmers developed a software system that logs in, tracks, and records the final disposition of police service requests and generated status reports. Staff from the CAPS Implementation Office double-check problems in the field to make sure that they get fixed. Changes were made in city ordinances to facilitate expedited building demolition and car tows, two frequent service needs.

But even this seemingly simple process ran afoul of police culture. Initially, officers were skeptical that the city's cumbersome bureaucracies would be sufficiently agile to meet their requests, and they feared they would be left twisting in the wind after promising residents that something would be done about a problem. At a training session we observed, officers laughed when the head of the streets and sanitation department claimed that her agency would come through for them. There was emotional as well as practical resistance to getting police involved in filling potholes. In the early years, many officers simply refused to fill out request forms. A vocal faction of beat officers resented their new role as the first link in the process. They felt that they would not only be held responsible by

CITY SERVICE REQUEST
CHICAGO POLICE DEPARTMENT   DATE

DISTRICT _____ BEAT _____ LOCATION ___ ___ ___ ___ ___ _____
                                          (NUMBER)   (DIR.)   (STREET NAME)

SERVICE DESCRIPTION:		GRAFFITI REMOVAL:	WAIVER SIGNED: □ YES
□ LIGHT □ WATER LEAK		MATERIAL: □ BRICK □ PAINTED BRICK	□ NO
□ HOLE □ CLEAN		SIDING (SPECIFY) _____	
□ CAVE IN □ BULK			
□ CART □ HYDRANT		OTHER _____	
□ SIGN □ HEAT			
□ TREE		OWNER (IF KNOWN) _____	

ABANDONED BUILDINGS: □ VACANT   □ OPEN   □ BRICK   □ FRAME
                       □ GARAGE   □ SECURED   FLOORS _____

□ STREET   □ VACANT LOT
□ CURB   □ PARKWAY   ABANDONED AUTOMOBILES: MAKE _____   YEAR _____
□ CHA   □ MIDDLE OF STREET
□ CORNER   □ SIDEWALK   LICENSE PLATES: □ YES □ NO # _____ STATE _____ YEAR _____
□ ALLEY   □ VIADUCT
□ HOUSE   □ SEWER BLOCK   CITY STICKER: □ YES □ NO # _____

                               HAZARDOUS AUTO: □ YES □ NO   FLOAT: □ FULL □ PARTIAL
□ ALL   □ ONE   □ TRAFFIC
□ OUT   □ CUT   □ TRIM HIGH COLOR _____ (TOP/BOTTOM)
□ NEW   □ OPEN   □ TRIM LOW
□ PLANT □ STUMP □ DAMAGED   VIN _____
□ REMOVE □ RESTORE
□ MISSING □ REPLACE   OTHER INFORMATION _____
□ INSUFFICIENT
OTHER _____

CRIMINAL HOUSING TASK FORCE: **NUISANCE PAY PHONE:**
BUILDING LOCATION _____   □ REMOVE

NUMBER OF UNITS _____ OWNER'S NAME _____   □ HUMAN SERVICES
                                                             REFERRAL
COMPLAINT _____
_____   □ LIQUOR CONTROL
                                                             REFERRAL

COMPLAINANT INFORMATION:
NAME _____ ADDRESS _____   **NEIGHBORHOOD
                                                          RELATIONS OFFICER
APT NO. _____ HOME PHONE _____ WORK PHONE _____   ONLY**
ORGANIZATION _____   _____

NARRATIVE: _____ PRIORITY
_____   (CHECK ONE)
_____
                                                          □ EMERGENCY
REPORTING OFFICER _____ STAR NO. _____
                                                          □ NON-EMERGENCY
R.D. NO. _____ I & I NO. _____
                                        (INITIALS)

CPD - 21.208 (REV. 1/96)   WHITE COPY - SEND TO MAYOR'S OFFICE OF INQUIRY AND INFORMATION, CITY HALL, ROOM 100
                            BLUE COPY - RETAIN IN NEIGHBORHOOD RELATIONS OFFICE

Figure 3.2. CAPS Service Request Form

residents for ignored service requests but also that there was a fundamental unfairness to the assignment, because "they don't call streets and sanitation workers when there's a robbery!" One officer lamented, "Everybody complains to us. Why can't the community call their alderman to complain? What do potholes have to do with police work?" In the area he worked in, we found that beat officers could not be bothered reporting collapsing sidewalks or open fire hydrants. In another beat we studied intensively, officers resented serving as what they dubbed "the pooper-scooper police." In the most graffiti-ridden area we could find, beat officers had not filed a single request for a site cleanup. In the beginning, this feeling was a general one. In the spring of 1995 we surveyed 7,300 police officers from every district of the city. Asked if "police officers should try to solve noncrime problems in their beat," only 30 percent agreed. Seventy percent were pessimistic when asked if CAPS would result in "more unreasonable demands by community groups." Two-thirds of them feared it would lead to "a greater burden on police to solve all community problems."

But during the program-development period the service-delivery component was one of the most successful elements of CAPS. The evaluation found that, in contrast to matched comparison areas, physical decay went down in all three of the most troubled prototype districts (Skogan and Hartnett 1997). In districts where abandoned buildings, graffiti, and trash were ranked among the most serious problems, these problems declined substantially in comparison with trends in similar areas. Several districts made effective use of the new service-delivery emphasis to target specific problems. In time, service requests became a routine way for responding to residents' complaints at beat meetings. The CAPS Implementation Office stationed civilian service coordinators across the city to see that problem-solving projects had the support that they required. Some policing initiatives routinely coupled intensive enforcement efforts with extensive cleanup projects. This included "superblock" projects that focused community involvement and infrastructure rebuilding efforts on very small areas, and the city's weed-and-seed-style Distressed Neighborhood Program. Even while police are still securing these areas, city crews can be seen towing abandoned cars, clearing alleys, trimming trees, and erecting new streetlights. The city's "Clean and Green" cleanup program is run by the CAPS Implementation Office. Now service requests are entered directly into the service-tracking system using personal computers located in police district stations. The system allows station personnel to check the status of individual requests and print out reports on service requests for distribution at beat meetings.

One novelty of this new service-delivery model is that it draws a closer, faster connection between residents and service providers. As one police officer described it: "I think it's empowered people. It's put them in touch with city services. They used to depend on the alderman, which was good if your alderman was strong, but otherwise things didn't get done. That's not true any longer. People can control the policing that occurs in their neighborhoods."

As a district commander noted, "The way this is set up, it really levels the playing ground for everyone. Everyone is entitled to—and gets—a good level of services."

We will see in chapter 6 that the link between service need and service delivery is substantial. There was a strong tie between citizen priorities, as measured in surveys, and the service-delivery rate for their beat, measured using agency records. Citizen involvement in CAPS played a role in steering service delivery as well. Service-delivery rates were higher—controlling for need and other factors—where beat meeting attendance is high and in beats where residents who came to the meetings were especially concerned about a problem. Citizen involvement helps the squeaky wheels get greased.

In another move, the city created a roving task force to enforce its anti-gang and anti-drug house ordinances. The team includes police, building inspectors, and health inspectors. They can initiate both criminal and civil cases against owners who refuse to negotiate with city attorneys or comply with an abatement plan that brings their building under control and up to code. An extensive program was developed to assist landlords in screening and evicting tenants. The city's law department, with its expertise in handling civil cases, stations attorneys in selected police stations. There they work directly with beat officers on problem buildings, and on gang and drug house projects. In parallel, jurisdiction over many building cases and civil charges arising out of health code violations and rules regulating gang and drug houses was removed from the regular courts and passed to a new city administrative hearing bureau. The bureau typically processes cases swiftly and facilitates settling cases through formal agreements between city attorneys and landlords or business owners.

Chapter 6 describes the role of the police department's agency partners in more detail. It describes how the service request process, coupled with efforts by city hall to ensure that other agencies delivered on their commitment to respond, created a system that successfully steers services in response to citizen demands. Other cities have failed to develop unified approaches to problem solving because of the differing bureaucratic needs of the organizations involved. A neighborhood officer in Fort Worth, Texas, remarked to me that he was fortunate to have a brother-in-law working for the street department, because other neighborhood officers did not have the connections they needed to get special help from the city. But in Chicago, community policing is the city's program, not just the police department's program, and at the end of the day that is one of its greatest strengths.

Hitting the Wall

By the end of 1995 the major features of Chicago's community-policing program were in place on a citywide basis, and in the spring of 1996 CAPS was formally codified by the release of a new departmental general order that put everything down on paper. The challenge at that point was to make the plan work, but evidence slowly began to accumulate that in many instances the plan was not working very well.

This should not have been a surprise. For a long list of reasons, police departments are extraordinarily hard to change. We have already seen evidence of the effect of police culture in the unwillingness of officers to become "pooper scooper police" by filling out service request forms, however meritorious that might seem to downtown planners. The more general rule is that they do not want to do things that are not "real police work." Another aspect of police culture is their aversion to civilians playing any role in telling them what to do or evaluating their performance. In Chicago, the visible role placed by civilian planners, citizen advisory boards, and vocal community activists in planning aspects of CAPS ran directly into this wall. Like police everywhere, they believed that no one who is not "on the job" could possibly understand their work. Even the top brass in police headquarters were dismissed as "out of touch with the street" when they tried to change business as usual. In fact, trying to do so defined them as being out of touch.

CAPS was also not properly managed, at every level. It relied too much on individual goodwill and motivation to get the job done the CAPS way, and not enough on supervising the performance of employees closely and holding them accountable when they did not get the job done. One problem was sergeants. Sergeants like to think they are the most important people in police departments, and that is probably right. They turn policy into practice by setting the daily working agenda for their officers. But at this level, commitment to CAPS was spotty at best. Our surveys found that beat team sergeants were much less supportive of CAPS than were their superiors (Skogan and Hartnett 1997). One reason for this was that they were far from handpicked, and often did not even want the job. In many districts the job of supervising beat teams was automatically passed down to the newest sergeants as they came on the job, because it was an onerous task that they had to do *in addition* to their "real" job. Often their regular assignment did not encompass the beats that they were handed, and they had little opportunity to interact with beat team officers outside of the quarterly team meetings. This created an imbalance of responsibility among sergeants, because those with beat team duties faced a greater workload without additional compensation. Many quit as soon as they could, leaving the job to an untrained replacement. One beat team sergeant spoke for most we interviewed: "I'll just say that the sergeants that are the beat team leaders are really the ones driving the CAPS program on a district level. . . . So they should give us more money. Why the hell would I do this? It's a lot of work. It's a lot of responsibility, where another guy right next to me doesn't have [the same responsibility]. I might get a higher efficiency rating, but . . . money. Give us money. What's at the end of the rainbow?" The actual day-to-day supervision of beat teams remained in the hands of field operations sergeants, who were not responsible for seeing that key components of community policing like problem solving or interaction with the community were carried out with any dedication.

Above the level of sergeant, no one was in charge of CAPS most of the time. As one senior manager put it, "From the stripes to the oak leaves . . . [i.e., from sergeants to the most senior top brass] . . . everyone was left out." Making community policing work was one of the jobs of the district commanders, but their list of responsibilities was two pages long. In light of the many things that could go wrong in a district—including charges of brutality, too many "bad" (unsupportable) shootings, and revelations of corruption—no commander was going to be fired for hosting bad beat meetings. The commanders also could not work twenty-four hours a day, so most of the time real authority rested with watch commanders, who were there around the clock. But they had no role in CAPS at all. None of its elements was on their list of managerial responsibilities, and there had even been no CAPS training for watch commanders—an oversight that CAPS managers later rued.

Another on the list of obstacles to police reform around the country is resistance by midlevel managers, who see their authority being undercut by decentralization, calls for greater officer autonomy, and other organizational innovations commonly associated with community policing. In Chicago, the barons whose fiefdoms were threatened were area deputy chiefs. They sat above the district commanders, each overseeing five of them. This was one of the most important management layers in the organization. CAPS planners knew that, over the long haul, downtown could not micromanage the activities of the districts; that had to be the job of area chiefs, who were closer to the action and commanded resources that they could commit to special projects. But area chiefs also were not involved in CAPS, and they were not monitoring its implementation in their areas. In this instance it was because most area chiefs did not *want* to take responsibility for CAPS, and no one would make them do it. CAPS managers understood that community policing would never be the routine stance of the organization until the area chiefs took charge, but they had no authority over the chiefs, who remained resistant to change.

CAPS implementation also stalled because of turnover at the top. One reason why police reforms often fade is that the tenure of chiefs is short, but the opponents of change are in it for the long haul. The top-down, command-driven structure of policing grants a great deal of influence to whomever is chief, and often incoming top executives want to establish themselves by sweeping out the old while their boom is still new. Expensive projects initiated by an earlier—and sometimes discredited—administration are vulnerable to cutbacks. At the end of 1997 the superintendent who oversaw the launching of CAPS saw his career cut unexpectedly short by a personal scandal. He was forced to resign, and everyone in the organization held their breath and refrained from doing anything out of the routine until they saw which way "the new guy" would go, supporting CAPS or not. Their nervousness was reinforced when the department's most important proponent of community policing—the original CAPS manager—was passed over for the promotion after making a determined bid for the job. Knowing that his career in Chicago was finished, he left to take on the herculean task of reforming the police department in Washington, D.C. The wait and see period turned out to be a long one. It was to be almost eighteen months before the new superintendent began to make it known where he wanted CAPS to go. In the meantime, only brave managers hitched their star (in this case, literally, their gold police badge) to making CAPS a further success.

At the bottom, officers on the street were deeply unhappy about how the department was being managed. A battery of job satisfaction questions administered to the 7,300 officers who were surveyed in 1995 found only 5 percent thought the most qualified people were picked for jobs; only 18 percent agreed that the organization was open to suggestions for change from its employees; only 22 percent thought that management treated its employees well; and more than half reported their supervisors paid no attention to them when they had an idea of their own. Chicago police respond to this by following a set of "rules for blue shirts" that dominate police culture in the city. The first is that "blue shirts [that is, patrol officers] don't tell white shirts [sergeants and above] what to do." Among other things, this means that news that something they have been told to do is not working often does not pass back up the chain of command. Unwelcome news has traditionally not traveled very far in Chicago. Another rule is that "blue shirts do not tell blue shirts what to do." That is, you do not monitor or correct your peers—that is the job of white shirts. CAPS' founders—and modern administrators everywhere—envision themselves at the helm of flexible, responsive organizations able to adapt rapidly to changes in their environment, staffed by self-directed teams of professionals motivated by the mission and policies of their agency. However, it is hard to make this happen without improving blue-white relations.

Our examination of CAPS implementation found that little was happening at the core of the department's new problem-solving process. Downtown planners had devised a "bubble-up" planning model. It was to begin with beat-level plans that carefully identified priority crime and disorder problems, and proposed how to solve them. These plans were to be a grassroots effort by beat officers and their sergeants, one that incorporated their local knowledge and the concerns expressed by area residents at beat meetings. Plans were to be passed to their district management team, which was charged with setting priorities among competing demands for police resources. The district management team could, in turn, go to the area chief for help with problems that went beyond their resources. However, out in the field we found that beat plans were being made up haphazardly and filed away, never to be seen again. Beat sergeants were supposed to ensure that a piece of paperwork—a Beat Plan Implementation Log—was completed everytime something was done about each problem, which would enable district managers to keep abreast of progress in solving priority problems. But when we looked in the file drawers, these forms were blank. We also found that few district plans actually relied on grassroots information in any event, and when the districts drew up their plans, the sergeants who were supposed to implement them mostly reported to us that they had never seen one.

One plainspoken district commander told us what he thought of the planning process:

> You wanna know how I'd rate [my district plan]? It's an academic exercise. The whole thing should be scrapped. The plan means nothing. We fly by the seat of our pants. That's the nature of this business. The plan is a joke. They tell me to do it, I do it. It's got all the elements of a graduate school education in a second grade paper. It sits in a drawer. I take it out when I have to do something to it. Then I return it to the drawer until the next time I'm told to do something to it.

Many other formal requirements of CAPS were being met by "going through the motions." Information sharing across shifts was carried out very inconsistently. The department's sophisticated crime mapping and analysis system was largely being used to produce maps and lists for community meetings, and not to plan police operations. Our surveys of police found that beat officers believed they had little opportunity to take time away from their radio calls to do preventive work, with most being reluctant to even request it of their supervisors. Very significantly, no new management-level training was going on, so recently appointed commanders—most with scant CAPS experience—knew little about their new roles and responsibilities.

Many parts of the organization remained untouched by change. Despite the hopes of the planners, CAPS remained a patrol division program, operating without the involvement of other important units. Most notable were detectives, who ran a virtual "department within a department" through the late 1990s. In a city with a minority of whites and in a department with a healthy fraction of African American and Latino officers, in 1992 fully 91 percent of detectives were white.[15] This was a reflection of their "cloutful" status: it generally took the active support of friends and relatives in high places in the department to arrange a detective assignment, and having friends and relatives among the ranks of politicians helped as well. A succession of chief detectives pursued the same avoidance strategy, which was to smile warmly at the mention of community policing and indicate that detectives were planning to get involved soon. There were many other nooks and niches in the organization where police who did not like CAPS could also hide out and get ahead, including the organized crime division, the narcotics unit, and various roving squads of plainclothes tactical officers. Their anonymity and disconnection from any community contact helped them "take heads" and "kick ass" with relative impunity, in the name of good, aggressive policing. Because the ultimate measures of good police work remained in making arrests and seizing guns and drugs, those were the jobs that everyone wanted. Vacant positions in the department were always in the uniformed patrol division, which was responsible for community policing.

As this suggests, through the entire period of the 1990s the Chicago Police Department also was unable to come up with an alternative measure of good police work. *Together We Can* had promised otherwise. It noted that "the roles and responsibilities of almost all Department members will change dramatically. These changes must be reflected in our performance evaluation system as well."[16] However, while CAPS promotional materials proclaimed that police would work with residents to identify and respond to neighborhood priorities, the organization had no independent way of confirming those priorities or discovering what their officers were doing to respond to them. Officers and more than twelve thousand residents had been trained in problem solving, but the organization not only did not keep track of problems that were supposedly being worked on but also could not indicate if anything in particular was being done to address these problems. The final stage of the department's official four-stage problem-solving model was "assess success," and *Together We Can* noted that, "whereas in the past we have measured primarily activities, our new strategy demands that we evaluate results as well."[17] But the organization had no way of assessing if any problems had been solved. The department could not even track the time officers took to respond to incidents, because years in the past officers had gotten out of the habit of radioing in when they arrived on the scene, and no one wanted to take on the unpopular task of trying to make them start doing it again. In the policing world, finding ways to assess the effectiveness of a broad range of police activities— including community policing—is known as "measuring what matters" (cf. National Institute of Justice 1997). In Chicago, a great deal that was supposed to matter was not being measured at all.

We found that things were far from perfect on the community involvement front as well. As will be documented in chapter 4, surveys found that the most common and fastest-growing source of information about CAPS was television, but television does not appear to stimulate beat meeting attendance or involvement in CAPS activities. A round of observations of meetings in 253 beats found these meetings good at the mechanics (they were being held frequently and maintaining resident involvement, and an adequate number of police representatives were present), but that they were failing to foster much problem solving or facilitate organized efforts by neighborhood residents. Few residents were contributing anything toward solving problems, and in the part of the meeting where those present were to report on what had done since the last meeting, residents did not have much to say. Observers assessed the "action component" of each meeting on the basis of discussions of beat activities, calls for volunteers, and announcements of other meetings or projects, and judged that only one-third of the meetings had any. On our ten-point measure of beat meeting quality, the average meeting received a score of five.

So, by the time CAPS reached its sixth anniversary in 1999, it was languishing. No one was following through on widely recognized organizational deficiencies; well-meaning people were reduced to waiting for direction. Our report for the year indicated that CAPS was "at a crossroads, with important matters remaining to be settled." As one lieutenant put it, "The spark has gone out. The energy is gone." CAPS was dead in the water.

Reinventing CAPS

But even before the report was officially released, wheels had been set in motion to address some of these deficiencies. Senior managers had an advance copy, and had been briefed even earlier as part of an ongoing dialogue between the department and the evaluation team. These managers conducted their own investigation paralleling that in the report, hoping to demonstrate that the evaluation team was wrong. Astonishingly, their operatives reported back otherwise. This was to their credit, because the police department was not an organization that liked getting bad news. One internal investigator told us that, in many instances, "it's *worse* than you said." The most senior and conservative of the top brass was not particularly enthusiastic about community policing, but he was disturbed that department policies and directives were being ignored. Lower-level employees, in his view, did not get to pick and choose their strategic direction.

At an ensuing high-level planning session he read excerpts from our report aloud, including what that commander quoted above had to say about the "academic" nature of district plans, and the reform efforts that followed were conducted under his protection. The chief himself kept a close eye on the investigation, checking frequently to learn what the staff was finding, and he was extremely supportive of the effort.

The police department did not shift gears *because* of the evaluation report; it was just a catalyst. The principal role of the evaluation report was that its impending release (and accompanying press release) created an event to which the organization would have to respond. Bad news was not well received at city hall, and the mayor's operatives would want to know what was already being done about the issues it identified. The police department had to have a response ready, an important reason for briefing key members of the department in advance of the release of the report. This situation empowered up-and-coming managers to step forward with proposals about what to do. They did not always agree with one another. They fought furiously among themselves over both policy and power, and who was going to run what when the dust settled. This was especially true among the civilians in the process, who felt less constrained by the command and control tradition of the organization. Another reason the chief had to keep a close eye on the process was that the managers occasionally needed an umpire who could call a time-out. There were winners and losers in this struggle, and after it was settled, the losers either moved on to positions outside the department or retired.

Diagnosing the Problem

The first step was to discover what—exactly—was working and what was not. This task was put in the hands of a former commander who had implemented a vigorous version of CAPS in her district and now held an even more senior rank. She formed a team that included officers who had helped make CAPS a success in her district, and they conducted an assessment of the implementation of CAPS. Team members interviewed managers and officers, attended meetings, observed beat meetings, sat in on roll calls, went on ride-alongs, and assessed the use and actual utility of paperwork. They learned that a great deal was revealed by unannounced district visits. Meetings scheduled on paper sometimes did not take place, files that were supposed to be maintained regularly could not be found, and little crime analysis was being done. They were particularly disheartened when they looked into the operation of beat team meetings. Their visits revealed that many were not actually being held, but that officers were still filling out overtime slips to collect for attending. One beat sergeant brushed past a surprise visitor from the internal inspection team, because he was on his way to the golf course when he was supposed to be holding a team meeting ("But I have my tee time," he complained). Our report had been fairly optimistic about beat team meetings, but this was because observers always called in advance to arrange attending, and in some districts that became an occasion for actually holding one. Warned by the report that they were proving disappointing, the investigating team also closely examined all aspects of the district advisory committees. They interviewed more than twenty committee chairs, observed their meetings, and scrutinized the bylaws of committees that had them.

The diagnosis stage of the renewal process got things off to a good start because it was empirical. Rather than sitting in downtown offices and drafting more directives ordering that things be done—that would have been business as usual in the department—the team wanted to understand why they were not being done, and how that could be fixed. After months of working in the field, they reported their findings to the superintendent and attached a list of more than forty recommendations for change, almost all of which were approved.

Fixing the Program

The many specific reforms that the chief approved can be summarized under a few major headings. The department thought—and we agreed—that the most important issue facing the organization was accountability. The department needed to clarify the responsibilities of each member, assess whether he or she had fulfilled it, and take action if he or she had not. The most important move in this direction was the designation of a "management team leader" (known to everyone as "the CAPS lieutenant") in each district. The creation of this post solidified responsibility for a wide range of district activities on one set of shoulders. The CAPS lieutenant was given responsibility for beat and district planning, the conduct of beat meetings, beat team sergeants, the district's community-policing office, analysis of crime and disorder data, and coordinating requests for support from other parts of the department to address priority problems. This lieutenant was also charged with "ensuring that beat plans are reflective of actual crime on the beat" and that "the most chronic crime and disorder problems are addressed." The department order describing the CAPS lieutenant's duties ordered them from "A" to "B" to "C," and the list extended all the way to "Z." Specific responsibilities also were created for the watch commanders who ran the districts twenty-four hours a day. Among other things, they were charged with planning and finding officers to staff efforts to tackle problems prioritized in beat plans, keeping beat team members on their assignments as long as possible, and making sure that beat teams had time to do community work when they needed to.

The post of CAPS lieutenant was an important departure from business as usual in the department because he or she was held responsible for that A to Z list twenty-four hours a day. An important feature of the Chicago department was that—except for the district commander—no one was responsible for anything except for what happened when they were on duty. This assembly-line mentality extended to managers and supervisors, and not just line officers. I have found it difficult to explain this to foreign visitors. In parts of England, for example, one patrol sector sergeant (who oversees an area roughly equivalent to a large beat in Chicago) is all a sector gets, 24–7–365. The sergeant sets out a work plan for his or her officers for all days and shifts, and gets a call at home if some emergency arises. They get paid significantly less than does a sergeant in Chicago, to boot. The CAPS lieutenant is now similarly responsible for seeing to it that the program works, not just that people are working on the program when the lieutenant happens to be in the office. Creating the position was a step toward creating a modern management culture in the organization.

Concurrently, a unit was formed downtown that was staffed largely by the officers and civilians who had investigated the old situation and found it wanting. It was charged with jump-starting change within the department by conducting training, and monitoring the implementation of the new organizational plan. District commanders and area deputies received their training from this unit one-on-one. The chief and other higher-ups always dropped in during these training sessions, to emphasize their importance. Then team staffers made multiple visits to each district to train local managers in their new roles. The CAPS lieutenants received particular attention from the trainers. In addition, the lieutenants organized a "support group" (more new terminology for a police department) that held monthly lunches. There they received updates from headquarters and talked through the difficulties they faced making their new position work. A team was formed to provide virtually continuous training for beat team sergeants, for there was constant turnover in the position.

Changes were also announced for one of the most visible elements of CAPS, beat meetings. A series of meeting requirements was announced that matched line by line the evaluation criteria that we had developed to assess them. To increase the limited amount of problem-solving discussion at beat meetings, new guidelines were drawn up to ensure that beat meetings hewed closer to the official model. The guidelines prescribed that participants prioritize new crime and disorder problems, hold preliminary discussions about them, identify tasks and a timetable, and seek volunteers and assign them tasks. Residents and beat officers were to review their progress on a specific problem, analyze it, and design new strategies to be undertaken by community members, the beat team, and city agencies to address it. The meetings had to have a formal agenda, and crime maps and city-service reports were to be distributed each time. Both the beat team sergeant and the CAPS managing lieutenant had to sign off on the official meeting report that these things had taken place. If all the new requirements actually were met, a beat would have gotten a perfect score in our 1998 study, which concluded instead that "the glass is exactly half full." This was no accident; beat meeting procedures were redesigned *in order* to get a perfect score from us, and also because our scoring criteria reflected the department's unrealized plan for the meetings.

New life was breathed into the department's languishing planning process. The CAPS lieutenant now had to approve and sign beat plans after reviewing beat meeting reports and crime statistics to ensure that they were addressing real problems. Then, using these as raw material, district managers were charged with creating district-level plans outlining the specific activities they would undertake to deal with local priorities. They are "strategic" documents because they identify the priority problems facing the district, outline strategies to address them, and identify the partnerships that are needed with residents and other city agencies in order to solve them. Like beat plans, these are multipage forms. The planning paperwork comes with detailed instructions, and everyone on the management team is trained in how to go through the process. They are to use the department's information systems to identify and analyze calls for service, crimes, and arrests. Priority problems usually span several beats—this is why they become district priorities.

Would any of this happen? This was not the department's first foray into problem-driven planning. It foundered before because it was the personal project of only a few zealous managers at police headquarters, and they had neither the time nor the localized knowledge necessary to keep abreast of these evolving documents and assess their utility. Once before, beat sergeants had been ordered to produce them, but when the evaluation team looked into the process we found it to be a hollow exercise. Some documents were made up without reference to actual conditions on the beat; others were written to take credit for actions that community organizations had already undertaken on their own; many beat officers swore they had never seen their units' plans. Things were no better at the district level. District plans did not have any compelling operational significance or community support, and because they were of no help in getting additional resources (the remainder of the department had not bought into the process), in the absence of pressure from downtown they were ignored.

This time there was an implementation blitz aimed at making these new procedures a reality. Senior managers went over each draft district plan, dissecting it line by line. A big difference between this decade and the mid-1990s is that all of this paperwork is now maintained online, and senior managers and inspectors at police headquarters can easily access and review beat and district plans and implementation records. More responsibility for reviewing and approving them was passed to the area deputies. They are the district commanders' immediate bosses, and meet with them quarterly to review progress on the districts' operational plans. Unlike the top brass downtown, the area chiefs are in a position to weigh and assess the district's plans, and with the assistance of new planners and analysts on their own staffs they are able to evaluate district effectiveness. The area chiefs are positioned to help districts with ambitious plans, for they can commandeer assistance from detectives, narcotics units, roving tactical teams, and other areawide and citywide units. They also can take resources away from districts that do not seem to have priority uses for them and assign them elsewhere in the area.

CompStat . . . Chicago Style

The next significant administrative move raised the profile of management issues in general. An Office of Management Accountability (OMA) was established in February 2000, directed by a very senior manager who previously was head of the entire patrol division. OMA's mission is to ensure that the department remains focused on its core missions. It is also responsible for pushing the organization harder in the direction of systematic crime analysis, and it generally watches for managerial and organizational bottlenecks and tries to fix them. As one official document put it, OMA is to ensure "that [district] management teams use their collective wisdom, specialized expertise and police practical experience, in partnership with the community, to develop and implement effective and creative strategies to impact chronic problems." OMA grew quickly by absorbing other management units. The unit that was conducting planning and CAPS training programs came first. Then the auditing and internal control unit (the department's internal inspectors) came into the fold. An office was created to monitor the implementation of community policing by the districts. It keeps track of beat meeting attendance and reviews all of the forms, reports, and plans created at the beat and district level. The office conducts CAPS training for all new sergeants and community policing lieutenants, and for the civilian beat facilitators who are supposed to help lead beat meetings.

OMA placed in motion a number of management initiatives we dubbed "CompStat . . . Chicago Style," because in general form they resembled the management accountability system imposed on the New York City police in the early 1990s.[18] The most famous aspect of New York's system is CompStat sessions. These are headquarters meetings at which precinct commanders are quizzed about their management decisions, and frank judgment is rendered on their successes and failures. The computerese in the title comes from CompStat's single-minded focus on "hard" numbers that can be extracted from New York's information systems, principally recorded crimes. These flash across large screens during the course of the meetings. CompStat was known around the world before the birth of OMA, and many members of Chicago's department visited New York to observe the review sessions in action.

As in New York, the most visible manifestation of this elaborate planning and accountability process is the "headquarters accountability session." At first typically attended by 80 to 110 people, these sessions were held to focus the attention of districts, area commanders, and the top brass on managerial and performance issues. One district is showcased each time. The sessions mostly focus on their effectiveness in tackling the specific problems they have identified in their district plan. A district typically might focus on garage burglaries in four beats and street prostitution in three beats. Some months before, they went through a process of prioritizing these problems and describing in their plan the resources that they would allocate to solving them. Headquarters sessions focus on how effectively they have since executed their plan, and its impact on the problems they prioritized. The stakes are high, for their capacity as managers is on display. Being told that a review meeting is coming up soon creates a clear and stress-inducing deadline for a district to work toward; one CAPS lieutenant exclaimed, "It's like studying for the bar exam!" These accountability sessions represented a dramatic departure from business as usual in Chicago, where districts and units enjoyed considerable freedom from scrutiny as long as they did not make any visible waves.

Management accountability in Chicago is principally about crime, but CAPS and community-related issues are on the agenda as well. District managers are expected to utilize a broad range of city services as part of their attack on priority "crime triangles." If contributions to solving a problem could be made by city-service agencies (for example, by car tows, installing new lights or signs, or bringing in the code enforcement inspection team), OMA analysts forage through city databases to count the number of service requests that were filed targeting the district's problem areas. If the district's plan promised to involve the community (and many do), the head table calls on a representative of the CAPS Implementation Office to rise and give an account of the meetings and marches held in the area and their efforts to organize block clubs and other resident self-help groups. Then the staff will display a map to see if their organizing efforts match the beats that have been prioritized in the district's strategic plan.

OMA also struggles to independently assess whether or not districts are responding to residents' priorities. This is integral to the department's commitment to community-oriented problem solving, but identifying community concerns from the lofty heights of police headquarters is difficult. It would be easier to follow San Diego's lead and simply focus problem solving on crime patterns that are identified using the department's computers, but CAPS' plan calls for factoring in the public's concerns when district priorities are set. One approach used by OMA is to study closely the paperwork filed by officers attending each beat meeting, and pull out their version of what was discussed. This became much easier when these reports and all of the beat and district plans became online documents in the early years of the new millennium. Analysts also read the minutes of district advisory board meetings and reports from their subcommittees, and examine patterns of calls to the city's non-emergency 311 city-services hotline.

The concerns brought up by the community are diverse in nature. At headquarters meetings we attended, they ranged from "Peeping Tom" incidents to gang recruitment and shootings. Other problems that have been identified in this way include tire slashing, public drinking, skateboarding and bicycling on sidewalks (a staple problem in senior citizen areas), after-hours liquor sales, street prostitution, and someone who was shooting rabbits in a park. At the accountability sessions, commanders were confronted with the community concerns identified by OMA analysts and quizzed about what they were doing about them. At first, OMA's real interest was in the *procedures* that districts had in place to identify community concerns and respond to them. Someone in each district is to be responsible for doing just what OMA does—comb through material to identify community concerns that are not being addressed. A senior district manager—often a watch commander—should assign officers to work on them, monitor their progress, and decide when issues are successfully resolved. Early on, more than half of the districts did not have such a process in place, but they did not make that mistake at their second headquarters session. Once they had procedures in place, OMA's focus shifted to the effectiveness with which districts responded to community concerns.

In another key management move, the department's internal inspectors were merged into OMA. Traditionally they had focused on the availability of soap in locker rooms and whether police officers purchased and properly displayed city vehicle stickers on their family cars. Now inspectors appear unexpectedly to examine district records and procedures, and they have been given the additional task of attending beat meetings and completing checklist reviews of how well beat meetings measure up to the department's standards. For example, inspectors check availability of printed agendas and crime reports; note whether progress on previously discussed problems is reviewed and new problems identified; watch to see if the official problem-solving model is applied during the discussion; and observe whether tasks are identified for residents, police officers, and city service agencies. Inspectors also verify the number of residents and police officers present, as a check on meeting reports filed by beat sergeants. In addition, sergeants from the CAPS Project Office typically attend beat meetings every week to observe how they are being conducted and provide feedback to beat team officers.

How Did Chicago Do?

The program Chicago devised touched base with the three major elements that make up community policing initiatives around the country: they involved the community, adopted a problem-solving orientation, and reorganized to ensure that the structure of the organization supported those efforts.

Community policing requires developing partnerships with community members and the civic organizations that represent them. Effective community policing requires responding to citizen input concerning both the needs of the community and the best ways by which the police can help meet those needs. To accomplish this, departments need to reorganize in order to provide opportunities for citizens to come into contact with their officers under circumstances that encourage these exchanges. In Chicago's plan, beat meetings are the most important mechanism for building and sustaining close relationships between police and the public. The 250 or so meetings held each month provide a forum for exchanging information and a venue for identifying, analyzing, and prioritizing problems in an area. They provide occasions for police and residents to meet face to face and get acquainted with officers assigned to their area. This was facilitated by the formation of teams of officers with fixed shifts and a long-term commitment to working in the beat. Five to seven officers attended the meetings, and most were beat team members or their sergeant.

Community policing also promises to strengthen the capacity of communities to fight and prevent crime on their own. This is an extension of an idea that is older than community policing, that in a democratic society police need the cooperation and assistance of the people if they are going to function effectively. In Chicago, neighborhood residents can routinely be seen painting over graffiti, walking their dogs in areas frequented by prostitutes, attending prayer vigils in the midst of street drug markets, and joining court watch groups that bring pressure on judges and prosecutors to take "minor" cases more seriously. A staff of civilian community organizers was hired to form block clubs, drum up attendance at beat meetings, and coordinate focused problem-solving projects. An important question is whether this helps develop local leadership and an organizational infrastructure in newly activated neighborhoods. Involving the public also calls for greater transparency in how departments share information about what they do and how effective they are. Chicago's crime maps, top ten crimes lists, and other information shared at beat meetings help bring the local "big picture" to discussions of local problems, reflecting the analytic approach called for by problem-solving policing.

Community policing usually involves adopting a broad ranging problem-solving orientation. As a police strategy, problem solving represents a departure from the traditional approach to policing, which is too often reduced to driving fast to crime scenes in order to fill out reports of what happened. Chicago moved quickly to train both officers and community residents in their new problem-solving responsibilities. Community organizing and problem-solving training sessions were held for the general public, and eventually about twelve thousand residents were trained. The department's bottom-up planning process called for beat teams to identify and prioritize their most pressing local problems, and for districts to allocate the resources it would take to resolve the most important of them. In a community-policing context, problem solving involves the public in identifying and prioritizing a broad range of chronic neighborhood conditions. In Chicago this was one of the most important roles carved out for beat meetings. We shall see in chapter 4 that residents were not shy about identifying problems and demanding action.

One of the consequences of opening themselves up to the public at beat meetings and in other venues is that police inevitably get involved in more and different issues than they did in the past. Of course, they cannot resolve all of the new problems that come up, so they need to form partnerships with other agencies of government. From the outset, Chicago linked community policing to the delivery of city services, and set up administrative mechanisms to ensure that the partnership worked effectively. An interagency task force coordinated inspections of buildings and negligent landlords identified by residents and the police, and city attorneys were assigned to prosecute them. A new city department was created to address housing management issues more effectively. For a long list of familiar bureaucratic and political reasons these kinds of interagency projects can be difficult to get off the ground, and not all cities succeed. Other city and municipal agencies usually think that community policing is the police department's program, not theirs. In Chicago, community policing is the city's program.

Finally, across the country, decentralization is closely linked to the implementation of community policing and problem solving. More responsibility for identifying and responding to local problems is delegated to commanders in charge of the geographical districts that make up a city. Departments do this in order encourage the development of local solutions to locally defined problems, and to facilitate decision making that responds rapidly to changing conditions. Sometimes there are also moves to shed layers of bureaucracy and speed communication and decision making within the organization. Police also have to learn how to structure and manage a decentralization plan that gives midlevel managers real responsibility yet holds them accountable for measures of their success. Here community policing intersects with another movement in policing, the emergence of a culture of systematic performance measurement and managerial accountability.

The focus of Chicago's management accountability process remained broader than many. CompStat-style headquarters review sessions continued to put pressure on the districts to respond to the public's concerns, coordinate with the mobilization efforts of the CAPS Implementation Office, and sustain attendance at beat meetings. At the district level, responsibility for overseeing these and other activities was fixed in one set of hands, the CAPS lieutenant. Chicago abolished the rank of captain in order to flatten the organization, leaving just three civil service ranks (Skogan and Hartnett 1997). Most of the department's elite units—including detectives, narcotics investigators, special tactical teams, and even the organized crime unit—are required to share information and more closely coordinate their work with the geographical districts. The department's management accountability process calls them on the carpet when they fail to serve as support units for uniformed patrol officers (Skogan and Steiner 2004a).

In addition to decentralizing management, community policing typically calls for assigning officers to fixed geographical areas and encouraging them to take the initiative in finding ways to deal with issues specific to the communities they serve. Chicago accomplished this by reorganizing the daily work of thousands of officers around small beats. Their daily routines were reshuffled to accommodate the new plan. The department prioritized 911 dispatching rules in order to keep these teams working in their beats, and assigned each team a sergeant to coordinate their activities across watches.

This being said, the jury is out on what centralized, data-driven management augurs for community policing. Can it survive Comp-Stat? Many of the features of modern accountability management push in the opposition direction. Community policing continues to ask officers to think and act in new and unaccustomed ways, and many of its presumed benefits do not show up in police information systems. To a significant extent, in this new post-CompStet management environment, what gets measured is what matters. Top managers decide what is a success, and hold midlevel managers to their standards. The accountability process is about harnessing the hierarchy to achieve top management's objectives, which are, in turn, driven by the data they have at hand, and at the top level those data say little distressingly about community priorities. The thrust of New York City's CompStat and similar management initiates all over the country is that measured accomplishments get attention and unmeasured accomplishments do not. As a result, there is a risk that the focus of departments will shift away from community policing back to the activities that better fit a recentralizing management structure driven by data on recorded crime.

Community policing also stresses the importance of developing the general-purpose skills of line officers through education and training, and it frequently features talk about empowering rank-and-file employees and encouraging them to act autonomously. This way of thinking stresses that workers at the very bottom of the organization are closest to the customer, and are to use their best judgment about how to serve the neighborhoods where they are assigned. However, these are, at best, low priorities for CompStat-style accountability management. Community policing is an attack on the traditional hierarchical structure of police departments. It calls for the bottom-up definition of problems. Police researchers attribute many of the problems of contemporary policing to the mismatch between the formal hierarchical structure of police organizations and the true nature of their work, which is extremely decentralized, not amenable to "cookie-cutter" solutions, dependent on the skills and motivation of the individual officers handling it, and mostly driven externally by 911 calls rather than management strategies. Perhaps the accountability process has ridden to the rescue of the traditional hierarchical structure, trying again to impose that hierarchy on work that does not fit its demands. Is the accountability process the last refuge of the command-and-control mentality of the past, and can community policing survive it?

However, the initial CAPS plan was a strong one. Critics charge that many community-policing programs are in reality no more than a press release, and that few of them survive once the media look the other way. To be sure, there were problems making it actually work in Chicago. As the next chapter notes, one irony of community policing it that it can be difficult to get the public involved, and to sustain participation in the areas that need it the most. On the police side there can be resistance in the ranks, and police researchers have found that it is hard to actually get officers to actually *do* anything resembling problem-solving policing. The city drafted a plan and set it in motion; in the chapters that follow, this book examines how it actually played itself out over time, in the three Chicagos.

FOUR

Involving the Community

A central feature of any community policing initiative is the breadth and variety of avenues it provides for citizen participation. At a minimum, police want to be able call on residents to act as their "eyes and ears" by calling 911 promptly when something happens and stepping forward to serve as witnesses. Residents may be asked to help identify and prioritize neighborhood problems for action. In more participatory community policing programs, departments can do this using public meetings; in a 2000 federal survey of departments, more than 95 percent of all big cities reported holding regular meetings with residents and with special-purpose groups such as those representing senior citizens and domestic violence victims (Hickman and Reaves 2003). In some places, police gauge citizen priorities by taking calls through special telephone hotlines, or even by conducting opinion polls; in 2000, a majority of large departments were conducting surveys of the public (Reaves and Hickman 2002). Many agencies invite selected residents to help shape police policies and operations by participating on advisory boards and steering committees. Another popular form of involvement is attending citizen police academies that expose residents to various aspects of police operations. In 2000, 87 percent of large agencies were running these programs.

The public may also be expected to be proactive—to act independently on behalf of the community by getting involved in problem-solving projects. These self-help initiatives can range from Saturday morning alley cleanups to marches confronting drug dealers or street prostitutes. In 2000, 79 percent of departments serving cities over 250,000 in population reported that they had trained residents in community mobilization and problem solving (Reaves and Hickman 2002). Opening themselves to an active partnership with the community was another aspect of policing that *Together We Can* pledged to reinvent. "The 1960s and 1970s were a time of tremendous social turbulence, rising crime rates, and a strong sense of fear among many urban residents. But citizen attempts to reach out and engage the police in meaningful crime-fighting partnerships were typically rebuffed by the 'thin blue line' metaphor that most police departments had adopted. Frustrated and fearful, citizens began to abdicate their responsibility for creating and maintaining order in their own neighborhoods."[1] The commitment to responsiveness and information sharing evidenced by many police agencies adopting community policing ideally would be matched on the civilian side with the enthusiastic involvement of a representative segment of the concerned public in these new activities. However, the extent to which both police officers and neighborhood residents actively embrace community policing is highly variable. Assumptions about their initial enthusiasm for the program can be made too casually. Police and residents may not have a history of getting along with each other, and in many poor neighborhoods the past is too often filled with broken promises. Getting involved in an active way can also be dangerous, especially in neighborhoods dominated by street gangs and drug dealers. The cooperation of community-based organizations is often required to sustain involvement over the long haul, as individuals tire or move on to other matters. However, poor and minority communities often lack much in the way of organizations outside of their churches, and the police may have to involve themselves in building this civic infrastructure. Like the police, members of the public also need to be trained in their new roles. Community policing involves a new set of jargon as well as assumptions about the new responsibilities that both police and citizens are to adopt. All of this will have to be explained before any of the participants can fully appreciate the new roles that they are expected to adopt.

This chapter and the next report on citizen involvement in Chicago's community-policing program. One of the most significant features of CAPS was the extensive role envisioned for the public in its operations. The city's model called for neighborhood residents to help identify problems and formulate solutions to them. They were also called upon to play an active role in solving them. On their side, police announced a commitment to working with residents and taking their concerns seriously when setting policing priorities. New venues were created to facilitate this involvement, including regular neighborhood meetings and district advisory boards. However, in a city the size of Chicago there is inevitably a considerable distance to be traveled between announcing that police (now) are welcoming public involvement and making it actually work in practice. Chicago's successes and shortcomings will illuminate some of the difficulties likely to be faced by other departments as they adopt a community-policing model.

These chapters are based on observations of citizen involvement in action. Between 1995 and 2002 the evaluation team attended more than one thousand neighborhood meetings to observe what went on there, and to survey the police and residents who attended. The paperwork filed by officers who attended every beat meeting held between 1995 and 2003 was also collected for analysis. These brief reports described more than twenty-five thousand meetings. In 1998 the CAPS Implementation Office inaugurated an extensive community-organizing effort and we monitored its activities in a sample of nineteen beats that were selected from the many that were involved in the program. There we conducted dozens of personal interviews, sat in on planning and training meetings, attended public meetings, and rode along with beat officers. Almost two thousand residents of these and a matched set of beats that were not involved in the program were surveyed as well. This chapter also makes extensive use of the twenty thousand survey interviews conducted citywide between 1993 and 2003. In addition, we conducted dozens of personal interviews with the CAPS Implementation Office and police department staff members involved in organizing and supporting beat meetings and turning out residents for community events and problem—solving projects.

Marketing CAPS

Beginning in the mid-1990s, Chicago launched an aggressive—and expensive—program to market community policing to the general public. The most important reason for this was, of course, political. The city was investing a great deal in this new program, and the mayor wanted to reap the benefits of its popularity. But in addition, all levels of government now recognize the importance of educating the public in tandem with legislating on their behalf. In the health and safety arena, for example, media campaigns spreading the messages that "smoking stinks" and that everyone should "buckle up for safety" have played an important role in increasing the effectiveness of the standard levers for implementing public policy, including taxation and enforcement. The CAPS marketing slogans included "Get with the beat" and "Safe neighborhoods are everybody's business."

Program marketing played an important educational function in Chicago because CAPS represented a departure from past practice.

At the outset, not many Chicagoans were clear about what community policing was and what it was supposed to accomplish. CAPS asked them to *do* something, however, so it was important to broaden awareness of the new opportunities for participation that it created and encourage residents to get involved. Beat meetings are supposed to be a locus for finding solutions for problems and involving participants in problem-solving projects, and not just a place to register complaints. As a consequence, residents not only needed to turn out; they also had to understand their role in problem-solving policing. Finally, the public needed to understand at the outset how CAPS was changing business as usual in this important and very expensive public agency, because they were about to get the bill. By the fiscal year 2000 the Chicago Police Department's budget exceeded one billion dollars. Because the schools are carried on a different budget, this is the city's biggest expenditure item. Police depend on the communities they serve for financial as well as moral support and, as taxpayers, the public needed to understand the new department strategy that they were being asked to pay for.

Regular surveys of city residents tracked the visibility of CAPS. Awareness of community policing expanded considerably during the second half of the 1990s. This was established by asking two questions. The first was whether respondents had heard about "a new program announced by the Chicago Police Department, a community policing program that calls for more cooperation between police and residents of Chicago." If a respondent did not recognize this description, they were asked a second, "aided recall" question. They were told that the program was often referred to as "CAPS," and then asked if they had heard of that. This picked up a large number of respondents, because the program was being marketed around the term. Based on responses to these two questions, 53 percent of Chicago residents knew about the program in 1996; by 1998 recognition was at 79 percent, where it essentially remained.

Table 4.1 presents the percentage of respondents who knew about the CAPS program among major population subgroups. Between 1996 and 1998, a period when overall awareness of the program was expanding, recognition of CAPS increased substantially within every group. Awareness of CAPS went up most (30 percentage points) among those under age thirty, before dropping a bit in subsequent years. It took a bit longer, but by 2001 CAPS awareness rose just as much among Chicagoans over age sixty-five. CAPS awareness went up by 25 percentage points or more among many other groups, in-

Table 4.1 Personal Background and Awareness of CAPS 1996–2003

	1996	1997	1998	1999	2001	2003
Total percent	53	69	79	79	79	80
Whites	52	73	79	80	80	81
Blacks	58	73	84	84	87	89
Latinos	50	60	72	73	68	70
Latinos Only						
Spanish speakers	48	52	65	68	58	56
English speakers	54	72	81	81	83	86
Age 18–29	46	56	76	76	71	69
Age 30–49	61	73	83	83	83	84
Age 50–64	54	74	79	80	83	86
Age 65 plus	46	57	65	74	76	77

	1996	1997	1998	1999	2001	2003
Number of cases	1,868	3,066	2,937	2,871	3,141	
Nongraduates	42	54	62	68	64	65
High school grads	56	73	83	82	82	83
Renters	50	66	75	75	72	74
Homeowners	58	73	83	83	87	85
Lower income	47	59	69	72	68	68
Moderate income	58	76	84	84	85	86
Females	51	66	76	76	78	80
Males	58	74	83	84	79	79

Note: Subgroup percentages for all but racial groups are based on data weighted to standardize the racial composition of the samples across years. Data weighted to correct for household size and telephone access.

cluding males and females, renters and homeowners, and poor and moderate-income households (the latter division was set an annual income of twenty thousand dollars). By 2001, CAPS awareness had risen by about 30 percentage points among both African Americans and whites. However, things were more complicated among the city's Latinos. Respondents who preferred to be interviewed in Spanish (or could *only* be interviewed in that language) are described in this book as "Spanish speakers," and they did not do very well. English-speaking Latinos reported about the same gains as did blacks and whites, 32 percentage points between 1996 and 2003, but for Spanish speakers the overall growth in CAPS awareness was only 8 percentage points. This gap portends many of the findings reported in this and later chapters, for it turns out that the city's growing Spanish-speaking population was left behind on many dimensions.

In another portent of a larger pattern, the initial gaps *between* the groups depicted in table 4.1 were also not erased. In 1996, cleavages were apparent between high school graduates and those with less education; they were separated by 14 percentage points. In 2003 the education gap had grown a bit, to 18 percentage points. During the first years of CAPS there was a gap in awareness between low- and moderate-income people (11 percentage points), and it grew a bit (to 18 percentage points) by 2003. The awareness gap also grew between renters and homeowners, and it narrowed only between men and women. Differences in CAPS awareness among racial groups were also large. In every year, CAPS awareness was greatest among African Americans, and that gap never closed. Latinos as a whole gained in awareness through the 1990s, and then lost a bit of ground. The role of language in this shift is apparent in table 4.1. English-speaking Latinos kept pace with the rest of the city, but among Spanish speakers, more than half of their 1996–1999 gain was lost by 2003. CAPS awareness in this group dropped by a full 12 percentage points between 1999 and 2003, from 68 percent 56 percent. In 2003 the language gap among Latinos was 30 percentage points, among the largest we observed in this seven-year span.

The high level of CAPS recognition documented by the surveys was not an accident. It was instead the product of a sophisticated and aggressive marketing campaign coordinated by city hall's CAPS Implementation Office. The mass media campaign began in early 1997. At various times it featured promotional spots on radio and television, ads in local newspapers, posters at rapid transit stops and high traffic areas, buses brightly festooned with CAPS advertisements, and billboards. The total budget for the 1997 media outreach effort was more than 1.5 million dollars; it exceeded 1.6 million dollars in 1998, and was budgeted at about that level in 1999. The 1998 radio budget of 650,000 dollars included announcements on Spanish-language stations. The television budget was about 835,000 dollars, for spot commercials in English and Spanish on both broadcast and cable channels, including a sports network. For years the city sponsored *Crime Watch,* a bimonthly series of half-hour television documentaries that played frequently on the city's two cable channels. During 1998 the CAPS Implementation Office also spent about thirty thousand dollars for newspaper ads, another thirty thousand dollars for advertising on billboards and posters, and seventy-five thousand dollars for advertising on Chicago Transit Authority vehicles and platforms.

The CAPS Implementation Office promoted CAPS in a variety of other ways as well. Schedules for beat meetings were posted on the Internet, and "surfers" just had to click their general part of town on a map in order to call up a list of meetings and many pages of information about their police districts. Meeting schedules were also displayed on the city's cable television channels. Program materials were distributed to community organizations, libraries, businesses, churches, and schools. For example, 130,000 copies of *On the Beat* newsletter (fifty thousand of which were in Spanish) were distributed in September and October of 1998. Targeted mailings were distributed in selected areas, paid for by local sponsors ranging from banks to a property management company. City workers received information about CAPS and how to participate, and were reminded of the schedule for beat meetings in their areas by announcements stuffed in their pay envelopes.

Beginning in 1997, the city hosted a number of citywide events promoting the program. The CAPS Implementation Office sponsored an annual, daylong CAPS workshop, attended in 1998 by six hundred of the city's community activists. The workshop featured seminars on topics ranging from running effective beat meetings to court advocacy. In June 1998, 750 residents attended similar workshops at a Block Club convention. In August, many Chicagoans attended a national conference on community policing that was sponsored by the city. October of 1998 featured the first yearly CAPS "appreciation" event, a party that was attended by 750 CAPS volunteers, and in November three thousand residents attended a neighborhood assembly at the city's convention center. These events were repeated in 1999, but beginning in 2000 the large assemblies were divided up and run separately in five areas of the city.

On a smaller scale, CAPS outreach workers were involved in other events around the city. They attended about 130 of the festivals that flourish each summer in Chicago. Booths were set up where they explained CAPS, and encouraged participation in beat meetings. They also promoted involvement in programs sponsored by the districts' advisory committees, including court advocacy. Staff members are continuously involved in local marches, rallies, prayer vigils, and smoke-outs (which are group barbecues held at gang- or drug-infested sites). Twenty CAPS workshops were held in various Asian languages during April and May 1998. National Night Out in early August is the occasion for events in all twenty-five police districts. Finally, a long list of promotional materials was available for distribution, including magnets, pens, pencils, rulers, hats, T-shirts, and sticky notes sporting the CAPS logo.

The surveys asked those who were aware of CAPS, "How did you hear about it? Did you receive some printed information on community policing? Did you hear about it on TV or the radio, did you see a sign or poster, or did you hear about it from someone else?" They replied in their own words, and the interviewers (who are trained to do this) classified their responses. Figure 4.1 presents the percentage of Chicagoans who recalled learning about CAPS in various ways, comparing results from the 1996 through 2003 surveys. Respondents were allowed to name up to five ways in which they learned about CAPS or community policing. A majority (about 60 percent in most of the surveys) identified only one source, but about 15 percent named as many as three or more information sources, so the percentages add up to more than 100 percent.

Figure 4.1 indicates that many information channels became more effective in reaching people over time. The most dramatic increase, from 15 to just under 50 percent, was in learning about CAPS from television. It was covered not only on news and public-affairs programs, but also on the city's two public-access cable stations. The cable stations feature frequent replays of a half-hour *Crime Watch* series produced by the city, and there is occasional coverage of CAPS on other city cable programs. During the 1990s the city also purchased time on English- and Spanish-language television stations to broadcast spot commercials.

The second most frequent way people recalled hearing about CAPS was hearing about it from other people. The "buzz" surrounding

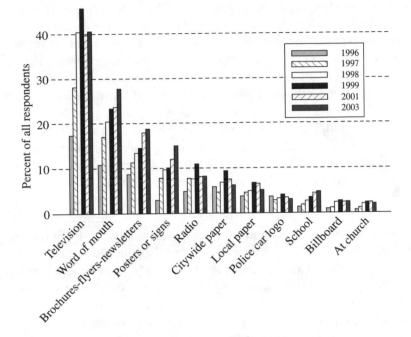

Figure 4.1. Sources of CAPS Awareness, 1996–2003

CAPS, spread through word of mouth, rose every year as illustrated in figure 4.1. Talk about the program reached 11 percent of all Chicagoans in 1996 and 28 percent in 2003. In 2003 it was cited as a source of information by 35 percent of those interviewed. We shall see below that this was very important, because personal contacts turned out to be the best way to actually get people involved in the program. There were also noticeable increases in the extent to which people reported hearing about CAPS through posters or signs (which went up by a factor of five), and from brochures, flyers, or newsletters (which doubled in importance from 1996 through 2003). Printed matter was mentioned by 19 percent of those interviewed in 2003, and 15 percent of respondents indicated seeing posters or signs. As detailed above, the city's civilian-staffed CAPS Implementation Office plays an important role in distributing program materials to community organizations, libraries, businesses, churches, and schools. A small but steady percentage of families reports receiving CAPS information carried home by their children from school, another Implementation Office project. Radio became a fairly common source of awareness by 1997.

Newspapers were less cited as a source of information about community policing. In 2003, 13 percent of all adults indicated they had read about CAPS in a citywide or local community newspaper. Attentive newspaper readers tend to be older, better-educated, higher-income homeowners. In 2003, people over age sixty-five were almost four times as likely to cite newspapers than were those under age thirty. The difference between college graduates and those without a high school diploma was almost as large, and very few Spanish-speaking Latinos reported relying on newspapers for information on CAPS.

The contrasts between television, newspapers, and word of mouth as sources of CAPS awareness are particularly striking. Television and personal communication were most frequently cited by less-educated respondents, while newspapers were mentioned often by those with more education. Television was most frequently cited by young people; older residents recalled hearing about CAPS or reading about it in a newspaper. Latinos relied on television; among those who had heard about CAPS in the 1998 survey, 63 percent cited television as their source of information. Spanish speakers stood out in terms of television; 73 percent of them, compared to 52 percent of English speakers, reported being aware of CAPS due to television. Written matter—posters, signs, flyers, newsletters, brochures, billboards, and citywide newspapers—were more likely to reach English speakers, despite the city's intensive effort to distribute Spanish-language materials. Even personal conversations were more likely to engage English speakers than Spanish speakers, by a ratio of three-to-two. Whites read about CAPS in newspapers; typically, one-quarter of them mention newspapers, compared to less than 10 percent of Latinos and 10 percent of African Americans. African Americans heard about CAPS from other people, by a smaller margin. Personal conversations were cited more often by older residents and homeowners, and especially by people who were involved in community activities. The more involved people were in community organizations and institutions such as local school councils, the less likely they were to identify television as a source of information about CAPS. The mix of ways in which people learned about CAPS was important; as chapter 5 details, some were more influential than others in actually turning people out for meetings.

During the 1990s, these surveys provided useful "market research" for the program. Through memos, briefing sessions and regularly published reports, the evaluation helped identify who was getting the message and who was not. The surveys also identified what channels were reaching the most residents and—equally as important—which were best at reaching the hard-to-reach. In 1998, when awareness of CAPS approached 80 percent, we advised the group running the CAPS marketing campaign to shift their focus from promoting awareness to stimulating involvement in CAPS activities. While impressive, involvement had not grown in parallel with program awareness. A statistical analysis of the data indicated that exposure to the program through television was particularly unlikely to generate actual involvement in CAPS. It was the most important engine for moving awareness forward, but it was not turning people out for events.

Beat Meeting Participation

In Chicago's plan, beat meetings are the most important mechanism for building and sustaining close relationships between police and the public. The meetings are to provide a forum for exchanging information and a venue for identifying, analyzing, and prioritizing problems in an area. They promise to provide occasions for police and residents to meet face-to-face and get acquainted. As we saw in chapter 3, this was facilitated by the formation of teams of officers with fixed shifts and a long-term commitment to working in the beat.

The city and the police department invested a great deal of energy in turning residents out for the monthly meetings. District officers distributed flyers and hung posters in businesses and apartment building entryways. The neighborhood relations offices in the districts encouraged organizations to get involved and send their members to the meetings, and some maintained mailing lists from sign-in sheets completed at the meetings. One district arranged to have beat maps and a list of upcoming meetings stapled to the lids of pizza boxes delivered in its area. Computer-savvy residents can check the meeting schedule for their beat by means of the Internet. The CAPS Implementation Office sent field workers door to door in selected areas, encouraging residents to attend meetings. All of the newsletters, flyers, billboards, and television spots described above emphasized the importance of attending beat meetings.

Trends in Beat Meeting Attendance

Attendance at beat meetings can be monitored using data drawn from brief forms completed by officers who attend. These forms detail where and when meetings were held, who was there, and what was discussed. Along with the department's internal inspectors, we periodically checked the accuracy of police records on the basic features of the meetings by comparing them with reports by observers about the same meetings, and found them highly reliable. Figure 4.2 charts trends in beat meeting participation between 1995 and 2003. It is based on data describing 25,300 meetings held during the period. The left axis reports monthly attendance counts, while the right axis presents the cumulative total of attendees since CAPS became a citywide program. Chicagoans attended beat meetings 59,200 times during 1995 and on 61,120 occasions during 1996. In 1999, it was 67,100, and in 2000, 66,260 turned out for beat meetings. In 2003, 60,000 people attended a total of 2,888 beat meetings. Referring to the cumulative total on the right axis, by the end of 2003, Chicagoans had attended beat meetings on more than 582,000 occasions. It is apparent that attendance was very seasonal, reflecting Chicago's weather. Attendance is chronically low in December and January, and reaches its maximum in July or September (the peak attendance each year is presented in figure 4.2). December 2000 was the lowest turnout month of the period; only eighteen hundred hardy souls turned out for beat meetings during that month of near-record cold and near-record snowfall.

Many other types of meetings and participatory events associated with CAPS are not accounted for here. This includes the downtown meetings held for building managers and security directors, and small informational sessions with neighborhood activists. CAPS-sponsored rallies, block parties and neighborhood assemblies, and other mass events are held virtually every weekend, and the mayor can be found leading a march almost every Saturday morning. The figures above also do not include participation in special district-level Spanish-language meetings. A substitute for beat meetings, they bring together police and residents who can work together in Spanish.

Neighborhood Attendance Rates

Before the program began, concern was voiced about where and why beat meetings would be a success. The predominant view was that they would be wildly successful where they were needed the least. It was assumed that white homeowners clustered in well-off and blue-collar neighborhoods on the northwest and southwest sides of the city would be first to climb on the bandwagon. They already liked the police—a view that was confirmed by our surveys—and many

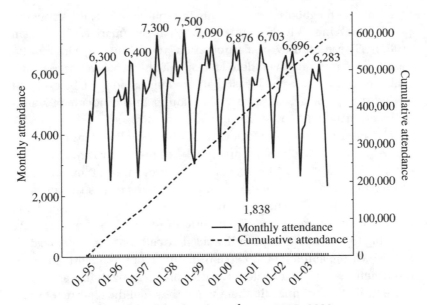

Figure 4.2. Trends in Beat Meeting Attendance, 1995–2003

white police officers and other city workers live in those areas. The more-educated and higher-income whites huddled closer to the lakeshore shared these predispositions, but they did not have as many pressing problems.

On the other hand, many residents of poor and minority neighborhoods in Chicago had a more troubled relationship with the police. The survey findings (see chapter 9 for more on this) were consistent with the view that, for many poor African Americans and Latinos, the police were to be counted among the *problems* in their communities, not as a solution to them. More, and more intensive policing to them seemed as likely to lead to new complaints about harassment, indiscriminate searches, and conflicts between police and area youths as it would be to solve serious crime problems. Racial polarization seemed to underlie much of what was going on in Chicago in the early 1990s and community policing potentially faced an uphill battle in the city's black and brown neighborhoods.

The CAPS evaluation team was not particularly optimistic for other reasons as well. During the 1980s there was a great deal of research on the extent of participation in anticrime activities and organizations. This was sparked by the community crime prevention movement of the late 1970s and 1980s that promised to reduce crime by involving neighborhood residents in what later became known as problem solving. (Much of this research is summarized in Skogan [1988]). These studies of participation in voluntary, community-based anticrime programs delivered about the same message as the racial polarization hypothesis that predominated in Chicago, but with a strong social class twist. They found that residents of better-off areas turn out more readily for anticrime projects. For example, as part of an anticrime effort, the City of Minneapolis attempted to organize new block clubs in previously unorganized areas. Professional organizers spent two years on the project, but they only succeeded in the lowest-crime, best-off blocks (Skogan 1990a; Pate et al. 1987). Around the country, it had proved difficult to sustain the involvement of residents of communities that need community policing the most. Surveys indicated that better-off, more educated, home-owning, and long-term area residents more frequently knew of opportunities to participate in anticrime organizations and were more likely to participate in them when they had the chance (Schneider 1986; Whitaker 1986; Lavrakas and Herz 1982; Podolefsky and DuBow 1981; Skogan and Maxfield 1981). Studies of the geographical distribution of community organizations focusing on crime problems indicated that they were less successful in poorer, renting, high-turnover, high-crime areas (Garofalo and McLeod 1988; Kohfeld, Salert, and Schoenberg 1983; Henig 1978, 1982). Research indicated that organizations emerge and persist most easily in the most cohesive communities, those where residents are bound together by ethnic solidarity, church and family ties, and intimate acquaintance. The irony, of course, is that neighborhoods that most easily sustain neighborhood-based anticrime initiatives usually already enjoy lower rates of crime, because the community is so strong.

Further, research had consistently found that residents of poor, higher-crime areas tend to view *each other* with suspicion (Taub, Taylor, and Dunham 1984; Taylor, Gottfredson, Brower 1981; Boggs 1971). Dennis Rosenbaum (1987) concluded that crime-prevention programs requiring social contact and neighborhood cooperation are less often successful in areas with high levels of fear. Crime is corrosive, for it undermines trust among neighbors. This violates one of the assumptions behind neighborhood watch and other programs that attempt to promote mutual cooperation to prevent crime—for example, it may not seem wise to inform the neighbors that you will be out of town when you fear their children (Greenberg 1983). CAPS, on the other hand, was asking residents to gather in a public place and speak out on issues that might well involve the children of people who were present. As we will see below, fear of retaliation for attending and speaking up at beat meetings was more common in poorer areas of town.

Examining the issue of where beat meeting participation was high and low involves combining meeting reports for a year in order to calculate the average monthly attendance rate for each beat. Attendance rates must be used because beats vary greatly in size. In 2000, the smallest 20 percent of the city's beats averaged forty-four hundred adult residents, while the largest 20 percent averaged more than nineteen thousand adults. These discrepancies are deliberate. The boundaries of the city's police beats were redrawn in the early 1990s in order to equalize workloads (measured by calls for service weighted by an estimate of how much time they took), not to standardize their populations. We saw in chapter 3 that this did not work out very well, and by the end of the 1990s, ensuing shifts in the city's population and crime rates had complicated the allocation of workloads to beat teams even more. A further complication is only adults generally come to beat meetings, and the mix of adults and children in the population varies greatly from place to place across the face of the city. So, the denominator for each beat's attendance rate is the number of residents aged eighteen and older. Many of the measures examined here were logged in order to correct for the fact that a few very high attendance beats would otherwise have a disproportionate effect on the citywide picture.

Once yearly attendance rates are calculated, data from other sources (including census, crime, and school and health indicators) can be used to describe the social and economic correlates of beat meeting attendance. It is important to note that the correlations that result are descriptive, not causal. They describe where in the city turnout is high, not necessarily why, although they give a few clues about why. The data reveal that meeting attendance was often highest in places that might have benefited from them the most. Table 4.2 examines attendance data for 2002, along with data from the 2000 U.S. Census, city land use data banks, and the findings of our 2001 and 2003 surveys when they are aggregated to the beat level. In general, attendance rates are higher in poor, high-crime, decaying neighborhoods, not lower as many anticipated. Residents were also more active in beats where other institutions and ways of getting things done have failed to serve them very well.

One block of measures in table 4.2 describes the link between

Table 4.2 Social and Economic Correlates of Beat Meeting Turnout, 2002

Correlation with (log) Beat Meeting Attendance Rate			
Disadvantage		Crime and Social Disorder	
percent female-headed families*	.57	personal crime rate*	.61
percent college education	−.33	911 drug call rate	.58
unemployment rate	.50	property crime rate*	.27
percent African American	.58	loitering problems (survey)	.41
linguistic isolation	−.40	gang violence problems (survey)	.35
percent born in Mexico	−.42	drug problems (survey)	.40
Institutional Effectiveness		Physical Decay	
infant mortality rate	.50	percent buildings in bad condition	.36
gonorrhea rate	.51	percent of buildings abandoned	.30
school achievement scores	.41	percent land vacant	.40

* logged measure

School achievement series are for 1998.

meeting attendance and economic disadvantage. The first is the percentage of family households in each beat that were headed by
women, an important index of poverty. There are also census measures of the unemployment rate, and a measure of affluence, the percentage of adults with a four-year college degree. Meeting attendance
rates were consistently higher in worse-off areas. Another important
measure of beat disadvantage is linguistic isolation. In Chicago, linguistic isolation—the percentage of households in which no one
speaks good English—is closely related to immigration from Mexico
and Central America. Unlike other disadvantage measures, linguistic
isolation is correlated with *lower* levels of beat meeting attendance.
So too is the percentage of beat residents who were born in Mexico
and the percentage who speak Spanish at home (−.37, not shown).
These findings foreshadow a recurring theme in Chicago—the underrepresentation of Latinos and the limited benefits they saw from the
program during the course of the 1990s and early years of the new
millennium. On the other hand, attendance was positively correlated
with the size of the African American population in each beat, and
this also reflects a recurring theme.

Beat meeting participation was higher in high-crime, disorderly,
drug-ridden areas. This is illustrated in another block of table 4.2.
The correlation between attendance and the personal crime rate was
+.61. The link between property crime and participation was lower,

but still positive, and it remained significant in multivariate analyses. The table also examines an alternative crime measure, the rate at which residents of each beat contacted the city's 911 center during 2002 in order to make a drug-related complaint. The correlation between this measure of crime and beat meeting participation rates was +.58.

City residents are worried about a number of problems in addition to crime. This is represented by responses given by beat residents to a survey question about "groups of people hanging out on corners or in the streets." Residents were asked whether this was a big problem, some problem, or no problem in their neighborhood. The table combines the results of surveys conducted in 2001 and 2003, in order to assemble enough respondents (ten or more) to characterize most police beats. As it illustrates, the correlation between the extent of resident concern about loitering and beat meeting turnout was +.41. Likewise, residents of areas plagued by gang violence and street drug markets were also more likely to turn out for beat meetings in larger numbers. The bad news for the neighborhood is that high beat-meeting attendance is driven by concern about crime and other indicators of neighborhood decline.

The success of beat meetings in areas where other institutions have not worked well is illustrated by the relationship between beat meeting attendance and school and health factors. Attendance was higher in areas where residents have severe health problems; this is illustrated using the infant mortality rate for each beat; in 2002, the correlation between infant mortality and beat meeting attendance was +.50. Attendance was also higher in beats with high rates of gonorrhea and (not shown) tuberculosis. Meeting attendance was also higher in beats where the schools have failed. I constructed a composite achievement test score for the elementary schools serving each beat (there are more elementary schools than beats in Chicago), averaging the proportions of students in each who scored in the bottom quartile on four standardized exams. The correlation between meeting attendance and this measure of low achievement was +.41. Higher meeting attendance was also associated with low attendance and graduation rates, and high levels of truancy. Attendance was also higher in places plagued by physical decay: where buildings were in bad condition (as assessed by city raters), where a large percentage of buildings were abandoned, and where there was a lot of vacant land. Because these were residential beats, this often flagged that the city had already torn down a substantial number of buildings.

Because they were related to one another, only some of these factors continued to be linked to beat-meeting attendance rates in multivariate analyses that take them all together. But in every analysis *violent crime* is the strongest factor linked to participation rates. In addition to the personal crime rate, a list of violence measures—including homicide and gun-related crimes—are also correlated with beat meeting attendance. The link between participation and property crime, which is high in better-off areas of the city as well as in poor ones, is weaker, and it emerges only after controlling for the violent crime rate.

These patterns are significant, for they run counter to many of the pressures that historically have shaped police-community relations in poor and disenfranchised neighborhoods. While the norm is to expect a "middle-class bias" in volunteer-based social programs, turnout rates for Chicago's beat meetings are positively related to many measures of need. This does not mean they are immune from the middle-class biases described by research on involvement in anticrime activities. As we will see in the next chapter, there is a strong establishment bias in *who* shows up for the meetings. But the number who show up is relatively high in areas where other ways of getting things done often do not work very well, including beats where school performance is poor and health problems are rampant. Residents turned out especially often in predominantly African American beats, and where their neighborhoods were dangerous. Measured by the level of resident involvement, CAPS beat meetings have had their biggest successes in some of the city's most disadvantaged places.

Who Gets Involved?

Official records account for *how many* people come to meetings each month, and questionnaires passed out to participants can gather personal information on those who attend. But it requires a general population survey to understand why some residents do *not* attend while others do. So, in addition to asking about CAPS awareness, the citywide surveys quizzed respondents about their participation. First they were asked whether there had been any effort to hold community meetings in their neighborhood, or if any meetings had been held to deal with crime problems. Awareness of these opportunities for participation in their neighborhood is an important first step in building citizen involvement in CAPS. Those who knew about local meetings were asked if they had attended, and those who said they had done so were asked if any police were present. If they were, the gatherings were classified as beat meetings, and respondents were asked to assess their effectiveness on several dimensions.

Through the latter half of the 1990s and into 2000s, about 60 percent of Chicagoans reported that community meetings about crime were being held in their area. Among those who knew about the meetings, 28 percent (or 14 percent of all Chicagoans) reported attending at least one beat meeting. Respondents who went to any meetings in the past year reported attending an average of 3.6 of them. Just over 50 percent went to one or two meetings, and only 10 percent went to more than seven meetings a year. How did they know where to go? In surveys distributed at beat meetings during 1998, participants were asked how they heard about when and where meetings were held in their beat. They could choose multiple sources of information from a list, and some did. Of all the sources of information mentioned, the most important (37 percent) was brochures and flyers announcing the meeting. Personal conversations came next, at 22 percent. Thirteen percent read about the meetings in a local newspaper. Most (46 percent) indicated that they had heard from a neighbor; another 20 percent had heard from the police about the meeting.

Why do people attend? Several factors are involved. The first is civic engagement: the more involved Chicagoans are in church and community affairs, the more likely they are to know about CAPS, be aware of beat meetings, and actually attend the meetings. Neighborhood activists hear about the meetings and other CAPS activities from one another, and they are also more likely to receive flyers and brochures. Marketing also contributes to turnout: there are distinct differences in how people learn about CAPS, and these affect whether they show up for meetings. Further, it is very important to understand frequent attenders, because they turn out to be critical for the success of the program. Another factor—the extent to which people are propelled to attend meetings in their beat because they are concerned about neighborhood problems—is considered in the next chapter, on the representativeness of beat meetings. It turns out that participants are more concerned than are their neighbors about a broad range of neighborhood concerns, and they are more optimistic than their immediate neighbors about the ability of the police to do something about them. Another conclusion in chapter 5 is that the turnout factors considered here contributed to a strong establishment bias in the meetings themselves.

Community Engagement

Figure 4.3 illustrates the strong relationship between civic engagement and CAPS involvement; the data are from the 1998 city survey, but every year the picture looks about the same. The surveys measure civic engagement using responses to four survey questions: whether the respondents or anyone else in their households are involved in a neighborhood watch group or citizen patrol, the local school council (Chicago's PTA), a church or synagogue, or a block club or community organization. Respondents with a high involvement count had many different kinds of linkages with their neighborhoods. The measure also assumes that involvement in organizations and groups on the list is a household rather than individual activity. Our randomly selected adult survey respondents might not be active, but think of themselves as represented because someone else in the household is. The result is a measure of "breadth" rather than "depth" of involvement, for it does not account for the number of organizations that households were involved in within a category. As the percentages arrayed across the bottom axis of figure 4.3 indicate, 37 percent of respondents indicated that their household was not involved in any of those activities and another 37 percent were involved in just one. At the upper end, 2 percent of households were involved in all four of these kinds of organizations. The average household was involved in just one type of group.

Figure 4.3 documents the linkage between civic engagement and levels of CAPS awareness, meeting awareness, and actual beat-meeting attendance. The differences are striking. Awareness of CAPS stood above 90 percent for those involved in three or four kinds of organizations, and awareness of neighborhood anticrime meetings was almost as high. Beat meeting attendance rose steadily with levels of civic engagement, rising above 40 percent among those involved in at least three kinds of local organizations. A detailed analysis suggests that each kind of organization was important in contributing to the rising levels of CAPS involvement depicted in figure 4.3. While church involvement may seem unrelated to community policing, during 1998 about one-third of all beat meetings were *held* in Chicago's churches, especially in predominantly African American communities where both CAPS and church involvement are particularly strong. Only

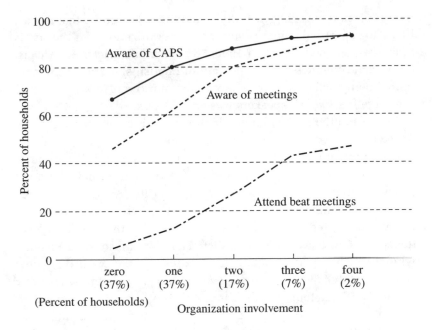

Figure 4.3. Community Engagement and CAPS Involvement, 1998

families with children living at home reported being involved in school affairs, but among them, some heard about CAPS from materials brought home by their children from the city's public and parochial schools. People with children living at home were more likely to know about CAPS, by about five percentage points. Among those belonging to a block club, 92 percent had heard of CAPS, and 86 percent had heard about anticrime meetings in their neighborhoods. Not surprisingly, people who were heavily involved in community organizations were also more likely to report that they had learned about CAPS through word of mouth, a factor that is linked to actual turnout.

However, there are limits to relying on participants in church and community organizations to fuel involvement in CAPS. The first is that most Chicagoans are not very involved in them. As noted above, the household average in 1998 was about one kind of organization, and that was most often church. Big attendance rates are racked up by people involved in three or four organizations, but these numbers involve less than 10 percent of households. A second disadvantage of relying on an existing network of activists is that their participants are very unrepresentative of the population. Older, higher-income, more-educated homeowners predominate the list of groups most likely to report engaging with the community. The group that is least likely to report belonging to any of the organizations on the list is Spanish-speaking Latinos. In 1998, 56 percent of African Americans, 52 percent of whites, and 49 percent of English-speaking Latinos reported being active in one or more community organization, while the figure for Spanish speakers was only 34 percent.

This is not the only point at which we observed an important role for civic engagement. Not only is it related to CAPS awareness and beat-meeting attendance, but other research has found that community engagement is strongly linked to involvement in neighborhood problem solving. During 1995 and 1996, the City and the Chicago Alliance for Neighborhood Safety (a nonprofit group focusing on crime issues) conducted problem-solving training for thousands of residents. The CAPS evaluation conducted a follow-up study to examine who among the participants actually did anything with their new skills. A total of 354 randomly selected trainees were interviewed by telephone about four months after their sessions were conducted. The follow-up found the most important factor distinguishing those who got involved was their level of involvement in community-based organizations. Overall, about 60 percent of those who were trained reported trying to do something about their neighborhoods' most pressing problems. The more involved participants were in other groups and activities, the more they got involved in CAPS-related problem-solving activities. Among the trainees who were affiliated with four or more organizations (the list in that survey was longer), more than 80 percent became involved in identifying and solving a local problem. Like respondents in the city survey, trainees who were more involved in the organizational life of their communities were also more likely to attend beat meetings and to have gotten involved in other CAPS-related activities (cf. Skogan et al. 1999). All of this suggests the wisdom of the saying that, "if you want something done, give it to a busy person."

Television

In his famous book *Bowling Alone,* Robert Putnam (2000) indicts television for undermining the kinds of volunteer activism described here. There are many plausible reasons for this, including that television competes for people's time, simply leaving them fewer hours to network with their neighbors or participate in community activities. Putnam thinks that television encourages passivity and stay-at-homeness, emotionally disconnecting people from the outside world. They experience the world secondhand, and think they are well informed. He charges television with promoting a "consumer's" view of the world's offerings. Rather than acting on their own behalf to "produce" the world they want, they support this or that cause by sending a check. Our data cannot go as far as these explanations, but the evaluation surveys find that television is by far the biggest promoter of CAPS awareness and it is the source of awareness that has grown the most dramatically over time. The question is, does it help turn people out for CAPS activities?

The answer is that, while television was central to expanding public awareness of CAPS, it played little role in encouraging Chicagoans to attend beat meetings. By illustration, the 1998 survey found that 29 percent of respondents who knew about CAPS and recalled learning about it on television actually attended a meeting; the comparable figure for those who did not mention television at all was 36 percent. On the other hand, talking about the program with someone else had just the opposite relationship to attendance; 41 percent of those who heard about CAPS from someone else attended a meeting, versus 28 percent who did not recall hearing from someone else about CAPS.

Obviously, not all of these differences can be attributed to exposure to the program. As noted above, different kinds of people learned about CAPS in different ways, and respondents could report multiple sources of CAPS information. These information-related differences almost certainly affect their involvement in the program as well. For example, respondents who recall learning about CAPS through newspapers also are more positive in their views of police, and both of these factors are also related to actually getting involved. However, in a multivariate statistical analysis (not shown here) that controlled for a long list of confounding factors, Chicagoans who heard about CAPS from someone else were 1.87 times *more* likely to actually attend a meeting. The separate impact of television was nonsignificant. These findings are in line with research by political scientists on turning out voters at election time. In contrast to mass mailings and telephone calls on election day, randomized experiments find that face-to-face, door-to-door canvassing assures the highest turnout; it is also cheaper per actual vote, because of its great effectiveness (for an example of this research see Green, Gerber, and Nickerson [2003]). In a "natural experiment" presented by elections in New Jersey, New York, and Pennsylvania, Jonathan S. Krasno and

Donald P. Green (2005) concluded that television advertising has minimal impact on actual voter turnout, a finding that is frequently corroborated by political scientists.

The limited positive impact of television, the largest and fastest-growing source of CAPS awareness during the 1990s, may help explain why beat meeting attendance did not expand in line with awareness. Based on the yearly surveys, the percentage of Chicagoans attending beat meetings remained at about 12 to 14 percent of the adult population. Over time, awareness grew a great deal—fueled principally by television—but the extent of involvement, measured by the percentage of adults attending at least one meeting, did not grow much at all. The limited influence of television may help explain the puzzle of low CAPS involvement among Latinos. As noted earlier, the city's Latinos who knew about CAPS distinctively identified television as their source of information about the program. This was even more true among Spanish-speaking Latinos, who participated in CAPS at even lower rates. Television was simply not helping.

Frequent Participants

A key factor sustaining beat-meeting involvement is the role played by relatively small cadres of frequent participants. They attend a large fraction of their beats' meetings every year, and in doing so they drive up attendance totals. The mathematics of the contribution of frequent participants to overall beat-meeting attendance is simple. For example, the 2003 city survey asked beat meeting participants how many meetings they had attended in the past year. Most attended just one or two meetings, and 66 percent of attendees reported visiting three meetings or fewer. However, the remaining one-third of participants attended a lot more. The average beat meets about ten times a year, so we classified those who attended five or more meetings annually—about half the total—as frequent participants. They make up 20 percent of all beat-meeting participants, but multiplying this by the frequency with which they attend reveals that frequent participants constitute *56 percent* of all those who show up in the course of a year. More participants—25 percent— show up just once for a meeting, but over the course of a year they account for only about 20 percent of their beat's total attendance.

As a result, a beat's attendance rate is very sensitive to the size of its cadre of frequent participants. Beat sergeants blessed with a loyal contingent of participants can bask in the glow of high attendance rates, while those burdened with a less frequently active population face the never-ending task of recruiting new faces each month. We also found that because frequent attenders also tend to be the people who participate in marches and other CAPS-related events, so fostering their involvement pays off for a broad variety of CAPS programs. Developing a local cadre of frequent participants is the surest road to sustaining high rates of citizen involvement. Although it probably plays only a minor role in getting people to return, by 2001 it was routine for the districts to offer participants inducements to do so. Throughout Chicago, beat meetings conclude with a raffle for prizes donated by various manufacturers, including smoke detectors, porch lights, fire extinguishers, steering-wheel locks, T-shirts, and sports caps.

Who are these frequent participants? Figure 4.4 describes them by charting the percentage that fall into the frequent-participant (five or more meetings) category. Differences among the groups are quite distinctive. Perhaps the most notable are linked to race and language. The disadvantage Latinos face is evident. Only 13 percent of English-speaking Latinos, and just 9 percent of Spanish speakers, fell in the frequent participant category. More than a third of African American participants and one-quarter of whites were frequent participants, on the other hand. Age differences were very strong as well. Older Chicagoans were the most likely to participate frequently: 37 percent of those over age sixty-five were classed as frequent participants, contrasted with only 18 percent of those under age thirty. Age is also associated with two other factors examined here: having children at home and participating in the labor force. Those with no children at home were twice as likely to report attending many meetings in the course of a year, and those with no job to go to the next day were more likely to attend than those who were working. Participation in neighborhood organizations, a factor that was examined earlier in this section, was linked to frequent participation as well.

Residents who show up often are also more concerned about the neighborhood. The survey included a battery of questions asking about the extent of various neighborhood problems. Figure 4.4 divides respondents into high- and low-concern groups, based on their responses. (These questions are examined in much more detail in the chapter 6, in the discussion of problem solving.) The more concerned people were, the more frequently they attended beat meetings. In short, frequent participants are rooted in their community; they have time on their hands; and they are worried.

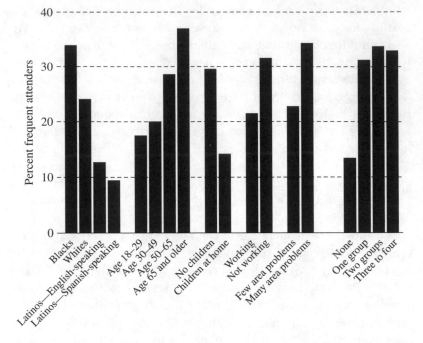

Figure 4.4. Frequent Beat Meeting Participants, 2003

In this light it is important to note that elements of this demographic profile also work in concert against Latino involvement. On
most dimensions Latinos are concentrated in the infrequent involvement category. Latinos are younger. In the 2003 city survey only 6
percent of Latinos—as compared to 25 percent of African Americans
and 21 percent of whites—were in the age sixty-five and older category, a high-participation age group. Latinos were by far the most
likely to have children living at home. Among Latinos as a whole, 66
percent reported having children at home, compared to 43 percent of
African Americans and 22 percent of whites. For Spanish-speaking
Latinos, the figure was 72 percent. Finally, Latinos are particularly
unlikely to be connected to their community through organizational
ties, including church attendance. In the 2003 survey, 64 percent of
Latinos reported being active in *no* neighborhood groups or institutions. Among whites, 55 percent reported being similarly cut off,
while the figure was only 50 percent for African Americans. The
demography of the city's growing Latino community thus worked
against their frequent involvement in beat meetings and involvement
in CAPS problem-solving efforts.

Another reason to foster a local cadre of beat-meeting participants is that they also become heavily involved in action projects. The role of activists in community problem solving will be addressed in detail in chapter 6. It reports that loyal meeting participants play a central part in that story.

In summary, surveys of the general public, beat-meeting participants, and problem-solving trainees all point in the same direction. Members of Chicago's growing community of Spanish-speaking Latinos are the least likely to know about CAPS and that beat meetings are being held. They are the least likely to participate often in beat meetings, and they are least likely to be involved in the neighborhood institutions that promote awareness and support involvement in community affairs. The only avenue by which they city has been able to "reach out and touch them" with the CAPS message has been television—which appears to be a medium without a significant action component. The distribution of beat-meeting awareness, the influence of other community organizations and institutions, and the demographics of frequent participation each have other potentially divisive consequences as well, for they all are consistently biased in the direction of older, sometimes retired, home-owning, more educated, better-off residents. *More* people turn out in troubled neighborhoods, but, in general, those who show up for beat meetings represent the top slice of the community. We will see later that these language, lifestyle, and class biases play themselves out at the meetings, contributing to a systematic bias in the representativeness of Chicago's beat meetings.

What Happens at Beat Meetings?

What goes on when people gather for beat meetings? This is a difficult and expensive question to answer. Because they are held night after night, in hundreds of church basements and park field houses all over the city, it is hard even for the police department to know what is going on. An officer who attends fills out a brief form counting the number who came and summarizing what was talked about, but not much information is recorded and other observers might report a different view of what transpired. Citywide surveys indicate that a large percentage of residents who attend think the meetings are useful and lead to improvements in their neighborhood, but these tell us nothing about why or how.

In order to examine the dynamics of beat meetings more closely, observers attended more than a thousand of them between 1995 and 2002. They completed forms recording specific details about the sessions, including where they were located, who attended, and what was talked about. They counted the number of police officers and residents who attended and classified the roles played by police and other city employees. Using a checklist, they noted the issues that were raised by residents during the course of the meeting. They reported on the languages that were spoken and the kinds of printed materials that were distributed. They noted which participants identified problems and solutions to problems. The observers were students trained to make judgments about such matters as how effectively police and civilian leadership conducted the meeting. At a prearranged moment (they arranged in advance to be on the agenda) they rose, explained who they were, and distributed questionnaires to both the police and residents who were in attendance. Most of the details presented here concerning what goes on in beat meetings are drawn from studies conducted in 1998 and 2002. In 1998, observers attended one meeting each in 253 beats and surveyed 5,293 residents and 1,050 police officers. In 2002 they observed 291 meetings in a random sample of 130 beats and surveyed 3,495 residents and 643 police officers. The surveys asked about conditions in the beat, the quality of local police service, involvement in CAPS-related activities, and people's assessments of the meetings they had attended. The questionnaires for residents were available in both English and Spanish.

Beat meetings are usually held on the same night of the month and in the same location each month. In 2002, many of the beat meetings we observed were held in local churches (28 percent), park district field houses (23 percent) and schools (15 percent). Each beat is supposed to have a civilian facilitator—someone identified by local police who can help them plan and conduct the meeting. Most do, but people come and go from this volunteer job. A facilitator was present at seventy-five of the beat meetings we observed. An average of seven police officers (and as many as twelve) were there. The police contingent usually included the beat team's sergeant, beat officers who were on duty at the time, and a few team members from other shifts. Almost all meetings began at 6:30 or 7:00 p.m., and in 2002 the average gathering lasted fifty-eight minutes. Police have attempted to accommodate the city's burgeoning Latino population by producing Spanish-language CAPS materials, but at 83 percent of the meetings handouts were available only in English. Twenty percent of the meetings opened or closed with a prayer.

Beat meetings are supposed to provide a forum for identifying and discussing neighborhood problems. This proves universal; not a single meeting has gone by without some problem being debated. We collected the most detailed data on what was discussed at beat meetings in the 1998 study. The observers were armed with a checklist of seventy-two issues and concerns. This was drawn up based on earlier observations of meetings. Table 4.3 combines observations of what was discussed into nine broad categories of problems and indi-

Table 4.3 Topics Discussed at Beat Meetings, 1998

Percent of Beats Where Major Categories of Problems and the Most Frequently Mentioned Specific Issues Were Discussed

Social Disorder	88%	**Physical Decay**	58%
loitering, congregating	50	abandoned buildings	30
public drinking	25	graffiti	17
liquor outlets	24	trash and junk	16
noise	24	loose garbage	12
suspicious persons	18	abandoned cars	11
bad landlords	16	sidewalks, street repair	5
Gang Problems	51%	**Parking and Traffic**	57%
violence	22	parking	32
intimidation	18	speeding/reckless driving	22
gang graffiti	15	traffic congestion	9
Personal Crime	47%	**Drug Problems**	66%
shootings	20	sales and use	55
street crime	16	drug houses	23
domestic violence	10	gang involvement	17
Property Crime	51%	**Citizen Involvement**	31%
burglary	23	turnout problems	21
theft	18	not working together	15
garage break-ins	14	need for follow-through	15
car theft	13	retaliation	12
Complaints about Police	47%	**Criticize Public Services**	11%
911 call response	31	**Criticize Public Officials**	8%
not enough police or low police visibility	21		
criticize CAPS implementation	12		

Note: Less frequently discussed topic categories are excluded from the detailed sublists.

cates the percentage of beats at which each topic came up. It also presents the most common specific concerns that fit within each general problem category. The percentages add up to more than 100 percent because multiple problems were discussed at every meeting.

What was discussed at beat meetings is related to the character of the neighborhood. This can be examined by linking the observer's reports to social, economic, and demographic data about each area. In general, residents of poor African American beats talk about drugs. Residents of heavily Latino beats discuss gangs, especially in areas with a high concentration of recent immigrants. Property crime comes up most frequently in better-off, predominantly white areas, along with conversations about parking and traffic issues.

Drugs are one of the most commonly discussed problems; residents expressed concern about drug sales or use at two-thirds of the meetings in 1998, and at 62 percent in 2002. Our observer noted this discussion on the South Side of the city:

> A quite lengthy discussion took place about conditions on _____ Street between ____ and ____. Several residents complained about the adults as well as youths in the area selling narcotics. They were selling the narcotics on the streets. The buyers would then proceed to an abandoned building on the block to use the drugs. The drug trafficking caused a lot of traffic congestion on the block. Drivers would literally have to wait until the dealers sold their product and the customer was happy. The residents said that in the last few months, the problem seemed to escalate. The narcotics were being sold in greater numbers and at all times of the day. The abandoned building that addicts were using became a haven for squatters and their children. As a result of all the discussion about that problem, the police decided to make that their new mission. They promised increased police patrol. The tactical sergeant also promised more surveillance and undercover work in that area.

People who attended beat meetings where drugs were discussed reported in questionnaires that they were concerned about many other problems as well, including street crime and gang violence. Drug problems were discussed frequently in meetings held in poor and predominantly African American beats where violent crime rates were high and many of the incidents that took place involved guns. These were also beats where residents reported the most dissatisfaction with police working in the area.

Physical dilapidation is another frequent topic at beat meetings, discussed by residents at 58 percent of the meetings in 1998 and 47 percent in 2002. This category includes concern about abandoned or run-down buildings, abandoned cars, graffiti and other forms of vandalism, litter and trash, illegal dumping, loose garbage in alleys and overflowing Dumpsters. An observer made this note during a beat meeting:

> They . . . had very serious concerns in regard to a dilapidated building in their block that was being used for drug sales. The drug seller's people were also squatting in the basement of the building. The main concern was that the four adults who were squatting also had three children under the age of four with them. The building had no running water or working electricity, but the neighbor had seen the landlord trying to assist the squatters to tap into the water. The neighbor who owns the building next to it complained about the rats in this dilapidated building. He stated that contact had been made with 311 [the city-service hotline] but there had been no response. At the conclusion of this conversation the police proceeded to leave, stating they were going to this building to check all this information out. This neighborhood beat meeting was filled with frustration from residents, the facilitator, and police. The facilitator can be quoted about the residents' overall feeling: "These people are prisoners in their own neighborhood."

Discussion of physical decay issues was most frequent in poorer areas that had many vacant buildings and low rents, and were plagued by both personal and property crime as well.

Parking and traffic issues, in contrast, were discussed most frequently in better-off areas. In 1998 they came up in 57 percent of the beats, and in 2002 in 44 percent. Residents expressed concern about the lack of adequate parking, speeding, running stop signs, and reckless or drunken driving. Discussions of traffic problems predominated at a meeting attended by one of the observers:

> A resident discussed a problem near a school on her block. She said that parents waiting to pick up their kids would double-

park in front of the school and back up traffic for miles. When residents asked these people to move their cars and drive around the block to wait, the drivers usually did not respond. The officers said that they would consider heavily ticketing the area, and that if they did so at the school then they would have to heavily ticket the whole beat. One resident suggested that she videotape some of these cars and show how much chaos they are causing in the street. These tapes could then possibly be shown at the school's annual open house to parents. Another resident discussed the problem of people running a stop sign near her home. She said that many children cross the street there after school. She sees several cars a day fly through the intersection. The woman asked the police if they could post a car there during the afternoon and hopefully stop some of this.

Parking and traffic issues came up most frequently in areas where few other problems concerned residents. The police who attended meetings in these beats agreed, for they also gave them low problem ratings. Beats emphasizing parking and traffic had low turnout rates, and few who attended meetings there reported much CAPS activism. They were predominantly higher-income, white-collar areas with high rents and home values.

Gangs.   Beats where discussion focuses on gangs have a much different profile. Overall, gangs and gang-related violence were brought up at more than half of the meetings observed in 1998. The specific concerns that were voiced included intimidation by gangs, outbreaks of gang graffiti, gang recruiting, and gang loitering. An observer noted:

It was at this point that the attendees became really vocal, particularly when a man brought up the gang problems in the neighborhood. The attendees began to give personal accounts of sightings of gangs, particularly around the park district. For example, the man who brought up the gang issue said his wife was nearly shot outside the intersection of ____ and ____ by gang members when waiting for their daughter to return from school. He had lived in the neighborhood for eighteen years and had called 911 so many times he had "worn out the buttons on his phone." He was extremely frustrated with the police response to the gang situation and referred to the neighborhood as a "war zone." In particular, he felt that the neighborhood was "losing control of the park." The subject of police response to the gang situation was apparently a hot issue with many of the attendees. Another man said that he had seen gang members carrying guns and using young gang members as lookouts. In addition, there were complaints that the squad cars and the police were not effective deterrents to the gangs.

In Chicago, gangs were a visible problem in heavily Latino beats. Residents who came to meetings were also vocal about graffiti problems and public drinking. Gang problems were frequently discussed in areas with large families, where schools were overcrowded, and where unattached males were concentrated. Gang problems were most frequently discussed where people had little education and many households were in the U.S. Census Bureau's linguistically isolated category.

Property crime   was discussed at 51 percent of the meetings attended in 1998. The issues that came up most frequently were home and garage burglary, car break-ins and theft, car vandalism, and general theft. Confidence games aimed at senior citizens were also discussed. An observer noted:

> Residents said that two nights before, some people stole a car in their back alley. These people then went on a joyride through the alley, knocking over garbage cans and damaging property. They finally drove out of the alley, dumped the car in an abandoned lot, and set it on fire. The residents said that they called 911 a couple of times and that the police only showed up after the car exploded. They were questioning why the police didn't show up right away, saying that if they had, the police could have arrested the individuals before the car was set on fire.

Property crime was a subject for discussion in better-off areas of the city, and in predominantly white beats with concentrations of senior citizens. Residents who attended beat meetings there reported little concern about personal crime.

Personal crime   was discussed at 47 percent of the meetings in 1998. The issues raised by residents included robbery, purse snatching, domestic violence, and sexual assault. At one beat meeting: "One resident brought up the recent attacks against elderly people in the area. Teenagers have been asking older people if they have change for a twenty-dollar bill, and when the people reach for their wallets, the kids hit them with bats and take their money. This has been happening while the elderly people are walking, driving, or waiting at bus stops."

Social disorder   in its various forms were discussed at 89 percent of the meetings held in 2002, and 88 percent in 1998. This category includes a long list of minor offenses, as well as conditions that are not criminal but that frequently disturb neighborhood residents. Concern about groups of people loitering in the streets was expressed at 50 percent of beat meetings in 1998, followed by problems associated with alcohol and with noise. The list of social disorder problems also included prostitution, panhandling, curfew or truancy violations, disturbances by teenagers, public exposure, gambling, trespassing, and landlords who lose control of their buildings. Concern about skateboarding and bicycle riding on sidewalks comes up frequently in meetings involving lots of senior citizens. Concern about social disorder is so widespread that it is not closely associated with any particular neighborhood feature. Observers noted these examples at beat meetings:

> The first problem discussed was a large group of children running amok on a particular block. The resident said the group sometimes numbered in excess of forty children. These kids would leave garbage in the yards and streets. Another problem, possibly related, took place after school was dismissed for the day. A resident complained that after school, streets would be mobbed with children running around and causing trouble. These children broke the resident's windows twice in the same week as well as at other times.

> Two residents complained that there was a huge party going on in the street in front of their home. They said there were a few hundred people drinking, smoking marijuana, and drag racing. They were also urinating on front lawns and causing trouble on the block. A building owner at the meeting said she is having a problem with her building. She said there are human feces all over in front of and next to the building.

> The next topic of discussion was prostitution rings, including those in which children were being pimped out to do sexual favors in various alleys and streets around the beat. One resident complained that she saw the prostitutes everyday, behind her

garage, engaging in sexual activity with various men. She said she was trying to get her neighbors and tenants involved but was not sure how to stop it.

Policing   is another of the issues residents discuss in beat meetings. In fact, negative comments or complaints about the police were aired at 44 percent of the meetings in 2002, and 47 percent in 1998. There was also specific praise for police at a third of the meetings, sometimes the same ones. The most commonly cited policing concern (voiced at more than 30 percent of the meetings in 1998) was dissatisfaction with responses to 911 calls. A beat meeting observer noted: "A woman described how she had called 911 because she saw a man passed out on the sidewalk. She explained that it had taken half an hour for the squad car to arrive and that the officers had not even gotten out to see what was wrong with him. The beat officer present explained that such individuals are 'usually drunk.'" Residents also complained that officers came slowly, or not at all, in response to their calls. Others reported how discourteously 911 call takers spoke to them. The "911 response" category also includes reports that officers violated the department's commitment to protecting the anonymity of callers when requested. "One man from the ____ block club yelled that he's tired of getting 'set up' by police who come to his door, based upon his reporting of activity. He said calls are seldom anonymous, as police almost always walk up to his door. He said he was too old to get shot." The perception that there are not enough police on patrol, or that they are not visible enough in troubled areas came up in about one in five beats. In addition, dissatisfaction with the way in which CAPS is being implemented was voiced at 12 percent of the meetings. "Residents asked police for a foot patrol post there. They explained they have resources only for one and the businesses farther south have it. The residents were angry that the businesses with more money and less crime had a foot patrol and they couldn't get one where they wanted one." Negative comments about the police were more common in predominantly African American areas that are neither extremely poor nor well off— where many lower-income homeowners are concentrated. Crime rates are not particularly high in these areas, although school truancy is. Surveys of officers at the meetings where complains about policing are frequent reveal that they do not come to beat meetings very regularly and have little contact with residents who do, except when they attend.

Citizen Involvement.   Finally, at about a third of the meetings there was discussion of problems with citizen involvement in CAPS. Beat-meeting turnout, a lack of police-citizen cooperation, and the need for more follow-up on problems that were discussed headed that list, and there was also frequent discussion of threats of retaliation against residents who became visibly associated with the police. A few well-known instances of firebombings, and even one murder, in retaliation against CAPS activists have made it clear that these fears can be well founded. A Roman Catholic nun working in Chicago's Little Village described the problem this way: "There's a fear factor of the gangs retaliating against the person and his or her family. There's also the belief that CAPS is in cahoots with the gangs. I heard a rumor from a CAPS attendee at [a beat meeting]. People had gone in good faith to talk about a homicide that took place. When they arrived they immediately recognized the beat facilitator as a close relative of the gang member that was responsible for the killing, and they noticed his lack of interest in the matter."

In 1998 our observers noted discussion of potential retaliation or actual reports of incidents at 12 percent of the meetings they attended. Expressions of concern about retaliation were voiced most frequently at meetings in heavily Latino beats and in places where concern about gangs and drugs was particularly high.

How Did Chicago Do?

There was good and bad news about resident involvement in CAPS. Awareness of the program grew over time, and it is especially significant that it grew among all major demographic groups. By 2003, almost 90 percent of African Americans knew about CAPS, exceeding the level of awareness among whites. On the other hand, only a little more than two-thirds of Latinos were aware of what is going on, a number that fell between the late 1990s and 2003. This was linked to the declining engagement of Spanish speakers with the program, a long-term problem for the city. Among those who knew about community policing, about one-third—or about 15 percent of the city's adult population—reported attending a beat meeting during the course of the year.

Actual involvement in CAPS remained essentially stable between 1995 and 2003. Average beat meeting attendance remained at about sixty-five hundred residents per month, belying the expectation that it would fade as the novelty of the program wore off. While that is an impressive number, involvement did not expand along with awareness of CAPS. One culprit for this may be television. Much of the growth in CAPS awareness during the second half of the 1990s was fueled by television, but as best as can be judged statistically— without the randomized experiments it would take to confirm it— television does not stimulate turnout. The most active residents we survey are the least likely to report hearing about CAPS on television, while those who rely on television are distinctively less likely to turn out.

What counted the most was personal contact. Over time, the cumulative number of Chicagoans who had heard about CAPS or talked about it with another person grew, especially among African Americans. This helped sustain overall levels of involvement, and validated the city's strategy of investing in a staff of community organizers charged with drumming up turnout and facilitating neighborhood problem-solving projects. CAPS awareness and involvement were also sustained by the network of community organizations that already honeycomb more fortunate city neighborhoods. This worked to the advantage of whites and homeowners, who were more likely to be involved in non-church-related community organizations, but these were not the places where the organizers put in their time and effort.

Perhaps most significantly, CAPS involvement was highest in the places that needed it the most. It was highest in beats where city institutions had failed to deliver health care and effective educational outcomes. It was highest in poorer areas where people had less education. Most dramatically, it was highest in the city's most violent, drug-infested neighborhoods. The bad news is that attendance was driven by area crime; the good news is that residents of many of the city's most troubled neighborhoods had a place to go to get help.

Representing the Community

In Chicago's model, beat meetings are the vehicle for grass-roots consultation and collaboration between police and the community. At the meetings, the two sides are to come together to identify local priorities, discuss how both police and residents can best address them, and review their progress in doing so. They are the city's official mechanism for providing communities leverage over the operation of one of its most important service delivery bureaucracies. This leads to two obvious questions: *Who* is "the community" that is being represented? and *How well* are they represented? My experience in evaluating community-policing projects in Houston, was that white homeowners dominated the civilian side of the partnership to the exclusion of both African Americans and Mexican Americans (Skogan 1990a). From the outset led me to be skeptical that their counterparts in Chicago would find close cooperation with the police to be an easy thing to carry off. However, we saw in the previous chapter that in the aggregate, poorer communities had higher turnout rates, albeit for the unappealing reason that they were propelled to attend because of crime. However, exactly who turns out and how well they represent the concerns of their neighbors remains an open question. The possibility that CAPS participants would be unrepresentative of the community was encouraged by the way in which Chicago resolved the potentially complicated question of "Who is the community?" The answer was that it is the residents of a police administrative unit, along with assorted building owners, business operators, and any others with a stake in the area. How was their representativeness to be ensured? That simply depended on who showed up.

This resolution was not casually arrived at. It was the result of a political struggle between police and politicians, on one side, and a fragmented collection of community and issue-oriented organizations on the other, that was played out during the early years of the program. In that struggle, the organizations "outside" wanted "inside." Some of them were neighborhood-based community organizations, while others presented themselves as representing broad coalitions of "progressive" Chicagoans. In local parlance, this means that they were multiracial in composition and anti-Daley in orientation, and some had been around long enough that they had been opposed to more than one Mayor Daley. For them, the resident-involvement component of CAPS presented an opportunity to assert some control over a citywide, grassroots network of beat meetings and district advisory committees that seemed almost purpose-built for their needs. They demanded that beat meetings be organized and led by local groups, and not the police. In their view, residents should control the agenda of the meetings, and invite police to participate on the community's terms. To ensure representativeness, they wanted civilian involvement in all significant aspects of the program to be directed by leaders who were either elected by beat residents or somehow emerged from locally prominent organizations. The organizations that were pushing this view of CAPS had an agenda that extended further than crime. They saw resident involvement in the city's community-policing program as another vehicle for building the autonomous capacity of residents to help themselves and to lobby effectively in the corridors of power for the outside resources that they needed to address their most pressing problems. The activists who led most of the organizations knocking on CAPS' door knew that all of this would take time and energy, so they also wanted grants and contracts to support the professional organizers that it would take to carry off this vision of resident involvement.

Police and city leaders would have none of this. Politicians were worried that beat meetings would provide a venue they could not control, one where complaints about elected officials and efforts to unseat them might be initiated. In this post–political machine era, few aldermen had a mechanism for reaching the grassroots in their constituencies that approached the magnitude of what the police were creating. The thought of hundreds of constituents meeting regularly outside of their control, attending gatherings that potentially provided a venue for their opponents to stir up trouble and make a name for themselves made them nervous. Police feared that the meetings would be taken over by "loudmouths" who would vent their spleens given any uncontrolled opportunity, and by "gimmie guys" who would try to bend police priorities to suit their personal interests. An officer explained to me that he could not be "the friend of the people" and enforce the law against them at the same time, for his new partners would abuse the relationship by trying to get him to fix parking tickets and overlook minor infractions of the law. During the early debate over the character of beat meetings, rumors spread through the department that part of the CAPS plan included having the officers report to civilians, and this increased their skepticism of the whole enterprise.

In the end, it was a one-sided struggle, for the mayor, the city council, and the police held all the power. Ultimately, the police department is in control. Police are the official hosts for beat meetings, and they control the agenda. They decide when and where the meetings are to be held, which can be a topic of conflict when beats are divided by race or inconvenient physical barriers. Beats do not elect leaders. Beat-team sergeants are responsible for finding civilian beat facilitators to help conduct the meetings, and a police officer is always a coleader. From the outset, the department insisted on assigning police officers the clumsy "facilitator" title, and stoutly resisted calling them beat representatives, meeting chairmen, or by any term suggesting they had an official voice or status. Beats also do not take votes on issues, by and large, although we have observed a number of meetings taking "straw votes" to decide between some options facing them. For example, some vote to decide what problem to focus on for the next six months or so. However, there are no public records of what transpires at meetings that can be used to hold anyone responsible for what goes on there. The community is represented at beat meetings by whoever happens to hear about them and chooses to attend. There are other ways to formally constitute public bodies—for example, they could be made up of heads of a list of formal organizations, or be official nominees of the mayo—but those options were not considered seriously because they would have vested beats with some degree of political autonomy. Chicago proceeded with a "depoliticized" version of representation at beat meetings, because that was the politically safe route to take. Looking back later in disappointment, a leader of the community-empowerment side of this battle lamented: "It could have been a community-building and empowering process, could have developed a democratic partnership with police, could have involved tens of thousands in ongoing cooperative problem solving. The implications of its potential frightened the City and so the administration gave us what we have now, a program that, measured against what it could have been, is clearly a failure."[1] Does this mean that the public has no real stake in what takes place at beat meetings? They are certainly not New England town meetings, where every able citizen who turns out gets to vote on municipal and school budgets that total millions of dollars even in the smallest communities (Bryan 2004). On the other hand, things do go on at beat meetings that can affect the future of the neighborhood. These include setting the agenda for police and community action, monitoring the effectiveness of police responses to community priorities, and mobilizing residents to act on their own behalf. These activities are certainly important enough to stress the importance of the representativeness of the citizenry assembled at beat meetings and the quality of the police and civilian leadership that is exercised there.

Setting an Action Agenda

The core function of beat meetings is to exchange information about problems, identify possible solutions to neighborhood problems, and help shape police priorities. Officers who work the beat from several shifts are usually represented at the meetings so they can all participate in the discussion. As chapter 3 indicated, they have been trained to employ a five-step process that features identifying and analyzing problems, developing and implementing solutions to the problems, and assessing the effectiveness of what they have accomplished. These problem-solving steps were also woven into the curriculum of a massive training program for neighborhood residents conducted in 1995 and 1996. One goal of this training was to help participants focus on chronic crime and disorder issues, rather than on their individual woes.

One task of observers who were dispatched to monitor what happens at beat meetings was to note whether problem identification and discussion of solutions to them was taking place. What they found is summarized in table 5.1. The 1998 study covered meetings in 254 beats, while the 2002 study was confined to a random sample of 130 beats. A 1995 study involved 161 beats clustered in selected districts, so the sample did not, strictly speaking, represent the entire city. Between the 1998 and 2002 studies there were paired observations in 120 beats, and 72 of the beats observed in 1995 also fell into the 2002 study. Because they were involved in two major studies, this discussion focuses on what took place in the fairly random sample of 120 matched beats, and it emphasizes the 1998 and 2002 studies because they are more recent. However, as table 5.1 indicates, other comparisons would come to the same general conclusions, for the matched beats are quite representative of the city as a whole.

Table 5.1 Agenda Setting, Monitoring the Police, and Mobilizing the Public, 1995, 1998, and 2002

Components of Model Beat Meeting Rating	All Beats in Each Study			Matched Beats	
	1995	1998	2002	1998	2002
Problem Identification Were problems or issues identified at the meeting?	97	100	100	100	100
Identifying Solutions Were solutions proposed for problems that were identified?	96	77	74	80	76
Officer Feedback Did police officers report back on previous problem-solving efforts?	51	60	72	65	73
Resident Feedback Did residents report back on previous problem-solving efforts?	35	35	44	32	47
Volunteers Called For Were volunteers called for or sign-up sheets passed around?	51	41	25	42	25
Action Component Did residents leave the meeting with a commitment to future action?	nd	35	24	38	26
Number of beats	161	254	130	120	120

Note: "nd" indicates measure not included in 1995 study.

Observations in the field indicate that there was a great deal of variation in the extent to which different elements of Chicago's problem-solving model were actually enacted at beat meetings. As table 5.1 documents, there was no difficulty in identifying problems; this was a universal feature of beat meetings. Most such discussion was initiated by residents; in 2002, police dominated the discussion of problems at only 10 percent of meetings, down from 16 percent in 1998 (these figures are not presented in table 5.1). An observer at a North Side beat summarized the "new business" section of a meeting:

The main issue discussed by the residents concerned the homeless problem. Many of the residents complained that the homeless were setting up tents in the park. One particularly vocal resident said, "In a neighborhood fraught with prostitution and drugs, how can the police department tolerate these types of problems?" He was very angry that the police were not doing enough to solve the problem, constantly asking why there was not more patrolling and more arrests being made. The officers responded by saying that they were patrolling the area all the time, but the homeless keep coming back with tents. Because many of the homeless leave their property behind in the park, the officers also said that they have been patrolling the park with a dump truck to pick up all the excess property left behind.

Solutions to the problems that are broached are less often discussed, however. Solutions were proposed at about three-quarters of all meetings in 2002; this was down a bit from 1998 and very much less common than in 1995, when CAPS was new. The observers also noted who was most likely to suggest solutions, when they were discussed. Police took the leading role in proposing solutions at more than half of the meetings; police and residents made a fairly equal contribution at 28 percent; and residents took the lead at only 17 percent of the meetings (these figures are not presented in table 5.1). Sometimes the solutions that are proposed are quite specific. At one meeting

[The beat officer] said that most of the burglaries occur while residents are away at work during the day. He said the best solution for prevention of burglary was to "get to know your neighbors." In addition, he said residents should install lights outside their houses, particularly by their garages, to use as a deterrent. Overall, he said the best solution was to "be a little suspicious." He gave some preventive tips to keep offenders from hiding in residents' garages like walking into the garage back first so residents can have a view of the door, and offenders cannot sneak in. In addition, he suggested residents buy "Beware of Dog" signs to give offenders a "moment of hesitation that will make them think twice."

Residents generally demand action from the police, however, and sometimes those discussions become small lessons in the limits of police power in a democracy. At another beat meeting: "Residents had many concerns relating to police responsiveness to problems. One resident went as far as to ask why the police couldn't be intimidating and harass the troublemakers like they used to when he was a kid. One officer explained that it was now considered harassment or brutality, and people would call 'OPS' on the officers more easily now."[2] Solutions tended to be discussed at meetings held in better-off beats. Meetings at which participants were more often college graduates involved the most discussion of solutions to problems; those with a good representation of Spanish-speaking residents (but this was painfully few meetings) tended *not* to include discussion of what to do about problems that were being brought up.

Monitoring Police Effectiveness

An interesting feature of beat meetings is that they evolved over time. The idea of having civilian facilitators came up only after some experimentation with holding beat meetings in the prototype districts, before CAPS became a citywide program. Training for police officers and beat facilitators in how to run better meetings did not begin until 1997. As noted in chapter 3, the districts were required to produce written meeting agendas and to make crime maps and other informational material available only in 1999, as part of a general push to increase the quality and standardize the conduct of the meetings. One of the most significant shifts has been the emergence of beat meetings as a venue for holding police responsible for working on issues identified by the community. This was not part of the original CAPS plan. It came about in part because we prodded the department to make attending beat meeting more worthwhile for residents, and this matched their commitment that beat officers should be more overtly responsive to community concerns. Follow-up reports by police regarding what they have done since the last meeting to address the concerns that were identified at that time help make it clear to participants that attending pays off—that they should attend because something actually happens as a result. It also helps ensure that police and city-service agencies actually follow up on problems discussed at these sessions.

Chicagoans are not shy about making their dissatisfaction known at the meetings. At one Northwest Side beat meeting, an observer reported:

> The atmosphere in the room was high-strung and the dialogue between the residents and officers at times became hostile and confrontational. The residents became highly frustrated with the police response to their concerns. Almost every problem that was brought up by residents was met with a similar response: the police couldn't do much; "our hands are tied" as one officer stated. The police focused the discussion around the limitations of their powers and rarely made an attempt to brainstorm solutions. At one point the officers tried to move on to another topic, and a resident angrily interrupted saying, "You haven't given any solutions. Something has to change [in the neighborhood]. You keep telling us what you can't do."

The reporting-back requirement is now enshrined in paperwork. Officers are officially required to report to residents on progress made on previously identified problems. The form that officers complete describing what happened at each beat meeting includes a section in which they list the actions they reported taking in response to concerns raised at the last meeting. These can be compared across meetings to check their consistency, and the beat-team sergeant has to sign the form, attesting that it is an accurate representation of what went on. The district's CAPS lieutenant also signs the form, indicating that he or she has reviewed the meeting report. Because both the department's internal inspectors and the office monitoring CAPS implementation independently inspect these meeting reports, the officers filling them out take it seriously.

As table 5.1 indicates, our observers noted that in 2002, police officers contributed reports of their latest problem-solving efforts fairly often—at 73 percent of the meetings, up from 65 percent in 1998. In this regard, well-functioning Chicago beat meetings are a remarkable institution. At best they provide a tight link between residents' preferences and the operation of their government. Police get rapid feed-back about the service they are rendering, directly from consumers. It is difficult to identify any other governance institution that does so as quickly and intimately.

Mobilizing Residents

In the CAPS plan, beat meetings were to be a place where residents could "get their act together" and organize their own problem-solving activities. Some beats work this way. Several districts we studied worked to improve their beat meetings in this regard. Some provided complaint forms for residents to fill out, so that problems that concerned individuals would not dominate the meeting and those present could focus on big issues. Some districts and beats varied their meeting structure to promote better problem solving. One district held separate problem-solving meetings every other month, and another held abbreviated problem-solving training in one beat needing help. Reports of resident problem-solving efforts made at the meetings may help sustain the enthusiasm of partici-pants for the process, and may encourage others to join in. The beat facilitator at one meeting we observed summarized recent events in the area:

> The beat had attempted three marches and thirty people (in-cluding children) attended the marches. They marched four blocks from _____ Street to _____ and to __th, and "mopped out" the area. People from the state attorney's office also showed up. She [the beat facilitator] asked residents to come out for the marches. She also said that in the current week, they are planning to march every Thursday of the month (changed to Sundays, because people complained). Those who cannot march were given the option of passing out flyers regarding the march. The beat car will also be participating.

However, the observers did not see this kind of activity taking place very often. They watched for reports by residents about problem-solving actions they had taken since the last meeting. As table 5.1 shows, this kind of feedback was fairly common, in the mid-thirties in 1998 and the mid-forties in 2002. However, in 2002 there was more feedback by residents describing their problem-solving efforts in better-off, predominantly white beats where people call 911 with problems less frequently than most, and these may be places where resident involvement was perhaps least needed.

The observation forms completed at each meeting also asked whether volunteers were called for during each meeting, or if sign-up sheets were distributed for a specific activity. The observers noted that this occurred just over 40 percent of the time in 1998, but at only 25 percent of beats in 2002. Observers were also trained to make an overall judgment of whether or not residents left each meeting with a commitment to taking some clear action before the next meeting. They thought this was the case in only 38 percent of the beats in 1998, and in 26 percent in 2002. There were certainly beats where this did occur. One observer reported: "After discussion of public drinking, people were beginning to brainstorm about possible solutions to some of their problems. There was already a person recruiting people for a protest to get more police officers. There was a resident who wanted to organize a block club. Another resident suggested that people should have a list of neighborhood phone numbers so they could call the police collectively. Another resident was going to get a petition started to vote their community 'dry,' which means that there would be no establishments licensed to sell alcohol in the community." However, it is evident that many beat meetings strayed from their role in mobilizing residents for action. Many of the meetings are essentially "slow 911 sessions" at which residents air their individual grievances to the assembled police officers. One CAPS trainer characterized these as "laundry" meetings, where residents "drop off the shirts, come back in a week and they're done." Others are "show-and-tell" sessions at which police or agency representatives talk and residents listen. Police frequently promote the expectation that the role of residents is to be their "eyes and ears," calling them for fast assistance when something bad happens; statements to this effect were made by police at 75 percent of the meetings that we observed in the 1998 study. A beat-team sergeant described the atmosphere at his beat's meetings this way: "Beat meetings, the ones that I've attended, still do not understand or partake in what is termed the police-community partnership. Every meeting that you'll ever go to, they'll say 'I have a problem at so-and-so street, what have you done?' Now, depending on what the problem is, everything I hear is a complaint. Instead of 'Oh, what can I do to help?' it's, 'Solve that!' So there's not any police-community partnership. It's usually just a complaint session. We just try to appease the community."

Impacting the Community

Another way to rate the significance of beat meetings is to look at what the participants say they have accomplished. The evaluation surveys monitored the views of beat-meeting participants. Respondents who indicated that they attended one or more meetings during the past year were questioned about three of the core functions of beat meetings: the exchange of information about the neighborhood, the formulation of action plans, and solving neighborhood problems. There was broad satisfaction with beat meetings, and satisfaction did not vary much by race. Well over 80 percent of Chicagoans of all racial backgrounds reported that they had learned something as a result of attending. Roughly 70 percent believed that actions had been taken in their neighborhood as a result of the meetings, and this figure did not vary much by race either. About half of the respondents in each group gave the meetings a "very useful" rating for finding solutions to neighborhood problems, and more than 90 percent thought they were at least somewhat useful.

Representing Community Interests

One problem with the catch-as-catch-can character of the representational system that was adopted in Chicago is that only a limited number of people actually attend. A "good" meeting by local standards draws about thirty residents, and in the average beat this is just under 0.4 percent of the adult population. By contrast, in the average beat about 30 percent of age-eligible residents turned out for the 1999 mayoral election. Attending beat meetings is *harder* than voting, of course. The meetings last an hour or more and they take place in the evening, after a long day's work. The makeshift spaces in which many are held can be uncomfortable as a meeting site, and participants may struggle to hear what is going on. And beat meetings are held an average of ten times a year, not once every few years. Vermont town meetings do better—about 20 percent of registered town residents attend despite the fact that they can last most of a day and are held in tough winter weather, but they only meet yearly (Bryan 2004).

Size may matter, however. Given the importance of the functions of beat meetings, it is important that they represent the character of the neighborhood. Because of the unofficial status of those who attend, whether these relatively small meetings represent residents' interests is a particularly important question. Even a small meeting can do this effectively if those who attend adequately mirror the concerns of the general public, but they may well not. This raises representational questions about beat meetings. Do they reflect the composition of the beat? Do they represent the problems concerning beat residents? And do they represent residents' views of the quality of police service?

Demographic Representation

The first question is, To what extent do those who attended beat meetings resemble their neighbors? The answer involves comparisons like those presented in figure 5.1. It describes the relationship between the demographic composition of beats and the background of those who attend meetings held there. Across the bottom of each chart is information about beat residents. This beat profile is based on projections for 1998 that were made using 1990 and 2000 U.S. Census data. The contrasting data on beat meeting participants is drawn from questionnaires completed by 4,673 residents who attended meetings in 195 beats for which there is complete data for this analysis.

In a perfect world, all of the beats—represented by the points in the chart—would string together in a straight line, because residents of the beats were proportionately represented at the meetings held there. Figure 5.1 describes an imperfect world. Studies of political participation typically find strong class effects in voter registration and turnout. Better-off, middle-class, and more-educated people, and those who hold jobs in the managerial and professional domain register and turn out to vote more frequently than their counterparts. These class differences become even stronger when more demanding forms of participation are involved, including attending meetings, participating in forums, and speaking to elected officials. The wisdom is that education and other class-related factors are linked to having more "civic skills," such as the ability to plan meetings, speak in public, write reports, and critically interpret government reports. It is easy to underestimate what a fearsome experience it is for many people to get up in front of a group to say something. People with these skills are, in turn, more likely to be comfortable in formally organized settings and more motivated to attend and take a role in civic functions—perhaps including beat meetings. They are simply more

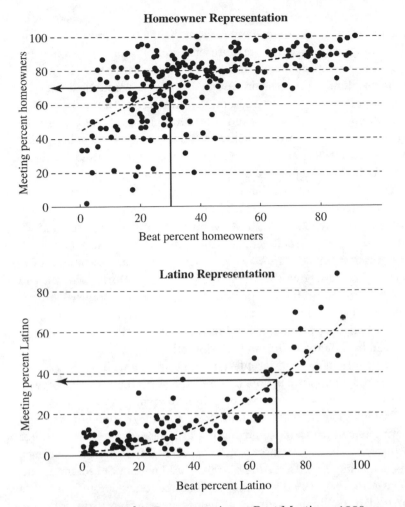

Figure 5.1. Demographic Representation at Beat Meetings, 1998

likely to know about these opportunities to participate as well. In short, there are many reasons to anticipate that there will be a strong bias in turnout at Chicago's meetings.

This turns out to be the case, and strongly so. The top panel in figure 5.1 examines the match between the percentage of beat residents and meeting participants who owned their home, an important feature of any neighborhood. As it indicates, homeowners were significantly overrepresented at the beat meetings we observed. At the average meeting, 75 percent of the participants were homeowners, compared to a beat average of 40 percent. More than 90 percent of the meetings had a greater percentage of homeowners present than lived in the beat, and homeowners were the majority group at 87 percent of the meetings. The overrepresentation of homeowners is especially apparent at low levels of beat home ownership; this is signaled by the decelerating regression line that is the best statistical description of the relationship between the two measures. Home ownership rates among participants are close to 100 percent at the top, so the line has to level off. As the arrow in the figure illustrates, beats that averaged about 30 percent homeowners were represented by meetings where about 70 percent of the participants were homeowners.

Figure 5.1 presents similar data charting the representation of the city's Latinos. It illustrates that Latino participation in beat meetings tended to be low except in beats where a "critical mass" of Latinos resided. There it skyrocketed, as illustrated by the rapidly accelerating regression line. But there were relatively few concentrated Latino beats in the city above the "take-off" point (only thirty-two beats in the city were more than 60 percent Latino in 1990), so gross underrepresentation of Latinos was the norm. Even at the 70 percent Latino mark, the proportion of Latinos at beat meetings was generally less than half their fraction in the population.

Beat meetings overrepresented other groups as well. As suggested by research on political and community participation, the biggest gap was in education. For example, in beats where about 30 percent of residents had a college education, almost 75 percent of beat-meeting participants reported having a college degree, and college graduates made up a majority at 70 percent of all of the meetings. This is consistent with Sydney Verba, Kay Lehman Schlozman, and Henry E. Brady's (1995) argument that education promotes the skills that lead individuals to dominate more demanding forms of civic participation. Older neighborhood residents were also overrepresented. On average, meeting participants had lived in their neighborhood nine years longer than the average area resident. Women were the majority at about 75 percent of the meetings. Women were more overrepresented in African American areas, in poor beats, and beats with concentrations of public housing. However, only race generated the large disparities illustrated in figure 5.1. In his study of New England town meetings, Frank Bryan (2004) found an interaction between social class and community context; the working-class participation rate was higher in towns with a large, critical mass of working-class residents. In Chicago, it is race, not class, that provides the context within which civic participation takes place.

Thus, on several dimensions the representation provided by Chicago's beat meetings demonstrates a strong establishment bias. In many social programs that rely on volunteers, better-off and more-established members of the community are quickest to get involved and contribute to the effort. Research on involvement in neighborhood anticrime organizations finds that higher-income, more-educated, home owning, and long-term area residents more frequently know of opportunities to participate and are more likely to get involved when they have the opportunity (cf. Skogan 1988). In the case of beat meetings the largest discrepancies in involvement favor college graduates, homeowners, older, and long-term residents. In Chicago this bias is manifested not in turnout *totals*; we saw in chapter 4 that overall turnout rates are highest in poor, high-crime areas. Instead, the bias is in *who* turns out. It is important to underscore that this overrepresentation takes place within beats. It is not better-off people from some other neighborhood that are taking fullest advantage of the program; it is the neighbors of those who do not. In poor areas they are scarcely an "elite," just a little better off, and they might still do a good job representing the interests of their small community.

Latinos were the most underrepresented racial or ethnic group. During 2003 experienced bilingual interviewers questioned ninety-three community leaders and social-service providers who were active in heavily Latino areas, in order to assess their views of Hispanic involvement in community policing. They were in broad agreement that Latino underrepresentation in CAPS was partly driven by the fears of new immigrants. The growth of the Latino community in Chicago, with all of its attendant problems, is driven by immigration from Mexico. Most are legal residents, but some are not. Undocumented immigrants, in particular, flock to areas of Latino concentration, for there they can find work and keep a low profile. Their numbers are unknown—estimates of the number of illegal immigrants may be the most shaky number published by the federal government—but everyone we talked to believed they are in the city in large numbers. Remaining anonymous was somewhat easier than in the past, for the U.S. Immigration and Naturalization Service (and its post-9/11 successor agency, the U.S. Citizenship and Immigration Services) had not conducted aggressive raids of workplaces around Chicago in some time, but undocumented immigrants continued to avoid attracting attention to themselves. In addition to their possible personal vulnerability, concern about the status of others—including family members, friends, or even other people living in their building—leads them to shy away from involving the police in their problems. This multiplies the influence of immigration-related concerns, further expanding the network of people for whom "the protection of the law" is elusive.

These concerns affected this group's involvement in CAPS. A senior police manager observed that one reason residents in his area did not attend beat meetings was the fear that their immigration status might be revealed at a beat meeting. He said, "They fear that police would be 'agents of deportation'; they are afraid to jeopardize their legal status, and have difficulty communicating with the police." As a long-time resident of a heavily Latino neighborhood put it, "Latinos have a feeling that by going to the police department they are turning themselves in." He switched to Spanish and said, "I'm from Mexico. I don't have papers—I don't go to the police department." Another activist advised, "The police need to make it clear that they are not here to deport people. The police need to reassure people that involvement in CAPS won't impact negatively their lives and also to create confidence in people to participate."

Chicago made efforts to involve Latinos more deeply in its community-policing effort. The publicity campaign supporting the program featured paid promotional announcements and a police-staffed talk show on Spanish-language radio; booths at festivals held in Latino neighborhoods; and wide distribution of posters, flyers, and newsletters in Spanish. Spanish-speaking community organizers worked for the city to generate involvement in beat meetings and problem solving. The city's emergency communication system was staffed to handle foreign-language calls, and the police department itself had about eight hundred Spanish-speaking officers. The department's cadet diversity training included some role-playing exercises revolving around linguistic issues. But despite these efforts, integration of the city's Latino residents into CAPS proved difficult.

Interest Representation

A second question is, to what extent did those who attended beat meetings represent the views of residents, concerning the problems they faced? In his study of public involvement in Chicago's schools and community policing, Archon Fung (2001) stressed the importance of protecting the ability of all citizens to deliberate and make their voices heard. If police lay back and "let nature take its course," the meetings might be captured by factions with particular interests to advance. The views of better-off residents might predominate, to the disadvantage of their counterparts. We have seen that the meetings overrepresented established members of the community, based on a comparison of beat populations with profiles of meeting participants. Because of this bias it is possible that beat-meeting participants have different priorities than their not-so-well-off neighbors. For example, they may be more worried about high taxes or low property values. Different elements of the community may have different views of gentrification. Younger adults with children living at home may be more worried than their retired neighbors are about conditions at the local school. Residents who spend more time outside may be more concerned about street crime than are those who stay at home and watch television. People whose garages are stuffed with expensive mountain bikes and snow blowers may be very nervous about burglary, while upper-floor renters of apartments may be more concerned about finding a place to park on the street.

On the other hand, an important feature of beat meetings is that they bring together people who all live together in a fairly small area. Some may be college graduates and others high school dropouts, but in Chicago they probably walk to the same transit stop and shop at the same supermarket. Living together, their fates are linked to those of their neighbors despite differences among them. CAPS speaks more to the quality of life in the vicinity and the level of service being provided by the city and the police, than it does to their own pocketbooks. This is not true in bodies representing larger constituencies, or in representative institutions that bring people together from diverse places. There, individual class, lifestyle, and racial differences frequently signal differences in interests of many kinds, as the better off and the worse off among them will generally live and shop in different places and send their children to different schools. But Chicago's beat meetings bring together little groups of neighbors. In the end, they inevitably face the same contextual problems and share many common day-to-day concerns, regardless of the diversity of their personal histories.

To examine the representation of neighborhood priorities at beat meetings, comparisons can be made between reports of neighborhood problems gathered from surveys of beat residents and the findings of surveys conducted with participants at the meetings. The data indicate that meeting participants were *more concerned* about problems than were the residents of their beat. In general, those who attended gave higher ratings than did their neighbors to a broad range of problems. Second, the data indicate that those who come to beat meetings *broadly represent* the views of beat residents, but more accurately for some issues than for others.

To make these comparisons, the results of citywide surveys conducted during 1997, 1998, and 1999 were aggregated to the beats in which the respondents lived. This analysis examines 195 beats (72 percent of the city's 270 residential beats) where at least ten meeting participants completed questionnaires *and* ten residents were interviewed in the city surveys. These beats are represented here by a total of 6,921 resident interviews and 4,697 meeting participant surveys. Comparisons between residents and beat-meeting participants could be made for assessments of the magnitude of seven neighborhood problems that were included in both surveys (the questions are described in detail in chapter 6). Both groups were asked to rate whether each was a "big problem," "some problem," or "no problem" in their neighborhoods.

In these comparisons it is apparent is that Chicagoans who came to beat meetings were much *more* concerned about conditions in their neighborhoods. Figure 5.2 compares the ratings given to seven neighborhood problems by meeting participants and the general public. Two of the biggest gaps are for drugs and gang violence. Just under 49 percent of the residents of the 195 beats thought that street drug sales were either somewhat of a problem or a big problem, compared to 80 percent of those attending beat meetings in the same area. In the case of gang violence, 45 percent of residents and 74 percent of residents thought this was an issue in their neighborhoods. Some other gaps were similar, including that concerning abandoned buildings (31 percentage points) and abandoned cars (also 31 percentage points). The difference between neighborhood residents and those who represented them was smaller for burglary and street crime (about 20 percentage points separated them), and it was about 25 percentage points different for graffiti problems.

It is also apparent that the two groups differed in the *intensity* with which they viewed problems in their neighborhoods. In many instances, it was in the "big problem" category that the two groups differed the most; the findings for concern about street drug markets are the most dramatic examples of this. Compared to their neighbors, beat-meeting participants came with more, and more intense, concerns to express. These individual-level survey findings are consistent with the beat-level data on meeting participation described earlier chapter 4. In

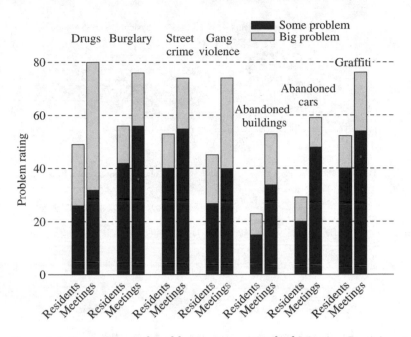

Figure 5.2. Perceptions of Problems among Matched Meeting Participants and the General Public, 1998

that data, participation rates were driven principally by crime; here we see how individual participants are more intensely concerned than even their immediate neighbors about local conditions.

Figure 5.2 viewed beat-meeting participants and their neighbors in the aggregate, but the real representation questions need to be addressed by comparing their views beat by beat. The issue is to what extent the concerns of neighborhood residents are being represented by those who attend the meetings in their beats. Three panels in figure 5.3 address the extent to which residents' perceptions of beat problems were reflected in the level of concern that participants brought to beat meetings. They compare the average ratings of problems gathered in the city surveys with ratings of the same problems supplied by meeting participants. Responses to questions about three forms of physical decay—abandoned cars, abandoned buildings, and graffiti—were combined to form a neighborhood physical decay index. Questions about the extent of problems with burglary and street crime formed a personal and property crime index, while questions about gangs and drugs constituted a measure of their own. Fig-

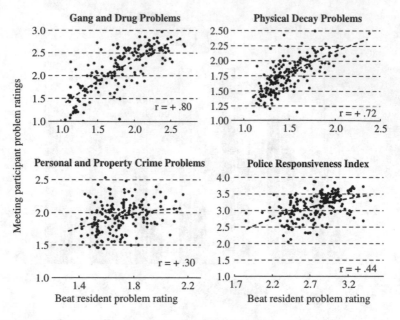

Figure 5.3. Interest Representation at Beat Meetings, 1998

ure 5.3 presents average resident and beat-meeting participant scores on these measures for each beat.

The strong relationship between resident and participant ratings of gang and drug problems is apparent; the correlation between the two measures was +.80. Likewise, there was a strong link between beat and participant assessments of the extent of physical decay in their area; that correlation was +.72. In these domains, where residents were concerned, those who showed up at meetings were concerned as well. Where residents were not concerned, many beat-meeting participants shared that view. Chicagoans could feel fairly confident that those who attended meetings in their beat generally reflected their views about the seriousness of gang, drug, and neighborhood physical decay problems.

The link was weaker between beat-meeting participants' views of crime problems and what the general public thought about burglary and street crime. As the figure indicates, the two measures were correlated only +.30. The picture would not have changed much if comparisons were made between resident and participant views of the individual problem measures, for neither correlation was particularly strong. Public concern about street crime translated a bit more directly into concern among meeting participants—the correlation between the two measures was +.48. For burglary, the resident-participant correlation was +.22. Careful inspection also reveals that there was less variation across beats in the views of both groups, when it came to crime. The high-to-low range for each group was smaller, and more beats were clustered near the city average.

One plausible explanation for the limited correspondence between resident and participant concern about crime is the issue's visibility. Most of the other problems probed by the surveys have visual manifestations. As noted in chapter 2, there is nothing subtle about a Chicago street drug market, or the activities of large and powerful gangs. Obvious evidence of the magnitude of these problems can be shared by broad segments of the community. Graffiti victimizes everyone who views and is offended by it, and unless it is cleaned up, the victimization continues. By contrast, theft and street crime victimize individuals and households, and they are crimes of stealth. People may hear and gossip about victims of these offenses, but they rarely see such crimes in progress. After the fact, theft and street crime leave few visible scars. They do not present the kind of shared, visible, repetitive experience that other problems in our inventory can manifest, even if they are widespread in a community.

Another possible explanation for the relatively weak link between residents' views of crime and those of beat-meeting participants is representational. To what extent do biases in the representation of social and economic groups account for any lack of correspondence between the views of the general public and those that are carried into beat meetings? The views of beat-meeting participants vary somewhat, so demographic imbalances in representation like those already described may have an impact on the correspondence between the priorities of the general public and the issues that concern just those who attend meetings.

Determining the significance of this demographic imbalances involves contrasting the impact of imbalances in the representation of various groups at the meetings upon the fit or lack of fit between the views of meeting participants and their neighbors. The groups that made the largest differences at beat meetings were Latinos, women, and older residents. The overrepresentation of women and older people affected the views represented at the meetings because they tended to be less worried about crime problems than their younger and male counterparts. The varying mixes of younger-versus-older participants and men and women at the meetings had an effect on the gap between beats and meetings. Having too many women was correlated +.36 with the underrepresentation of concern about crime, and having too many participants over age sixty-five was correlated +.30 with the underrepresentation of concern about crime. But the strongest effect was due to underrepresentation of Latinos at the meetings, because they were very concerned about a wide range of neighborhood problems. The correlation between a shortfall of Latinos at the meetings and the underrepresentation of crime problems (measured by the three-item index) was +.45. In contrast, there were only small differences between older and younger people, and between men and women, when they were asked about visible and repetitive problems like physical decay, social disorder, and drug and gang problems, so demographic misrepresentation had a much smaller effect on the match between the views of residents and beat-meeting participants concerning these issues.

Representing Concern about Police

Beat meetings are not simply a forum for identifying and prioritizing neighborhood problems. They also play a role in monitoring police activities in the area. As noted earlier, an official agenda item for each meeting is a report by police about what they have been doing in response to problems identified at previous meetings. Although we have never seen police put a slice of time on the printed agenda to discuss complaints about themselves, these complaints also came up frequently. As noted above, in 1998 the observers noted that criticism was leveled at the police at 47 percent of the meetings. At about a third of the meetings, there was also discussion of problems with the extent of citizen involvement in CAPS. Beat meetings can actually provide a forum for residents to voice their concerns and try to hold police accountable for working on them, both separately and in partnership. Representing the satisfaction or dissatisfaction of residents with policing in their area should be one of the meetings' most important functions. In practice, however, this form of interest representation does not appear to be a very direct one.

The lower-right panel in figure 5.3 illustrates the relationship between resident views of the quality of police service in their neighborhoods and the views carried into beat meetings by those who attend. The index of opinion about police is based on responses to questions about how well police deal with problems of concern to residents, work with residents to solve local problems, and respond to community concerns (the questions are described in detail in chapter 8). Figure 5.3 indicates that beat meetings provide a very general guide to public opinion in this regard. The 1998 correlation between beat and participant attitudes was +.44, providing a direct but not particularly strong link between the two. The correlations between the individual components of the index were all in about the same range, between +.36 and +.43.

There are at least two reasons for this tenuous linkage. First, many meeting participants are *more positive* than their neighbors about the quality of police service in their neighborhoods. For example, about 70 percent of those attending meetings in 1998 thought police were doing a good or very good job at dealing with problems that concerned beat residents, while the comparable figure for residents was 60 percent. The divide was greater—15 percentage points—in the proportions who thought police were doing a good job working with residents to solve problems. We have seen that those who attend the meetings are more concerned than were their neighbors about a broad range of local problems, but they are less concerned about the police.

This optimism probably has several sources. Those who choose to attend beat meetings may already be more optimistic about police, while those who are not favorably inclined toward the police just stay away. This gap may grow wider because those who attend and have a bad experience do not come back, and critics who speak up may feel unwelcome to return. At the same time, those who attend may come to know and appreciate the concern shown by the police who are there. They would also see any positive accomplishments that stem from the meetings. These explanations are consistent with the finding that frequent beat-meeting attendees are more positive about the police than are those who attend only once or twice; and light attendees are, in turn, more optimistic than those who do not come at all. The gap in optimism about police that emerges between participants and the general public is also consistent with the extremely high levels of satisfaction that participants reported with what took place at the meetings. As we saw in chapter 4, 80 percent or more of meeting attendees routinely report that they learned something at the meetings, that action had taken place in their neighborhood as a result of the meetings, and that meetings are useful for finding solutions to local problems.

Another reason that there was not a strong relationship between the views of the general public about police and the views of beat-meeting participants is that there were large racial differences in the size of the gap between residents and participants. The distance between African Americans who showed up at beat meetings and their African American neighbors who did not attend was particularly noticeable when it came to views of the police. The gulf between residents and participants was almost as great for Latinos. Because large numbers of less satisfied segments of the public stayed away, or came but did not return, the representation of residents' views of police service was less effective in African American and Latino communities. There, the climate of opinion at beat meetings made police-community relations appear to be rosier than they really were. The *differential gap* between beat residents and CAPS participants depending on their race further attenuated the link between beat-meeting participants and their neighbors. The overrepresentation of older residents also attenuated the link between resident and beat-meeting opinion. Due to the underrepresentation of younger people—who do not like the police much—at the meetings, beat meetings provided a more favorable venue for police than they would if adults of all ages were more fully represented.

Representation and the Police

What did police officers think about all of this resident involvement, and did they agree with residents when it came to neighborhood priorities? To assess police opinion, observers also distributed questionnaires to the police officers who attended beat meetings. The content of the studies varied from study to study. Beat meetings were only about three years old in 1998, so that year questionnaires for the police included questions about citizen involvement. There was complete data for about 1,030 officers, who could be linked to the meeting at which they filled out the questionnaire. Those who responded were regulars: almost 70 percent of the officers indicated that they attended every beat meeting, and another 17 percent replied that they attended approximately every other meeting. The questionnaire, which had to be brief, included four questions about beat meetings. Officers were asked how satisfied they were with attendance at the meetings. Thirty-three percent were very satisfied, and 43 percent were somewhat satisfied. Not surprisingly, a strong correlate of this response was high average attendance at meetings held in the beat. Officers who reported that they were very dissatisfied worked in beats that averaged nineteen residents per meeting; those who were very satisfied worked in beats that averaged almost thirty residents per meeting, all year around. In the survey, 64 percent indicated that their team "very often" considered resident priorities when identifying their priority problems, and another 24 percent indicated that they did so "somewhat" often.

Officers were also questioned about their relationship with residents who attended the meetings. The 1998 survey focused on this issue because of the trepidation with which many officers had approached the meetings when they first were held. Many feared that they would provide a convenient forum for "police bashing." However, more than 50 percent of those surveyed indicated that the meetings were "very congenial," and another 42 percent that they were "somewhat congenial." This did not leave much room to identify any pockets of real troublemaking, but the degree of friendliness with which they were received was linked to characteristics of their beat. Relations between police and residents were reported to be better in predominantly white and well-off beats with low rates of violent crime. Things were less congenial in beats where there were concentrations of public housing, a large at-risk youth proportion (age fifteen to twenty-four), and where schools and health programs were not meeting the needs of residents. Officers who attended beat meetings frequently were more likely to feel their presence was well received. About one-third of those who attended less than half the meetings thought residents were very congenial, while the comparable figure among officers who reported attending every meeting was almost 60 percent, and virtually none of them thought relations were strained. Age was strongly linked to how welcome they felt as well. Among officers in their twenties, 44 percent felt residents were very congenial; among those in their forties it was 57 percent; and among those in their fifties it was 62 percent.

Finally, the views of some officers were affected by the racial composition of the meetings they attended. White officers felt the most welcome at beat meetings where most of the residents attending were white. For example, white officers who reported that residents were "very congenial" were attending meetings where residents (based on the observations) averaged 68 percent white and 22 percent African American, while white officers who reported that relationships at the meetings were strained were attending meetings that averaged 26 percent white and 67 percent African American. Interestingly, Latino officers who reported that relations between residents and police attending the meetings were strained were most likely attending a meeting, conducted in part in Spanish, hosting a large proportion of Latinos. On the other hand, the views of African American officers were unaffected by the racial composition of the meetings they attended, and a large majority felt welcome everywhere.

The 2002 beat-meeting study included more questions about the neighborhoods in which the meetings were being held. Police were questioned about the extent of a list of neighborhood problems, so their views could be compared to those of residents at the same sample of meetings. We saw earlier in this chapter that residents who attended were much more worried about crime than were their close neighbors. However, the surveys conducted at the meetings indicate that police were generally in agreement with attendees about the extent of crime problems. While they differed in detail, by and large they gave the highest ratings to the same problems, and agreed on those that were somewhat lower down on the list.

Figure 5.4 examines the view of participants attending beat meetings held during the summer and fall of 2002. A total of 3,396 residents and 632 police officers were surveyed, and the questionnaire included similar questions about the extent of a list of crime, social disorder, and physical decay problems in the beat. This figure examines the distribution of the "big problem" ratings given by each group. For each, it sums all of their "big problem" ratings into one pie, allocating the total among them. The two groups were generally in agreement about the nature of their beat's problems. For example, 15 percent of residents and 18 percent of police gave the highest rating to abandoned buildings, while 34 percent of residents and 30 percent of police gave a top rating to public drinking. Among the larger differ-

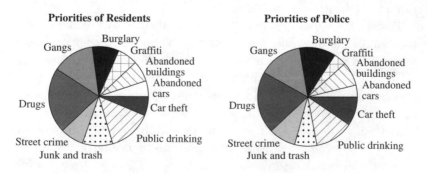

Figure 5.4. Police and Participant Priorities

ences between them were ratings given to car theft (22 percent by police, 14 percent by residents) and "trash and junk on the streets and sidewalks" (23 percent by residents, 17 percent by police). In the case of street drug markets, the figures were 50 percent for residents and 48 percent for police. The two groups were within one percentage point of each other in their rating of the extent of problems with gang violence. As the pie charts indicate, police and residents attending beat meetings generally shared the same concerns.

What Makes Beat Meetings Work?

Beat meetings are one of the most distinctive features of community policing in Chicago. No other city has attempted such a large-scale citizen mobilization effort, or sustained it for as many years. What have been Chicago's lessons about what makes them work? Based on a decade of observing beat meeting, surveying police and residents, and discussing them with the civilian community organizers charged with increasing turnout, I think that a combination of organizational and process factors needs to come together in order to ensure effective citizen involvement.

Organizational Features

A key feature of beat meetings in Chicago is that they provide widespread *opportunities to participate*. By-and-large, most beats meet nearly every month. In 2002, for example, the 270 beats that are significantly residential in character met an average of ten times during the course of the year. Beat meetings occur regularly in all parts of the city. Meeting frequency is not correlated with a community's class or race, or with its crime rate or strength of community organizations in the area. The number of people who turn out is linked to these factors, of course. However, the frequency with which beats meet is not tied to the size of the turnout, so even if few people attend, subsequent meetings will still be held. Meetings take place on a regular schedule—for example, on the third Thursday of every month—and at the same time and place. The meetings are held in locations that are well known to members of the community, and other civic events take place there on a regular basis as well.

These are safe environments. The police keep them that way, and residents can attend with some confidence that they will get home safely afterward. In some beats there is concern about potential retaliation by bad elements in the community if people speak up against them at meetings. A few well-known instances of retaliation against CAPS activists have made it clear that these fears can be well founded. In 1998 our observers overheard group discussion of potential retaliation or actual reports of incidents at 22 percent of the meetings they attended. Expressions of concern about retaliation were voiced most frequently at meetings in heavily Latino beats and in places where concern about gangs and drugs was particularly high. Police have devised a number of simple tactics that enable people to voice their concerns under those circumstances. In some beats they pass out cards on which trouble spots can be identified and the cards returned at the end of the meeting. Other districts feature prominent citizen "suggestion boxes," and residents anywhere can call their district's Community Policing Office directly to voice their concerns.

Beat meetings also facilitate resident involvement because someone is always responsible for organizing and conducting them. On occasion, our observers have arrived for meetings to find that no one in the crowd outside had a key to the building, but almost always the problem gets rectified quickly. Crime maps and other current materials are usually available at the sign-up table, and meetings at least start with—though they may not follow—an agenda. Civilian facilitators play a visible role at meetings, as do the police. In 2002, one police area (a group of five districts) held a Saturday training session for beat-team sergeants and their civilian facilitators. There they learned how to run a good meeting; at one point the department showed a video of a staged "beat meeting from hell" in order to illustrate how *not* to conduct them.

Why is this important? As noted earlier, there has been a great deal of research done on citizen involvement in anticrime activities, and it usually documents strong biases in participation. Some of this research involves identifying geographic locations of meetings or active groups and examining the social and demographic correlates of those locations. Other studies employ surveys that ask people about their individual involvement in various crime-prevention efforts. These studies usually find that programs relying on voluntary participation are most common where they are least needed and involve people with only modest crime problems. There is a strong middle-class bias in activism. Home-owning neighborhoods already endowed with strong organizations field the most impressive anticrime projects, while in poorer and higher-crime areas, a few isolated volunteers struggle to build any capacity at all in their community. In high-crime areas, people tend to be more suspicious of their neighbors or their neighbors' children. There, older residents, whom we have seen provide the backbone for beat meetings in many areas, are more likely to stay home in order to stay safe. However, research indicates that the real key to participation rates is the distribution of *opportunities* to participate. People cannot show up if there is nothing to show up for, and it is a poverty of opportunities that most afflicts poor, high-crime neighborhoods (Skogan 1988). But in Chicago, beat meetings are held everywhere, not just in places blessed with strong organizations and a large supply of skilled, sophisticated leaders. Women and senior citizens turn out in large numbers, even after dark, because the meeting places are safe. The police do not get discouraged by low turnout, and return next month regardless. They have a key to the church social hall.

In this regard, the turnout efforts of the civilian Implementation Office also play a key role in making the meetings work. Assigned to some of the most difficult areas of town, and often speaking languages that will give them entrée into immigrant communities, their efforts help compensate for class and ethnic differences in people's initial predilections to get involved, and perhaps in their willingness to turn out in the face of competing work and family-related demands on their time. While CAPS is a volunteer program, cities would be blind to ignore the fact that volunteerism can be highly selective and that participation cannot be left to chance. Empowering the community can be hard work.

In short, police have used their organizational capacity to create quite egalitarian as well as frequent and visible opportunities for participation. In Fung's (2004) model of empowered participation, one of the police officers' jobs is to see to it that people throughout the polity have the ability to get involved in this way. As documented above, people come to beat meetings because they are concerned about neighborhood problems, and crime is the number one correlate of beat meeting attendance rates. In Chicago, even residents of poor and high-crime areas have a place to go. Beat meetings provide them with an opportunity to participate that might not be there without the organized structure provided by the city's community-policing program.

Process Factors

There are also features of the meetings themselves that appear to attract participants and cement their loyalty. The most important are feedback and payback. One reason people attend is that they are concerned about their community. However, they typically are not well informed about crime or the efforts being made by police and local activists to respond to it. Traditionally, police departments have not been particularly transparent. They expect the public to be their "eyes and ears" but reveal as little information as possible about their plans or effectiveness. From the beginning, Chicago's beat meetings were to be venues for the actual sharing of information that could help both police and residents more effectively address community problems. In 2002, beat-meeting observers watched for information sharing and found quite a bit of it. Department guidelines call for the distribution of crime information at the meetings, and their crime analysis system produces a variety of reader-friendly maps and reports. Our observers found that police shared this kind of information with residents at 90 percent of the meetings. Feedback also comes in the form of reports by police and residents on what they have been doing to address local problems, and what has been done about concerns brought up at the *previous* beat meeting. From the residents' point of view, meetings provide an important venue for holding beat officers accountable. In short, meetings enable the community to monitor whether police are holding up their end of the partnership. The 2002 observational study found that police were reporting back on their efforts at almost three-quarters of the meetings.

Chicago was less successful at using the meetings as a locus for organizing community problem-solving efforts. Beat meetings can provide a venue where residents celebrate their own efforts, and perhaps successes. But while observations in 2002 revealed that police were reporting to the community with some frequency, residents had something to say at less than 50 percent of the meetings. Only about one-quarter of meetings seemed to include any action component. Mostly, people left with no commitment to action before the next meeting.

Payback comes from the ability of residents needing help from a city agency to attend a meeting and see their problem written up in a CAPS service request. If residents show up, they can get something done. There was no shortage of problem identification at the meetings the observers attended; problems were raised by residents at every session. The mix of issues discussed at beat meetings is surprisingly diverse, and a large percentage of the conversation concerns issues that are not resolvable using traditional policing tools. In 2002, the third most frequently discussed category of problems was physical dilapidation, which came up at 47 percent of the meetings. The number one category of problems discussed was social disorder, which came up at 89 percent of meetings. Social disorder includes a long list of relatively minor offenses and some conditions that are not criminal at all, but that frequently disturb neighborhood residents. Neighborhood drug problems (62 percent) and property crime (38 percent) topped the list of traditional policing concerns, but calls for more emphasis on parking and traffic problems came up at 44 percent of the meetings.

Social factors are important for sustaining successful beat meetings as well. A potentially important feature of beat meetings is networking. Meetings can provide a venue for neighborhood residents to get acquainted and begin building relationships that will sustain joint activities outside meetings. In 2002 we surveyed beat-meeting participants to gauge the extent to which they encountered each other outside of the meetings, including "seeing them around," attending other meetings at which beat regulars were also present, and speaking with them on the phone. The survey also included questions about how involved they were in a broad variety of local problem-solving efforts. It turned out that being networked had the strongest link to being a beat-meeting activist. Networkers were more likely to be frequent participants at beat meetings as well. This recommends efforts to increase the networking potential of meetings. This could include developing "phone trees" that put lists of participants in each other's hands, with a license to make contact about local concerns. It also highlights the importance of the social aspects of beat meetings. Some beats routinely offer social periods preceding or following their meetings. Some offer coffee and snacks that bring people together at the back of the room. At better meetings, officers and residents huddle after the formal session is over to hash out issues too specific to involve the entire group.

Another factor contributing to successful beat meetings is that people who attend are not in complete agreement, and frequently are unhappy with the service they are receiving from the police. In his study of New England town meetings, Bryan (2004) found that controversy over issues increased turnout, which was lower in placid, more consensual towns. He also found that a bit of diversity helped;

turnout was higher in more class and ethnically heterogeneous town (but remember these were mostly small New England villages). Diversity was one reason why people had different interests, which brought conflict into town decisions. He concluded that conflict and a little distrust led to "discussion spiced with conflict," and made attending town meetings both more interesting and necessary to protect one's interests.

Was CAPS an *Alternative* Way of Getting Things Done?

An important question raised throughout this book is whether CAPS brings new capabilities to neighborhoods in need or simply reinforces the status quo with regard to the life chances of ordinary Chicagoans. In it's very name CAPS was billed as the city's "alternative" policing strategy, suggesting that it would somehow work differently than in the past. There was some evidence concerning this in chapter 4, which documented that beat-meeting involvement was highest in poor, high-crime places. This section considers more of the many ways in which neighborhoods have traditionally gotten things done in Chicago, and contrasts those with beat meetings. The other channels include organized collective action and the exercise of informal social control, two important paths to effective crime control. Another way of getting things done in Chicago is through politics, which importantly means being part of the mayor's electoral coalition. The distribution of the capacity of neighborhoods to respond on their own to crime, or to have ready access to city government through politics, is here contrasted with CAPS' vehicle: beat meetings. It turns out that an important feature of beat meetings was that they worked differently than the contrasting ways that things got done. They showed surprising strength in parts of town where other mechanisms for tackling crime and disorder were not working very well.

To examine this, figure 5.5 plots the relationship between crime rates for the period 2001–2003 with measures of the ways in which things get done: through informal social controls, strong community organizations, political clout, and meetings for the city's beats. The question is if these ways of getting things done were operating where help was needed the most. The figure presents the regression line that best describes the data, but omits the hundreds of actual data

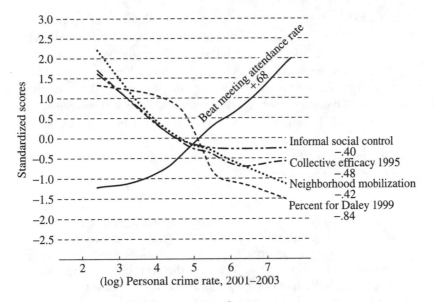

Figure 5.5. Neighborhood Capacity and Crime, 2001–2003

points in order to make room for several indicators of neighborhood capacity. It reports the correlation between each measure and neighborhood crime, an index of how tightly those data points would fit the lines that are depicted there.

One way that things get done in Chicago is through autonomous neighborhood action. This includes exercising informal social control and organizing neighbors in reaction to threats to neighborhood security and well-being. Measures of this kind of independent action were constructed from combined evaluation surveys for 2001 and 2003. Together, the two surveys totaled almost fifty-three hundred respondents. Requiring at least ten respondents to characterize an area yielded data on 199 police beats, with an average of 24 respondents per beat. Using the surveys, the beat-level *strength of informal social control* was measured by averaging responses to three questions. Respondents were asked if it was very likely, likely, unlikely, or very unlikely that their neighbors would intervene in these hypothetical incidents: "If some children were spray painting graffiti on a local building; if there was a fight in front of your house and someone was being beaten or threatened; if a teenager was harassing an elderly person." These are measures of the willingness of residents to actively represent the norms of the community by intervening to safeguard them when they are threatened. Many theories of crime view the exercise of informal social control as one of the principal ways communities maintain order on their own initiative. In Chicago, stopping a fight seemed least likely to spark neighborhood intervention, while harassing an elderly person seemed most likely to draw a response. Overall, about 20 percent of Chicagoans averaged toward the "unlikely" end of the continuum; most were more sanguine about what their neighbors would do.

Reactions to two hypothetical scenarios were combined to create an index of *neighborhood mobilization*. Respondents were asked:

Suppose that because of budget cuts the police station closest to your home was going to be closed down by the city. How likely is it that neighborhood residents would organize to try to keep the police station open?

Suppose that the city announced that public housing was going to be built in your neighborhood. How likely is it that neighborhood residents would organize to try to keep the public housing out?

In each instance they were asked if action by their neighbors was very likely, likely, unlikely, or very unlikely. Acting to stop the closing of a police station was seen as more likely than resisting public housing, and in total about 70 percent of Chicagoans averaged toward the "likely" end of the continuum.

As figure 5.5 illustrates, both informal social control and the perceived likelihood that residents would mobilize in the face of outside threats were lowest in high-crime places. This is not surprising; criminologists would count them among the forces *controlling* crime. But it is a reminder that expecting people to pick themselves up by their bootstraps has not worked very well in high-crime places, and that residents there need outside help.

The figure also examines the distribution *collective efficacy*. This concept combines the willingness to maintain public order with the extent of mutual trust among residents. Communities that have a high degree of collective efficacy are exceptional in many regards. They are particularly good at defending themselves against crime and disorder problems, because residents of these tight-knit communities trust one another and are willing to take action in the best interests of the community. In these communities, in fact, what is perceived as beneficial for the common good is often indistinguishable from that which benefits an individual. Residents expect reciprocity:

they assume that others will take the initiative when it is their turn. Regular acts of generosity, support, and even courage are common in the communities characterized by high levels of collective efficacy. Research by Robert J. Sampson, Steven Raudenbush, and Felton J. Earls (1997) examined the impact of collective efficacy on rates of crime for Chicago's census tracts, and found it was associated with a 40 percent reduction in homicide.

Figure 5.5 reexamines the Sampson et al. data, which are aggregated to match Chicago's police beats. There were enough respondents in their large 1995 survey to characterize 257 beats, with an average of 34 respondents per beat. Collective efficacy was lowest in what later were high-crime places. At the beat level the correlation between the two measures was -.48. While collective efficacy promises to be an important force for neighborhood renewal, it remains unclear how areas where trust and reciprocity are low can develop or reclaim these features of community life. Neighborhoods that need trust and reciprocity the most by and large have the least. Collective efficacy is lowest in neighborhoods of concentrated poverty and in racially or ethnically heterogeneous areas, and highest in stable, home owning, predominantly white parts of town. High-crime areas do not enjoy the networks of trust, shared values, and informal organizations that provide the social glue holding together better-off areas.

Another important way that things get done in Chicago is through *politics*. The political influence of beats could be assessed in at least two ways. Political scientists might focus on sheer voter turnout, measured by the rate at which age-eligible voters made it to the polls. The supposition would be that high voter turnout leads politicians to pay more attention to a beat's interests. However, "don't back no losers" is an extremely important principle in Chicago's generally unprincipled politics (Rakove 1975), and there is evidence that more attention is paid to residents of neighborhoods that hew to that rule. Who you reliably vote for may be more important than just turning out in large numbers, especially in a politically polarized city characterized by seemingly rock-solid block voting. In Chicago these divisions are largely along racial lines.

Figure 5.5 presents the distribution of support for the incumbent mayor in the 1999 election, the most recent data available. The data are for all 270 residential beats. This proves to be the strongest correlation of the lot, −.84. The magnitude of the correlation is a reflection of the racial composition of the city's higher-crime beats, combined with the racially polarized nature of Chicago's politics. At the beat level, the correlation between the percentage of the vote that went for "hizonner" and the percent of the population that is African American was −.94 in the 1999 election, one of the stronger correlations in social research. The figure suggests that the antagonistic political role played by residents of high-crime beats may not help them win largesse from government, and the next chapter documents that support for the incumbent mayor is one of the most important factors boosting the delivery of city services.

However, beat-meeting attendance marched to its own drummer. Beat-meeting attendance was strongest in high-crime areas. It was high where neighborhood activism and trust were the lowest, and where residents fell outside the mayor's political coalition. As the figure illustrates, for this time period the correlation between the two measures was +.68. By this measure, Chicago's beat meetings had the potential to serve residents of high-crime neighborhoods very effectively.

Beat meetings thus provide an alternative channel for securing neighborhood safety, and a new and nontraditional way of securing the benefits of government. As we shall see in chapter 6, beat-meeting attendance rates and the concerns expressed by participants at the meetings independently affect the distribution of selected city services, including graffiti cleanups and the rate at which abandoned cars are towed away. Such services are also affected by beat politics, but in Chicago, politics tends to steer these services in the direction of white homeowners. Beat meetings provide residents with an additional—and different—channel for influencing government. In fact, when describing CAPS to groups in Chicago, I often ask in jest whether CAPS is a "new political machine." My quick rundown of some of the functions of the old political machine—assessing resident's needs, delivering services where they are needed, mobilizing the public through marches and rallies, turning them out for mass assemblies, and generating support for the mayor—sounds like community policing in Chicago. The now-hollowed-out machine is no longer very good at what it once did, but there are other ways to accomplish some of its functions.

How Did Chicago Do?

The representational structure created by Chicago's beat meetings helped translate residents' priorities into action. They provided a forum in which small groups of neighbors could meet with—and sometimes confront—the officers who worked in their beat, and discuss local concerns and priorities. Residents were somewhat less involved in providing and implementing solutions to the problems they brought up. Compared to the vision of CAPS' planners, there were too many "laundry" meetings at which residents "dropped off their problems" to be solved. On the other hand, the meetings frequently featured feedback concerning the quality of neighborhood policing. Complaints about the police were aired at 44 percent of the meetings in 2002, and 47 percent in 1998, although many took the tone of "there are not enough of you around" or "we don't see you often enough." This happened more often in predominantly African American areas. Based on surveys of those who attended, however, there were no major racial differences in how effective participants thought the meetings were in getting things done and resolving specific neighborhood problems, and the level of consumer satisfaction with the meetings was quite high.

There was a strong establishment bias in participation in the meetings. Beat meetings did a better job representing already-established stakeholders in the community than they did at incorporating marginalized or disaffected groups, who probably had fewer mechanisms for voicing their concerns. The problem priorities that participants brought to the meetings generally reflected those of their neighbors, but it is ironic that neither concern about burglary and street crime nor dissatisfaction with the quality of police service was particularly well represented in this community-policing program. Those who came to the meetings generally saw eye-to-eye with the police who were present, on the other hand, and police were generally pleased with the representativeness of the meetings and the friendliness with which they were received.

These representation issues were not just symbolic ones. They were significant because community policing created a unique forum—the *only* such forum in the city—where small groups of neighbors could regularly and directly engage in constructive dialogue with public officials. These issues provide a kind of "New England town meeting of the Midwest," albeit one where votes are not formally binding. However, the priorities that residents bring with them to beat meetings do play a role in the actual operation of CAPS. We shall see in chapter 6 that they have an independent effect on the delivery of city services, one of the key components of Chicago's community-policing program. They seem to work as well as they do because beat meetings provide a remarkably uniform set of opportunities to participate, officers who are working in the area are in attendance, there is a great deal of information exchanged, residents get important feedback from their police officers, and if residents have a problem and come to a meeting, their chances of getting something done about the problem are quite good. Finally, beat meetings were the most vital—involving large numbers of people and (we shall see this in the next chapter) turning them out for problem-solving projects—in some of the most disadvantaged parts of town. These were places where schools and the health care system were not working well, and where other important ways of getting things done in Chicago were not strong either.

SIX

Tackling Neighborhood Problems

In the CAPS model, police are to move beyond driving to the scene quickly in response to individual 911 calls. As described in chapter 3, they are to adopt instead a proactive, prevention-oriented stance toward neighborhood problems. Their first step is to identify problems and prioritize them, and then to analyze their locations, victims, and offenders. Subsequently, police design strategies that might deal with the chronic character of priority problems, thinking "outside the box" of traditional police enforcement tactics. Then they implement their strategies and assess their effectiveness. This widely used model of problem solving was developed to address traditional crimes (see Eck and Spelman 1987; Spelman and Eck 1987). However, an important feature of Chicago's community-oriented approach to problem solving is that police have taken responsibility for a wide range of neighborhood problems. The problems that the community-oriented approach addresses do not have to be conventional criminal matters. Around the country, effective community policing inevitably involves an expansion of the police mandate to include concerns that previously lay outside their competence. In Chicago, the expansion of the police mandate had two sources. The police took on new responsibilities because they needed to be able to respond to the concerns expressed by residents at beat meetings and other public venues, and because Chicago took seriously the "broken windows" view of crime and neighborhood decline.

First, taking on a much broader range of problems was one of the prices of citizen involvement. When beat officers meet with residents, all manner of problems come up. The public does not make neat legal or bureaucratic distinctions about the forces that threaten to drive their neighborhood down. Residents can be as worried about garbage-strewn alleys, graffiti on garage doors, and landlords renting to threatening-looking people as they are about burglary and car theft. This was documented when we analyzed twenty-five hundred reports filed by officers after their monthly meetings with residents during 1998. At the meetings, officers recorded discussion of 11,221 problems. The largest set—constituting 36 percent of the concerns that were brought up—fell into a "social disorder" category that is examined in detail in this section. Residents talked most about loitering, prostitution, public drinking, and various fears about teenage conduct. Next on the list came discussion of a traditional target of policing: drug markets (24 percent of discussions). The third most common topic of concern, constituting 12 percent of the issues brought up at beat meetings, was physical decay. This included discussion of graffiti, vandalism, abandoned buildings, and trash and junk in vacant lots. Even at police-sponsored beat meetings, talk about individual victimizing crimes like robbery and burglary arose only 9 percent of the time, tied exactly with complaints about parking and traffic problems. When CAPS was developed, its planners knew that if their officers' response to community concerns was "that's not a police matter," many residents would not show up for subsequent meetings. They needed to have a plan in place to deal with issues that concerned the public.

A second reason for taking a more expansive view of neighborhood conditions and the importance of doing something about them was that Chicago takes what is known as the "broken windows" argument seriously. In 1982, criminologists James Q. Wilson and George Kelling advanced the idea that social disorder and physical decay undermine the capacity of a neighborhood to defend itself. They focused mainly on problems classified here as social disorder. Wilson and Kelling's list included public gambling, public drinking and urination, street prostitution, congregations of idle men and bands of youths dressed in (apparently) gang-related apparel, and activities like panhandling, disturbing the peace, loitering and vagrancy. Residents take them as signs that others have given up, and they give up as well. Those who can do so move away, and many of the remainder hunker down to stay out of trouble.

The broken windows view is that the emergence of visible signs that the community has ceased to care or intervene also invites predatory troublemakers from outside the neighborhood to join unruly insiders, further pushing the neighborhood downhill. Gambling and drinking can lead to robberies and fights; prostitution and drug sales attract those who prey on the customers. Social disorder thus begets an even broader range of problems and can, in short order, inundate an area with serious and victimizing crime. The title of Wilson and Kelling's argument suggests that the signs of physical decay need to be addressed as well. The decline of community control may be read in dilapidation, abandoned buildings, broken streetlights, trash-filled vacant lots, graffiti, and garbage-strewn alleys blocked by abandoned cars.

The belief that "broken windows" are a cause of crime and neighborhood decline was the second force pushing expansion of the police mandate in Chicago. There, it is widely recognized that crime is rooted in a range of neighborhood conditions and events, and that it is necessary to address both criminal and criminogenic conditions if the city is to take its mission of preserving the city's neighborhoods seriously. A 1996 police department document describing its rationale for community policing noted: "CAPS recognizes that graffiti, abandoned vehicles and buildings, malfunctioning street lights and other signs of neighborhood disorder do have an adverse effect on both crime and the public's fear of crime. By addressing these relatively minor problems early on, police and other government agencies can prevent them from becoming more serious and widespread crime problems."[1]

As a result of this expansion of the police mandate, the department now finds itself involved in orchestrating neighborhood cleanups and graffiti paint-outs. Districts have "problem-buildings officers" who inventory dilapidated and abandoned structures and track down property owners. Police stand with residents at prayer vigils and guard barbeque "smoke-outs" in prostitution zones, distribute bracelets that will identify senior citizens if they fall down, and take note of burned-out streetlights and trees that needed trimming. Officers drop into stores to ask merchants to display signs requesting that patrons refrain from giving money to panhandlers. Beat meetings steer officers toward problems like the sale of loose cigarettes and individual cans of beer at convenience grocery stores, as well as toward the open-air drug markets that plague too many city neighborhoods.

An important feature of Chicago's approach to solving these problems is that it does not just involve arresting people. Unlike New York's "zero tolerance" approach to addressing community problems by making tens of thousands of arrests for minor offenses, Chicago's solution for broken windows is to fix them. It is also supposed to be strongly *prevention* oriented in its approach to both crime and associated neighborhood problems. The police department's 1993 description of its brand-new program stated: "It is this focus on prevention through a stronger government-community partnership that holds real hope for addressing some of the City's most difficult neighborhood problems—and for doing so in a way that is far less expensive than constantly reacting to those problems after the fact."[2]

To accomplish addressing problems early on, the city confronted a wide range of neighborhood problems with a diverse package of solutions, with the police being just one tool for addressing these issues. In Chicago, community policing is the city's program, not just the police department's program.

Another important feature of problem solving in Chicago is that CAPS envisioned an active role for the community in addressing problems. *Together We Can* argued, "Government, through the police department, must empower the community by getting them actively involved in the job of creating and maintaining neighborhood order. The police cannot be everywhere, but the community can. Together, then, we can improve the quality of life and reduce the level of fear in our neighborhoods."[3]

To accomplish this, the city trained thousands of residents in its problem-solving model. In beat-level training sessions held throughout the city, teams of police and civilian trainers went through the five-step problem-solving process and the crime triangle. A large team of professional organizers was added to the city payroll to support these community efforts, and to coordinate them with the work of city-service agencies.

This chapter examines how elements of the problem-solving process were put into practice. It first describes some innovative problem-solving partnerships that police developed with other agencies. It then examines the extent of resident involvement in problem solving, because the rhetoric of community policing in Chicago has a strong "self-help" component. Another section assesses the effectiveness of the department's beat-level problem-solving efforts. The next chapter details trends in the problems that were a special focus of agency and community partnerships: physical decay and social disorder.

Agency Partnerships

While it was apparent to CAPS planners that they needed a capacity to respond to a broad range of troublesome and perhaps criminogenic problems, it was also clear police were not going to actually do all the work. Police officers might learn at a beat meeting that rats in the alley are a priority concern among residents, the beat teams were not going to bait the traps. To get things done, police had to forge new relationships with a range of city-service agencies. As noted in chapter 3, establishing these new relationships was often not easy. The various bureaucracies involved were divided by their differing priorities and operating routines, as well as by their notions of what "speedy service" entailed. At the outset these other agencies thought that community policing was the police department's program, and not theirs. Many of the agencies eventually involved in CAPS performed familiar tasks, including trimming trees (to cast more light on street drug markets, for example), towing abandoned cars, and installing stop signs at dangerous intersections. But in addition, new units were created or got involved for the first time in coordinated problem-solving projects. Their efforts are aimed at the social-disorder and physical-decay problems the evaluation tracked using surveys and reports from beat meetings.

Code Enforcement

One problem-solving tool is the city's Strategic Inspections Task Force (SITF), which was formed in 1996. Prior to the formation of the SITF, each department handling inspections acted largely independently, following its own schedule and using its own personnel. The new task force took responsibility for coordinating some of the efforts of individual departments by banding teams of inspectors to work together to focus on buildings that were special targets of the police. SITF teams are composed of inspectors detailed from the city's buildings, fire, and police departments. Inspectors from the Chicago Department of Revenue are called in if a building with a business license is targeted, and health inspectors turn out for actions involving restaurants. Four teams are in the field at the same time, working in bulletproof vests and guided to their targets and protected by district officers. In one police area (a group of five districts), in order to support the work of SITF, the area deputy chief created a team that specialized in identifying problem buildings and discovering the often-hidden identity of their owners. In 2001, this project won the Quality in Law Enforcement Award from the International Association of Chiefs of Police.

SITF inspections are conducted on a rotating schedule in each police district. A team can inspect seven or eight properties per day. Inspectors look for signs of gangs and illegal activity as well as building-code violations; in addition, they compile a list of recommendations about how to fix the building. Equipped with digital cameras, inspectors include in their reports pictures of the conditions they find. The results are given to city attorneys stationed in each of the city's five police area headquarters buildings. These attorneys initiate actions against owners before administrative hearing officers or in criminal court. Through reports it generates, SITF keeps its city partners and the community apprised of the status of buildings it inspects. Teams also conduct reinspections to ensure that landlords follow up on the renovation plans they negotiate with the city. SITF teams can also recommend "fast-track" demolition of particularly unsafe buildings.

The task force handles a substantial number of cases; in 2002 it inspected almost six thousand buildings. Most SITF cases involve enforcing city codes, which fall under the jurisdiction of the city's administrative hearing process described below. For example, one South Side duplex was referred to the city attorney by district police after a narcotics arrest was made there. The SITF inspection revealed eleven building-code violations, resulting in the city's filing a case against the building owner in the administrative hearing unit. The owner subsequently agreed to a negotiated settlement that included correcting the violations, attending local beat meetings, and paying a fine.

The Illinois Criminal Justice Information Authority conducted an evaluation that included an analysis of SITF. The study found that crime decreased where SITF and city attorneys operated, not only in targeted buildings, but in a half-block area around each property as well. This deterrent effect was lasting, continuing even after inspection teams left the area (Higgins and Coldren 2000). SITF also has successfully driven building owners to comply with code standards. A senior SITF administrator reports that most owners, when cited for building-code violations, fully comply or attempt to fix the problem. And of the remaining cases that go on to a hearing, he estimates that half are quickly resolved as buildings are brought into compliance. Landlords who fail to comply are subject to further prosecution.

Drug and Gang House Enforcement

The city's Drug and Gang House Enforcement Section (DGHES) plays a prominent role in problem solving. Chicago's Department of Law formed DGHES to use the city's 1996 drug and gang house ordinance to prosecute negligent property owners. City attorneys are assigned to each of the five police areas. They focus on crime in and around gang or drug houses and abandoned buildings. Most of their cases are referred by SITF teams or by the police districts. The drug and gang house ordinance holds property owners responsible for physical conditions and criminal activities in and around their buildings. DGHES attorneys use municipal-code violations and crime patterns to target selected buildings, with the goal of renovating them and deterring future negligence.

DGHES was formed because the city's attorneys wanted to get more involved with the community and viewed the recent creation of the SITF as a vehicle for doing so. They thought their possible role had been overlooked when CAPS was planned. As one DGHES administrator put it, "No one looked at how civil enforcement can impact quality-of-life issues. Wouldn't it be great to have a municipal prosecutor be part of the pie—to deal with problem solving in districts [using] the CAPS model?" After experimenting for a year in a few pilot police districts, the project expanded citywide in 1998.

Cases come to an attorney's attention mainly through the police. Each district has police officers designated to act as its liaison for drug and gang house projects. Officers refer five or so problem properties to the district's DGHES attorney every six weeks. Properties are chosen based on community complaints, arrests, and calls for service. The city attorneys attend police district management team meetings, so they also know which buildings are in the department's priority areas. A few cases come to the city attorneys from aldermen or first surface at beat meetings. A DGHES committee also prioritizes cases involving owners of a string of bad buildings. Over time the program has shifted its focus somewhat, taking on bigger cases involving the most serious crimes. As one staff member put it, they "take a big problem and have a big solution, rather than more properties with small fines and small solutions."

To pursue cases, DGHES attorneys cite municipal-code violations documented by SITF and crime data revealed by police databases. They target property owners rather than the persons committing the criminal activity, though these may be the same. In order to initiate prosecutions there must be at least one felony or two misdemeanors related to a particular property. Landlords are served a notice requiring them to meet with the DGHES attorney and a police representative at a resolution meeting. Owners can attend with or without a lawyer; owners who fail to show up face a jail sentence.

The goal of a resolutions meeting is to determine what will be done to abate the problem at hand. The meetings often lead to negotiated solutions for problem buildings. DGHES attorneys have the interest of the community in mind as they tackle these cases, so solutions vary. Attorneys may seek to fine building owners or to force them to install new security measures at the building, to repair code violations, to evict problem tenants, or to close and board up the building. If illegal apartments have been carved into a building, they must be removed. Landlords can be required to post "no loitering" signs and upgrade exterior lighting. They often find themselves agreeing, as part of a settlement, to attend beat meetings and to take the city's landlord training course (see below) to learn how to screen potential tenants. Sometimes the solution lies in informing an absentee landlord about the problem or providing assistance to an inexperienced landlord. "We give them leniency if they're willing to fix the problem. We seek fines and remedies, including security guards and physical improvement to the property," stated one assistant corporation counsel.

Most cases involving residential landlords are resolved through an agreement signed by the landlord and the attorney. Charges against families or individual homeowners can be more difficult to resolve through negotiation, in part because they have fewer resources. If the parties cannot agree, the issue is taken to an administrative hearing officer (see below), or to criminal court. If the initial problem is very severe, an agreement is broken, or the landlord does not respond to the notice of violation, cases go directly to an administrative hearing or criminal court. The city has a stiff criminal housing management ordinance that can be used in the most egregious cases. Regardless of whether the case is resolved through agreement or by a formal decision, police and DGHES staff monitor the property in question for compliance with the abatement plan.

Neighborhood residents attend resolution meetings to a varying degree; some DGHES attorneys emphasize resident involvement because they believe it encourages better settlements or stiffer sentences from judges and hearing officers. Others view the program as having become more routine and professional, and, as a result, insulated from day-to-day community involvement. After several years of casual management, the program began to maintain a database of its activities. When the city's finances began to crumble in the early years of the new millennium, its reports began to showcase the dollar amount collected through fines rather than the informal settlements that enabled landlords to use their money to fix their properties.

Administrative Hearings

One arm of the city's apparatus to enforce codes and statutes is its Department of Administrative Hearings. Founded in 1997, it was the first municipal administrative adjudication agency in the nation. It provides a "quasi-judicial" forum for adjudicating violations of municipal ordinances, including those brought forward by the SITF and city lawyers working with police. Instead of judges, trained attorneys serve as hearing officers. Persons cited for municipal ordinance violations attend, either with or without lawyers of their own. The city is represented by an assistant corporation counsel. Community members can appear as witnesses or sit in on the hearings, which are open to the public; community participation is encouraged by DGHES attorneys. Hearing officers cannot jail anyone; that still requires action by a judge. Administrative hearing decisions, though less formal than a regular court, are nonetheless binding. Hearing officers can level monetary fines, order restitution, suspend various licenses, and direct violators to perform community service. They can also issue "orders of compliance" that, if violated, automatically become a criminal offense.

One case we followed illustrates how DGHES attorneys and the SITF worked together, using the administrative-hearing process to tackle a case involving a liquor license. One of the DGHES assistant corporation counsels described it:

> I gave my opening argument, and five minutes into it their attorney asked for a brief recess. He said, "My client has no chance of winning this case—what does the City want?" I immediately met with community leaders [who were present] and we agreed that we wanted his license. . . . The agreement was to voluntarily surrender his license, close and board up the store, evict everyone from the apartments, board and secure the apartments, and then sell the building. . . . We have pictures of him at the license commission surrendering his license with the community members watching. Today the building is still secured. There's no criminal activity on that corner; neighbors say it's very quiet. The property is a real success. It's for sale now. Some people in the community are trying to get money together to buy the building. What I'm most happy about is that the attorney was willing to fight me until he saw how involved the community was. The message was clear: they didn't want this kind of business here. This was community policing.

The great majority of cases set for trial are eventually settled, with admission of liability a major goal, because the City's attorneys want to remedy crime and quality-of-life problems at the property. Interestingly, judgments against landlords of problem buildings commonly include a requirement that they regularly attend the beat meetings in their areas. An observer ran across a beat meeting attended by a city attorney who was there to report on the progress of a case:

> A drug and gang house attorney for the city thanked everyone who came to court for an abandoned building case. She said that the owner refused to cooperate. She had brought copies of the court order against the landlord, so that residents will know when she is violating the order. She said that court is the "last thing we want to do." She said that the order requires the woman to come to beat meetings, where she will not be allowed to cause disruptions. The woman is required to listen to the problems of the community and if she causes difficulties she will not get credit for coming to the meeting.

In 2000, this branch of city government heard more than four hundred thousand cases. Among the city agencies able to use the hearing system to enforce its codes are the building department (for building-code violations as well as gang and narcotics drug house activities); streets and sanitation (for overflowing garbage bins); the licensing bureau (for unlawful or unlicenced businesses); the zoning department (for illegal residential conversions); and the health department (for unsanitary stores, outdated food, and rat infestation). In 2002 the agency heard more than thirty-eight thousand health and garbage-related cases alone. The police are also large-scale participants. By the end of the 1990s they were routinely making use of tickets (called Administrative Notices of Violation, or ANOVs) rather than making arrests for curfew violations, disorderly conduct, trespassing, public drinking, and other "quality-of-life" offenses that are included in our survey-based measure of neighborhood social disorder. These required the recipients to show up for residential hearings.

This administrative process was created to increase the efficiency of ordinance enforcement. A looser standard of judgment prevails when compared to the courts, making it easier to fine people. At an administrative hearing, only a "preponderance of the evidence" is required to collect a fine; proof "beyond a reasonable doubt" is not required. The inspector or police officer who issues a violation notice is not required to be at the hearing, a very important cost savings for the city. In the past, many police officers were reluctant to write tickets for these offenses because the tickets were likely to be thrown out or treated lightly by lawyers and judges alike. Under the new system, sanctions are essentially automatic, and police officers do not have to show up at the hearing at all. In practice, issuance of the citation that brought the recipient to a hearing is routinely accepted as evidence enough, and it is difficult for anyone to be found not guilty.

For police and the city attorneys assigned to work with them, one important role of the administrative hearings system is that it facilitates negotiated settlements that achieve their *real* goal—to clean up bad buildings, not just to collect fines. One case we followed closely involved a two-story building with a liquor store on the first floor and apartments above. It was connected to a small courtyard apartment building around the corner. In a twelve-month period, the complex generated 960 calls to 911, which got the attention of the police. Bands of loitering men, including many who were drinking, routinely gathered in front of the liquor store, and drug dealers worked out of the apartment building. Inside, the building was in complete disarray, with sewage running openly across the basement floor and rats everywhere. The area deputy chief and the attorney representing his area tackled the building, beginning with an SITF inspection of the premises. Implementation Office organizers turned up at the ensuing administrative hearing with a busload of residents who had been complaining about the building at beat meetings. The police commander startled the defense counsel by referring to these residents as his "witnesses." At the hearing, the building owner was fined fifty thousand dollars for building-code violations. However, the real function of this impending financial blow was to encourage him to agree to a formal abatement plan drafted by the attorneys involved. In the end, the owner paid a ten thousand dollar fine and spent the remaining funds on carrying out the terms of the abatement plan. The liquor store operator was ordered to leave because he had violated the terms of his lease (something the landlord had somehow overlooked before). This automatically triggered an instant revocation of his license without any involvement at all by the liquor commission (see below). The building owner also agreed to hire two armed security guards who would patrol the corner during agreed-upon periods of the day. The guards (and the police) were given a list of tenants, so that persons not on the list could be challenged and forced to leave. The police contributed a team that backed up the guards, and district cars patrolled the area heavily. While police were there in large numbers, city agencies undertook a coordinated "service blitz"; they cleaned the streets and alleys, aggressively towed cars, and improved street lighting. Police have occasionally attempted to make undercover drug purchases in the area, to make sure there has been no backsliding. And, of course, the building owner had to respond to all of his building-code violations.

Liquor Regulation

Criminologists long ago established a close causal connection between alcohol and crime, especially violence between individuals. There is a strong association between alcohol sales and a long list of crimes and disorders, including assault, robbery, sexual assault, and prostitution. Statistically, there are untoward effects of both package carryout and on-site-consumption establishments. The density of nearby liquor outlets also statistically reduces residential property values, and customers can create parking congestion on nearby residential streets. One link between liquor establishments and other problems is that conditions "inside" can spill "outside." Taverns may generate noise, including after hours, when they close. Drinking may continue outdoors, and urinating in public, throwing beer cans at passing cars, and hurling abuse at citizens passing by is not unheard of. A resident of one of the city's poorest African American beats described the situation there.

> The main problem with the drinkers is that they urinate on people's homes and gardens. Also, the bums who buy liquor at that store also buy food from the nearby restaurant. They too urinate on people's homes and defecate. It is really bad. The smell is terrible and the residents who live around there have no choice but to clean it up to try to get rid of the stench. [Are there any other types of problems resulting from public drinking?] Oh yes! There is increased litter from the empty beer bottles and food wrappers that are thrown all over the street. There are customers parking in front of the liquor store playing their loud music and disturbing the peace.

In many Chicago neighborhoods, groups of men can be observed drinking outside convenience grocery stores and liquor outlets where they bought their goods, especially establishments that sell individual cans of cold beer, airline-size bottles of liquor, and "loosies" (individual cigarettes). Package stores may also fail to carefully monitor the age of their customers. At the conclusion of a successful campaign to close twenty-seven liquor outlets in one small precinct on the far South Side, a resident voiced her view of the problems the outlets created: "It belittled the neighborhood. . . . It was a problem, all this hanging-out, begging, wondering who was going to get robbed, wondering who's going to ask you for rock or weed. All you saw was negativity." Chicagoans noticed. In the 1999 city survey, for example, 20 percent indicated that public drinking—just one manifestation of liquor issues—was a big problem in their neighborhoods, and another 30 percent reported that it was at least some problem. Latinos were most likely to report it as a big problem (28 percent did so); younger respondents were more concerned than older ones; and better-off people were generally less concerned than were the not-so-well-off. One resident whose view counts for a great deal is the mayor, who told me that one of his predecessors issued far too many liquor licenses during her short stay in office, and he wanted a significant reduction in the number of taverns and package stores operating in and near residential areas.

City ordinances provide the police and neighborhood residents with several mechanisms for tackling liquor issues. At beat meetings, residents share information with police about problems created by "bad" establishments. The liquor commission—one of the city's more hard-working and corruption-free agencies—routinely holds informal meetings at which members of the public can bring problems to the attention of the licensing authority. If five or more residents file a complaint, the liquor commission compels the licensee to appear at a meeting to consider the complaints and to discuss with residents and a commission representative whether there are remedies for the problem. The commission must balance the rights of landlords and license holders with those of nearby residents. While holding a great deal of formal authority, the commission frequently attempts to broker informal, negotiated solutions to specific problems that satisfy the needs of the protagonists. In cases where these solutions fail, the commission can levy fines and suspend or revoke the licenses of individual establishments.

A more draconian instrument is a "vote dry" referendum. City statutes allow area residents to vote to prohibit the sale of alcohol in a particular electoral precinct (a very small area) or at a particular address in their precinct. During the mid-1990s, representatives of the mayor's office, the liquor commission, the city's attorney, and the CAPS Implementation Office participated in seminars and conferences explaining how to use this tool, and the city distributed promotional materials. Informational meetings are held regularly in each police district. The city's cable channel aired a program on local liquor referenda. "Bad Liquor Establishments: What You Can Do!" aired on a fairly continual basis and listed the times and locations of area "vote dry" meetings.

That South Side resident who described the impact of public drinking in his community reported what he and other CAPS activists were doing about it:

> Members from the community and myself have talked to the owner of the building where Dixie Liquors operates. We told him about the problems we were having with that business and the owner told us that when their lease expires, he would not renew it to them. In reality, he ended up giving Dixie Liquors a six-year lease. So we decided to approach the problem differently. We are meeting with the liquor commission to dispute Dixie Liquors' license and hopefully have them shut down. We met with them (the Commission) in July 26 of this year, and we will meet the liquor commission again on August 26. We also organized a petition to get this problem put on the voting ballot when elections come up.

On the police side, action against troublesome liquor establishments traditionally was cumbersome and time consuming, because of the liquor commission's hearing arrangements and the representation of licensees by their attorneys in an environment that formally respected their right to be in business. However, things got much easier when—as described above—an area deputy chief developed the tactic of addressing liquor problems through the interests of the landlord, who typically was someone else. In practice, buildings hosting problem liquor establishments can usually be found in violation of a list of city building, health, and safety ordinances. Goaded by the threat of a hefty fine in an administrative hearing, landlords usually find grounds for terminating the liquor store's lease, which leads to the automatic revocation of the store's license to do business, without further hearings at all.

School Safety

Schools should be natural partners in any community-safety program. They certainly can be loci for problems. Rambunctious youths are corseted there all day, and they surge through the surrounding neighborhoods during their journeys to and from school. National surveys of students indicate that levels of fear and even criminal victimization can be high in schools, and that it is easy to get drugs and even weapons in and around many schools. In Illinois, a 1990 statewide survey of public high schools found that one in four students feared violence in school and one in five feared the journey to and from school. One in three Illinois students reported they had carried a weapon to school; one in three said that they knew someone who had dropped out of school due to trouble with gangs; and half of them indicated that it was easy to get marijuana in their school.

Society certainly wants schools to solve their own problems when they can, and during the period that CAPS was being formulated, Chicago's schools had their own disciplinary and safety initiatives in place.[4] By the 1990s, the era was long past when teacher-enforced school disciplinary codes did the job. During the 1990–1991 school year, 6,250 persons were arrested on school property for crimes involving the physical safety of children (Williams 1994). In 1990 the school board had already positioned 750 security guards in the schools. Special state funding then enabled the board to hire even more, and between 1990 and 1995 these add-ons rose in number from 59 to 528. During the early 1990s, high schools began to install walk-through metal detectors, and all schools were using them or even handheld scanning devices by 1999. Beginning in 1990, the police contributed a special school patrol unit that by 2000 had grown to about two hundred officers. Additionally, security cameras in lunchrooms and hallways were installed.

The pace of change picked up following a shakeup in school financing and administration. A thoroughgoing restructuring of Chicago's public schools began in 1995, when the Illinois legislature made changes in the governance and funding of the city's schools that effectively handed control to the mayor. In short order, the new administration made dramatic changes in virtually every aspect of operations. Many new disciplinary and security programs were instituted, some involving just the school bureaucracy itself, and others involving partnerships with police and the CAPS Implementation Office. Beginning in 1996, schools became more aggressive about expelling troublemakers, after alternative schools run by private contractors were set up to receive them. The state's 1995 Gun-Free Schools Act—which was later expanded to cover knives, pipes, alcohol, and drugs—provided additional legal incentives to expel students found with guns. A change in the system's disciplinary code called for the mandatory expulsion of students carrying firearms. Although school disciplinary statistics are very unreliable guides to either levels of problems or actual disciplinary practice, it appears that things got tighter during the 1990s. In 1996, one school reported 106 expulsions for every 100 students! Then, in October 1998, the Chicago public schools announced a draconian "zero-tolerance" policy with regard to the more serious offenses in its Uniform Disciplinary Code; this further toughened a zero-tolerance policy announced in 1995. School board policies allowed pat-downs and personal searches of students based upon suspicion by teachers or administrators, as well as wholesale locker and desk searches, using dogs, looking for weapons and drugs. In 1998, the school system launched a peer mediation program and conflict resolution initiative that trained youth to deal with their anger before it escalates into violence.

There is community involvement in school safety as well. Beginning in 1990, parents were recruited to stand guard on school grounds; later, this program was greatly expanded. In 1999 the CAPS Implementation Office added a "walking school bus" project. They organized students and parents living along various routes to a school into convoys that picked up and dropped off members as they moved through the neighborhood. A corporate donor bought them distinctive Windbreakers and handheld signs to carry as they transported children safely to the neighborhood school. By 2000 there were parent patrols around 450 schools, and about 100 active walking school buses.

Of course, efforts that are not on their face "security measures" can also have an impact on school climate and student performance, and these, in turn, can have spin-off consequences for school and neighborhood safety. In addition to the security projects described above, post-1995 there was a sea change in school management and performance assessment in Chicago. Drastic revisions were instituted in the curriculum; selected schools began to remain open until 6:00 p.m. for optional math and reading programs; many thousands of failing students were held in school during the summer months; and a massive construction program replaced or renovated a host of school buildings. Dress codes drafted by parent groups were instituted in many schools beginning in 1996, as was a requirement for daily homework assignments for every class. Not the least of these changes was an empowerment of parents and neighborhood residents. The elected local councils affiliated with every school gained a significant voice in administrative, budgetary, staffing, and even curricular matters within their school's doors. Archon Fung, a Harvard University professor who has studied both community policing and school reform, concluded that together CAPS and the Chicago Public Schools are "the most participatory, democratic public organizations of their kind in any large American city."[5]

Coordinated Service Delivery

CAPS planners knew that many issues that are uppermost on the minds of neighborhood residents—including abandoned cars, graffiti-scarred buildings, and intersections that are unsafe due to fallen stop signs—cannot be solved by police. The planners anticipated that when police met with the public with the announced agenda of identifying and responding to local concerns, a broad range of issues would emerge, and an affirmative response would need to be ready. The mechanism CAPS planners initially developed was the service-request process described in chapter 3. It enabled police officers and the civilian CAPS Implementation Office staff to trigger a response from every relevant city agency. The process worked because a tight management system was developed that set clear standards for the delivery of each type of service (usually measured in hours or days) and held the city's diverse bureaucracies accountable for following through in a timely fashion. More recently, the Implementation Office has taken major responsibility for coordinating the delivery of services. Each police area has a full-time service coordinator. One staff member we interviewed estimates that he writes about one hundred service requests every day he is in the field.

While CAPS service requests helped steer the delivery of routine service requests, the Implementation Office also took responsibility for coordinating the involvement of service agencies in special projects conducted by police and resident groups. Operation CLEAN (City Services Law Enforcement and Neighbors) is one example of this. According to a program description, its goal is "to deliver, in a coordinated manner, a massive amount of city services to high crime areas in an effort to improve the quality of life for residents. . . . These quality of life issues affect public and officer safety and rank high among the underlying causes of crime and disorder problems in target areas." Blitzes by CLEAN include aggressively towing abandoned cars, removing graffiti by using the city's Graffiti Blasters (so named because they use high-pressure soda blasters), tree trimming, rat poisoning, sewer cleaning, clearing and mowing vacant lots, repairing streets and sidewalks, installing new street signs and lampposts, and painting fire hydrants and other public structures. Building and business inspectors come in to identify responsibilities for owners, and the SITF hits buildings particularly hard when they are suspected of harboring drug activity. Implementation Office staff members, beat facilitators, resident activists, and police walk targeted areas together to determine which services are needed, and later track agency follow-up efforts. A service coordinator reported keying in 669 individual service requests as he got organized for one day's Operation CLEAN. Implementation Office staff walk door to door during the cleanups, encouraging people to participate in community organizations. A related "Clean & Green" program provides community organizations with rakes, brooms, shovels, and trash bags, so that they can clean things up on their own as well.

The coordinated delivery of city services is an integral part of community policing in Chicago. It is linked to what are believed to be the causes of crime and neighborhood decline, and to the need to be responsive to the concerns expressed through participatory structures created by the program. It is also there because the mayor, who is very interested in the effectiveness of municipal services, saw the process as another mechanism for forcing his many bureaucracies to focus on their ultimate customers and generate more "consumer" (and, of course, voter) satisfaction.

Figure 6.1 monitors the distribution of two high-volume services that respond to problems that are of concern to the public and are widely discussed at beat meetings: graffiti and abandoned cars. For example, the 1998 citywide survey found that half of Chicagoans thought graffiti was either some problem or a big problem in their neighborhood, and 32 percent expressed similar concerns about abandoned cars. Residents who turned out for beat meetings were more emphatic; in the same year, 76 percent of residents who attended beat meetings thought graffiti was a problem in their neighborhoods, and 59 percent were concerned about abandoned cars.

Figure 6.1 examines how effectively the city targets services in response to these concerns. First, a "service need" measure was created by combining responses to citywide surveys conducted in 1996, 1997, and 1998. About eight thousand city residents were interviewed in those surveys. The combined sample was large enough that at least 10 respondents were interviewed in 222 of the city's 270 residential police beats. Responses to questions about neighborhood

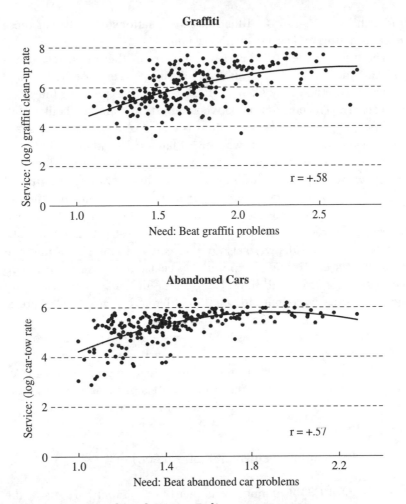

Figure 6.1. Beat Needs and Service Delivery, 1997–1998

problems (which are described in detail in the next chapter) were averaged within beats to calculate an estimate of the extent of concern
for graffiti and abandoned car problems in each beat. City data banks
contributed measures of the distribution of the relevant service responses for 1997 and 1998. In those two years there were almost
180,000 graffiti site cleanups and 83,000 car tows. Over the period,
the average beat was cleaned 646 times and 225 cars were towed
away. Since beats vary greatly in population, rates of service per ten
thousand residents were calculated using estimates of the population

for each beat. Figure 6.1 illustrates the relationship between these need measures and service-delivery rates.

The link between need and the delivery of these two services is substantial. Both graffiti clean ups and car tow rates rose with public demand, although they leveled off a bit in areas expressing the greatest concern. The correlation between reports of concern about graffiti and the (logged) site cleanup rate was +.58. For concern about abandoned cars and car tows, it was +.57. Statistically, other factors were correlated with service delivery as well. Land-use factors influenced graffiti cleanup rates, including the relative number of nonresidential (commercial and manufacturing) structures, the concentration of small businesses, and the sheer density of buildings. Businesses were not represented in our resident survey, but they have problems too. Graffiti clean ups were also more frequent in heavily Latino and immigrant areas, in densely populated beats, and in areas with concentrations of older buildings. Controlling for the survey measure of need, car tows were more frequent in older and nonresidential areas, lower-income beats, communities with large concentrations of parking lots and auto repair establishments, and in both Latino and African American neighborhoods. Later in this chapter we will see that citizen involvement played a role in steering service delivery as well. Beat-meeting turnout and the priorities of those who attended played an independent role in directing the delivery of services.

Resident Involvement in Problem Solving

The vision of CAPS planners was that the principal partners of the police in problem solving would be neighborhood residents, as well as the groups and associations that represented them. A police department "fact sheet" noted: "While traditional policing relied almost exclusively on the police to fight crime, CAPS creates a partnership of police, residents, government agencies, and other members of the community. The community shares responsibility with the police for setting the crime-fighting priorities in their neighborhoods and for designing and implementing problem-solving strategies."[6] Before CAPS got off the ground, officers serving in the districts that were chosen as test-beds for the new program were trained in a five-step model the department had adopted to guide the problem-solving efforts of police and residents. During 1995, seventy-five hundred officers assigned to the department's uniformed patrol division received two days of problem-solving training. They reviewed key organizational elements of CAPS and the problem-solving model, as well as how to document problems in their beat's action plan and to work with the community. Later there was yearly training for sergeants in crafting beat plans and managing beat meetings. Beginning in 1997, the department held training sessions for selected officers assigned to beat teams, and for civilian beat facilitators.

Formal training in problem solving began in 1995 for large numbers of residents. Pairs of police and civilian trainers conducted sessions that introduced the general public to the concepts of community policing and problem solving. They taught residents how to identify, prioritize, and analyze problems; how to form strategies for mobilizing the community around problem-solving projects; and how to evaluate their community's accomplishments. Trainers tried to hold an orientation meeting and three follow-up training sessions in every beat, and while they fell a bit short of that goal, more than twelve thousand residents attended at least one training session.

There is evidence that many trainees got involved in problem-solving projects after undergoing training. To assess this we conducted a follow-up survey of 354 randomly chosen training participants, about four months after their first training experience. The survey found that trainees took some kind of action on 63 percent of the priority problems they identified for their neighborhood, and three-quarters reported urging others to attend beat meetings (for more details on training, see Skogan et al. [1999]).

The results of police and resident training can be seen in action. During 1998, observers attended hundreds of beat meetings and noted what took place there. At a meeting on the Far North Side they happened upon police and residents working their way through the crime triangle as they addressed a public-drinking problem.

The main topic of the meeting was problems with sports teams in H____ Park. The problems include drinking in the park and then driving, loud music, trash, urinating on trees, and staying past the park's closing hours. One woman says it is not just drinking sports teams that is the problem, it is also young kids and drugs in the park. At this point the sergeant steps in and says this is a perfect opportunity to do preventive work—to use the CAPS method of problem solving and stop problems in the park before they begin again this year. First, they determine that it is a CAPS problem because it won't go away on its own, and it affects more than a handful of people. Then they brainstorm the three aspects of the CAPS triangle. The location is H___ Park, and especially the parking lot along C____ Avenue. The victims are park patrons and people who live along C____ Avenue, and a new potential group of victims is the seniors who will be moving into a new senior home at M___ and C___. The offenders are sports-team players, gangs, and perhaps liquor stores selling to minors. The sergeant then says that to have a solution you have to address at least two sides of the crime triangle. The group talks about strategies: to talk to people on C____ to maybe get them to form a block club and get them involved in the CAPS group; to install better lighting and more trash cans; and to post signs in English and Spanish regarding park rules and fines for having liquor in the park. There is some talk about the fact that fines are rarely given or paid. The female police officer says that if the community comes to court, it pressures the judge to actually make people pay fines ("we've seen it work"). Someone suggests that since most people work, it would be good to get the seniors involved in court advocacy because they have the time to go to court. There is also talk about a neighborhood watch in the park and about getting the gates to the park closed on time. Also, someone suggests putting signs regarding park policy on liquor in nearby liquor stores.

An observer came across a "problem-solving refresher" when he sat in on a beat meeting on the North Side.

The first presentation was given by CAPS trainers. They conducted a problem-solving demonstration for almost one-and-a-half hours. The crime triangle and five-step problem-solving processes were discussed by applying them to the problem of children being left unattended, and to a cluster of drug, gang, and violence problems on a particular street corner. Offenders, locations, and victims were identified and analyzed, and strategies were brought forward. Residents volunteered to get tax ID numbers for buildings in which trouble occurs so they could go after specific people. Officer ____ would pursue DCFS (the state's Department of Children and Family Services) action for the children left unattended. Stepped-up police presence would occur. The demonstration was explained clearly and was very understandable. There is to be a report next month.

At the district level, police and the CAPS Implementation Office organizers frequently sponsor more assertive activities. For example, in one district we studied intensively, activists conducted what are called "stand-ups" twice monthly in front of problem businesses, during the spring, summer, and fall of 1999. On a chilly Saturday morning in mid-April, an observer stood with a group of twenty residents outside a corner liquor store. The crowd included members of the District Advisory Committee and other residents who were part of the district's community networking subcommittee. The liquor store was targeted because loose garbage was perpetually strewn around its sidewalk. "We have to crack down on these businesses and stop thinking that we don't deserve better," explained one DAC member. They each took turns entering the store and "getting in the face" of the operator, while the others chanted slogans to passersby.

CAPS Implementation Office organizers working in predominantly African American areas are especially fond of prayer marches and vigils as community-action tools. Organizers, residents, police, and community leaders parade through problem streets to demonstrate their unity and confront troublemakers by stopping in front of the drug hot spots, joining hands, and singing or saying a prayer aloud for the community. In one police district, church groups conducted "emergency outreach prayer vigils" at the sites of drug-related shootings. District officers notified participants when an incident occurred, and they converged on the scene to pray. Another district held a Year 2000 Prayer Vigil at the change of the millennium. In some districts prayer vigils were held at the site of *every* homicide, to voice the concern of the community about the loss of its members. In the 11th District, prayer vigils became regular, districtwide events, sponsored by the police and involving pastors and gospel choirs who assembled in the district's most dangerous sections (Meares 2002). Though it is not clear what long-term effects prayer vigils have on gang homicides or drug houses, they do give the community the chance to point out hot spots to police and let the dealers and gang members know that the community is aware of what they are doing and that it disapproves.

There are other forms of assertive vigilance. "Smoke-outs"—barbeque picnics—are held in drug market areas, with officers from the district attending to provide protection for residents. "Positive-loitering" campaigns are organized to harass prostitutes and potential customers. Positive-loitering campaigns are efforts to increase the frequency with which law-abiding residents occupy public spaces in order to discourage street prostitutes, loiterers, drinkers, and other disorderly persons. They do so by scheduling dog walks and walking groups during periods of time when these problems are at their most intense. According to activists we interviewed, smoke-outs and positive-loitering projects were underway in eight districts. One DAC began a positive-loitering campaign after watching crime levels skyrocket along a riverfront walkway in the district. Residents assembled and strolled around or walk their dogs, keeping an eye on passersby and, on occasion, confronting troublemakers. In an inter-view, an Implementation Office organizer described a project in her area:

> Of the several problems in the district, one of the main ones is prostitution. . . . The problem was brought up at the beat meeting, after residents caught prostitutes doing business in their gangways and garages, or found traces of the business (e.g., used condoms). She [the Implementation Office organizer] proposed positive-loitering, and they [residents] agreed to give it a try. . . . They started out with thirty people and were es-corted by a police car. They began to alternate days and times so that the prostitutes would never know when they'd be there. Soon the prostitutes ran when they saw the group coming, while the police would stop them and check for warrants, ar-resting them if there were any outstanding. By the time of the next beat meeting, attendance rose because they had done such a good job with that problem that the word had spread. It was decided that they needed to carry signs to target the johns. So the next time they were out, they carried signs. When a com-munity member complained of seeing prostitutes from 9 p.m. to 11 p.m., positive loiterers came during those times. They got up to sixty volunteers. One day they just started chanting. The next step in their minds was to go to court to follow up on ar-rests. They were becoming so familiar that the prostitutes rec-ognized them in the courtroom and left. They began to talk with the judge and develop a good relationship with him. He listened to them and said it was good of them to come and show community support, but he reminded them that the pros-titutes had rights and he had to be impartial. However, he did give them and the police pointers on what they were doing wrong and what could be done to make these cases stronger.

Youth programs provide another focus for district activists. In the activist survey, a majority of respondents from every district reported CAPS-related youth projects. With the police, residents sponsored Explorer Scout Troops and baseball teams. The DACs raised funds to support youth programs, field trips, sporting activities, and after-school programs operating in their districts. Beginning in 1999, the districts began to organize peer juries—groups of high school students who volunteer to serve on a "jury" that renders sentences for first-time juvenile offenders who agree to participate in the program. Residents serve as adult monitors, helping jurors and officers handle cases and overseeing the fulfillment of community-service sentences. One district had a youth subcommittee composed entirely of teenagers who live or go to school in the neighborhood. A beat-team sergeant summarized his view of resident involvement in CAPS this way: "We all know that with the traditional role of policing, we did a great job of locking people up and taking them to court. But we weren't solving the problems. We were putting out fires, but we weren't solving the problems. The thing I like most about working with the community is that it holds the community accountable. Making them equally accountable for quality-of-life issues brings more effective results in problematic areas. That's one of my big things. I really believe in that stewardship."

Frequency of Involvement

Chicagoans who attend beat meetings report being active in community problem-solving efforts and other community-policing activities. To assess the extent of their involvement, thirty-seven hundred people were surveyed who were attending beat meetings during the summer and fall of 2002. The survey included questions about various forms of CAPS activism. Residents were asked if they had participated in each activity during the past twelve months "in your beat or district." Overall, 70 percent of those who attended reported participating in at least one of the activities that were listed. Table 6.1 presents detailed findings from the survey.

The activities described in table 6.1 fall into two distinct clusters. One is *aggressive activism*. Activities in this cluster are listed on the left-hand side of the table. They include marches, prayer vigils, smoke-outs, positive-loitering, parent patrols, and neighborhood watches. Participating in marches and rallies was the most frequent activity in this category. Twelve percent reported participating in "smoke-outs, CAPS picnics or barbeques." These events are aggressively anticrime, for they are deliberately held in the midst of street drug markets or prostitution zones and are intended to drive both sellers and their potential customers from the area. "Walking school buses" are parent

Table 6.1 Beat Meeting Participant Activism

Percent of Meeting Participants Involved in CAPS Activities in Past Twelve Months

Aggressive activism		City/CAPS projects	
Marches or rallies	26	City or area neighborhood assembly	18
Prayer vigils	13	CAPS fairs, forums, or education programs	16
Smoke-outs, CAPS picnics or barbeques	12	Attended court for court advocacy or a Court Advocacy subcommittee meeting	11
Positive loitering	9	"vote dry" or liquor control projects	12
Parent patrols or walking school bus	6	Worked with the CAPS office to organize a neighborhood group	14
Neighborhood patrols or watches	21	Contacted police or elected officials about a problem	39
Percent involved in aggressive activism**	43	Percent involved in CAPS neighborhood projects**	63

** See text for definition of activism measures.

groups that walk through a neighborhood each morning wearing distinctive jackets, stopping along the way to assemble a group of children to escort safely to school. Neighborhood watches or patrols were popular, reported by 21 percent of those attending. Overall, 43 percent of those attending beat meetings reported being involved in at least one of these efforts.

Activities reflecting involvement in city- and CAPS-sponsored *neighborhood projects* are listed on the right side of table 6.1. These ranged from attending neighborhood assemblies to being a court advocate, working on liquor control projects, and organizing neighborhood groups. As noted in chapter 3, court advocacy is an official CAPS project that is sponsored by the districts' advisory committees, and 11 percent of those attending beat meetings reported some involvement in that effort. Neighborhood assemblies and CAPS fairs or forums are events organized by the CAPS Implementation Office. Twelve percent of those surveyed indicated some involvement in efforts to close down troublesome liquor establishments. An observer reported the following presentation at a South Side beat meeting:

The neighborhood relations officer then introduced _____, a member of _____ Baptist Church. He explained to residents that members of his church and other residents were working to make the 9th and 34th wards "dry" and that the only way to get undesirable people off the streets is to close the liquor stores. Last year, four hundred church members circulated petitions to get a referendum asking to close liquor establishments placed on a ballot. They were successful in getting some liquor stores closed. The members plan to start circulating petitions in June until August. He told residents that they would be paired up with another person to get signatures and he would pass out flyers later.

Overall, 63 percent of those attending beat meetings in the summer of 2002 reported being involved in at least one neighborhood project. "Contacting police or elected officials about a problem," which is a fairly passive form of involvement, was the most frequent activity reported in the survey (at 39 percent), and it fell in this category.

There were some differences in patterns of involvement in these two clusters of activities. Older, long-term residents of the community tended to be involved in neighborhood activities but not in aggressive activism. Men and African Americans were most likely to report being involved in both CAPS projects and aggressive activism. Reports of activism were highly related to being a frequent participant in beat meetings and being active in the community. To examine this, I created beat-level measures of participation in CAPS neighborhood projects and aggressive activism. This confirmed that cohesive beats—beats where those who come to meetings attend frequently, know and work with one another outside of the meetings, and belong to other kinds of community organizations as well—spawn more CAPS activism.

CAPS was designed to stimulate and bring focus to this kind of neighborhood activism, and a 64 percent involvement rate among beat-meeting participants was a considerable accomplishment. The question is, Were these efforts focused where they were needed the most? To examine the distribution of CAPS activism, responses by participants in meetings in each sample beat were aggregated to produce a beat-level measure of the overall extent of their involvement in the activities listed in table 6.1. Enough residents (ten or more) were surveyed to do so in 124 beats. The index is the average count of activities reported by residents of each beat, so places where people were involved in multiple activities received a higher score than places in which people were involved in no or only a few projects. The beat average ranged from less than one activity to just over five activities. These scores could be compared to other features of the beats, to assess the fit between beat problems and the extent to which people were active in addressing them.

It is apparent by a host of measures that, by and large, the beats that needed CAPS activism the most were the most active. The correlates of higher rates of activism include high levels of poverty and rates of broken families, many households with children, lower incomes, less education, high unemployment, and low housing values. Like beat-meeting attendance rates, beat-meeting activism was driven, in part, by high levels of violent crime and frequent 911 calls about drug problems. Activism was less frequent in predominantly white and more affluent areas, on a host of measures. Figure 6.2 illustrates four of these relationships. The top panels describe the link between beat activism (on the vertical axis) and the rate at which beat residents call police about drug problems, and the average neighborhood problems rating that respondents living in the beat gave in surveys conducted in 2001 and 2003. Activism was higher in areas with some of the most serious drug problems, and in places that residents thought were problem ridden. As the bottom-left panel illustrates, beat activism was lowest in the city's primarily white beats. It was highest in predominantly African American areas, and above average in heavily Latino beats.

The lower-right panel of figure 6.2 illustrates that this kind of neighborhood activism is not simply a reflection of support for the police. In fact, aggregating the findings of the 2001 and 2003 city surveys reveals that CAPS activism was higher in places where residents were more skeptical about police performance, while some of the highest support for the police was found in places where people were not very active at all. Multivariate analyses of these data reveal that CAPS activism was driven by crime and drugs, and by resident and participant perceptions of the seriousness of neighborhood problems. The good news is that, like beat-meeting participation rates, the efforts of the city's beat activists were generally targeted at the places that needed help the most.

Resident Involvement and Service Delivery

An important question about CAPS is whether citizen activism and involvement in setting beat priorities make a difference for their neighborhoods. This is a difficult question to address, for the character of neighborhoods in a large city like Chicago is influenced by a broad range of forces. In contrast to factors like large-scale immigra-

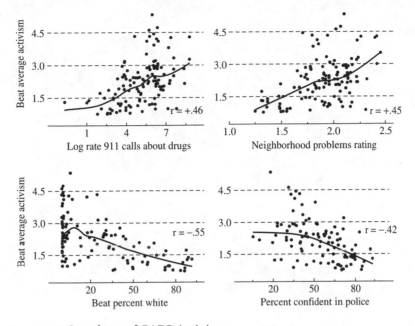

Figure 6.2. Correlates of CAPS Activism

tion, a shift from manufacturing to services as the economic engine of the city, and the exodus of the childrearing middle class to the suburbs, beat activism probably is of relatively minor importance. At the local level, CAPS activists compete with a list of political and economic influences for affecting the course of neighborhood development. One place to look for the effect of beat activism is closer to home, in its impact on how community policing is conducted. Does the program respond effectively to the concerns of residents, as their concerns are articulated through beat meetings and other fora? Do "the goods get delivered" in response to citizen priorities? Even then, there inevitably will be other forces at work affecting how the program operates and who enjoys its benefits, so the question becomes, What is the role of beat activism in comparison to other factors determining who gets what from the program?

The delivery of city services is one of the CAPS functions that should be responsive to resident input. The issue is, How closely does the delivery of services match the priority that beat residents and activists give to problems? This question can be addressed systematically, using beat-level data constructed from surveys and administrative records. Figure 6.3 describes the general relationship be-

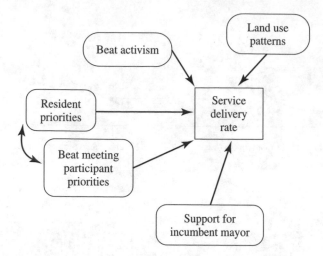

Figure 6.3. Citizens' Priorities and Service Delivery Patterns

tween some of the factors that may influence the distribution of city services.

As described above, measures of the priorities of beat residents were created by aggregating three years of citywide survey data to the beat level. A parallel measure of the priorities of residents attending beat meetings was created by aggregating questionnaire responses by 4,673 residents who attended meetings in 1998. Only beats with at least ten city-survey respondents and ten beat-meeting participant respondents are included in the analysis. Another factor that may affect who gets what from community policing is beat activism—the extent to which residents get involved in beat affairs. This is represented by the 1998 beat-meeting turnout rate (the number of participants per one thousand adults). In Chicago, politics provides another priority-setting process that channels benefits to this neighborhood or that, and politics needs to be taken into account in any portrait of the distribution of city services. In this case it is represented by the percentage of each beat's vote that went to the incumbent (and ultimately successful) mayoral candidate in the 1995 general election. City data banks contributed indicators of the distribution of the relevant service responses for 1997 and 1998. Logged rates of service per ten thousand residents are used here. It is also important to take into account the built environment in each beat, for many areas of Chicago are characterized by a mix of residential, commercial, and other land uses, and those too have an impact on specific service needs. Relevant measures of land use are included as controls, to clarify the relationship between resident priorities and service delivery. For the analysis described below, there was complete data for 195 of the city's 270 primarily residential beats.

The statistical relationship between these factors is summarized in table 6.2. It indicates the strength of the correlations between service-delivery rates and the factors sketched in figure 6.3. It also summarizes their relative impact when taken together in multiple regression. In that case, the tables should be read down the column; the standardized regression coefficients presented there are comparable to each other within the analysis of each service. They represent the relative importance of each factor in shaping the delivery rate for that service. The two types of service present fairly independent tests of the influence of public priorities on service delivery, for the correlation between them was relatively low (+.22).

Table 6.2. Correlates of Beat Service Delivery Rates

Variable	(log) Graffiti clean-up rate		(log) Car-tow rate	
	Standardized coefficient	Bivariate correlation	Standardized coefficient	Bivariate correlation
Resident priorities	.30	.68	.29	.48
Meeting attendee priorities	.18	.67	.29	.62
Meeting attendance rate	.21	(−.06)	.20	.42
Vote share for the incumbent mayor	.36	.63	−.22	−.34
Nonresidential land use	.18	.46	−.18	−.13
Pct. of parcels small businesses	.18	.32	—	—
Building density	.13	.20	—	—
Pct. parcels automobile uses	—	—	.34	.22
R² (adj.)	.66		.64	

Table reports standardized regression coefficients. All coefficients and correlations are significant $p < .05$ unless indicated by '( )'. N = 196

The link between service-delivery rates and politics varied from service to service. Being part of the mayor's electoral coalition was strongly linked (the correlation was +.63) with graffiti cleanups, independent of residents' priorities and the priorities of beat-meeting activists. This was driven, in part, by the strong association between the size of a beat's Latino population and the extent of graffiti problems, joined by the fact that Latinos gave the incumbent mayor significant support in the 1995 election. On the other hand, support for the mayor was negatively related (-.34) to action against abandoned cars. Relatively few car-tow complaints were lodged in the city's better-off white neighborhoods; complaints were moderately concentrated in Latino and African American beats, and voters in the latter were particularly indisposed to vote for the incumbent.

But in both cases there were substantial direct links between beat residents' priorities and who got what from the City, and beat meeting attendance rates were important as well. The concern of the general public was the first or second most important correlate of service delivery rates. City agencies were fairly successful in targeting problems of concern to the public. In light of the fact that neighborhood and participant attitudes were assessed on the basis of as few as ten survey responses, limiting their accuracy, the strength of these correlations (+.48 for car tows and .+68 for graffiti cleanups) is impressive. In addition, where beat-meeting participants were especially concerned compared to their neighbors, service-delivery rates were somewhat higher still. These correlations were also high (+.67 for graffiti cleanups and +.62 for car tows), and beat meeting priorities were correlated with service-delivery rates even when the views of beat residents were taken into account. In addition, the "squeaky wheels" were "being greased." This is evidenced by the additional effect of beat-meeting attendance rates on graffiti cleanups and car tows. The attendance rate–tow rate correlation was high (+.42) for tows, but the relationship between beat-meeting attendance levels and graffiti cleanups was only apparent in the multivariate analysis. This was due to the "suppressor effect" of low beat-meeting attendance among the bulk of the city's Latinos, a group reporting a high level of concern about neighborhood graffiti.

To summarize, we have seen here that the representational structure created by Chicago's beat meetings to a significant extent translates residents' priorities into the program in action. As documented in chapter 5, there is a strong establishment bias in participation in the meetings. Beat meetings do a better job representing already-

established stakeholders in the community than they do at integrat-
ing marginalized groups with fewer mechanisms for voicing their
concerns. This being said, there were strong correlations (.48 to .68)
between residents' priorities and the delivery of city services that
speak to two widely discussed neighborhood problems, graffiti and
abandoned cars.

How Did Chicago Do?

Because it involved a commitment to deal with a broad range of neighborhood problems, and not just crime, CAPS involved the creation of
new partnerships and working relationships between the police and
municipal-service agencies. Other city institutions—especially the
schools—were already working on some of the same problems, of
course. In parallel with CAPS, the process by which the city had long
regulated liquor establishments was modified to include significant
community input. New institutions were also created, including an
administrative hearing bureau. Cross-agency task forces mobilized the
legal powers of diverse bureaucracies to tackle issues prioritized by
district officers. All of this took time, because it is not the natural instinct of bureaucracies to share control over their agendas and budgets, but CAPS' success reflected the important fact that community
policing in Chicago was the city's program, not just the police department's program.

Another feature of the CAPS plan was its commitment to involving the public in neighborhood problem-solving efforts. During the
mid-1990s, thousands of civilians were trained in problems solving,
in parallel with the new training that was delivered to more than
nine thousand patrol division officers. A civilian agency was created
to drum up support for problem-solving projects, start block clubs,
and turn people out for monthly beat meetings. Over 40 percent of
the residents surveyed at beat meetings reported getting involved in
some fairly aggressive activities, including marches, prayer vigils,
neighborhood patrols, and smoke-outs. More popular was attending
assemblies and forums, working to organize neighborhood groups,
and contacting public officials to get action on local problems. At 64
percent, I would judge participation in these activities to be high,
and just as important, it was most frequent where it was needed the
most: in high-crime, drug-ridden, minority communities. Finally,
there is evidence that the distribution of services provided by the

city to address their problems was fairly responsively targeted. The priorities of neighborhood residents and those who attended beat meetings were both linked to higher service levels, as was the overall beat-meeting attendance rate. When it came to services, beat meetings provided an extra push in the direction of the "squeaky wheels."

Finally, police all over the city—not just officers assigned to special units or with special training and resources—were supposed to get involved in problem solving at the beat level. We knew this was going to be hard to pull off. Research in other cities indicates that police do not take easily to abstract concepts like "problems" and that steps in the problem-solving process that stand in the way of action—including gathering more information using department data systems and analyzing the underlying causes of the problem—typically get short-changed. In a ten-year "report card" (Skogan and Steiner 2004a) we gave the department a "C" for its problem-solving efforts, faulting them for a lack of supervision, continued training, and analytic capacity. In too many beats, the same problems persisted year after year even though they had been identified as priorities. Asking both police and residents revealed that most of what the police were up to was extremely traditional. As in other cities (cf. Cordner and Biebel [2005], on San Diego), police rarely gathered "data" of any kind except what they observed in the field, and they mostly applied traditional enforcement tactics, such as driving by more often, stopping cars, and trying to arrest people. But both police and residents reported broader public involvement in a range of problem-solving activities, including organizing block clubs, forming patrols, mobilizing city services, and trying to awaken their apathetic neighbors to the problem. Both police and residents described fairly extensive use of resources from outside the department, including city services and door-to-door efforts by the CAPS Implementation Office.

SEVEN

Trends in Neighborhood Problems

Repeated administration of the evaluation surveys enables us to examine trends in the extent of neighborhood problems over time, beginning in early 1994. This was after CAPS was announced and the development of the program began in the prototype districts, but a year before it expanded to encompass the entire city. The surveys asked about neighborhood conditions using categories that are readily understood by the public, and they included many concerns that are not easily gauged using agency statistics. All were targets of police problem-solving projects and city service agencies. The surveys, which were conducted in both English and Spanish, were large enough to track changes in the views of major subgroups of residents. This turned out to be a very important feature of the analysis, for citywide averages disguised significant differences in the experiences of Chicagoans. In the main, African Americans reported very substantial improvements in their quality of life, and things got better for the city's whites as well. However, Latinos showed little overall improvement and, among immigrants, things grew decidedly worse over time. Chicago ended up a racially divided city, much as it had begun, but the nature of the divisions shifted in fairly dramatic fashion.

Physical Decay

An important subset of the problems plaguing the city's neighborhoods were the signs of visible neglect, abandonment, and deliberate vandalism that were visible in too many neighborhoods. The first evaluation surveys revealed that many Chicagoans were very concerned about these issues, sometimes almost to the exclusion of concern about conventional crimes. A 1996 police department internal fact sheet explaining the role of city services to its own employees noted, "When residents of the five CAPS prototype districts were asked by evaluators to name the top problems in their communities, they frequently cited graffiti, abandoned buildings, vacant lots, and other neighborhood disorder problems, in addition to serious crime problems."[1] The memo described how the CAPS city-service request form described in chapter 2 would "allow officers to address relatively minor problems and conditions before they grow into more serious crime problems."[2]

In the surveys respondents were requested to rate a list of things "that you may think are problems in your neighborhood." They were asked to indicate whether "you think it is a big problem, some problem or no problem in your neighborhood." Responses to four of these questions were used to assess the extent of neighborhood physical decay:

Graffiti; that is, writing or painting on walls or buildings;
Abandoned houses or other empty buildings in your area;
Vacant lots filled with trash and junk; and
Abandoned cars in the streets and alleys.

Figure 7.1 summarizes trends in reports of neighborhood decay during the course of the 1990s and into the early 2000s. It presents, by race, the percentage of respondents who thought these were a "big problem" in their neighborhood.

Graffiti

Graffiti presented an important test of the effectiveness of the city-service component of CAPS. Graffiti is a common fact of life in many neighborhoods. In 1994—the first year for which there is survey data—it was the most highly rated problem among Latino residents. Overall, 22 percent of Chicagoans thought graffiti was a big problem in their areas; for Latinos, the figure was 38 percent; and among whites, it was 17 percent.

One theory about its origins is that graffiti is "infectious"—where it appears and is not quickly erased, its visible presence will quickly stimulate still more graffiti (cf. Skogan 1990a). The city's anti-graffiti program involves strategies besides cleaning it up, but its aggressive approach to cleaning up graffiti rapidly reflects contagion theory. Perhaps the most visible element of the city's graffiti-elimination program is its teams of "Graffiti Blasters." They come armed with nineteen high-pressure soda sprayers and, without charge, they blast graffiti from the property of any willing property owner. Before 1993, the

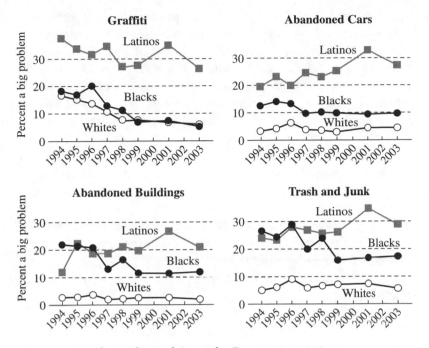

Figure 7.1. Trends in Physical Decay by Race, 1994–2003

responsibility—and the cost—for graffiti removal lay with the property owner, as the city only maintained public property. Now the city considers these owners the victims of crime, and spends about four million dollars a year to clean up private property. From 1993 through 2002, more than nine hundred thousand buildings were cleaned of graffiti, some repeatedly. Paint and clean-up supplies are also available for community groups bent on removing graffiti on their own. The logo for this program reads "Give graffiti the brush!"

Chicagoans also associate graffiti with gangs, and read its emergence as a sign that gangs are moving into their area. Discussions pondering the significance of specific instances of graffiti take place at numerous beat meetings. One activist in a North Side study area described her routine after she noticed gang symbols that had not been around before: "I do rounds through the area, taking note of where new graffiti has popped up and reporting it to the police, as well as following up with the Graffiti Blasters. I do this once every week without fail. Even if it's not my property I'll call and wait for the Graffiti Blasters to show up." Some officers considered eradicating graffiti to be a useful strategy in their struggle against gangs. In a beat that identified gang violence as its priority target, a team member noted that: "the Graffiti Blasters got rid of graffiti to help prevent turf wars. The presence of graffiti, when it is of gang symbols, often leads to turf war. The Graffiti Blasters getting rid of the graffiti before it becomes a big problem has helped to suppress the gang problem by preventing turf wars." In interviews, community leaders and social-service agency staff members in some of the city's most concentrated Latino areas agreed that graffiti is, importantly, a gang phenomenon. In the new immigrant areas on the Near South East Side of the city, the most important gangs are the Latin Kings, the Two Sixers, the Bishops, and the Ambrose. As a top police official described it, these gangs are strongly territorial. While they all are involved in the drug trade, they still retain the tradition of fighting for control of turf, over women, and to act out their "machismo" self-image. Gang violence starts with the marking of territory with graffiti, then enforcing the boundary if crossed by a member of another gang—by a drive-by shooting, if necessary.

At a beat meeting on the West Side, police and the civilian beat facilitator gave the following advice about using city services to handle graffiti problems:

> The beat facilitator told residents to call police if they found graffiti on their garages. He emphasized that the more calls police get, the more resources are allocated to them. A police officer told the residents to call Graffiti Blasters instead, and passed out information about the program. A resident said she called 911 about the graffiti and nothing happened. The female officer explained the process of calling the non-emergency [311] number and filing a report over the phone. The officer passed out waivers to the residents to shorten the process of having the graffiti removed (the waivers give the city permission to use soda blasters and cleaning materials on the resident's property).

In addition to forming Graffiti Blaster teams, the city approved an ordinance banning the over-the-counter sale of cans of spray paint, one of the perpetrators' favorite tools. The ordinance was challenged in federal court by the National Association of Paint Manufacturers, who argued that the ban was an unconstitutional blow against interstate commerce. The first judge to hear the case agreed that the benefits of the ban did not outweigh its costs (this despite my expert testimony in court that graffiti was bad for neighborhood property values), so the judge's application of this legal "balancing test" found for the paint manufacturers. Later, he was overruled by a federal appeals court, and the ban again went into effect (*National Paint & Coatings Association, et al. v. City of Chicago,* 1995).

As figure 7.1 documents, reports of serious graffiti problems declined among all groups between 1994 and 1999, before leveling off for whites and African Americans. Graffiti was cited as a big problem by 22 percent of Chicagoans interviewed in 1994, and by 11 percent in 2003. However, all of this concern was among whites and African Americans. Concern among Latinos jumped sharply in 2001 and remained at its 1998 level in the last survey, in 2003. The gap between Latinos and others in the city was the largest for graffiti, which now appears to be a problem primarily plaguing Latino neighborhoods.

Abandoned Buildings

At the other end of the spectrum, only 11 percent of respondents interviewed in 1994 reported that building abandonment was a big problem in their community. But that number varied greatly by group, with only a few whites, but many African Americans (and, by 1995, Latinos) reporting that abandoned buildings were a concern for them. Building abandonment is a question of economics. It is heavily concentrated in the city's poorest areas, where it is most difficult to make reasonable rates of return by investing in housing because people do not have much to pay. In poor areas of the city absentee landlords and struggling property owners may be unwilling or unable to maintain their buildings. Though often constructed of brick and stone (a legacy in the building code enacted in the wake of the Great Chicago Fire of 1871), the ravages of time, weather, and decades of neglect have left many buildings in poor neighborhoods with crumbling mortar, pooled paint, rotten framing, broken windows, and leaky roofs. If left empty for long, scavengers pick them clean of items of value, including stained glass, light fixtures, elaborate wooden molding, copper electrical wiring, and bathroom fixtures. Even aluminum siding will be stripped overnight and exchanged for cash at recycling centers. Squatters may move in, and drug dealers find it easy to set up shop. Eventually many of these hulks are razed as part of the city's aggressive "tear-down" abandonment strategy, because they are no longer habitable and no one can be found make the investment necessary to return them to use. At a beat meeting our observer noted:

"A resident complained about an abandoned building. The beat officer said the building is 'terrible, terrible, terrible.' He said the owner has never done anything to secure the building from squatters. A resident said that it is illegal for the building to be open. The beat officer replied that he and his partner have put in service requests every week for the past few months. A resident volunteered to call city services. The sergeant told the resident to be sure to mention the police requests."

There are several city programs for moving against abandoned buildings, including the Strategic Inspections Task Force (SITF) described earlier, but of all the problems in Chicago, building issues can be the slowest to be resolved. The rights of property owners must be respected, so owners must be involved before their buildings can be demolished or rehabilitated. But owners can often be difficult to track down, as Illinois allows landlords to hold property in secret land trusts that enable them to hide their identity from tenants. Police have to use building department records, tax files, tools on the Internet, and old-fashioned detective work to run them to earth.

However, over time there was no real overall change in the extent of resident concern about abandoned buildings. In 1994, 28 percent of Chicagoans reported it was some or a big problem in their neighborhoods, and in 2003 the figure was 26 percent. As figure 7.1 documents, decreasing concern by African Americans was counterbalanced by heightened concern about abandoned buildings among the city's Latinos. By 2003, Latinos were about 10 percentage points more likely than blacks to report serious building-abandonment problems.

Trash and Junk

In the 1994 survey, about one-quarter of African Americans and Latinos, but only 5 percent of whites, reported that loose trash and junk were a big problem in their neighborhoods. In two poor African American beats that we studied in detail, many vacant lots were used as makeshift parking lots for cars, trucks, and abandoned vehicles. The lots were not only ugly, they posed a health hazard, for tall weeds, accumulating trash, and abandoned vehicles inevitably become nesting spots for rats. Overgrown vacant lots are convenient hiding places for stashes of drugs and weapons that drug dealers do not want to keep on their person. Vacant lots also attract illegal dumpers, who deposit their loads there rather than paying hefty fees charged by licensed landfills. Loose trash and junk generally require a city-service response. The following discussion took place at a beat meeting on the Near South Side:

> A woman asks the tactical officers to ride down and check the end of the alley where there is a lot of overgrowth, couches, and even grills sitting under a tree where people loiter in the abandoned lot. An officer responded that he has been by the lot and he only saw old guys hanging out there, and what first must be taken care of is the grass and weeds. The woman continues to complain about the weeds in the lot and how high they are. The officer tells her he will write up a work order and call city services to file a complaint, and that he will speak to her after the meeting to get all the information from her.

Vacant lots require maintenance and supervision to prevent them from becoming problems for the community. If owners will not maintain their properties, cleaning them becomes the responsibility of the city's streets department. If the property is owned by the city, complaints can lead to their enclosure by a fence to prevent further dumping. Private owners of lots requiring cleaning are ticketed in order to recoup some of the cost. As documented in figure 7.1, African Americans' level of concern about loose trash and junk dropped through 1999 and then leveled off. Concern remained high among Latinos, on the other hand, countering other citywide gains during the 1990s.

Abandoned Cars

In 1994, abandoned cars were nominated as a big problem by 20 percent of Latinos and 12 percent of African Americans. Abandoned cars are easy targets for city towing, but—like building problems—there are legal niceties that must be observed unless a vehicle is creating a direct safety hazard. At a beat meeting on the Near Southeast Side:

> A resident complained of a car that has no license plates and has not moved in several weeks. The officer said that they would take care of it, but that [residents] should not wait for a meeting to complain about this. Several residents confirmed that there is rapid response to towing requests. A resident noted that an abandoned car on her block had been ticketed but that it was still sitting on the street. The CAPS organizer [from

the Implementation Office] informed residents that a car without proper stickers left on the street for seven days is considered abandoned and should be called in to the city.

Figure 7.1 documents that concern about abandoned cars actually
grew a bit during the period we monitored. While concern among
African Americans and whites essentially remained steady, over
time Latino respondents were more likely to report that abandoned
cars were a big problem in their community.

Decay and the Three Chicagos

Continual surveys of residents indicate that there was no "citywide"
trend in CAPS-related physical decay issues over this nine-year period. Instead, the surveys point to race-related variations in trends
over time. In a nutshell, surveys indicate that whites began with few
serious concerns about physical decay issues, and things did not
change much for them. Except for graffiti, even during the early
years of the program few whites were concerned about neighborhood
decay. African Americans began with many serious problems, but
they reported improvements in neighborhood conditions over time.
Initially, they were nine times more likely than whites to think that
abandoned buildings were a big neighborhood problem, for example,
and five times more likely to give the highest rating to junk and trash
problems. But during the 1990s, reports of serious neighborhood
decay problems by African Americans declined sharply. Concern
about abandoned buildings dropped by half, from 22 percent to
11 percent, and concern about refuse-filled lots and graffiti declined
by about 10 percentage points. The city's Latinos, on the other hand,
began with serious problems and saw little improvement over the
course of a decade. Even an apparent turnaround in serious graffiti
problems stalled in the early twenty-first century. By 2003, it was
whites and African Americans who were in the most agreement
about improvements in their neighborhoods—although African
Americans certainly still had a way to go before they could claim
parity. Nothing improved for Latinos, and some problems even grew
worse. We will return to an examination of causes of these trends in
a later section of this chapter. It reports that concern about physical decay was driven by language, immigration, growing poverty,
and the increasing concentration of Latinos in the city's emerging
Spanish-speaking barrios.

Social Disorder

The repeated administration of surveys also enables us to examine trends in social disorder over time. Responses to three survey questions were used to assess the extent of neighborhood social disorder. Unlike the other questions, these about the extent of loitering and public drinking were not included until 1995, the year that CAPS became a citywide program. The conditions described were:

Public drinking;
Groups of people hanging out on corners or in the streets; and
Disruption around schools, that is, youths hanging around making noise, vandalizing, or starting fights.

In 1995, correlations among responses to these questions averaged +.52, and had a combined reliability of .76. They, too, will be examined as a combined measure in some of the analyses that follow.

Loitering

In 1995, loitering was the most highly rated problem in the survey. That year, 23 percent of Chicagoans reported that loitering bands of people were a big problem in their neighborhood, and another 33 percent thought they were some problem. Loitering received this high priority in part because many Chicagoans associate loitering with a host of related problems, including gang activity, violence, street gambling, public harassment, drug sales, public drinking, and other activities. When asked about his neighborhood's biggest problem, a respondent to a special neighborhood survey replied: "Teenagers. No respect. There's no curfew; you hear them cursing, hanging on the corners." Others pointed to problems like "People on the corners in the liquor stores cause fear to other people"; and "Guys hanging on the corners all night long."

Loitering became a major political issue in Chicago when the city council instituted an "anti-gang loitering" ordinance giving police officers the authority to arrest loiterers known to be gang members who do not move along when ordered to do so (cf. Rosenthal 2001). The ordinance took effect in 1993 and led to about ten thousand arrests each year. It was ultimately declared unconstitutional by the United States Supreme Court, in the case of *City of Chicago v. Morales* (*U.S. Supreme Court Reports* 1999), but tens of thousands of Chicago residents signed petitions declaring that their neighborhoods would be safer places if such a law were in place. Later the city council passed a revised version of the ordinance that created a restricted number of sites in which loitering could be forbidden, and required police to be specially trained in enforcing the new ordinance.

Whatever the policy, loitering primarily afflicted minority communities. In 1994, only 11 percent of white Chicagoans rated loitering a big problem in their neighborhood, while for African Americans the comparable figure was 39 percent, and among Latinos it was 32 percent. Figure 7.2 summarizes trends in this view and indicates that little changed over time. Except for a 1999 drop in the rate among African Americans, which was later largely negated, members of all three groups reported about the same level of concern about loitering in 2003 as they did in 1995. Regarding loitering, the experiences of Latinos and African Americans were very much in agreement over the entire nine-year period. By 2003, loitering was still of great public concern, ranking just below street drug dealing on our list. While in 1995, 56 percent of Chicagoans thought it was some-

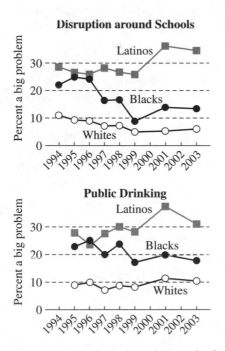
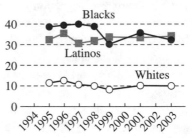

Figure 7.2. Trends in Social Disorder by Race, 1994–2003

what or a big problem in their communities, in 2003 the total was 57 percent.

Public Drinking

Overall, 17 percent of Chicagoans rated public drinking a big problem in their neighborhoods in 1995. Public drinking is a visible, everyday pastime in some of the poor Latino and African American beats that we have studied intensively. In one South Side area, groups of men (and a few women) regularly congregated near liquor stores—usually in vacant lots—or they sat on milk crates and curbs in alleys and on street corners, never straying far from carryout liquor outlets. There they sat, passing around bottles wrapped in brown paper, surrounded by overgrown weeds, empty snack food bags, cans, and broken bottles. When the police asked them to move, they never went far, shuffling around the corner or to the other side of the street, just enough to give the illusion of movement. Within minutes, however, the group would congregate again. An observer on the city's South Side noted:

> Without community pressure, beat officers may not come down hard on the drinkers. One noted, "I know them; they're out here everyday. [Several of the drinkers had, in fact, greeted him by name.] Mostly they're harmless, but they do litter, they urinate in public, and they set a bad example for kids. Adults drinking on the street all day do not make positive role models." In another beat, the day-watch officer had less patience. Once, after several unsuccessful attempts to clear away a group of recalcitrant drinkers with his loudspeaker, he drove his squad car onto the sidewalk to disperse them.

In addition, these bands may sometimes be selling drugs. A liquor store owner in the area said he had learned not to call police because he had been threatened in the past. "Once I did call police because they were dealing in front of my store. They broke my car windows and threatened me. I try to be polite and ask these people to move on, but they disrespect me, call me names, and threaten me. I don't think it should be my job to get involved. It is too dangerous. That is the police's job."

Noting that public drinkers usually congregate around their source of supply, police and neighborhood activists often look to the city's "vote dry" referenda to close down the liquor stores. An observer encountered this presentation at a beat meeting held on the Far South Side:

> The neighborhood relations officer then introduced Anthony _____, a member of _____ Church. [Anthony _____] explained to residents that members of his church and other residents were working to make the 9th and 34th wards "dry" and that the only way to get undesirable people off the streets is to close the liquor stores. Last year, four hundred church members circulated petitions to get a referendum asking to close liquor establishments placed on a ballot. They were successful in getting some liquor stores closed. The members plan to start circulating petitions in June and continue until August. Anthony told residents that they would be paired up with another person to get signatures, and he would pass out flyers later.

Reports that public drinking were either somewhat of a problem or a big problem in the area did not decline much during the 1990s, beginning at 52 percent and ending at 50 percent in 2003. However, these citywide figures disguised a drop in concern among African Americans and a big increase in concern among Latinos. This is illustrated in figure 7.2, which plots the percentage of Chicagoans indicating that public drinking was a big problem in their neighborhoods. At the high point in 2001, almost 40 percent of Latinos reported that public drinking was a big problem in their neighborhoods. During our fieldwork we also noted frequent problems associated with alcohol in areas where new immigrants are concentrated. As one civilian CAPS employee observed: "The Little Village area does have problems with night clubs. Both the larger venues and smaller corner bars that get packed with people getting drunk, cruising the neighborhoods, and potentially getting in trouble because of drunk driving. The bars are also selling liquor to minors."

But bands of men could also be observed drinking along the commercial arterial streets and in residential parts of the area. A district advisory committee (DAC) member from the Pilsen neighborhood thought "public drinking might be something cultural, since people in Pilsen tend to drink outside rather than inside a bar." Another DAC representative indicated that "drinking on the public way, urinating on people's property, and gambling on the corners (shooting craps) are all main problems in the neighborhood." Another city CAPS worker referred to public drinking as a social issue: "Once [men] have drinks they'll leave glasses outside and, in their buzzed condition they'll be intolerant of the spouse and kids," adding that such scenarios could lead to domestic violence.

School Disruption

Disorder around local schools was identified as a big problem by 18 percent of Chicagoans in the 1994 survey. School security issues were described by a police officer at a beat meeting on the Near West Side: "The sergeant brought up problems at _____ School. Because of the warm weather, problems that they normally expected in late March through May were starting now. Girls were getting more involved with gang activity. These elementary school girls were selling marijuana and carrying guns. He wanted to make parents aware and have them look for signs, such as gang-type graffiti on books, and what kids take and bring home in their book bags. Both boys and girls are susceptible." At another monthly meeting residents of the same beat debated what to do about problems around the same school:

> A resident asked what she can do when kids make a lot of noise in the street after 11 p.m. An officer told her to call the police who can pick the kids up and take them home. Another resident said there is a problem with kids out late on a school playground. She said there are not enough lights on the playground and that a lot of kids hang out there. An officer asked when the kids are there. She said they are at the school and then go to a house every Thursday through Sunday night. A neighborhood relations officer suggested the residents talk to the principal of the school to see if they can lock the gates after hours to keep people out.

Disruption in and around schools was of particular concern to parents. For example, 34 percent of Latinos interviewed in 1995 who had children at home also reported that school security was a big problem, while among Latino householders without children, the comparable figure was only 12 percent. School disruption is a real issue for the city's Latinos because they are the group with the most children. In the 2003 survey, 61 percent of English-speaking Latino respondents reported having children living at home, as did 70 percent of Spanish-speaking respondents. By contrast, the comparable figure was 26 percent for whites and 49 percent among African Americans.

Between 1994 and 2003 the largest overall drop in the social disorder category was in reports of school disruption. In 1994, 50 percent reported school disruption was not a problem at all in their neighborhoods, a figure that rose to 59 percent by 2003. Figure 7.2, which charts the percentage of Chicagoans indicating that school disruption was a big problem, illustrates that this decline was confined to whites and African Americans. School disorder problems did not improve for Latinos during the 1990s, and they spiked even higher in the first years of the twenty-first century.

Significantly, the findings of these surveys with adults are corroborated by students themselves. The Chicago Consortium for School Research conducts period surveys of high school students.[3] In 1994, 1997, 1999, and 2001, students were asked to rate how safe they felt in their schools. During this period students in predominantly African American high schools reported the largest gains in school safety, followed by those in racially diverse schools. Students in predominantly Latino schools reported improving conditions between 1994 and 1999, but then the trend reversed itself, and by 2001, statistically, they were the least safe group in the Chicago public schools.

Overall, however, the most substantial decline in social disorder in Chicago was associated with schools, because of large improvements noted by African Americans and whites. As we have seen, many positive changes and aggressive security efforts were underway in the city's public schools, in parallel with CAPS. On the other hand, school crime was down nationwide during this period as well. National survey reports of theft, rape, and assault declined by one-third between 1992 and 1999, and total victimization at school was down by 20 percent (*Chicago Tribune* 2000). The city may have simply been sharing in that general trend.

Social Disorder and the Three Chicagos

It is apparent that some city residents felt better off during the course of the 1990s, while others did not. Little changed in the city's predominantly white neighborhoods over this period. Few whites reported serious neighborhood social disorder problems even before CAPS became a citywide program, and over the ensuing period they still managed to witness significant improvement in school-related problems. None of the problems in the social disorder cluster were top rated by more than about 10 percent of whites.

The bulk of the improvements was registered by African Americans. They expressed substantial concern about social disorder during the early years of CAPS. In 1994, almost 40 percent of blacks thought group loitering was a big problem in their neighborhoods; the figures for school disruption and public drinking were 22 percent and 23 percent, respectively. But over time, African Americans reported modest improvements in neighborhood conditions. The percentage of African Americans expressing concern about disruption in and around schools dropped to only eight percent in 1999, before rebounding a bit to 14 percent in 2003. Concern about public drinking was also down a bit, before leveling off at the beginning of the twenty-first century.

On the other hand, there was little good news for the city's Latinos. As figure 7.2 illustrated, in 1994 and 1995, African Americans and Latinos reported about the same level of concern about social disorder. But by 1999, the experiences of the two groups diverged dramatically. Latinos reported deteriorating conditions in and around the schools serving their neighborhoods, and concern about public drinking jumped considerably.

What Happened to Latinos in Chicago?

The Chicago story begins with Latinos and African Americans at the beginning of the 1990s living in about the same conditions.[4] On five of the seven disorder and decay problems considered in this chapter, Latinos and African Americans gave their neighborhoods comparable ratings. But as the decade progressed, the story became more complex as the views of the two groups diverged. What lay behind these contrasting trends during the 1994–2003 period? Part of the answer can be found in demographic and survey data for these groups. In brief, the Latino community is under pressure from immigration and internal growth, and in response it has cleaved apart. Things have gotten better for established, English-speaking Latinos living in racially diverse areas; they have grown worse for Spanish speakers concentrated in the city's developing, heavily Latino barrios. Because the number of barrio-dwellers is growing faster than the number of their counterparts, Chicago's Latinos, as a group, have found themselves progressively worse off. By contrast, the city's African American community is not expanding. Its numbers are static, and there is not much immigration from the American South or elsewhere. While they are differentiated by class, trends in Chicago's African American areas have been much more uniform—and things have gotten more uniformly better—during this nine-year period.

The effects of immigration on the composition of the Latino population can be seen in the surveys. Because they arrive without much formal education, Latino immigrants have had the effect of pushing down average levels of education for the group as a whole. In our 1994 survey, 71 percent of those identified as Latinos reported having a high school degree; by 2003 that figure had dropped to 64 percent. The Spanish-language version of the survey included questions designed to reflect the educational experiences of persons from Mexico, but responses to these questions can also be combined with U.S. educational categories. The effects of immigration from Mexico reflect the national pattern. Immigrants from Mexico and Central America bring with them low levels of educational attainment, even in comparison to immigrants from South America or the Caribbean (U.S. Bureau of the Census 1999).

The results of continued immigration can also be read in respondents' language of choice in the surveys. Spanish-speaking interviewers screened and interviewed the randomly selected respondents when they preferred to be interviewed in Spanish. Using this indicator of linguistic preference, about one-third of Latino respondents were classed as Spanish speakers in the 1994 survey; in 1997 that figure was 49 percent, and by 2003 it was 54 percent, a tremendous demographic change.

A final key point about demographic change among Chicago's Latinos is that during the course of the 1990s they became more geographically concentrated. Between the 1990 U.S. Census and the 2000 U.S. Census, Chicago's Latino population grew from 546,000 to 754,000, and most of this growth was concentrated in a growing number of heavily Latino neighborhoods on the city's West and Near North sides. Figure 7.3 presents a map depicting areas of Latino concentration in 2003, based on our population estimates. Between 1990 and 2000, the number of Latinos living in beats that were at least 50 percent Latino in composition in 1990 rose from 290,400 to 491,600, a 69 percent increase. By contrast, the number of Latinos living in beats that were less than 50 percent Latino in 1990 grew by only two percent. By 2000, two-thirds of all Chicago's Latinos lived in majority-Latino police beats.

An illustration of the effects of these factors is depicted in figure 7.4, which combines the results of surveys and the 2000 U.S. Census.

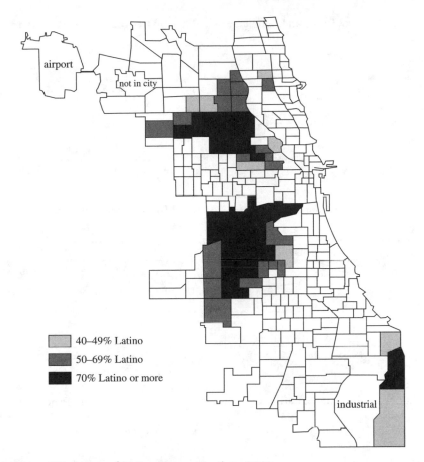

Figure 7.3. Areas of Latino Concentration, 2003

The impact of geographic concentration is depicted in the rightmost panels. They classify Latino respondents by the composition of the beat in which they lived, which could range from near zero to virtually 100 percent Latino in the lower-right hand panel. Figure 7.4 classifies beats into five categories, ranging from areas that were less than 20 percent Latino according to the census, to those that were more than 75 percent Latino. It charts this in relation to the beats' scores on measures that combine responses to the physical decay and social disorder on the 1999, 2001, and 2003 city surveys. The percent who averaged replying that these were a "big problem" in their neighborhood is displayed in figure 7.4. As the figure illustrates, among Latinos, reports of serious disorder and decay prob-

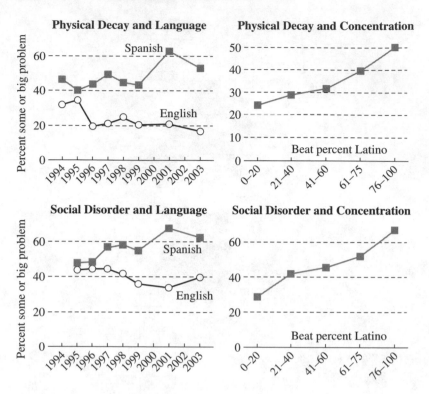

Figure 7.4. Language, Latino Concentration, and Neighborhood Problems, 1994–2003

lems grow in frequency with the concentration of their coethnics in their beat. The effects are roughly linear (the lines rise smoothly) for both. In beats that are less than 20 percent Latino, about 25 percent of Latinos report that—on average, for the three individual problem measures—social disorder is some or a big problem in their areas. In beats that are more than 75 percent Latino, the comparable figure was almost 70 percent. The trend line for physical decay is almost as steep. As we shall see below, the effects of neighborhood concentration persist when other individual and neighborhood factors are taken into account.

The diverging experience of English- and Spanish-speaking Latinos is depicted in the left panels of figure 7.4. Survey respondents who preferred to be interviewed in Spanish reported more extensive neighborhood problems than did their English-speaking counterparts, and this was especially true as the decade wore on. For example, in 2001, the individual-level decay-language correlation was +.41, and that for social disorder was +.38. Figure 7.4 charts trends over time in the percentage of respondents reporting that, on average, social disorder and physical decay were more than just some problems in their neighborhood, breaking down respondents by language. Spanish speakers always reported more problems, but over time the two groups began to report more divergent experiences. Much of the difference was due to reports of worsening conditions by Spanish speakers. One reason for this divergence was the increasing concentration of incoming Latinos in beats that were heavily populated by Spanish speakers. By 2001, conditions for Spanish-speaking Latinos were the worst for any demographic group we examined. This continued to be the case despite a small rebound by 2003.

How well do the social forces examined here explain the deteriorating conditions reported by the city's Latinos, especially during the crucial period in the late 1990s when things seemed to go wrong in a substantial way? Table 7.1 presents two multilevel analyses that probe the joint effect of individual and neighborhood-level factors that may help explain trends in concern about social disorder and physical decay among Chicago's Latinos. The dependent variables are indices combining replies to the four questions concerning the extent of physical decay problems (their combined reliability was .76) and replies to the three social-disorder measures, using school disorder as the measure for 1994 (in 1995 the three had a combined reliability of .77). The table examines the opinions of 2,940 respondents interviewed between 1994 and 2003.[5]

A long list of individual factors are included in order to account for the many changing demographic features of the Latino population over this period. The beat-level factors include factor scores that measure the extent of poverty and the degree of residential stability in each, along with measures of the concentration of Latinos in each beat. The neighborhood context data are organized so that the beat in which each respondent lives is described by interpolated or projected census data for the year in which he or she was interviewed. For example, respondents interviewed in 1993 are linked to estimates of 1993 census characteristics for their beat, while those interviewed in 2003 are linked to census estimates for that year. In total, Latino respondents were situated in 917 distinct year-beat contexts. Technically, this is a "fixed effects" model for estimating the joint impact of individual and context-level measures on fear of crime, so the results presented here are akin to those of a standard OLS regression

Table 7.1 Hierarchical Models of Physical Decay and Social Disorder, Latinos 1994–2003

	Physical Decay		Social Disorder	
	Coefficient	Standard error	Coefficient	Standard error
Intercept	1.61	.05	1.76	.05
Personal Background				
Spanish language	.31**	.03	.20**	.03
High school graduate	−.12**	.03	−.08**	.03
Female	−.02	.02	.00	.02
Homeowner	.00	.03	−.03	.02
Income over $40,000	−.07**	.03	−.10**	.03
Decades of residence	.03*	.00	.07**	.00
Employed	−.01	.03	.03	.02
Children at home	.05	.03	.06*	.03
Married	−.03	.02	−.03	.03
Age 60 and older	−.22**	.08	−.24**	.08
Beat-level Factors				
Poverty index (z)	.13**	.02	.15**	.02
Stability index (z)	−.10**	.02	−.14**	.02
Percent Latino (z)	.05**	.02	.06**	.02
Intraclass Correlation	11%		4%	
Variance Explained				
Within-neighborhood	10%		8%	
Between-neighborhood	81%		80%	
Number of Cases				
Individuals	2940		2940	
Contexts	917		917	

*p < .05; **p < .01; "z" indicates standardized variable.

model. The difference is that the intercept for the individual-level equation predicting fear is allowed to vary from beat to beat; this enables us to parcel out contextual ("between neighborhood") effects from individual ("within neighborhood") effects, while in OLS regression, the former are confounded with the latter.

Except for decades of residence in the neighborhood, all of the personal characteristics presented in table 7.1 are dichotomies, so their coefficients can be compared in magnitude. The coefficients represent the difference in fear, net of other factors in the model, associated with being on one side of a demographic category rather than the other. Across the entire period, the strongest individual correlates of physical decay and social disorder were being older (which was associated with reporting less concern about these problems) and being a Spanish speaker (which was linked to perceptions of more problems). The latter reflects the great linguistic divide among Latinos that was documented above. Two measures representing affluence—education and income—were also significant correlates of lower levels of disorder and decay. As noted earlier, immigration reduced overall levels of education and affluence among Latinos over time, and increased the frequency with which respondents could only be interviewed in Spanish.

Table 7.1 also reports the impact of beat-level factors reflecting the context within which the city's Latinos were living during this period. They were standardized, so the coefficients associated with them can be compared in terms of their magnitude. In the surveys, lower levels of disorder and decay were reported by respondents living in more affluent and stable areas. Here beat stability is represented by a factor score loading heavily on home ownership and low residential turnover in the area. The poverty measure reflects the extent to which beat households were below the poverty line, receiving public aid, and female-headed families. In addition, Latinos living in areas of Latino concentration also reported more disorder and decay, although the effect of this factor was only about half that of poverty and stability. Together, the individual-level and context-level neighborhood factors listed in table 7.1 explained about 18 percent of the variance in physical decay, and 15 percent of the variance in social disorder.

In short, both individual factors that are linked to immigration and neighborhood forces that reflect, in part, the impact of immigration had a substantial effect on the life chances of Chicago's Latinos. Poverty and neighborhood stability had the biggest effect at that level, and less affluent Spanish speakers were the most likely to report disorder and decay problems in their community.

The question of how accurately these factors account for *trends* in disorder and decay over time is examined in figure 7.5. It compares trends in the measures revealed by the surveys with trends predicted by the personal and contextual factors examined in table 7.1. Together, these factors did a fairly good job of explaining changes in levels of concern about disorder and decay over time. The left-hand panel of the figure plots survey and statistical predictions of reports of physical decay problems, and the data capture both the uptick in

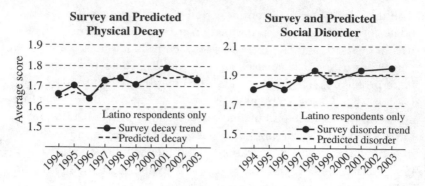

Figure 7.5. Trends in Survey and Predicted Disorder and Decay, Latinos 1994–2003

decay in the second half of the 1990s, and the fact that the trend flat-tened out in the early years of the twenty-first century. There was less over-time variance in the summary measure of social disorder, but the factors described in table 7.1 picked up the late-1990s in-crease in it as well.

The improving fortune of Chicago's African Americans was, by contrast, a relatively widespread trend. Changes for the better in re-ports of both decay and disorder problems ran in parallel for sub-groups within the black population. African Americans were divided by social class. The largest split was between homeowners and renters, who differed by about 10 percentage points on levels of social disorder, and seven percentage points on levels of physical decay. More-educated African Americans reported fewer neighbor-hood problems than did less-educated African Americans, and there were parallel differences by income as well. But although poor and better-off African Americans began with different *levels* of problems, trend lines for these groups dropped in unison between 1994 and 1999, then leveled off in the new century.

Were These Changes Due to CAPS?

As in other chapters, the best evidence of the impact of CAPS on these problems comes from the period before it became a citywide program. The 1993–1994 period offered an opportunity to contrast trends in neighborhood problems in the five prototype districts with what happened in similar, matched areas of the city. This stage of the evaluation (which is reported in Skogan and Hartnett 1997) focused on crime and physical decay, the two big targets of CAPS during the prototyping period. Surveys were conducted in the program and comparison areas before the initiative began, and again about eighteen months later. As part of the design of the two waves of surveys, a large number of respondents were interviewed both times, enabling us to directly contrast changes in their views of neighborhood conditions.

In concert with the citywide trends reported here, analysis of the survey data revealed only modest effects of the program on physical decay and disorder. In the surveys, the extent of neighborhood physical decay was measured by some of the same questions examined in this chapter. Respondents were asked to rate problems with vacant lots filled with trash and junk, abandoned cars, abandoned buildings, and graffiti. An overall measure of decay declined significantly in the three most troubled experimental areas. For two of these there was no parallel decline in matched comparison areas, and for the third district there was a smaller but statistically significant decline in the comparison area as well as the experimental area. In the worst-off area we studied, residents themselves prioritized two physical decay problems among their top four concerns. Both were the targets of concerted efforts by the police there, and both declined by a very substantial margin. The other two experimental areas were better off, and they were visibly cleaner and in better repair even before CAPS began. Respondents in one of those districts identified graffiti as a top four problem, but it did not decline significantly there during the months after the program began. There were two measures of social disorder in the 1993–1994 study. Disorder in and around schools was identified by respondents in one district as a top four problem, and over the course of the evaluation it declined noticeably but not significantly; there were no changes in the matched comparison area. Likewise, vandalism to parked cars declined, but not significantly, in another experimental area, but did not decline at all in its comparison area. These results were all read as promising, because many pointed in the right direction. The time frame for the evaluation was very short (only twelve months in three of the five districts) and there were reinterviews with only about 180 individuals in each of the targeted districts, so our expectations were modest with regard to the size of the program's potential effect and the statistical power of our measures.

How Did Chicago Do?

Together We Can, the city's blueprint for CAPS, argued that Chicago's neighborhoods could be improved "by addressing those conditions that contribute to unacceptable levels of fear and disorder."[6] It took a broad view of the responsibilities that the police were taking on. In the plan, the chief of police argued that Chicago needed "an intolerance not only for crime and violence, but also for neighborhood decay, open defiance of the law, and other disturbing and often dangerous conditions."[7] Chapter 6 reviewed some of the problem-solving organizations and activities that were fielded in response.

Surveys conducted between 1994 and 2003 found that the city's concerted attack on graffiti was one of its most generally successful projects. Otherwise, the pattern was for things to improve substantially in the eyes of African Americans, but to grow worse for Latinos. Over time, fewer and fewer African Americans reported serious public drinking and school disruption problems in their neighborhoods, and they reported fewer problems with abandoned buildings and vacant lots filled with junk and trash. But at the same time, Latinos reported greater and greater concern about most of those problems, as well as with abandoned cars. As a result, by 2003 the balance of concern about neighborhood problems had shifted dramatically in Chicago. The views of blacks trended toward those of whites, although they certainly did not end up in the relatively problem-free zone enjoyed by most of the city's whites. The worsening trend among Latinos turned out to be concentrated among the city's Spanish-speaking population; English-speaking Latinos ended up somewhere between whites and African Americans. An analysis of trends among Latinos indicates that much of these adverse trends were linked to factors associated with immigration. These included the growth in the size of the Spanish-speaking fraction of the city's population, their declining levels of education and general affluence, and their increasing concentration in unstable, poverty-stricken, predominantly Latino neighborhoods. By 2003 it could be said that none of the city's major groups was "average," and the success of CAPS depended on who you were and where you lived.

Trends in Crime and Fear

In describing the city's new community-policing program, the department's 1993 strategic plan *Together We Can* reassured readers that CAPS was not soft on crime. It stressed the importance of good traditional police work and effective crime fighting. It praised the current efforts of the force, noting that "the men and women of the Chicago Police Department have established the pace with respect to rapidly responding to calls for service, arresting offenders, and carry[ing] out other elements of the traditional policing strategy."[1] The report concluded that, "solving crimes is, and will continue to be, an essential element of police work."[2]

These points were not made casually. The management consultants who drew up a preliminary plan for CAPS had visited cities that tried, but failed, to implement community policing. They found that opponents of change had promoted the perception that adopting community-oriented policing would turn officers into "social workers." In Houston, Texas, midlevel police commanders and others who were resistant to community policing had successfully pushed the line that diverting scarce resources to this untried "social experiment" was leaving the public unprotected from crime (Booz, Allen & Hamilton, Inc. 1992). To preempt any similar assault on CAPS, top Chicago officials reiterated, in print and at public gatherings, that effective traditional police work was still required, and that it would be respected and rewarded by the department. CAPS was presented as a strategy for allocating resources and focusing the efforts of officers on each community's worst problems, beginning with crime. *Together We Can* also argued for a preventive approach to crime control, noting that research in Kansas City and elsewhere had found that many traditional policing tactics were of limited utility in keeping crime from occurring in the first place.

Some elements of community policing could be linked to crime reduction. One presumed plus of the program was an increase in information from citizens about crime and criminals. Even some officers who were otherwise skeptical about CAPS justified their new partnership with the community in terms of the network of informants it promised to deliver. Police might be more effective because they targeted persons and places identified by well-informed residents at beat meetings and other community forums. Police could hope that neighborhood mobilization around CAPS might contribute to greater watchfulness and wariness among the public. It might also lead to a greater willingness of residents to report crimes and (especially) step forward as witnesses, rather than just lying low and hoping to not be victimized. In 2002 we surveyed 643 police officers who were attending beat meetings, and more than 80 percent agreed with the statement that "without citizen cooperation, the majority of crimes would never be solved." A full 95 percent agreed that "the prevention of crime is the joint responsibility of the community and the police." CAPS also brought a new emphasis on information technology to the Chicago Police Department. From the beginning, crime analysis was considered a key component of the program. Computerized databases and mapping software were to provide a new knowledge base driving problem solving *and* traditional tactical operations.

Although fear of crime is considered by some to be a "soft" target for policing, *Together We Can* also identified its importance. In a section titled "Limitations of Traditional Policing" it concluded, "We have learned that citizen fear, not just the index crime rate, is important in measuring levels of neighborhood safety and public satisfaction with the police."[3] It went on to argue that fear was driven by neighborhood disorder as well as crime, and that "ironically, order maintenance was a function that was downplayed under the traditional model."[4] The document, which was the department's first "vision statement" concerning community policing, concluded that research had demonstrated that innovative policing tactics "can have an impact on citizen fear of crime and their support for police agencies."[5] It lamented that the department's "best efforts have not produced the necessary results: a reduction in crime and an increased sense of individual safety and neighborhood order."[6] Linking fear of crime and support for police was doubtless not an accident, either, for it helped legitimate this new measure of police performance. We will see in chapter 9, which examines citizen satisfaction with police service, that the claim was also true that during the 1990s, declining fear was associated with increasing confidence in the police. Police officers who attended beat meetings also bought into this part of the CAPS agenda. In the 2002 survey, 84 percent agreed with the statement "lowering citizens' fear of crime should be just as high a priority for this department as cutting the crime rate."

This chapter describes trends in crime and fear of crime in Chicago. Crime trends can be measured in several ways: using official figures gathered by the police and through repeated surveys that ask about neighborhood conditions and fear of crime. Each has advantages and disadvantages, and those are considered here. An early section of this chapter describes trends in officially recorded crime, which were very positive: recorded crime was down in almost every part of the city. It then considers an alternative measure of crime: assessments of its seriousness gathered through surveys. Surveys measures of crime are unconstrained by legal distinctions and people's willingness to report crimes to the police. The findings point in particular to the unique experiences of the city's large and growing Latino population. Next comes an examination of the parallel issue of trends in fear of crime. Although they are related, perceptions of crime problems and fear of crime do not necessarily change in unison. Fear is driven by a wide range of concerns and experiences, but it is no less real for its complex character. Fear of crime is an important social fact with consequences for individuals, neighborhoods, and metropolitan areas. In this light, the substantial decline in fear documented by the surveys bodes well for the city's future. A final section puts trends in Chicago in comparative perspective. Compared to other large American cities, Chicago did fairly well. In general, the drop in crime paralleled trends in other big cities, and was deeper than some. A rough comparison between national and local trends in fear of crime points to a deeper drop in Chicago than around the country.

Measuring Crime

The police department counts "recorded" crimes. Its databases include incidents that are reported to police, often by victims or their friends and relatives, *and* are determined by the officer who responded to be criminal offenses, usually after cursory investigation or an interview with the victim. As chapter 2 notes, many victimizations are not reported to the police. The proportion for Chicago is unknown, but the Chicago Police Department's own annual report accurately notes, "Annual changes [in crime] may therefore reflect a real change in the incidence of crime, a change in victims' reporting behavior, or a combination of the two."[7] Little is known about the possible impact of changes in policing styles on crime reporting. A little research in the United States and abroad suggests that effective neighborhood-oriented policing may encourage more reporting (Schneider 1976), while the perception that the criminal justice system is not taking reports seriously may discourage reporting (van Dijk 1982). Chapter 9 reports that Chicagoans' views of the police shifted in a positive direction during the course of the 1990s, so this may have boosted official crime figures. On the other hand, the growth of Chicago's Spanish-speaking population might also have impacted crime reporting—we will see in this chapter that Spanish-speaking Latinos are avoiding contact with the police whenever they can, including when they are victimized. But how much crime reporting in the city has changed or remained stable over the time period examined here remains an unknown factor.

Following victim reporting, the second step in the process that produces official crime statistics is police recording of what they are told. This is also a highly variable process. One study found that police decisions *not* to record reported robbery incidents and to dismiss them instead ranged from 2 percent to more than 60 percent, depending on the city (Skogan 1976c; see also Seidman and Couzens 1974). As noted in chapter 2, during a period in the early 1980s, police non-recording of reported robberies in Chicago stood at about 35 percent; for rape it was 50 percent, and assault 20 percent (Skogan and Gordon 1982). But like victim reporting, the impact of decisions by Chicago police on contemporary trends in recorded crime remains unknown.

However, data from the police on reported and recorded crime also have many advantages, and this chapter takes advantage of all of them. Police crime reports are available for small areas, and here they are examined separately for beats. The reports filed by officers can be broken down into detailed categories, and some of the discussion in this chapter is based on data that has been combined in new ways that have advantages over traditional crime categories. It is practical to reconstruct past trends from police files. The next section of this chapter examines recorded crime since 1991, several years before the evaluation actually began. Some offenses appear to be better reported and recorded than others (Skogan 1976a), and the analysis of crime trends in the next section includes a focus on several of those, including homicide, robbery, auto theft, and crimes of all kinds involving guns.

Much of the information recorded on police reports written at the scene is computerized, and the data on each individual incident were turned over to us for independent analysis. Because the department changed its beat boundaries twice during the course of this research, it was important to be able to arrange everything in a consistent format. The presentation here begins in 1991; before then, the information stored on the police department's data tapes was unstandardized and filled with errors, and it was impossible to geocode it accurately.[8] As it was, to include the early 1990s required hand coding thousands of individual incidents each year. Later, the department adopted a modern data management system and things got easier.

Trends in Recorded Crime

In Chicago, many categories of crime peaked in 1991 and then declined sharply. Over the 1991–2003 period, violent crime declined by 56 percent, and property crime by 37 percent. Figure 8.1 depicts trends in the crime figures submitted by the city to the FBI's Uniform Crime Reporting system. It excludes property thefts, down 26 percent, because they are so numerous it was difficult to display on the same chart. Murder and rape, the least frequent of the offenses presented here, are graphed on a separate scale (on the right) so their trends are visible. The yearly number of crimes is presented because the population of the city changed only slightly over the period. As the figure illustrates, there has been a steady decline in crime in each of these categories since its peak in 1991. The largest decline was in robbery, which dropped by 60 percent. Robbery is a closely watched crime category because it combines theft, risk to life and limb (for a gun is often involved), and predatory intent. It is seen by some as a bellwether indicator of urban trends. Between 1991 and 2003, the subset of robberies involving a gun went down (not shown) by a bit more: 63 percent. Criminal sexual assault (a local record-keeping category that approximates the FBI's rape statistic) declined 50 percent (also not shown). Aggravated assault declined by 51 percent. The assault category encompasses many kinds of offenses, including domestic violence, gang battles, bar brawls, violence in schools, and disputes between neighbors. Within this collection of offenses, gun-related crime declined more rapidly than did incidents without guns; assaults in domestic situations went down a bit more than others; and gang-related assault did not go down at all.

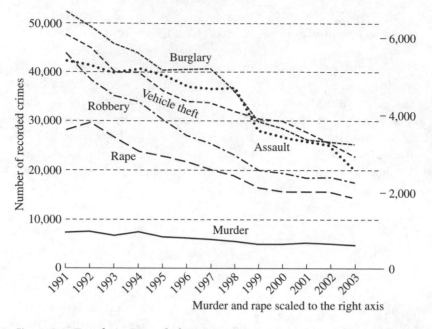

Figure 8.1. Trends in Recorded Crime, 1991–2003

Murder, by contrast, was least down over this period, by 35 percent. As in many other cities, the ability of Chicago's police to solve homicides has waned. In 1966, the Chicago Police Department claimed to have solved 94 percent of all murders, but the usual figure during the 1960s and early 1970s was in the high 80s. As late as 1986, Chicago claimed to have solved 80 percent of its murders. But then the rate at which police "cleared" homicide cases went into sharp decline. In 1990, the solution rate was 72 percent; in 1995 it was 62 percent. Between 1996 and 2000 alone, the clearance rate for homicide dropped by 10 percent, from 53 to 43 percent. Homicide clearances used to be higher because a large percentage were crimes of passion or fueled by alcohol. They involved offenders who were known or even related to their victims, or they arose out of fights in bars, and they were usually easy to solve. However, much of the nationwide decline in homicide during the course of the 1990s was in these categories.

In the early 2000s, drug-related youth violence, gang-related murders, and other more calculated killings make up a larger percentage of offenses. The changing character of victims and offenders is signaled by the fact that in 2001, the average murder victim had been arrested 8.3 times in the previous decade, and the average offender 8 times. When it is possible to figure out the motive, about half of Chicago's murders now involve either gangs, or the drug business, or both. But compared to the past, a much larger percentage of these cases are now classified as "motive unknown," "relationship unknown," and "stranger on stranger" cases, and these can be difficult to solve. In 1972, police reported they could not uncover much about offenders— for example, even their relationship with the victim remained unknown—in 8 percent of homicides. In 1986 that figure was 21 percent; in 1990 it was 29 percent; in 1998 it was 37 percent; and by 2000 it was 42 percent. As the number of homicides in Chicago declined during the 1990s, a larger percentage of what was left was difficult to solve, at least by the traditional routines of the police department.

There are other ways of classifying offenses, and crimes in some of the most significant alternate categories also registered significant declines. For this purpose we sorted and categorized more than 7.8 million crime incident records for the 1991–2003 period. A category of special significance is gun crime, for in many ways it is gun use that differentiates American crime from that of other nations (Zimring and Hawkins 1997). Combining all offenses in which a gun was used in some way, there was a 59 percent drop in the level of gun crime in Chicago. Holdups of commercial establishments and store customers were less common than street robbery, but they also declined by 59 percent. Another offense category that resonates politically is "street crime." To create a street-crime index, personal-crime incidents of all kinds were classified by their location to identify crimes that took place on the street or sidewalks, in alleys and parks, along the lakefront, or in parking lots and driveways. By this measure, street crime declined by 49 percent.

In the property-crime category, motor vehicle theft was down by 52 percent. This offense is accurately reported by victims and recorded by police, because of the high value of the average loss and the fact that most cars and trucks are insured against theft. Stolen vehicles are also sometimes recovered, which is another reason to keep accurate reports. Burglary, which typically involves break-ins of businesses, homes, or garages went down 62 percent. Burglary just of residences and garages dropped 47 percent. A separate measure of thefts from commercial establishments registered a 31 percent decline.

Race and Trends in Crime

Who enjoyed the benefits of the large drop in crime? To answer this, the city's police beats were grouped by their racial composition, based on the 1990 census. In 1990, there were 71 predominantly white beats, 121 heavily African American areas, 32 areas of concentrated Latino residence, and 46 diverse areas that were impossible to classify in simple fashion. There are 279 beats in the city, but only 270 of them are substantially residential (although often still mixed) in character. The remainder includes large commercial or industrial areas that are home to only a small number of people, and several beats located in the central business district. The aggregated groups of beats differed in size, so the analysis here reports yearly rates of crime per one hundred thousand persons living in each area. This principally accounts for the fact that some predominantly white beats in 1990 lost population by 2000, while many predominantly Latino areas gained population over the same period.

Figure 8.2 presents trends for selected personal crimes. As it illustrates, between 1991 and 2003 crime was down in all or most areas, but it declined most dramatically in predominantly African American beats. These were the same areas in which personal violence was disproportionately concentrated at the beginning of the 1990s. In predominantly African American beats, robbery dropped by 62 percent, rape (which is not shown here) by 48 percent, and homicide by 33 percent. A 33 percent decline in assault (also not shown) in African American beats was paralleled by a 39 percent decline in heavily Latino areas. Robbery in predominantly white areas dropped 45 percent, and for Latinos it was 56 percent. Crime rates generally declined the least in predominantly white areas, where they were not very high at the outset. However, in percentage terms, even residents of white beats enjoyed significant declines in violent crime during the course of the 1990s.

A significant trend illustrated in figure 8.2 is the decline in gun crime. In comparison to other areas, the most distinctive feature of crime in Chicago's predominantly African American beats is the use of guns. In every crime category, both the gun crime rate and the percentage of crimes that involve guns are highest there. In 1991, for example, 41 percent of all robbery in predominantly African American beats involved a firearm, compared to 34 percent in white areas, and 32 percent in predominantly Latino beats. Virtually every homicide in African American areas was by gun. Increased handgun use was

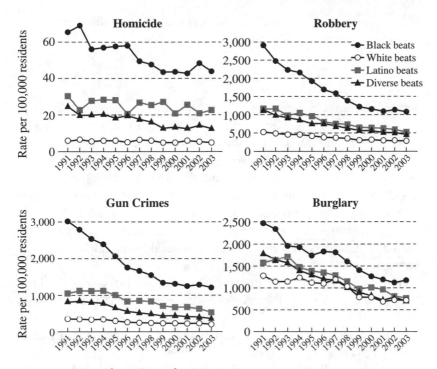

Figure 8.2. Trends in Crime by Race, 1991–2003

associated with much of the run-up in crime in these areas during the late 1980s (Wintemute 2000; Block and Martin 1997). Thus it was doubly significant that during the 1990s both the number of gun crimes and the percentage of personal offenses involving a gun dropped there the most. The gun crime rate dropped by 60 percent in predominantly African American areas. Gun crime also declined by 49 percent in heavily Latino areas.

Figure 8.2 presents parallel trends for an important property crime: burglary. The biggest decline in the burglary category was registered by African Americans, for whom it declined by 52 percent. For whites the comparable figure was 45 percent, and for Latinos it was also 52 percent. On the other hand, motor vehicle theft (which is not shown) dropped the most in predominantly white areas, by 60 percent, while rates were down 41 percent in African American beats, and 48 percent in predominantly Latino areas. General property theft (also not shown) was down 30 percent in white areas to 35 percent everywhere but in racially diverse communities. In general, racial differences in property crime were notably smaller than they were in the personal-crime category.

Crime in Decline

One of the most important features of the drop in crime in Chicago was that it was a general one. Crime was down virtually everywhere. Between 1991 and 2002, aggravated assault declined in 80 percent of the city's beats, and rape declined in 87 percent of all beats. Robbery was down in 98 percent of beats, and all crimes involving a gun declined in 97 percent of these police areas. Murder was down the least, in 70 percent of beats. These calculations were made by subtracting the 1991–1992 crime rate for each residential beat from its 2001–2002 figure. A two-year average was used to smooth out chance fluctuations in crime rates for small areas.

However, it is apparent that the real Chicago story was the initially high level of crime in African American beats. This was not unusual; in general, crime is extremely concentrated in a few communities, even in urban areas (Krivo and Peterson 1996; Massey and Denton 1993). By the beginning of the twenty-first century, Chicago was a substantially safer place than it was twelve years before, and residents of predominantly African American areas had seen much of that improvement. Declining crime in those beats largely powered the drop in violent crime in the city. Figure 8.3 presents two maps of the city that illustrate the dramatic consequences of this decline for the safety of African Americans in Chicago.

The left panel of figure 8.3 identifies fifty-two residential beats with the highest rates of robbery in 1991–1992. These high-crime beats all exceeded three hundred robberies per ten thousand residents. During that period they accounted for just 12 percent of the population of the city, but were home to 34 percent of the robberies. They were all predominantly poor, African American areas; at the median, these fifty-two beats were 98 percent black, and more than one-third of the households were headed by single women. In contrast, the right panel presents the *four* residential beats where the robbery rate exceeded three hundred in 2001–2002. All were above the three hundred threshold in 1991–1992 as well, but the remaining forty-eight beats had dropped below that level by the turn of the century. The fifty-two high-crime beats reported 27,380 robberies during 1991–1992, but they were home to just 8,159 in 2001–2002.

The magnitude of this decline can be further illustrated by calcu-

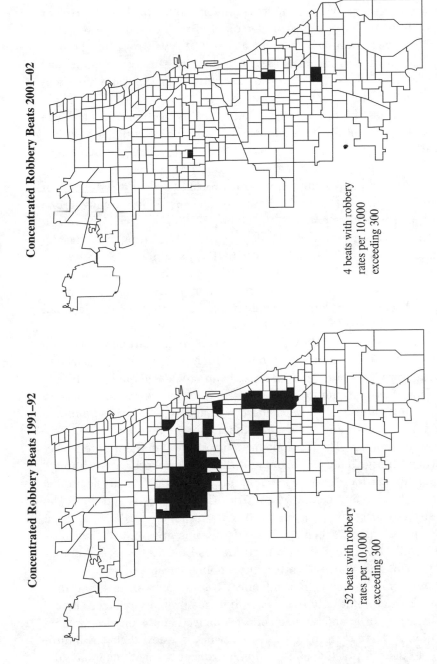

Concentrated Robbery Beats 2001–02

Concentrated Robbery Beats 1991–92

4 beats with robbery
rates per 10,000
exceeding 300

52 beats with robbery
rates per 10,000
exceeding 300

Figure 8.3. High-Rate Robbery Beats, 1991–1992 and 2001–2002

245

lating some "What if?" numbers. These forecast what would have happened if crime had *not* dropped in the fifty-two high-robbery beats. In the real world, the total robbery count in these areas over the entire period was just under ninety-five thousand. However, *if* robbery had continued to occur at its 1991 level, by 2002 the total would have been almost 182,000 robberies. In that hypothetical world there would have been about eighty-seven thousand more robbery victims in just those fifty-two beats.

What was the direct role of CAPS in this decline in crime? The best evidence of the added impact of community policing on crime in Chicago comes from the 1993–1995 period during which CAPS was developed in the experimental districts. Skogan and Hartnett (1997) concluded that the program probably led to a reduction in crime in three of the five areas. As measured by surveys, crime dropped in all five police districts, but did not outpace all trends in some of the matched comparison areas. Gang and drug problems declined significantly in three districts. For example, in the worst-off district, reports of serious street drug markets dropped from 62 to 49 percent, and from 66 to 53 percent in the next-worst areas. Officially recorded auto theft, burglary, robbery, and assault generally declined (or remained stable) in parallel with the survey findings.

After CAPS went citywide it became much more difficult to tie the program to changes in crime rates, which are seemingly correlated with every social ill and measure of economic disadvantage. Chicago police of course continued to innovate in other ways, in response to changing patterns of crime. The city's lagging decline in homicide did not pass without notice, and the mayor goaded the police to action in response. The local media concentrated on the difference between Chicago's murder count and that of New York City. Although the latter has more than twice Chicago's population, by the beginning of the twenty-first century, New York City had fewer murders. The year 2001 also saw an actual uptick in the local murder total, from 631 to 665 cases. When these trends became apparent in December 2001, the *Chicago Tribune*'s headline read, "City to Get a Dubious Title: No. 1 in Murder." In response, police became more aggressive about searching for violent offenders wanted on warrants, and they patrolled more heavily in areas with concentrated violence. The department's drug-enforcement efforts focused more on drug-related violence. They reorganized detective work in a few districts, returning to the old practice of assigning murder investigations to an elite homicide squad rather than parceling them out to detectives with more diverse caseloads. A series of forums chaired by the chief of police led to increased interagency cooperation in tackling violence in one of the city's highest homicide zones.

But focusing on establishing a direct link between CAPS and crime decline would be to miss what the program is really about. Across the nation, community policing is essentially about recapturing the legitimacy that police have, in large measure, lost in many of America's minority communities. The same opinion polls show that African Americans and recent immigrants have dramatically less confidence in the police, and are much more likely to believe that they are brutal and corrupt (Skogan and Steiner 2004a). They are the only growing part of the population in a surprisingly large number of American cities, and civic leaders know that they have to find ways to incorporate them into the system. Police take on community policing in part because they hope that building a reservoir of public support may help them get through episodes of nasty misconduct when they (inevitably) occur. Community policing might help police be more effective. Indirectly, it might help rebuild the social and organizational fabric of neighborhoods that previously had been given up for lost, enabling residents to contribute to maintaining order in their communities (Sampson, Raudenbush, and Earls 1997). However, as noted in chapter 1, I do not know of a single police department that adopted community policing just because it thought that it was the most direct route to getting the crime rate down.

Public Concern about Crime

Community policing relates to the public's concern about crime, and about fear. Measuring concern and fear is another way of assessing the extent of "the crime problem," broadly speaking. While police figures provide one vantage point for assessing trends in crime, others are available. Because police depend on the willingness of residents to report crimes, and then they further screen complaints to ensure that they meet legal and bureaucratic requirements, the discrepancy between crime as measured by citizen concern and by agency records can be substantial. In a multiple-city study, the difference between police and survey figures ranged from 60 percent to 85 percent (Skogan 1976c).

Survey measures of crime bypass these barriers by going directly to ordinary residents. They are positioned to report on crime as they experience it. This experience can include not just their own victimization but also what they hear from friends and neighbors, and in local shops. When reporting on conditions in their neighborhood, people can factor in what they can see with their own eyes, even if they are lucky enough not to be involved personally. Surveys also provide an alternative measure of important public (and law enforcement) concerns that are very ill measured in official crime data, particularly gangs and drugs.

As an alternative to official measures of crime, our periodic surveys questioned city residents about what was going on in their areas. Respondents were presented with a list of crime descriptions and asked to rate whether each was either "no problem," "some problem," or "a big problem" in their neighborhoods. The questions were included in the evaluation surveys beginning in 1994. They indeed proved to be an alternative measure, for the results did not always match official statistics. In general, there was broad agreement between the reports of white and African American respondents, and recorded crimes for beats where they are heavily represented. However, the picture for Latinos differs a great deal, depending on whether we look at official or survey trends.

Drugs and Gangs

Concern about drug problems is rampant in Chicago. In the 1994 city survey, respondents were asked about "drug dealing on the streets," and this ranked highest on a list of ten neighborhood crime, social disorder, and physical decay problems. More than half of Chicagoans thought street drug dealing was a problem in their neighborhoods. As noted above, this concern is not adequately reflected in police statistics. Drug offenses are generally measured by the number of arrests, but arrests most directly measure police effort rather than the extent of the problem. While residents do call 911 to complain about street drug markets and other drug-related offenses, their complaints are difficult for police to count because they represent suspicion and concern rather than discrete events such as robberies or burglaries. In addition, multiple people may well be calling about the same condition. But while they are hard to officially count, street drug markets are not hard to spot, and area residents have no difficulty recognizing they have a drug market on their hands.

The concentration of drug and gang problems in Latino and African American areas is apparent in figure 8.4. In 1994, 40 percent

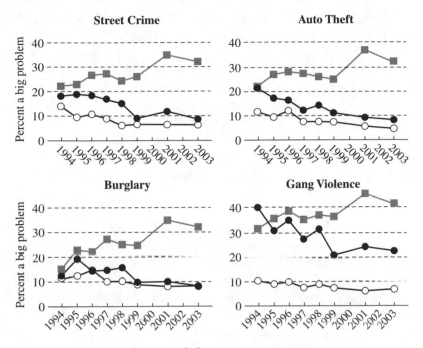

Figure 8.4. Crime Problem Trends by Race, 1994–2003

of African Americans and more than 30 percent of Latinos rated gang violence a big problem, while only 10 percent of whites put it in that category. Chicago's Latino community is home to fighting gangs as well as to those plying the drug trade. There is intercommunal warfare between gangs of Mexican and Puerto Rican origin, and between them and African American gangs along the periphery of their home turf. In contrast, drugs fund the operation of the large and powerful gangs dominating the city's African American beats. Outbursts of gang violence there are frequently tied to conflict over control of street drug markets and illegal arms sales. Turf wars easily escalate into shootouts with semiautomatic weapons that put everyone in the neighborhood at risk. Residents spoke at beat meetings with police about sleeping on the floor and away from the windows, or in the bathtub, to avoid stray bullets, and many knew families who have lost members to drug-related gang violence. The high level of concern about street drug markets among African Americans and Latinos can be seen in figure 8.4 as well. In 1994, almost half of all African Americans interviewed reported that drugs were a big problem in their areas, compared to "only" 23 percent of Latinos.

However, during the course of the 1990s, many Chicagoans reported improvements in gang and drug problems. The decline in concern about gang violence among African Americans was particularly noticeable; the percentage rating gang violence a big problem dropped almost in half, and this figure was down a bit for whites as well. Concern about street drug markets remained high among the city's African Americans, but dropped by about ten percentage points during the 1990s. Like the other trends described in figure 8.4, these declines slowed or came to a halt in the early years of the twenty-first century, but continued to hover at the lowest point.

Trends among Latinos are another story. Concern about gang violence did not abate during the 1990s, and leaped in surveys conducted in 2001 and 2003. This was quite in contrast to trends reported by African Americans. The percentage of Latinos rating street drug markets a big problem rose steadily during the 1990s and then spiked upward in 2001 before receding to near its 1999 high. Though relatively unconcerned about street drug markets in the early 1990s, by the new millennium Latino concern about drugs had doubled, passing that registered by African Americans. The different course traced by gang and drug problems among Latinos dampened overall improvement in the city, because their numbers were growing while the number of white residents—who reported fewer problems of all kinds—declined.

Personal and Property Crime

Figure 8.4 also presents trends in survey measures of three personal and property crimes. Respondents were quizzed about "cars being stolen," "people breaking in or sneaking into homes to steal things," and "people being attacked or robbed" in their neighborhoods. Trends in these three problems followed the same pattern. Concern about street crime and auto theft dropped the most. Whites thought things were a bit better, except in the case of burglary, despite their already low base. In the early 1990s, African Americans and Latinos reported about the same level of concern for every crime problem. Then, during the course of the 1990s, the experiences of African Americans and Latinos diverged. Over time, more and more African Americans reported that things were not so bad, and by 2003 their scores on all of these problem indices dropped by 10 percentage points or more. By 2003, the views of blacks had converged toward those of whites, and both groups expressed relatively low levels of concern about personal and property crime. But there was again little good news for the city's growing Latino population. In the first survey they reported about the same level of crime problems as did African Americans, but reports of concern by Latinos did not decline during the 1990s. Worse, their ratings jumped to new highs during the early years of the twenty-first century. By 2003, the city's Latinos were *three times* more likely than whites *and* African Americans to report that street crime, burglary, and auto theft were big problems in their communities.

What Happened in the Latino Community?

Why is this the case? The findings have already been previewed in the previous chapter on neighborhood disorder and decay. Part of the answer can again be found in demography.[9] The Latino community is growing, due partly to internal growth, but more from immigration. Conditions have gotten better for established, English-speaking Latinos living in diverse areas, while they have grown worse for Spanish speakers concentrated in the city's growing number of heavily Latino neighborhoods. Spanish-speaking Latinos are more likely to be poor and uneducated, and few are homeowners. Because newcomers are increasingly more numerous, as a group, Chicago's Latinos find themselves progressively worse off each year.

The diverging views of English speakers and Spanish-speaking Latinos are depicted in figure 8.5, which illustrates trends in a crime-problems index that combines responses to questions about neighborhood auto theft, burglary, street crime, and gang violence. Between 1994 and 2003, reports of neighborhood crime conditions were essentially unchanged among English speakers. All of the increases identified above were contributed by Spanish speakers, for whom this index more than doubled in value in less than a decade. In a multivariate contextual analysis, we found that language preference was by far the strongest (and one of only) of three significant individual correlates of perceived crime problems (Skogan and Steiner 2004b), when neighborhood-level factors were taken into account.

Figure 8.5 also plots the relationship between crime problems and two neighborhood-level indicators: ethnic concentration (the percentage of beat residents who were Latinos in the 2000 U.S. Census) and the beat poverty index used in many chapters of this book. The

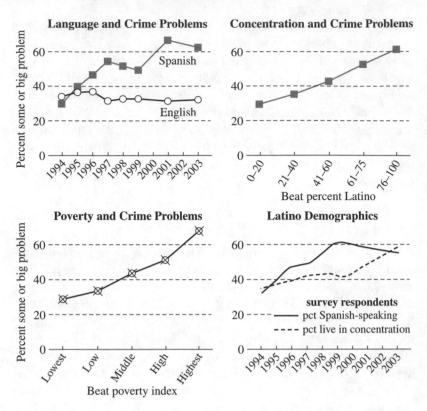

Figure 8.5. Language, Latino Concentration, Poverty, and Crime Problems, 1994–2003

figure documents sharply higher levels of perceived crime in places where Latinos live in poverty and in concentration. For example, less than 30 percent of Latinos living in beats with the least poverty rated crime as either some problem or a big problem during the 1999–2001 period, while 70 percent of those living in the most impoverished areas rated crime a problem in their neighborhoods. Likewise, Latinos living in more diverse racial settings were much less likely than those living in areas with substantial concentrations of Latinos to rate crime as a big problem. The problem for Latinos is that the frequency of both of these factors grew over time. A final panel in figure 8.5 displays trends in language and residential concentration, the former based on the survey and the latter on the census characteristics of the beats in which Latino survey respondents lived. The figure documents the increasing size of the concentrated,

Spanish-speaking component of the city's population during the course of the 1990s. In the same multivariate analysis, we found that neighborhood ethnic concentration and poverty together explained 84 percent of the variation between neighborhoods in perceived crime problems.

The improving fortune of Chicago's African Americans was, by contrast, a relatively widespread trend. Changes for the better in reports of crime ran in parallel for subgroups within the African American population. African Americans were divided by social class; the largest split was between homeowners and renters. More-educated African Americans reported fewer neighborhood problems than did less-educated African Americans, and there were parallel differences by income as well. But although poor and better-off African Americans began with different *levels* of problems, *trend* lines for these groups dropped in unison between 1994 and 1999, then leveled off together in the new century.

Latinos and Crime Reporting

We have seen two different portraits of crime in Chicago's Latino community. One—that painted by police-recorded crime—presented a rosy scenario, describing steady decreases in crime over a thirteen-year period. The other, based on surveys, pointed in the opposite direction. Why didn't the survey-based trends match those for recorded crime in heavily Latino neighborhoods? The problem is that the city's growing Spanish-speaking immigrant population is avoiding contact with the police. The data document this in a variety of ways, and by inference it appears that the unwillingness of new-comers to engage with the police extends to reporting crimes when they occur. Thus, not only were things growing worse in the city's emerging barrios, but the recorded crime figures kept by the police were not adequately representing what went on there.

Two analyses supported this conclusion. The first addressed the correspondence between trends in official crime rates for beats in each racial classification and survey reports of crime problems, separately for whites, African Americans, and Latinos. In the main, trends in of-ficial and survey measures of crime dropped roughly in parallel for the city's whites and African Americans. For example, survey-measured auto-theft problems reported by whites dropped by about 60 percent between 1994 and 2003, and police-measured auto thefts in predomi-nantly white beats dropped by almost the same amount. Compared to the beginning, by the end of the time period, both measures of auto theft, burglary, and street crime were decidedly down, for both whites and African Americans. However, official and survey measures did *not* readily correspond for the city's Latinos. The experiences of English-speaking Latinos who were interviewed generally paralleled official figures for heavily Latino beats. However, the contrast between trends reported by English and Spanish speakers was striking. While English speakers generally reported fewer crime problems over time, their counterparts progressively saw things getting worse. For Latinos, the disjuncture between trends in recorded crime and their everyday experiences can be traced directly to immigration.

A second look at the issue examined the frequency with which respondents reported contacting the Chicago police. In the surveys, citizen-initiated encounters with police are monitored using a nine-question checklist of the most frequent reasons that people contact them. These range from reporting a crime or suspicious persons to requesting routine information. In 2001, almost exactly 50 percent of Chicagoans age eighteen and older recalled contacting the police for one or more of these reasons. The most frequent reason to contact police was to report a crime (24 percent). Reporting accidents or medical emergencies was a close second (19 percent). Ten to 12 percent of those interviewed recalled reporting suspicious persons or noises, or things "that might lead to a crime." About the same proportion recalled giving the police information or contacting them regarding some other neighborhood concern or problem, and 17 percent reported contacting police to ask for advice or information.

However, the surveys indicate that reliance on police among the city's Spanish speakers is incommensurate with their concern about neighborhood problems. They have a lot of concerns, but they do not call to involve the police in resolving them. Among white and African American respondents, a comparison of contacting the police with indices of the extent of problems in their neighborhoods found that the more concerned Chicagoans were about a broad range of neighborhood problems, the more likely they were to mobilize the police. Only about one-third of Spanish speakers in the highest problem category recalled contacting the police, a figure far lower than that for whites and blacks. Spanish-speaking Latinos are heavily overrepresented in areas plagued by gang violence, street drug markets, public drinking, auto theft, and other serious problems. However, they suffer a double disadvantage, because while plagued by the worst neighborhood conditions, they are very reluctant to involve the police in their problems. The dramatic difference in the rate at which English- and Spanish-speaking Latinos initiated encounters with the police suggests that language and immigration factors play a very large role in shaping the relationship between the city's new-comers and institutions of government. In conjunction with the find-ings presented above on trends in crime, it also implies that official rates of crime—which depend upon ordinary citizens contacting the police to make official reports—may not adequately reflect the prob-lems facing those living in the city's heavily Spanish-speaking areas.

Fear of Crime

Fear of crime is a social and political fact with concrete conse-quences for big-city life.[10] The costs of fear are both individual and collective. Fear can confine people to their homes, and it undermines their trust in their neighbors and, especially, in their neighbors' chil-dren. Fear is a key "quality of life" issue for many people. Research also indicates that concern about crime has bad consequences for the neighborhoods in which we live. Fear leads to withdrawal from pub-lic life, and it undermines informal and organized efforts by the com-munity to control crime and delinquency. It is difficult to organize activities in neighborhoods where people fear their own neighbors. Fear undermines the value of residential property and thus the will-ingness of owners to maintain it properly. When customers—and even employees—fear entering a commercial area, the viability of businesses located there is threatened.

Most significant, in Chicago as elsewhere, fear of crime has been one of the most important factors driving residents to the suburbs, encouraging race and class segregation and undermining the politi-cal importance of American cities (Skogan and Maxfield 1981). In the 1970s, American cities began to feel the consequences of the flight to the suburbs of families who could afford to so do. Their flight was, in part, a reaction to mounting inner-city crime, as well as to perceived declines in the quality of schools and neighborhood life. Even by then, fear of crime had become a familiar component of the country's political rhetoric. Fear is a "wedge issue" that divides whites from other Americans, a divide that can be politically useful in certain cir-cles. Surveys indicate that many more people are fearful of crime than actually are victimized, and that fear undermines the quality of their lives (cf. Skogan and Maxfield 1981). Even criminologists have taken up this argument. Michael Maltz (1972) famously noted that, "unless the public *feels* safer in proportion to its increased actual safety, the full potential of [crime control] improvements will not have been reached."

Concern about fear and its consequences has led to the use of measures of fear to assess the effectiveness of crime-prevention projects and, more recently, community-policing programs. One of the first experiments in community policing was conducted in Houston, Texas, and Newark, New Jersey. It was known as "The Fear Reduction Project," reflecting its focus on citizen perceptions and behaviors as bottom-line measures of its success (Pate et al. 1986). The idea of the experiment was that citizens—as taxpayers, voters, and people who might choose to live and work elsewhere—needed to feel that their lives were better as a result of the new program. Chicago's plan for community policing encompassed this goal as well. As noted earlier, the department's original twenty-nine-page strategic plan concluded that reducing fear had to be a goal of the department.

Why should better policing affect fear of crime? One path is through the possible reassurance effect of police visibility and supportive contacts between police and residents. There is some controversy over whether police visibility increases citizen self-confidence and decreases fear. The results of an experiment in Kansas City (Kelling et al. 1974) have been widely interpreted as evidence that "policing doesn't make any difference" with regard to fear of crime. However, there is much evidence in the other direction. Many correlational studies have found that visible police presence on the streets is associated with lower levels of fear. In a quasi-experimental study of foot patrol in Newark, New Jersey, Pate (1986) found that foot patrols reduce levels of fear. Bennett (1989) drew the same conclusion from a quasi-experiment in Britain. Zhao, Scheider, and Thurman (2002) provide a wide-ranging review of this literature, concluding that the weight of the evidence is that visible police presence reduces fear.

Of course, it is possible that the causal relationship between confidence in the police and fear runs in the other direction, and that improving conditions and declining levels of fear increase satisfaction with the police, rather than the other way around. This reflects a general problem with establishing causation using one-wave surveys. However, the experimental intervention studies that have examined this link generally support the policing-affects-fear specification. Evaluation findings from the prototyping period in Chicago (see Skogan and Hartnett [1997] for the details) indicated that residents of most prototype districts detected positive changes in policing during its first year of CAPS. Because of the program, there were increases in the visibility of foot-patrol officers and informal police contacts with citizens. These were more commonly reported in the experimental areas after the program began. Residents of the prototype areas saw police more often, but they did not notice any significant changes in traditional enforcement efforts. They were reassured when they saw police doing community-oriented patrol. Controlling for many factors, police visibility was linked to positive changes in people's views of the quality of police service, and—especially for African Americans and renters—reduced fear of crime. Statistically, the effects of police visibility on fear were about the same as those of age and sex, two important factors in the fear of crime equation.

Components of community policing may extend reassurance through new channels, and not just through visible patrol. Being able to identify and respond to local priorities is one of the most important aspects of community policing, and in well-organized programs like Chicago's, there are management systems in place to make sure that officers address the concerns expressed by residents. If police are thought to be becoming more effective at dealing with neighborhood crime and disorder, and responding more effectively to the particular problems that are of most concern, people may feel more secure. On the other hand, this may vary by group; not everyone perceives the police in favorable terms, and more contact and familiarity with the police may not be seen to be an unalloyed good. More intensive and visible policing may be seen as intrusive, oppressive, and perhaps unfairly targeting residents. Skogan (1994) found that, in general, British Crime Survey respondents who recalled having seen police patrolling on foot in their neighborhoods felt substantially more positive about them—with the important exception of Afro-Caribbeans, for whom police visibility had no discernible favorable effects.

Another vulnerable group is victims. Traditionally the police have defined "good service" as police driving quickly to the scene when victims called. Research on police effectiveness in helping victims suggests that police are often not very good at it. In fact, victims are often *more* fearful as a result of their contact with police. Research has documented that victims have a list of specific and immediate needs. They want information, recognition, advice, support, protection, and reassurance from the police, but usually they do not get it

(Skogan 2005). In this light, it is important to note that in the early 1990s, Chicago police came off worst on the ten survey questions that we used to rate the police when it came to a question about providing service to victims. This is ironic, for by many measures, victims—and there are a lot of them—are the police's most important customers. In the early 2000s, Chicago police received about five million 911 calls each year, and the surveys indicate that more than half of all adult Chicagoans have personal contact with a police officer in the course of a year (Skogan 2005). The city has well-developed programs for responding to the targets of domestic violence and sexual assault, but otherwise crime victims are on their own.

Of course, we should also anticipate a direct link between fear of crime and neighborhood conditions. Fear is related to many of the conditions and experiences reported by respondents to the surveys. Not surprisingly, Chicagoans are more fearful when they think burglary or assault is a big problem in their neighborhoods. They are also more fearful when they can see around them visible signs that the social order is breaking down: they report more fear in places where public drinking, loitering, and graffiti are common, and they are distressed by the appearance of street drug markets in their communities. In Chicago, as elsewhere (see Lane and Meeker 2003), the relationship between neighborhood conditions and fear a strong one. We have already seen that social disorder, physical decay, and reports of neighborhood crime, drug, and gang problems declined for many (but not all) Chicagoans over the course of the 1990s. The very large declines in fear reported by the city's African Americans may, in particular, be testimony to the tremendous drop in crime in predominantly African American areas during the course of the 1990s, though whites' fear of crime declined as well.

Fear in Chicago

The evaluation surveys monitored trends in fear over time. This section examines trends in one of the most common measures of fear, responses to the question "How safe do you feel or would you feel being alone outside in your neighborhood at night?" Respondents were asked to indicate whether they would feel very safe, somewhat safe, somewhat unsafe, or very unsafe if they found themselves in that situation. This question has been included in surveys conducted by the U.S. Census Bureau, and it is commonly used in research on fear. It is not a behavior measure. Behavioral measures of fear—such as reports of staying indoors at night or driving rather than walking to avoid being victimized—are sensitive to a host of contingencies and life situations (such as having a nighttime job, or not having a car) that make them very complex to interpret. Responses to questions about their (perceived) risk of being victimized incorporate what people have already done to protect themselves (such as staying at home), and they can also miss the mark (Skogan 1993). The measure used here focuses on the potential for harm that people feel crime holds for them, or what they believe *could* happen to them *if* they exposed themselves to risk. It is a neighborhood-oriented, close-to-home measure of fear.

Figure 8.6 examines trends in fear during the course of the 1990s, and into the first years of the twenty-first century. It presents trends separately for key demographic groups—by age, gender, home ownership, and income. The trend lines chart the percentage of respondents who indicated they would feel either somewhat or very unsafe out alone in their own neighborhoods at night.

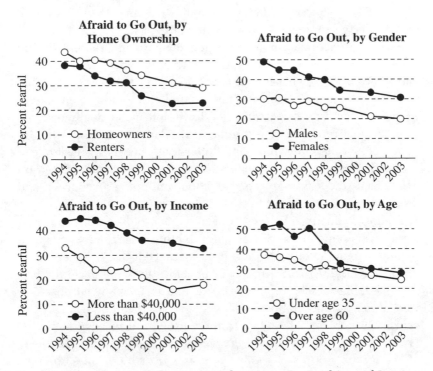

Figure 8.6. Trends in Fear, by Age, Gender, Home Ownership, and Income

The surveys reveal that fear of crime has been in general retreat over most of Chicago; there was an impressive decline in levels of fear over this ten-year period. By 2003, every group surveyed had fallen below the 40-percent-fearful mark, and seven of the eight groups were at or below 30 percent. As the figure indicates, divisions remain; even in the twenty-first century, men make themselves out to be less fearful than women. However, even among men, fear was down by 10 percentage points or so. Fear dropped almost twice as much for women, from 49 percent to 31 percent. It was down among both younger and older Chicagoans. Among those over age sixty, fear dropped from 51 percent to 28 percent. In fact, age differences in fear (here comparing the fears of those under age thirty-five and those sixty and older) virtually disappeared in Chicago at the end of the 1990s. This is very surprising, because age has been one of the most reliable correlates of fear (Fattah and Sacco 1989). In an early study of crime and the elderly, Cook and Cook (1976) concluded that "the major policy problem associated with the elderly and crime is probably not crime *per se*. Rather, the problem is related to the elderly person's fear of crime and the restrictions to daily mobility that this fear may impose." They argued that "the policy response to victimization of the elderly should be targeted to alleviating fear."[11]

Fear also declined among both homeowners and renters, and at about the same pace. The percentage of homeowners who reported being very or somewhat fearful about going out alone after dark fell from 42 percent to 29 percent; the parallel shift among renters was from 38 percent to 23 percent. The lower-left panel documents the limited gains reported by less affluent residents, those reporting incomes of less than forty thousand dollars per year. In this group, fear dropped from 44 percent to 33 percent. By contrast, among better-off Chicagoans, the fear index stood at 33 percent in the *first* survey, and dropped to just 18 percent by 2003.

Figure 8.7 documents trends in fear by race and—among the city's large Latino population—by language. By this measure, fear dropped by half among the city's whites, from 34 percent to 17 percent. Fear dropped among African Americans at about the same pace: the percentage of blacks who reported they would feel somewhat unsafe or very unsafe at night in the own neighborhoods declined from 49 percent to 25 percent. The city's Latinos turned out to have made the fewest gains over this period. In comparison to 1994, the 2003 level of fear for the group as a whole was down just a bit, from 43 percent to 38 percent. Earlier in the 1990s, African Americans were the city's

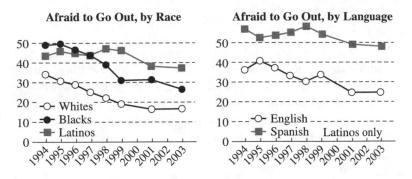

Figure 8.7. Trends in Fear by Race and Language

most fearful group, but by the turn of the century, blacks felt significantly safer than the city's Latinos.

The right-hand panel of the figure divides Latinos among Spanish
speakers and English speakers, based the language in which they
preferred to be interviewed when contacted by survey interviewers.
The panel documents the large differences in fear associated with
language. Spanish speakers are a growing group: by 2003 they made
up 54 percent of all the Latinos that were interviewed, foretelling an
important demographic shift in the Windy City's population (Skogan
and Steiner 2004b). In the mid-1990s, Spanish-speaking Latinos
were easily the most fearful large demographic group. Over time, fear
declined among both English and Spanish speakers, but the gulf between them actually widened.

Explaining Trends in Fear

What could account for declining fear? Past research does not provide much guidance for answering this question. Most of it examines
fear as a static phenomenon. The findings of these studies emphasize
the importance of the fairly fixed features of people—their race, age,
gender, affluence, education, and the like. Likewise, in Chicago,
women, the elderly, the poor, and racial minorities were substantially more fearful than their counterparts. However, for all of their
obvious importance, the fixed personal factors that play such an important role in discussions of fear of crime cannot explain substantial
changes in levels of fear over a relatively short period of time. What
can change rapidly are neighborhood conditions, and we have seen

that by many measures Chicago's neighborhoods became cleaner, safe, and more orderly.

Table 8.1 presents a multilevel analysis of fear of crime. It probes the joint effect of individual and neighborhood-level factors that may help explain the decline in fear in Chicago during the 1994–2003 period. The table examines the opinions of 16,878 respondents interviewed between 1994 and 2003.[12] The individual factors that are included were significant predictors of fear when they were examined separately. The beat-level factors include crime, which is represented by the log of personal crime and residential burglary per ten thousand residents of each beat. There are also measures of the racial composition of each beat, and two other demographic factors that help separate out the unique effects of crime as opposed to other features of these areas. As in the last chapter, the beat context data are organized so that the area in which each respondent lives is described by crime and (interpolated or projected) census data for the year in which that person was interviewed. For example, respondents interviewed in 1993 are linked to 1993 crime rates and estimates of 1993 census characteristics for their beats, while those interviewed in 2003 are linked to crime data and census estimates for that year. In total, respondents are situated in 2,043 distinct year-beat contexts.

The table includes the personal characteristics of respondents. All of them are by dichotomies, so their coefficients can be compared in magnitude. The coefficients represent the difference in fear, net of other factors in the model, associated with being on one side of a demographic category rather than the other. The analytic variables representing race identify all but white respondents; as the "omitted category" in this analysis, the other measures contrast the fear scores of their group's members with others and in comparison to white Chicagoans.

Controlling for other factors, women and older people were the most fearful. Those who were still working, younger people, and higher-income respondents were less fearful, overall. Without controlling for other factors, African Americans and Latinos were more fearful than whites, but taking neighborhood conditions into account revealed a radically different pattern. African Americans were— statistically—less fearful than whites. This means that in an unlikely world in which African Americans lived in places that were "just average" (if this was their score on measures of gangs, drugs, social disorder, residential stability, recorded crime, and confidence in the

Table 8.1 Fear, Personal Factors, Neighborhood Conditions, and Confidence in the Police, 1994–2003

	Coefficient	Significance
Intercept	2.13	.00
Individual Factors		
African American	−.13	.00
Latino	−.02	.30
Spanish-speaking	.09	.00
Other or undetermined race	−.00	.87
Female	.28	.00
Age 65 and older	.34	.00
Under age 30	−.07	.00
In the labor force	−.09	.00
College graduate	−.01	.41
Income $40,000 or more	−.05	.00
Homeowner	−.02	.00
Neighborhood Assessments		
Crime problems (z)	.13	.00
Drug and gang problems (z)	.13	.00
Social disorder problems (z)	.10	.00
Confidence in local police (z)	−.16	.00
Neighborhood Context		
Personal crime rate (z)	.05	.00
Residential burglary rate (z)	.03	.00
Percent African American (z)	.12	.00
Percent Latino (z)	.05	.00
Linguistic isolation (z)	.04	.00
Stability index (z)	−.03	.00
Policing		
Heard of community policing	−.04	.00
Heard about area meetings	−.04	.00
Variance Explained		
Within neighborhood	22%	
Between neighborhood	90%	
Number of Cases		
Individuals	16,878	
Contexts	2,043	

"z" indicates standardized measure; all other measures are 0–1 dichotomies.

police), they would feel even safer than whites and Latinos. Of course, this is not the real world, for African Americans are over concentrated in some of the worst parts of town and have much less confidence in the police. On the other hand, the extra dollop of fear associated with being a Spanish speaker did not drop much at all, and language was the only other racial or ethnic factor that remained significantly associated with fear. The influence of most other individual characteristics was not much affected, for Spanish speakers are less geographically concentrated and covaried less with crime, disorder, and relations with the police.

The analysis also includes respondents' views of neighborhood crime conditions and the perceptions of the police in the mix. Unlike their personal characteristics, we have seen that these perceptions shifted over time, some quite dramatically, and differentially for various population groups. Indices of the extent of crime, drug and gang, and social disorder problems were standardized, so that the coefficients presented for them are comparable. The coefficients represent differences in levels of fear associated with a one standard deviation shift (which is a very substantial change) in the level of each of those independent variables. All were strongly related to levels of fear, with perceived drug and gang problems having the largest negative impact.

Context-level measures of crime and associated demographic factors were also included in the analysis. All of these measures were also standardized, so the coefficients can be directly compared in terms of their magnitude. The extent of officially recorded crime corresponded to fear at this level: residents were more fearful in times and places with high levels of reported personal crime and residential burglary. Because crime rates were dropping in almost all areas of the city between 1993 and 2003, neighborhood crime decline was one factor behind the drop in fear. In addition, fear of crime was lower in more stable areas; beat stability is represented by a factor score loading heavily on home ownership and a low level of residential turnover in the area. Home ownership went up a bit between 1990 and 2000, from 40 to 44 percent of occupied units, but residential turnover went up, so changes in these factors could not account for much of the decline in fear. Fear levels were higher where there were concentrations of African Americans and Latinos, with the former evidencing the highest covariance with individual levels of fear. The final contextual level factor included in the analysis is linguistic isolation. Linguistic isolation is closely associated with the emergence of large, poor, Spanish-speaking immigrant neighborhoods in

Chicago, and these are places in which many survey respondents who reported worsening neighborhood conditions were concentrated (Skogan and Steiner 2004a).

In addition, assessments of the quality of policing were linked to fear, with an effect equaling that of drug and gang problems. The two dichotomous measures of awareness of Chicago's community-policing program each had about the same effect, which was in the range of that of being a homeowner.

Together, the individual-level and context-level neighborhood factors examined here explained 90 percent of the difference between beat-year contexts in fear of crime, and 22 percent of the individual-level variation in fear. Most of the latter is due to differences and changes in neighborhood conditions. In these data, the year-beat context within which individuals were situated explains 17 percent of the total variance in fear (this is the "intraclass correlation"). This figure is high for criminological research in general (Oberwittler 2004), and over twice that reported by Reisig and Parks (2004) for a study of the effects of neighborhood context on fear. On the other hand, it is almost exactly the figure reported by Robinson et al. (2003) for a block-level study of fear in Baltimore. Because Chicagoans are strikingly segregated by race and class, 37 percent of the between-context difference in fear was due to "compositional effects" (for example, neighborhoods exhibited more fear because many Spanish speakers were concentrated there), and this is reported as well in the table.

The question of how accurately the factors considered here account for *trends* in fear over time is examined in figure 8.8. That figure compares the fear trend documented by the surveys with trends predicted by various components of the model. The first prediction is based on the fixed personal characteristics of respondents, and it is apparent that those demographic factors account for scarcely any of the decline in fear over time. The "demographic prediction" of fear is virtually flat over time, and does not match the observed trend at all. This is consistent with the fact that the decline in fear in Chicago was broad based during the 1994–2003 period, and could not be easily explained by changes in the city's demography.

Adding respondents' assessments of neighborhood conditions, their awareness of community policing, and their confidence in the police helped a great deal. The yearly levels of fear predicted by demography plus those factors did capture some of the trend in fear, and the further addition of area crime and demography improved the fit a bit more.

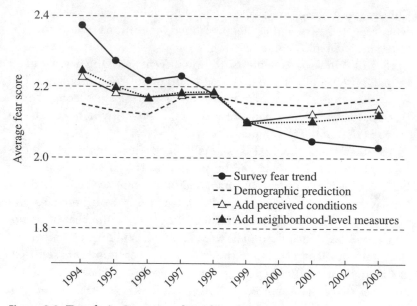

Figure 8.8. Trends in Survey and Predicted Fear

However, it is apparent in the figure that the factors examined here can account for only part of the drop in fear witnessed in Chicago during the 1990s and the early years of the twenty-first century. In particular, the predicted level of fear in the 2001–2003 period is farther from the mark than it was for the 1990s. The early years of the new century were a period in which confidence in the police stopped increasing among African Americans, and when their reports of neighborhood gang, drug, and social disorder problems ceased improving. Things also took a turn for the worse among Spanish-speaking Latinos during this period. Fear of crime continued to drop for both groups, on the other hand, suggesting that other factors *not* included in this analysis were at work during these years. The large size of the individual-level coefficient associated with being a Spanish speaker, even when controlling for neighborhood and policing factors, suggests that more needs to be understood about the sources of their fear.

There are certainly many plausible causes of fear that are not examined here, because adequate measures were not included in the survey. One is a direct measure of personal victimization, which, in line with declining recorded crime rates, should have declined over the course of this study. However, because victimization is fairly selective in terms of age and gender, one-time cross-sectional surveys frequently find that largely young and male victims seem *less* fearful than nonvictims. The effects of victimization on fear are more apparent in multiwave studies of the same individuals, which can control for people's previctimization level of fear in order to reveal how fearful they became following experiences they had between the interviews (see Skogan 1987).

Other causes of fear include what Skogan and Maxfield (1981) dubbed "vicarious victimization." People can have "secondhand" experience with crime through a variety of channels (see also Tyler 1980). One such channel is media coverage of crime. The evidence concerning media influences on fear is diverse and contradictory, and the methodological challenges to drawing clear causal inferences from survey research on this topic are formidable. With a number of statistical controls, researchers can find correlational links between self-reported television viewing and fear (e.g., Weitzer and Kubrin 2004; Eschholz, Chiricos, and Gertz 2003). However, people heavily "self select" the media they are exposed to, and there is always concern that not all of the selection factors—which may themselves be linked to fear—have been controlled for. Research on the impact of another source of secondhand information on crime—interpersonal communication—is less common. As Skogan and Maxfield (1981) documented, people talk and hear about crime on a frequent basis. When they do, they are more fearful, and when victims they hear about resemble themselves and come from the same neighborhoods, they are even more fearful. Given the decline in crime that Chicago experienced during the 1990s, it is plausible that talk about neighborhood crime diminished somewhat, and data on this point might improve our understanding of trends in fear. I am less sanguine that media coverage of crime tracked this new reality very closely, on the other hand.

Also not considered here is a list of concerns about ostensibly "noncrime" issues that research has linked to expressions of fear of crime. On this list are perceptions of growing racial diversity in the neighborhood, the appearance of immigrants in the community (Lane and Meeker 2003), and concern about cultural diversity more generally (Merry 1981). Another study might also consider additional neighborhood or contextual-level factors, including the extent of neighborhood cohesion or solidarity, and the willingness of neighbors to intervene to protect one another. These are components of "collective efficacy," which has been shown to deter violent crime

(Sampson, Raudenbush, and Earls 1997). Yili Xu, Mora Fiedler, and Karl Flaming (2005) document that collective efficacy is linked to fear, both directly and indirectly through its impact on neighborhood disorder and crime. What is unknown in the present context is whether Chicagoans' "noncrime" concerns and neighborhood solidarity have increased enough over time to account for declining levels of fear.

Finally, it is difficult to discount the possibility that citywide factors that did not vary much from beat to beat contributed to the drop in fear. This is signaled by the decline in fear across virtually all major social groupings. The correlational research design used here can only capture the effect of factors that varied from place to place within the city. However, while the statistical model takes into account differentially declining reported crime, violent crime in some category was down in *every one* of the city's 270 residential beats, predicting that everyone would feel at least a bit safer. Another example would be the ratings boost that the American police received nationwide following the events of September 11, 2001. This, coupled with increased concern about the security of the nation's cities, may have reverberated through multiple channels to reduce people's sense of security from conventional crime.

How Did Chicago Do?

There was an enormous drop in crime in Chicago during the 1991–2003 period. Crime was down in every category and in almost every beat. In particular, it was down in predominantly African American areas—to their huge benefit. We saw early in this chapter that the drop in crime rescued almost eighty-seven thousand people from robbery just in fifty-two high-crime, almost exclusively African American beats. Citywide, these projections are even more dramatic. If the 1991 murder rate had persisted over the 1992–2003 period, there would have been more than 11,100 homicides over that twelve-year span; instead there were fewer than 9,000 homicides. The drop in crime saved more than twenty-one hundred lives, by this accounting. The consequences of the drop in crime are even more stark in higher-volume offense categories. If the drop had not occurred, there might have been 196,000 more burglaries, 111,000 more victims of assaultive violence, and 172,000 more cars stolen. These are large numbers, and they help illustrate the social and economic significance of what took place in Chicago toward the end of the twentieth century.

Other big cities provide a benchmark against which to evaluate the extent of the drop in crime in Chicago. Figure 8.9 compares trends in big cities over the 1991–2003 period. The others are the nine cities with populations of about a million or more: Dallas, Detroit, Houston, Los Angeles, New York City, Philadelphia, Phoenix, San Antonio, and San Diego. The figure averages trends for the other nine large cities, giving each city equal weight. Compared to big-city America, Chicago lagged in homicide during most of the period. Between 1991 and 2000, big-city murder declined to about 50 percent of its original level. Then that rate stabilized, and even went up a bit, while Chicago's homicide rate continued to decline. In the end, the city met the national standard. Chicago also did well in the robbery category, as noted above, especially after 1998. Chicago essentially matched the very substantial declines that took place in big-city burglary and auto theft during the course of the 1990s. By 2003, big-city

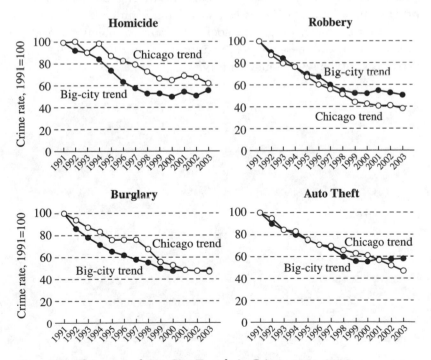

Figure 8.9. Chicago and Big-City Trends in Crime, 1991–2003

burglary and auto theft (in all of the cities including Chicago) stood at half or less than half their 1991 levels.

Surveys conducted in Chicago between 1994 and 2003 document that fear of crime dropped noticeably. The decline was a general one, although fear went down a bit more among some of the groups that were most fearful at the outset, including women, African Americans, and older residents. A downside of this general pattern of decline is that race, class, and gender differences in fear remained strong, and with few exceptions the *gap* between better-off and worse-off Chicagoans was about as large in 2003 as it was in 1994.

A statistical model incorporating these individual and neighborhood-level factors explained a substantial fraction—but far from all—of the decline in fear that was observed over time. Among the notable findings was the importance of immigration; after women and older people, Spanish-speaking residents were the most fearful Chicagoans. This factor takes on added significance because it is the fastest-changing feature of the city's demographic landscape. The effect of confidence in the police was a strong one, and awareness of the city's community-policing program contributed to declining fear as well. Both awareness and confidence rose during the 1990s, as the program took hold in the city. Not surprisingly, indicators of the extent of crime, gang, drug, and social-disorder problems were also linked to fear, and these too declined for many during the 1990s and early years of the twenty-first century.

NINE

Police and the Public

O ne goal of Chicago's-community policing initiative was to build (they would say "restore," on the assumption that they once had it) popular confidence in the responsiveness and effectiveness of the police. *Together We Can* noted this as "the growing separation between police and the people they serve."[1] It tied this gulf to the rigidly traditional model of policing that became the department's standard in the early 1960s, arguing that its focus on rapid response and preventive patrol had led to "the forced isolation of the police from the community."[2] Tying police almost entirely to responding to 911 calls "prevented officers from becoming knowledgeable about specific problems and individual people on their beats."[3] Community policing, the chief argued, offered "a historic opportunity to get back in touch with the people we serve."[4]

This chapter examines the changing views of Chicagoans about their police as CAPS took root in the city. Police gained significant support over time, and they did so among all major groups. Much of the explanation for this lay in improving neighborhood conditions. Many—but not all—Chicagoans felt their neighborhoods were growing cleaner, safer, and more comfortable as a place to live, and official rates of crime were declining. These improvements in quality of life benefited the police. Some of the remaining gaps between views of whites and African Americans can be attributed to personal experience, for there continued to be a great gulf between them in how they evaluated their encounters with police, and to the police-initiated street stops that initiated the most dissatisfaction heavily targeted young African American males.

Policing in Chicago

The image of the Chicago police certainly needed some polishing. Surveys find that police in the United States generally have the support of the public; in fact, they are held in higher esteem than are many other public officials. But support for them is not as high among residents of the nation's largest cities, and Chicago is a good example of this pattern. During the 1970s, the U.S. Census Bureau conducted surveys of residents of twenty-six of the nation's largest cities, and Chicago ranked near the bottom in terms of public confidence. In these surveys, the opinion *gap* between white and African American residents of Chicago was also the largest of any city (Skogan 1979). More recently, a 1998 federal government survey of residents of twelve cities found that Chicago placed second to last in terms of citizen satisfaction with the police who serve their neighborhoods (Smith, Steadman, Minton, and Townsend 1999). As the riot that scarred Los Angeles in the aftermath of the Rodney King episode reminds us, these opinions can have consequences.

The history of the Chicago Police Department does not help its reputation much. It is a story of misconduct and corruption occasionally punctuated by reform, and a department caught like many between the demands of a changing city population and an entrenched status quo bureaucracy protected by law-and-order rhetoric. Describing the department in the 1950s, policing expert Herman Goldstein wrote: "The CPD was weak by any standards. It had a poor reputation for service, corruption was widespread, partisan political influence was pervasive and determinative for all important decisions made in the department, and personnel were poorly trained, disorganized, at times dispirited, and even disgraced."[5]

He went on to describe what he dubbed "the mother of all scandals," a widespread criminal conspiracy among officers who stole and burgled while they were on duty and in uniform. When this came out in 1959, it lead to a wholesale purge of the organization by a new reform police chief, O. W. Wilson. He created the archetypal "professional" police department of its day, one organized around visible motorized patrol and rapid response to 911 calls. He largely broke the link between low-level politicians and the police, tipping it strongly in the direction of independence from—and perhaps unresponsiveness to—external influences. However, the winds of change were sweeping through the city and nation, and ensuing decades tested the effectiveness of this new model. Chicago's neighborhoods were churning as whites moved out in massive numbers and African Americans moved in to claim their nicer, safer spaces. Through the 1960s this led to continued racial strife and civil rights activism, including Martin Luther King's failed effort to march through the city in support of integrated housing (Cohen and Taylor 2000). The 1968

Democratic National Convention featured what one investigating commission later labeled "a police riot" (National Commission on the Causes and Prevention of Violence 1968), then the federal courts ordered the department to close down its "Red Squad" and cease spying on people the mayor did not like (Nimocks 1994).

By the early 1970s, charges of police brutality were being voiced by both the community and its elected officials. William Geller and Kevin Karales (1981) found that about that time, African Americans were shot or shot at by Chicago police almost four times as frequently as whites, taking into account their numbers in the population. Hispanics were only twice as likely to be shot or to be shot at. They also found that it was white officers, not African Americans officers, who were doing the shooting. An Afro American Patrolmen's League formed within the department voiced its disillusionment with the attitudes of fellow officers, and sued the city regarding discrimination in hiring, promotions, and assignments. A retired deputy superintendent of the department has described the scene: "During this period, when the superintendent would have occasion to go out into the black community to discuss police operations, invariably he'd be booed and blasted with charges of racism and brutality. Some Afro American Patrolmen's league members would openly be in the audience, and in some instances would shout him down."[6]

In 1975 a federal judge imposed a hiring quota on the department to address its racial imbalance, but it did not change much. A 1993 report to the United States Commission on Civil Rights urged that "the persistent pattern of underrepresentation in the police force as a whole and in the detective ranks in particular must be alleviated."[7] The investigating committee also concluded that predominantly African American police districts were understaffed relative to the crime rate. It formally found that "African Americans in the city of Chicago are suffering discrimination in the administration of justice,"[8] and recommended intervention by the U.S. Department of Justice.

To make things worse, throughout the 1970s and 1980s, a backdrop to every discussion of race and policing was a festering wound that bled the police department of its credibility: the Jon Burge scandal. For almost two decades, Burge, who was commander of the detective division, and those under his control systematically tortured black prisoners in the back rooms of police stations. They administered electric shocks to their testicles, poked them with cattle prods, suffocated them with garbage bags, and shoved a shotgun down their throats. A special prosecutor eventually set the torture count at 104, but others assembled even longer lists. All of this was widely known for more than a decade. Suits were filed, those convicted on the basis of confessions extracted through torture were released from prison, newspaper editorialists thundered, and community groups picketed the stations, but the city refused to take any action. The police union, ever one to shoot itself and the department in the foot, raised funds to stave off any prosecution in the case, and celebrated the defendants with placards on its St. Patrick's Day parade float. In 1992, just as our evaluation was about to begin and after twenty-one years of misconduct, the city suddenly reversed itself and fired Burge—while in response to civil suits it continued to stoutly deny that he had done anything wrong.

In 1997, while our evaluation was underway, the mayor moved to alleviate another crisis by appointing a commission on police integrity. He was responding to federal indictments of a ring of police officers who were extorting and robbing drug dealers operating on the city's West Side. The commission's report included a litany of corruption episodes in the city's recent history. The list included officers involved in murders for hire, extortion from tavern owners, kickbacks from vendors, bribing judges, and protecting gambling rings (Commission on Police Integrity 1997). In 2004, when the evaluation was concluding, a (recently) former deputy chief of the department was convicted of running a mob-connected jewelry theft ring, and he allegedly also brokered Mafia executions while he was chief of detectives.

In the 1990s, distrust of the police threatened the viability of CAPS in the very neighborhoods where it was needed most. Chicagoans were divided by economic status, with better-off residents sharing more positive views of the police, but the most significant cleavage over policing was along racial lines. During the first days of the program, savvy activists anticipated that dissatisfaction among the city's African Americans and Latinos would make community policing a tough sell in many neighborhoods. Concern about police disrespect for the public led some to question whether beat meetings would attract participants or if residents could be convinced to form partnerships with police around problem-solving projects.

In the early 1990s the perception was also widespread that police were just not very effective. Crime rates were at their highest in decades. The public linked crime to the persistence of open-air drug markets and drug-related shootings, and police seemed incapable of doing anything about them. At the first beat meetings held in the prototype districts, residents frequently complained about slow or non-existent responses to 911 calls, and they recounted tales of police indifference to their concerns and disregard for the plight of victims. People felt unprotected; they wanted more frequent, visible patrols, and they wanted patrol cars to stop when they flagged them down on the street. As we shall see in this chapter, during the early 1990s even the city's white residents did not think police were doing a very good job at fulfilling their core duties.

The changing demography of the city magnified the potential consequences of racial divisions over policing issues in Chicago. The communities that are most likely to feel the brunt of police indifference and abuse are the largest and the fastest-growing ones. During the 1990s Chicago's white population dropped by 13 percent, while the number of African Americans and Latinos in combination increased by 12 percent. Whites were also the oldest group, and Latinos the youngest by a wide margin, and we will see below that age is another important factor in shaping people's views of the police. But another reason to focus almost exclusively on race is that many factors beyond age were *not* tied to African American opinion about police, while they were for the city's whites and Latinos. For example, among whites, 39 percent of renters and 60 percent of homeowners had positive views of the police in 1994, using an overall index. For African Americans, the comparable figures were 28 percent versus 30 percent. Whites and Latinos were internally divided across income and gender lines, and by marital status and employment, but African Americans were scarcely divided at all along these important cleavage lines. For African Americans, race provides a "master status" that transcends many other social divisions among them. When it comes to policing, whites and Latinos evidence themselves as working or middle class, men or women, and renters or owners; African Americans are black.

The ramifications of these racial divisions are felt in political quarters. Because of the changing composition of the city, no mayor can now govern without building some sort of cross-racial coalition. Gone are the days when Chicago's mayor could dig in his heels and defend the interests of the city's white blue-collar homeowners against all contenders. During the 1980s the city's first African American mayor attempted to forge a "rainbow coalition" uniting the city's black and brown residents, but he was unable to divert enough jobs and services in the direction of Latinos to build a coalition that could survive his untimely death in office. His white successor built his political base around a coalition of whites and Latinos, and he had enough support from the city council to make it work.

As I have noted elsewhere (Skogan and Hartnett 1997), community policing had its origins—in part—in this political reality. Because of the city's racial complexion and resulting politics, it was probably not an option to respond to public outcries over crime just with "get tough" policies. They would have been popular in some circles, certainly in the city's shrinking white neighborhoods where they would not often apply. They might have been popular enough among middle-income African Americans, who were facing crime problems disproportionate to their economic standing. There was widespread support for the city's tough gang-loitering ordinance, and it promised to address a problem that loomed large in the city's poorest and most disenfranchised neighborhoods. But many African Americans and Latino immigrants had reason to fear the police as well. Our early surveys documented that large majorities of African Americans and Latinos were dubious about many aspects of police performance, and by the early 1990s they constituted a majority of city residents. Doing something *about* the police, not just with them, promised to be a less divisive strategy for the mayor, because it could also be billed to the public and the media as doing something about crime.

How could community policing fix relations between police and the community? The CAPS plan promised to address the gulf in several ways. Beat-community meetings and the new plan to keep officers on the beat as long as possible promised to be a vehicle for building familiarity and (perhaps) trust between community activists and police who worked the streets in their neighborhoods. For the first time, police and "the good people" of the community would have a chance to interact in a context that could show the former in a new light—hopefully as less rude and arrogant than many believed. One of the potential virtues of community policing is that it gives officers an opportunity to build support in the community. Harnessing the police and beat meetings to enhanced effectiveness in delivering city services promised to make the system more responsive to residents' concerns. CAPS could "deliver the goods" in a tangible way, and it could do so in response to a broad range of problems. Discussion of neighborhood priorities and the practice of police reporting at subsequent meetings on their efforts might actually help them be more effective at addressing physical decay problems, and it certainly might make them appear to be more effective at addressing crime and disorder problems as well. As we will see later in this chapter, improving neighborhood

conditions played a large role in reshaping people's views of the police in Chicago. Finally, new 911 dispatching policies and the formation of stable beat teams were to help ensure that familiar officers
would show up when police were called, and they would be the same
officers who attended beat meetings.

Trends in Public Confidence

The evaluation monitored public opinion in a series of surveys conducted between 1993 and 2003. During that period there were ob-
servable changes for the better in perceptions of several aspects of
police service. Opinion improved steadily between 1993 (when the
first small evaluation survey was conducted) and 1999, before leveling off at a new high in the early years of the twenty-first century. At
the same time, it is also apparent that the gulf between the races in
Chicago did not change much at all. Partly this is good news, for it
signals that improvements in the image of the police were not confined to only one group. On every measure, changes in opinion have
been apparent among whites, African Americans, and Latinos alike.
But on every dimension, the 15 to 20 percentage-point gap between
the views of whites and those of other racial groups closed scarcely
at all over the ten-year period during which the evaluation monitored the views of the general public. Chicagoans are happier about
their police, but just as polarized in their views.

The first dimension on which Chicagoans were asked to rate their
police officers is police demeanor. While not conceding that they
might have a problem in this regard, *Together We Can* stressed the
importance of "delivering the highest quality of service to our
customers—the citizens of Chicago—in a fair and impartial manner."[9]
Responses to four questions asking about police in their area were
used to index this aspect of public satisfaction.[10] Like all of the questions in this section, those interviewed were given four response
categories to choose from; the best and worst of the four categories are
reported below.

In general, how polite are the police when dealing with people
in your neighborhood? Are they [very polite to very impolite]?

When dealing with people's problems in your neighborhood,
are the police generally [very concerned to not concerned at all]
about their problems?

In general, how helpful are the police when dealing with people in your neighborhood? Are they [very helpful to not helpful at all]?

In general, how fair are the police when dealing with people in your neighborhood? Are they [very fair to very unfair]?

Chicago police have always done best on the demeanor dimension. Even at the outset, a majority of city residents believed that their neighbors were treated well by police, so there was not as much room for improvement on this measure. In the small citywide survey conducted in 1993, 86 percent of the city's residents thought police working in their neighborhoods were either very or somewhat helpful, as opposed to not very helpful or not helpful at all. Responses to these questions went together consistently in every yearly survey. In 1996, for example, they were correlated an average of +.57. In analyses that combine them into an index, the resulting police demeanor measure has a reliability of .83. The discussion below is based on combined indices for each of the dimensions used to evaluate the police.

A second measure was created of perceived police responsiveness. It was based on responses to three questions:

How responsive are the police in your neighborhood to community concerns? Do you think they are [very responsive to very unresponsive]?

How good a job are the police doing in dealing with the problems that really concern people in your neighborhood? Would you say they are doing a [very good job to poor job]?

How good a job are the police doing in working together with residents in your neighborhood to solve local problems? Would you say they are doing a [very good job to poor job]?

These questions addressed directly two of the central goals of CAPS: to increase the responsiveness of the police to concerns expressed by the public at beat meetings and other venues, and to engage the community in addressing them as well. In *Together We Can* the chief indicated that "this partnership will not be a superficial one. We must aggressively seek input from the community in setting priorities and in developing and implementing crime-fighting and problem-solving strategies at the neighborhood level."[11] However, at the outset there were large differences in how Chicagoans rated police on these three measures. In 1993, the police fared best on responsiveness, with more than 80 percent of respondents reporting that the police were responsive to neighborhood concerns. Only 42 percent thought police were doing a good job working with neighborhood residents to solve problems. Police action seemed less certain than their expressions of concern. Despite these differences in the magnitude of the ratings, responses to these three questions also went together consistently every year: in 1996, for example, they were correlated an average of +.65. The combined police responsiveness index had a reliability of .85.

The last measure that can be tracked over the entire period is of perceived police performance. It is also based on responses to three questions:

How good a job do you think they are doing to prevent crime in your neighborhood? [very good job to poor job]
How good a job do you think the police in your neighborhood are doing in helping people out after they have been victims of crime? [very good job to poor job]
How good a job are the police in your neighborhood doing in keeping order on the streets and sidewalks? [very good job to poor job]

In the first survey Chicago police did not rate highly on any of these aspects of their performance. They did best in terms of keeping order; 59 percent gave them either a "fairly good job" or "very good job" rating on this. Only 40 percent gave them a positive rating for helping victims, and just 12 percent thought they were doing a good job at this. Forty-eight percent gave them a passing mark on preventing crime. Responses to these items were correlated an average of +.63 in 1996, and the combined police performance index used later in this section had a reliability of .84.

Figure 9.1 illustrates trends in these measures over an eleven-year period. It charts the percentage of respondents averaging a positive rating (the two best of four rating categories) on each index. Separate trend lines are presented for whites, African Americans, and Latinos, the three racial groups that the surveys are large enough to monitor with accuracy. The 1993 survey was conducted only in English, so the data point for Latinos is omitted in that year. The figure also combines all of the measures of police effectiveness into a single index of service quality. Those who gave police a positive rating on one dimension also tended to give them a favorable rating on the other two, so this summary index provides a fair representation of residents' overall opinion of the police. It is not an average of the three scores

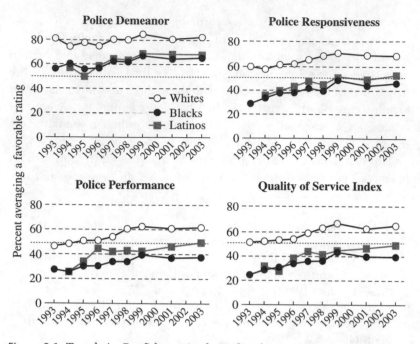

Figure 9.1. Trends in Confidence in the Police by Race, 1993–2003

presented in figure 9.1, but is instead based on all ten individual survey questions.

As noted above, police scored best on their personal relations with the public. Before CAPS began in 1993, almost two-thirds of those interviewed averaged a positive score on the police demeanor index, and that figure rose to 73 percent by 2003. The biggest increase in this category was in the percentage thinking that police treated residents of their neighborhood politely, which rose from 71 percent to 81 percent by 1999, before dropping a bit to 79 percent in 2003. The percentage who thought police were helpful went from 82 percent in 1995 to 90 percent by 2003. In 2003, 85 percent of Chicagoans thought police were either very or somewhat fair in dealing with their neighbors. There were notable differences between the races in how they rated the police, however. In general, whites perceived that police treated people well even in the early 1990s, and there was not much room for improvement. Positive perceptions of police demeanor rose by about 10 percentage points among both Latino and African American respondents and ended on a high note.

In contrast to the public's view of police demeanor, before CAPS was launched only 43 percent of Chicagoans had an optimistic view of police responsiveness to community concerns. Responding to this perception was one of the most important goals of CAPS. By 1995, beat-community meetings were being held regularly in every part of the city, and each police district had formed an advisory committee. The CAPS marketing campaign succeeded in driving program recognition from 53 percent in 1996 to 79 percent by 1999, and it stood about there in 2003. Perceptions of police responsiveness to community concerns improved steadily until 1999; overall, the responsiveness index rose by nearly 20 percentage points during the 1993–1999 period. Then, like the other measures examined here, perceptions of police responsiveness stopped improving. In 2003 about 56 percent of city residents averaged a positive view on this dimension. The largest gain in the area of police responsiveness was the percentage of respondents who thought police were doing a good job working with residents to solve problems, which rose from 39 percent to 58 percent in 2003. Problem solving jointly with residents was the newest and most innovative new aspect of CAPS. Perceptions of the police on this dimension changed the most among African Americans and Latinos, rising by almost 20 percentage points between 1993 and 1999. The views of whites, which were more positive even before CAPS began, improved by about 10 percentage points.

At the outset, Chicagoans were mostly negative in their views of how well police did their jobs. At early beat meetings, residents complained about unanswered calls to the city's 911 emergency number and that patrol cars would not stop when anxious residents tried to flag them down. But over time, the index measuring this aspect of police service improved significantly, rising from a low of 36 percent in 1994 to a high of 51 percent in 2003. Police efforts to prevent crime were widely recognized. The percentage granting them a positive rating on this aspect of their work rose from 44 percent in 1994 to 61 percent by 2003. Reports that police were doing a very good job or a good job assisting crime victims increased from 39 percent in 1993 to 58 percent at the end. Police got the highest marks for keeping order; positive scores on this measure hit 66 percent in 2003, up from 53 percent in 1994. These were solid gains, but in 2003 only 51 percent of Chicagoans were willing to give the police an average score in the positive range on performance, their weakest mark. Whites began the period with relatively negative views of police on-the-job performance. As figure 9.1 illustrates, on average, less than half the whites surveyed thought the police were doing a satisfactory job. Their views—like those of African Americans and Latinos—shifted by about 10 percentage points during the course of the 1990s, then leveled off in the new century. African Americans remained more dubious.

The summary index presented in the lower-right quadrant of figure 9.1 encapsulates many of the patterns described here. It is based on all ten evaluative questions, and the figure presents the percentage of respondents each year who averaged in the positive range. The summary index points to an improvement in white opinion by 13 percentage points, while positive opinions among African Americans grew by more than 15 percentage points between 1993 and 1999, before dropping a bit by 2003. Improvement was more continual for Latinos. In 1994, 31 percent of Latinos averaged a positive view of police service, a number that grew to 48 percent by 2003.

These were solid gains. The views of Chicago's major racial groups shifted in a positive direction over the course of the 1990s. These changes ranged from 10 to 15 percentage points, and they were substantial enough that the views of a majority of Latinos and African Americans *almost* made it into the positive range. But in the end, a majority of Latinos and African Americans were solidly satisfied only about police helpfulness, fairness, and concern. As the dark horizontal line highlighting the 50 percent mark in figure 9.1 emphasizes, even in 2003 there was still ample room left for improvement. After more than eight years of citywide community policing, a little less than half the public thought that police were doing a good job at preventing crime, helping victims, and maintaining order, and only about 55 percent thought they were doing a good job responding to community concerns. "Helping victims" was the lowest-rated form of service included in the surveys; by this measure, police were not seen as responding to the needs of some of their most important customers.

Were the shifts in opinion that did occur due to CAPS? The concluding section of this chapter compares trends in Chicago with the findings of nationwide surveys assessing confidence in the police. However, the best evidence of the impact of CAPS again comes from the experimental period during which the program was developed (see Skogan and Hartnett 1997). In the prototype districts, large changes in opinions about the police were confined to perceptions of their responsiveness to community concerns. The evaluation surveys found that perceived police responsiveness improved significantly in four of the five experimental districts, but only in one of their comparison areas. Perceptions of police effectiveness and demeanor also improved in predominantly African American districts, but not in their comparison areas. Combining the opinions of all surveyed residents of the prototype districts, attitudes toward the police changed most favorably among African Americans, who began with fairly negative views on every dimension. Views of policing also improved among whites, but their views were quite positive at the start. Attitudes toward the police also grew more positive among both renters and homeowners. The biggest shortcoming of the program in the prototype areas was among Latinos, who started out even more dissatisfied than the city's African Americans. Their views did not improve at all, and the prototype district in which Latinos were concentrated was the only one where opinions did not improve significantly overall.

Continued Discord Over Policing

A continuing concern is that while there were general improvements in assessments of the quality of police service in Chicago, in the new millennium the *gulf* between whites and others remained almost as wide as ever. In terms of perceived police responsiveness, whites were still more likely than African Americans—by 24 percentage points—to give police a favorable rating for dealing with problems that really concern people. The gap was the same when it came to perceptions of how good a job police were doing at preventing crime; in 2003, 74 percent of whites, but only 49 percent of African Americans, and 58 percent of Latinos thought the police were doing a good job at that. Based on the summary index, about 20 percentage points separated whites from other city residents, compared to about 25 percentage points eight years earlier. The views of many city residents grew more favorable, but the division between whites and racial minorities over policing hardly shrank at all. One summary of overall trends in Chicago is that "the glass" representing the views of city residents about police went from being "less than half full" to "a little more than half full."

Race is not the only dividing factor among Chicagoans when it comes to policing, although it is the most significant. Another dividing line across which people look in the direction of the police is age. That young people do not get on well with police has been an enduring theme in analyses of public opinion in the United States and elsewhere. Like studies in other cities, the Chicago surveys indicate that a large gap remains between young people and others when they rate the quality of police service. In 2000, the Chicago Alliance for Neighborhood Safety conducted a survey of 943 students in Chicago high schools (Friedman et al. 2002). Fully 47 percent of them reported that they had been stopped by police during the previous year. Among that group, 61 percent felt they were treated with disrespect by police, and 26 percent reported some form of physical abuse. African American and Latino youths were most likely to report being arrested as well as abused. The troubled relationship between police and young people even extends to crime reporting. Nationally, victimized youths are least likely to report their experiences to the police. In many crime categories, the reporting rate for National Crime Victimization Survey respondents in the youngest age category (age twelve to fifteen) is less than half that for victims over age twenty-five (Hart and Rennison 2003). Of course, younger people are also much more likely to *commit* offenses of a variety of kinds, ranging from personal crime to traffic violations, and this certainly does not help their relationship with the police. In addition to the simple effect of age, in Chicago there is an interaction between race and age. Young African American males are more negative than either their race or age would predict. As we will see below, they are also stopped by the police in tremendous numbers, and often feel mistreated when they are.

Age patterns are illustrated in figure 9.2. One section of the figure charts the relationship between age and the percentage of survey respondents who gave the police a favorable rating. This chart combines responses from the 2001 and 2003 surveys, increasing the number of respondents in each relatively small age category. As it indicates, younger African Americans (and to a lesser extent young whites) are more negative than their counterparts. African Americans under age thirty were the most negative, splitting roughly down the middle in their assessments. Overall, the effects of age are much stronger among African Americans than among whites. Among Latinos, on the other hand, there is little relationship between age and their views of the police. Latinos are more dissatisfied than whites, and their support does not rise with age. One of the most significant features of the city's Latino population is its youth. In 2003, for example, only 6 percent of Latino respondents were over age sixty, compared to 23 percent of African Americans. As a result, there were so few older Latinos, even in the combined surveys, that it was impossible to adequately represent their views if they were older than seventy.

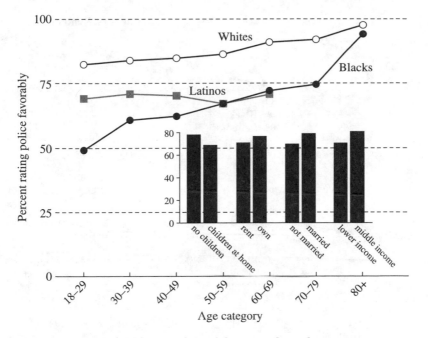

Figure 9.2. Personal Factors and Confidence in the Police, 2001–2003

Compared to age and race, differences among other groups of residents were relatively small. As figure 9.2 illustrates, there was about an eight percentage-point difference between those making less than forty thousand dollars per year and those over that mark. The gap was very similar between married and single people, and between homeowners and renters. The owner-renter difference affected only whites, however. African Americans who had children living at home were more negative than their counterparts, a difference that persists even controlling for age and other factors. This contrast was not significant for either whites or Latinos.

But although Chicagoans were divided, their views of the police improved virtually across the board. Over time almost everyone's confidence in the police increased. These trends are illustrated in figure 9.3. It charts the percentages in various social categories that averaged a positive score on the index that sums up respondents' assessments of the quality of police service in their neighborhoods. As it illustrates, opinions of the police grew more favorable among renters and owners alike, and among both higher- and lower-income

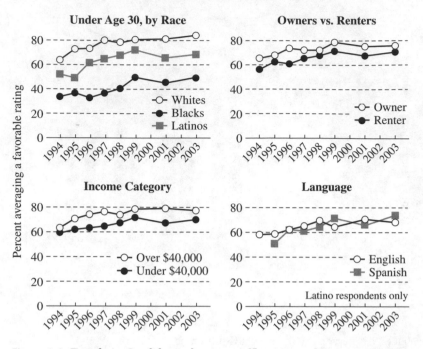

Figure 9.3. Trends in Confidence by Age, Affluence, and Language, 1994–2003

respondents. For example, in 1994 about 56 percent of renters and 66 percent of homeowners were favorable; and in 2001–2003 it was about 70 and 77 percent, respectively. The gap between higher and lower income groups (broken down in the figure at forty thousand dollars) was very small all during the 1990s, and both groups grew more favorable by about 10 percentage points during that period. English- and Spanish-speaking Latinos were largely in agreement about the police, and both groups became more favorable over the course of the 1990s, by 10 percentage points among English-speakers and 20 percentage points among Spanish-speakers. Figure 9.3 also examines trends in the views of younger Chicagoans, those under age thirty, because they are generally the group with the most troubled relationship with the police. It indicates that the views of young adults grew more positive over time. Confidence in the police rose substantially among young whites and Latinos, and—unevenly— from 34 to 50 percent among young African Americans.

Neighborhood Conditions, Community
Outreach, and Confidence in the Police

As all of this indicates, simple demographic shifts cannot explain improving views of the police in Chicago over time, for the change in attitudes was a general one. What factors can account for the trends described here, which seem to transcend the demography of the city? This section examines this question, and presents evidence that at least some of the improved rating of Chicago police was "earned" by improving neighborhood conditions, and a bit was earned by effective community outreach.

We also need to understand more about the enduring gap between the city's whites, African Americans, and Latinos. As noted above, although opinions of the police generally improved during the 1990s, the gulf between the races did not close. The close proximity between those on opposite sides of many other cleavage lines—which is also apparent in figure 9.3—suggests that factors such as economic status do not account for divisions between the races; differences in opinion by income, housing tenure, and other factors are simply too small. As noted earlier, many of the social and economic factors that divide whites and Latinos, in particular, seem to make little difference to African Americans, who are more united in their dissatisfaction. What factors account for the continuing racial divide? There is evidence that some of the continued gaps between the races can be explained by differences in people's personal experiences with the police, which are differentially divided by race and often negative in their consequences.

Improving Neighborhood Conditions

An enduring question for opinion researchers in this field is whether the public holds the police responsible for crime and disorder. The evidence is shaky. When Americans are asked what they think causes crime, opinion ricochets between social causes, drugs, and criminal sentences that are not harsh enough, and I have been unable to discern a trend in opinion concerning the causes of crime. However, police are undoubtedly the municipal agency that is most closely watched and criticized by the general public and the media alike, and about the only one whose annual statistical reports routinely make the nightly news. Of all the problems that we hold city agencies responsible for somehow solving, crime is probably the most compelling of our attention. Doris Graber's (1980) content analysis of network and Chicago news broadcasts revealed that 20 percent of all local news stories and 10 percent of all national stories concerned crime and criminal justice, with the police being mentioned frequently (and often quite critically). Katherine Beckett (1997) found that 90 percent of Americans report that the mass media is their most important source of information about crime and criminal justice. The CAPS publicity campaign stresses the role of the police, in conjunction with city services, in bringing the crime rate down.

Opinion research also indicates there should be a strong link between neighborhood conditions and assessments of the police in Chicago. In surveys, attitudes toward the police are correlated with perceptions of neighborhood crime (Maxson, Hennigan, and Sloane 2003; Reisig and Giacomazzi 1998), fear of crime (Cao, Frank, and Cullen 1996; Smith and Hawkins, 1973), and neighborhood disorder (Reisig and Giacomazzi 1998; Cao, Frank, and Cullen 1996). These studies were all conducted at the individual level, so both attitudes toward police and perceptions of crime were gathered in the same questionnaires. More sophisticated studies that embed survey respondents in their neighborhood contexts come to similar conclusions, however. In studies in different cities, Michael Reisig and Roger Parks (2000; but see Reisig and Parks 2003) and Robert Sampson and Dawn Jeglum-Bartusch (1998) found that variations in neighborhood homicide rates are linked to differences in how people assess the police, even when controlling for important neighborhood factors (such as poverty) and individual factors (including race and experience with the police). One plausible explanation for the improvements in public opinion that were depicted in figure 9.1 is that neighborhood conditions improved in Chicago during the course of the 1990s, sometimes by a great deal.

And in previous chapters we saw evidence of very positive trends in Chicago. Recorded crime was also down all over the city, and hugely so in predominantly African American neighborhoods. When asked about crime and social disorder problems, people's responses were somewhat more mixed. In particular, on many measures, conditions did not improve very dramatically for the city's Latinos, largely because of the impact of massive immigration and the development of new segregated Latino neighborhoods in Chicago. However, reports of crime and disorder problems declined substantially among African Americans, and also among whites, who faced far fewer problems even before community policing began.

To the extent to which these resonate as successes for the *police,* these trends could go a long way toward accounting for increasing confidence in the police. But does the public hold police accountable for these things, and will the public extend police any credit if things get better? Certainly many analysts proceed as if this is the case, when they use survey measures of concern about crime to statistically explain attitudes toward the police. The correlations are usually strong. Liqun Cao, James Frank, and Frances T. Cullen concluded from this that "it appears that citizens hold the police at least partially responsible for the disorder—the "broken windows"—in their neighborhoods. . . . Our respondents appear to perceive the police as the government's first-line representative, responsible for controlling neighborhood disorder."[12] For Chicago, the analyses that follow include measures of crime and disorder conditions at the individual and neighborhood levels.

Effective Community Outreach

We have also seen that one of the most significant features of Chicago's community-policing program is the extensive role created for public involvement. The city's model calls for neighborhood residents to help identify problems and formulate solutions to them. They are also called upon to play an active role in solving these problems. Meetings between community residents and the police who work in their neighborhoods have been a regular feature of CAPS since 1993. Beat meetings were first held in the experimental areas where CAPS was developed, and in 1995 they spread to the remainder of the city. For this analysis I make use of the database of reports on what happened at all 25,294 beat meetings held between 1995 and 2003. These were used to estimate beat-meeting attendance rates for every year between 1995 and 2003. This measure of community mobilization around CAPS reflects the sum of police organizing efforts and resulting public turnout in each area of the city.

The Impact of Conditions and Outreach

The joint impact of factors discussed here is examined in table 9.1. It presents a multilevel analysis of confidence in the police. In particular, we are interested in the impact of improving neighborhood conditions and the extent of neighborhood mobilization around CAPS, for they may help explain the positive trend in opinion in Chicago during

Table 9.1 Hierarchical Models of Confidence in the Police

	1994–2003		1997–2003	
	Coefficient	Standard error	Coefficient	Standard error
Intercept	2.92**	.02	2.92**	.02
Personal Background				
African American	−.07*	.02	−.05**	.02
Latino	.03*	.02	.03*	.02
Other races	.02	.02	.02	.02
Married	.04**	.01	.03**	.01
Age 60 and older	.18**	.02	.13**	.02
Under age 30	−.08**	.01	−.04**	.01
Young and African American	−.12**	.02	−.10**	.02
Years of residence	−.01**	.00	−.01**	.00
Employed	−.06**	.01	−.05**	.01
Individual Perceptions				
Heard of community policing	.03**	.01	.02	.01
Know meetings being held	.10**	.01	.09**	.01
Crime problems (z)	−.10**	.01	−.08**	.01
Social disorder (z)	−.13**	.01	−.12**	.01
Personal Experience				
Positive citizen-initiated	—	—	.05**	.01
Negative citizen-initiated	—	—	−.50**	.02
Positive police-initiated	—	—	.04**	.01
Negative police-initiated	—	—	−.29**	.02
Beat-Level Factors				
Beat meeting attendance rate (z)	—	—	.01*	.01
Percent African American (z)	−.04*	.02	−.05**	.02
Percent Latino (z)	−.05**	.01	−.05**	.01
Poverty index (z)	−.03**	.01	−.03**	.01
Robbery rate (log) (z)	−.06**	.01	−.05**	.01
Residential burglary rate (z)	−.02**	.01	−.01*	.01
Intraclass Correlation	17%		16%	
Variance Explained				
Within neighborhood	15%		25%	
Between neighborhood	90%		92%	
Number of Cases				
Individuals	16,708		12,829	
Contexts	2,046		1,314	

*$p < .05$; **$p < .01$; "z" indicates standardized score; all other measures are dichotomies; "—" indicates not measured or program element not yet in place.

the course of the 1990s. The table combines the opinions of white, African American, and Latino respondents in order to examine the impact of individual and neighborhood factors on views of the police.[13] The individual factors that are included were significant predictors of opinion when they were examined separately. The beat-level factors include a measure of concentrated poverty that combines various census measures of hardship.[14] Two measures of the racial composition of each beat were also included, helping to separate out the unique effects of crime rates as opposed to other features of these areas. Crime is represented by the log of the robbery rate per ten thousand residents of the beat. The data are again organized so that the beat context in which respondents live is described by crime and census data for the year in which they were interviewed. Technically, this is a "fixed effect" model for estimating the impact of context-level measures perceptions of police-service quality.

The left-hand panel of table 9.1 examines data for the eight surveys conducted over a ten-year period. The personal background factors were all measured by dichotomies, so their coefficients can be compared in magnitude. Age was clearly most influential of the personal factors. Older Chicagoans are more positive about the police, while those under age thirty are more negative in their views. African Americans are also more negative, and being both young *and* African American had an added negative impact. Married-couple households were represented by more optimistic residents. Personal factors such as income, education, having children at home, and home ownership were not significant once this short list of personal factors was taken into account, so they are not included here.

Table 9.1 also reports the effects of neighborhood factors that changed over time, some quite dramatically. Respondents' reports of the extent of crime and disorder problems were quite strongly related to assessments of the quality of policing. The coefficients associated with the two indices can be compared to one another, and they had about the same effect. (An index of physical decay problems was not linked to views of the police, on the other hand, and it is not included here.) Respondents were asked if they had heard about the city's community-policing program, and in another section of the questionnaire they were questioned about neighborhood anticrime meetings. As the table indicates, Chicagoans who knew of community policing and beat meeting were more confident about the police as well.

At the neighborhood context level, rates of officially recorded crime mattered as well. Even controlling for poverty and the racial composition of the beat, residents were more negative about the police in areas with high rates of robbery. Crime rates were dropping in almost all areas of the city between 1993 and 2003, and neighborhood crime decline was one factor behind increasing levels of support for the police. In addition, there was support for the police in more affluent areas, and less support where there were concentrations of African Americans and Latinos. The impact of neighborhood-level mobilization around CAPS could only be assessed in later years, for beat meetings did not begin to be held until 1995, so I have included them in the model presented in the right-hand panel of table 9.1. As it indicates, in places where the turnout rate for beat meetings was high, people were generally more favorable toward the police. Together, the factors listed in the table explained almost 87 percent of the difference between beats contexts in confidence in the police.

Separate analyses by race (which are not shown here) find that crime still enters into the equation when whites, African Americans, and Latinos are considered separately. Whites living in areas with relatively high robbery and residential burglary rates reported less confidence in the police. There are relatively few poor whites in Chicago, so there was not much scope for measures of beat affluence, and black-white segregation is so high that there is little variance in measures of their propinquity to African Americans. However, support for police was lower in higher-turnover beats and in places where whites live in proximity to Latinos. Latino opinion was linked to local crime rates and, in addition, was lower in poor areas with large concentrations of Latino residents. African Americans reacted negatively to high levels of personal crime, and concentrated-beat poverty also played a large role in shaping their views of the police.

Personal Experience with the Police

Beginning in 1997, the surveys also included questions tracking citizen-initiated encounters with the police and stops by the police. Citizen-initiated contacts are inventoried using a nine-question list describing the most frequent reasons that people contact the police. These range from reporting a crime or suspicious person to requesting routine information or informing police about an accident or other emergency situation. Throughout this period, about half of all adult Chicagoans recalled initiating an encounter with the police during the course of the past year.

In a 1971 book, Albert Reiss observed that the public relies on the police for a broad range of matters, not just for responding to specific crime incidents. He based this on studies of calls to police department emergency telephone numbers, so he could describe patterns of calls, but not the number or kinds of people who were involved. Surveys can do that and, in addition, they can account for citizen-initiated contacts of all kinds, and not just telephone calls. In the 2001 and 2003 surveys (which are combined here to increase the sample size for key population groups), the most frequent reason to contact police was to report a crime (26 percent of all respondents did so), followed by reporting an accident or some other emergency (19 percent). Between 11 percent and 13 percent of those interviewed recalled reporting suspicious persons or noises, or "things that might lead to a crime." Thirteen percent described contacting police regarding some other neighborhood problem; 12 percent gave police information; and 17 percent reported contacting police to ask for advice or information. Ten percent recalled contacting them about some matter that was not on our list. These percentages overlap, for respondents could contact the police for a variety of different reasons in the course of a year (for more details, see Skogan [2005]). Combining incidents involving possible and probable crimes, 35 percent of all adults contacted police about what they thought might be a criminal matter, while 40 percent approached them about other issues. How the police handle events of all kinds, not just the effectiveness of their "crime-fighting" activities, is likely to impact an appreciable proportion of the population.

Citizen-initiated contacts with the police are also quite common among all major population groups. There is a tendency for younger (under age forty), lower-income people with children living at home to contact the police more often, especially about crime. But with one exception, these encounters were surprisingly evenly distributed by race. More than half of whites and African Americans recalled contacting the police, and the figure was somewhat higher—57 percent—for English-speaking Latinos. The group with the lowest contact rate was Spanish-speaking respondents. Only about one-third of them reported contacting the police in the past year, despite generally adverse neighborhood conditions.

The surveys also asked respondents about their involvement in police-initiated encounters. About 20 percent of those interviewed report having been stopped by police during the past year, either while driving or while they were on foot. Seventeen percent recalled a police-initiated traffic encounter during the previous year, while an overlapping 7 percent described being stopped while on foot. There was also a substantial overlap between police-initiated and citizen-initiated encounters. Among those who were stopped by police, 61 percent also reported *contacting them* about some matter during the course of a year. Chicagoans who were stopped by police were also willing consumers of police services, under different circumstances. This may have consequences for their ratings of the quality of self-initiated encounters. Examining the 1982 British Crime Survey, Michael J. Maxfield (1988) found that a significant portion of the general dissatisfaction with policing described by persons who contacted the police was attributable to their past encounters with police in traffic stops and as the subjects of police investigations.

Not unexpectedly, the distribution of stops by police was strongly related to demographic and social factors. The strongest correlate of being stopped by police was age. Fully 42 percent of respondents age eighteen to twenty-five were stopped during 2001, in contrast to 7 percent of those over age fifty-five. The next most potent predictor of police stops was gender: 28 percent of males, but only 12 percent of females reported being stopped by police during the course of a year. Additionally, the racial background of Chicagoans was related to their risk of being stopped by police as well. In 2001, 26 percent of African Americans surveyed reported being stopped by Chicago police during the past year, in contrast to 16 percent of whites, and 20 percent of Latinos.

The combined effect of these three factors is illustrated in figure 9.4. It divides survey respondents into eighteen age-sex-race groups, and illustrates the percentage of each that reported being stopped by police during the previous year. In this figure, "young" respondents are age eighteen to twenty-five; "middle-age" spans the ages twenty-six to fifty-five; and "older" respondents are over age fifty-five. It graphically depicts the fate of the demographic group at highest risk: young African American males. The very high stop rate for young African American males—71 percent in the course of a year—contrasts with all other groups. Taking these three factors into account statistically, using logistic regression, the impact of age was greater than that of sex or race. Compared to those over age fifty-five, those in the youngest age category were 6.7 times as likely to be stopped, and those age twenty-six to fifty-five were 2.3 times as likely

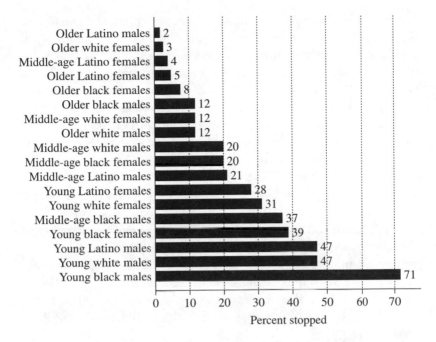

Figure 9.4. Age-Race-Sex Distribution of Stops by Police, 2001–2003

to be stopped. Note that the six groups depicted in figure 9.4 that included young males were among the seven most frequently stopped groups. Next came differences associated with gender. The three most stopped age and racial groups involved males, as were four of the top five, and males were 2.5 times more likely to be stopped than were females. Only two of the top half of these categories included white respondents, both young, while four of the six white groups were in the bottom half when ranked by police stops. Compared to whites, African Americans were 2.5 times as likely to be stopped, while—controlling statistically for age and gender—Latinos were stopped at about the same rate as were whites.

What transpires during encounters makes a difference in people's views of the police. One consistent finding of research is that encounters with police are less "outcome–oriented" than they are "processoriented"; that is, people are less concerned about someone being caught or (in many instances) getting stolen property back than they are in how promptly and responsibly they are treated by the authorities. Police are judged by what physicians might call their "bedside manner." Factors such as how willing police are to listen to people's stories and show concern for their plight are very important, as are their politeness, helpfulness, and fairness. Rapid response has positive effects as well; studies by Frank Furstenberg and Charles Wellford (1973), Antony Pate (1976), Steven Percy (1980), and others document the impact of the speed of police response on victim satisfaction. Information sharing is also very important; police willingness to give advice and to notify victims of progress in their case has a great effect on victim satisfaction, for example (Sunshine and Tyler 2003; Tyler and Huo 2002; Skogan 1989). The 1988 British Crime Survey found 56 percent of victims complaining that police did not keep them informed about their cases. This lack of communication between police and victims was strongly related to general measures of victim dissatisfaction (Mayhew et al. 1989). Research on police-initiated contacts finds that fair and courteous treatment, giving people reasons for stopping them, and explaining their rights all contribute to satisfaction with encounters (Bland, Miller, and Quinton 2000; Bucke 1997; Quinton, Bland, and Miller 2000; Stone and Pettigrew 2000).

In Chicago, respondents who had contacts with police were asked follow-up questions about what happened at the time and how satisfied they were with the way police handled the incident. They were asked about police response time and demeanor, and about the help they received and the fairness with which they were treated. Efforts by the police at establishing two-way communication were measured by asking whether police told those who called what actions police were going to take in response to residents' complaints. The survey also asked about the politeness and helpfulness of police in citizen-initiated encounters, and about their politeness and fairness in police-evoked contacts. In general, reviews of citizen-initiated encounters were favorable. About 70 percent of those who contacted police indicated that they "came right away," or that they scheduled an appointment to meet with the police (which was also coded a satisfactory police response). They were almost unanimous about the politeness with which they were treated (90 percent gave police a favorable rating). They were also very positive that the police paid attention to what they had to say (86 percent) and were helpful (82 percent). Police were least successful at making it clear to the public what they were going to do with their complaints (71 percent were favorable on this dimension). Not surprisingly, those who were pulled over or stopped while they were on foot were less satisfied with their experience. However, even a majority of them responded on the positive end of each evaluative question. They frequently reported about the fairness with which they were treated (66 percent were favorable) and police care in explaining the situation to them (64 percent favorable). They were least satisfied with how politely they were treated (59 percent) and police attention to what they had to say on their own behalf (62 percent).

Perhaps predictably, given the history of police-community relations in the city, reactions to the service being rendered when they called the police varied a bit by race. Latinos interviewed in Spanish were somewhat more likely than English-speakers to think that police did not pay careful attention to what they had to say. Whites were more likely to report that police came rapidly when they called. But overall, the relatively equal—and high—levels of satisfaction among persons of different races were an accomplishment. Research tends to find that African American victims of crime are significantly less satisfied than are whites when they contact them for assistance (see, for example, Homant, Kennedy, and Fleming 1984). In Chicago such differences were small.

There were larger and more consistent race and language-related differences in what police did on the scene when it came to police-initiated encounters, however. Overall, the police were described as delivering modestly acceptable levels of service; generally, about two-thirds of those who were stopped gave them favorable marks. But the overall figures disguise sharp racial divisions. African Americans and Spanish-speaking Latinos in particular were far less likely to report that police had explained why they had been stopped, or that police paid attention to what they had to say or explained why they did what they did. The situation was somewhat better for Latinos who were interviewed in English, but they too were significantly less likely than were whites to report receiving good service. Foot and traffic stops initiated by the police were received in critical fashion by any but the city's whites. Only about half of African Americans and Latinos found police to be polite, compared to 70 percent of whites who were stopped. Both groups were significantly more likely than were whites to feel that they were treated unfairly. These findings parallel those of some of the earliest studies of police interactions with the public, which found that African Americans were much more likely than whites to report experiencing insulting language, unnecessary searches of their person, and instances of police brutality.

Impact of Personal Experience

Not surprisingly, respondents' personal experiences strongly affect their general views of the quality of police service. The findings are bad news for the police, however. In general, the impact of encounters is "asymmetrical"; that is, having a positive experience helps a little bit, but having a bad experience hurts a great deal. The effects of how police handled their encounters with the public were independent of the personal background of our respondents, and in particular their effects—a bit good but mostly bad—were about the same among whites, African Americans, and Latinos.

The statistical impact of encounters with the police was summarized in table 9.1 above. It presented two multilevel analyses of confidence in the police, and the rightmost panel also includes measures of the quality of personal contacts with police. As before, the analysis also controls for the effects of race, age, and other personal factors, as well as for neighborhood characteristics, and adds beat-meeting turnout rates. In this case, we examine the opinions of 11,693 white, African American, and Latino respondents interviewed between 1997 and 2003 to examine the impact of personal experience.

Together, the factors described in table 9.1 explained 26 percent of the individual-level variance in views of the police. The variance explained is substantially higher than that for the analysis that did not include measures of personal experience in the models. Age was still influential, but the direct effects of age dropped by about 50 percent once experiences with the police (which are mainly the domain of the young) were taken into account. The direct effect of being an African American also dropped by about half. One reason for the declining strength of the coefficient associated with being an African American is that they were most likely to report being dissatisfied when they call and—especially—when they were stopped by the police, and that is now included in our model of satisfaction with police services. These findings parallel those of some of the earliest studies of police interactions with the public, which found that African Americans were much more likely than whites to report experiencing insulting language, unnecessary searches of their person, and instances of police brutality. In addition, being both young and African American continued to have an added negative impact. Fear of crime and perceptions of neighborhood conditions were still very influential, as were beat-level measures of crime, poverty, and race. There also was a significant link between the extent of neighborhood mobilization around CAPS (which was measured by beat-meeting turnout rates) and positive views by residents of the quality of local policing.

A key point in the right-hand panel of table 9.1 is the effect of recent personal experience with the police. It separately identifies those reporting positive and negative experiences during citizen- and police-initiated encounters, using the self-report measures of what happened at the scene. Statistically, the effects of these positive and negative experiences are being contrasted with each other (for respondents with both police- and self-initiated encounters to describe) and with not having any recent experience to report about. The latter is the omitted reference category.

Table 9.1 documents that the independent effects of *negative* experiences are quite robust. Positive and negative experiences were measured as dichotomies, as were all of the personal factors, so the coefficients are comparable. For both self-initiated and police-initiated encounters, it appears that the impact of bad experience was about *ten times* as influential as the impact of having had a good experience. In short, some of the most important determinants of general satisfaction with police are the negative things that happen when they encounter the police. These include police being seemingly impolite, unhelpful, unfair, inattentive to what respondents had to say, and unwilling to explain to respondents what was going on. Summary measures of these experiences account for more than one-third of the explained variance in attitudes toward the police. This highlights the extreme importance of the police treating people well as they conduct their routine business. At a time in which there is much discussion of "problem-oriented policing" and "intelligence-driven policing," there is evidence pointing to the importance of "process-oriented policing" as well.

The effects of experience varied a bit by race. In separate analyses by race (not shown), there was a positive effect of having a good experience when contacting the police only among whites; neither African Americans nor Latinos were impressed by good service when they called. In the aggregate, the impact of having a favorable police-initiated encounter was statistically significant. However, the coefficient is small and its statistical significance is due to the large number of cases involved; when considered separately by race, satisfactory police-initiated encounters had no significant impact. In short, people seem to expect good service, since receiving it has no substantial impact on their general views of the police. Nothing in the model approaches the importance of having a bad experience, on the other hand. Other factors pale in importance in the face of having a bad experience with the police.

There was little trend in reports of contacts with the police over the 1997–2003 period. The frequency of police-initiated contacts dropped a bit, from 25 percent in 1997 to 19 percent in 2003, which contributed to increasing overall satisfaction over time. The police-initiated encounters that took place became increasingly neutral over that period; the percentage of stops that were positively *and* negatively interpreted both declined. There were no particular trends in the frequency or character of citizen-initiated contacts.

These findings about the effects of police-citizen encounters are not good news. The hypothesis that the impact of encounters with the police might be "asymmetrical"—that is, that favorable contacts may not have positive consequences while unfavorable experiences deflate people's overall rating of the police—was first proposed by Herbert Jacob, based on his study of Milwaukee residents (Jacob 1971). More recently, Miller, et al. (2005) found comparable asymmetry in a study of police-initiated encounters in New York City, and I replicated this asymmetry in a reexamination of surveys conducted in seven different cities (Skogan 2006). There is debate over this issue. Reisig and Parks (2000) found a significant link between situational satisfaction and the general views of the public regarding the police, but the link between situational dissatisfaction and ratings of the police was much stronger. Their measures closely resemble those used in the Chicago study, as did their analysis model. The classic studies of police-public contacts (including Dean 1980; Poister and McDavid 1978; Smith and Hawkins 1973) all came to the same conclusion: positive experiences help. On the other hand, in a study that directly addressed issues of causal direction, Brandl et al. (1994) found that the effect of experience on general atitudes was not very large, and that a countereffect—that of people's general views of the police on how they interpreted their recent experiences—was stronger. In their view, people stereotype the police and selectively perceive even their own experiences. Brandt et al. do not make the link, since their 1994 article, social psychologists have begun to stress an opposing hypothesis—that general, preexisting attitudes shape how people interpret individual experiences. These psychologists find that people read their experiences in the light of their prior expectations; therefore, perhaps more than their experiences affect their general expectations. General attitudes affect their evaluations of the encounters they find themselves caught up in, rather than the reverse. By inference, this implies that the quality of service rendered does not matter very much, but few would want to press that point normatively. As a normative question, the answer seems quite clear: Americans are committed to both equality of treatment and an objectively fair level of treatment through almost every aspect of their laws and Constitution. But the empirical message is, unfortunately, "You can't win, no matter what you do. It only counts when it goes against you."

Explaining Trends in Confidence

The question of how well these personal, experiential, and neighborhood factors accounted for changing confidence in the police over time is examined in figure 9.5. It compares trends in confidence revealed by the surveys, with statistical predictions using the factors examined in table 9.1. Two statistical predictions are presented. The first extends from 1994 until 2003, and is based on the personal, perceptual, and beat-level factors available for the entire series. The shorter-term prediction incorporates the post-1997 addition of measures of respondents' personal experiences with the police. The latter prediction, in particular, is closely aligned with actual trends in opinion. Both predictions account for the post-1999 leveling-off of confidence in police, following a half-decade of improvement. As we have seen, concern about neighborhood conditions mounted among Latinos during the early years of the twenty-first century, and the percentage of them living in predominantly Latino areas grew then as well. Even among African Americans, reports of neighborhood gang, drug, and social disorder problems ceased improving post-2000. These turnarounds all predicted slowing improvement in confidence in the police.

How Did Chicago Do?

There is both good and bad news in this story of police-community relations. Over time, Chicagoans became more positive about the quality of police service in their immediate neighborhoods. This was a general trend, not confined to one class or caste, and it was good news for the police. But in 2003, after nine years of citywide commu-

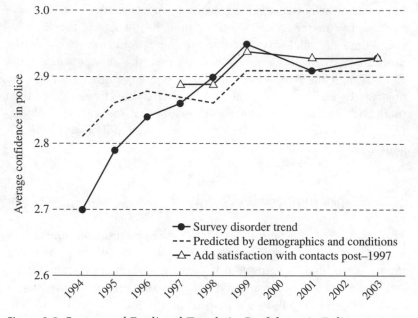

Figure 9.5. Survey and Predicted Trends in Confidence in Police

nity policing, there were still large gaps between the races. The views of African Americans and Latinos had not yet moved solidly into the favorable range, and there was plenty of room left for improvement.

The favorable trends were largely accounted for by improving neighborhood conditions and community mobilization around CAPS. For many, the city got cleaner and safer, and residents apparently thought this was due to community policing and the good efforts of the mayor. A good deal of the remaining gap between whites and African Americans—perhaps half of the direct effect of race—was accounted for by the frequency and dissatisfaction engendered by police-initiated stops, and these experiences accounted for a lot of the age-related dissatisfaction with police. Through their good works, the police earned what they received, and they paid a price for what they lost at the same time on the street.

Did neighborhood successes fully account for the marked upward trend in confidence in the police in Chicago over time? In this regard, it is instructive to observe the various trend lines presented in this chapter closely. In figure 9.1 it was apparent that support for the police grew during the 1990s, but leveled off during the early 2000s. Most measures of neighborhood conditions showed the same pattern, except for Spanish-speaking Latinos. Gang violence and school disorder stopped declining in the early 2000s, and the rates at which crime and fear were declining slowed noticeably. The matching trends are consistent with the inference that improving neighborhood conditions during the 1990s drove up support for the police, among all Chicagoans. To assess this statistically I added an individual-level trend measure to the 1993–2003 and 1997–2003 data sets, to test whether there was still a tendency toward more favorable views of the police in later years, once the factors included in the models were taken into account. There was still a significant positive trend in the 1993–2003 data set, but in the 1997–2003 analysis that included encounters with police and a beat-level measure of community mobilization around CAPS, that trend disappeared.

It may be significant that many of the trends reported here run counter to those revealed by surveys of the public's confidence in institutions of government and public officials more generally. In the United States, belief that elected leaders care "what people like me think" has been on the decline since the 1950s. Patricia Moy and Mark Pfau note that there is "a profound and consistent lack of confidence in the executive branch of the federal government," and document that the proportion of Americans who believe that "the government in Washington" can be trusted "to do what is right" dropped from 76 percent in 1964 to just 14 percent in 1994.[15] Yet during the 1990s, Chicago bucked the trend. There were positive shifts in views of policing, and support for the police grew among all major population groups. To be sure, there remained plenty of room for improvement. After more than a half-decade of community policing, public perceptions of police job performance just hit the 50 percent mark among African Americans and Latinos, and their perceptions of police responsiveness did not rise much above that level. But a larger proportion of residents in all groups reported that police were helpful, concerned, and fair, and the trend line for other aspects of their jobs was in the right direction.

How Did Chicago Do?

How did Chicago do, after more than a decade of community policing? This chapter reviews the most important challenges facing the city and the police department, to see whether their efforts were effective and how the city changed over the course of more than a decade. The chapter revisits the data to shed more light on who benefited from community policing. There were many reasons to fear that community policing—like many government programs—would mostly benefit the already well off. Everyone expected that white homeowners would get along with the police, just as the police would feel most comfortable allying with them. Decades of bitter struggle over the disproportionate exercise of force and discrimination within the department itself were unlikely to prepare the city's poorer African Americans to embrace the program. Research on voluntary social programs had also documented that more-educated middle-class people quickly learn about programs and find ways to use them to their benefit. They are more likely to be vocal and articulate spokespersons for their interests and for those of their neighborhoods, perhaps helping them get more out of CAPS.

So, the sections that follow review the fundamental challenges facing CAPS, and then reexamine what happened, and the distribution of outcomes by race. It will be no surprise to the reader that things came out worst for the city's Latinos, so after reviewing the main findings, there is a summary section that pulls together what we learned about the fate of the nation's largest immigrant group.

Challenge: Implement and Sustain a Significant Program

The first challenge facing the city was to actually implement a program and stick with it over the long haul. As I noted in chapter 1, community policing is a high-risk commitment, it may be expensive, other parts of government may fail to support it, and programs fail. Cities may start off with a strong neighborhood orientation, but then pull back in favor of other priorities following a change in leadership at the top. New York City's abandonment of Mayor Dinkins's commitment to dedicated community officers when Mayor Giuliani came to office is but one example of this. Chapter 1 described how Cleveland cut its payroll and closed its neighborhood mini-stations after federal funding for police salaries dried up. Seattle retrenched its training effort—a very important factor in fielding an effective community-policing program—in the face of union intransigence (they charged that the training was "political correctness indoctrination"). Officers in Fort Worth's special neighborhood policing unit had little support among their peers and virtually none from other city agencies.

Chicago actually implemented a program. Beginning in April 1993, the city spent more than a year experimenting with the details in a few test districts, before going citywide with the final product. Learning from the difficulties faced by other cities, they avoided creating special community-policing units, which inevitably would have been tagged something like "empty holster guys," as Houston's community-policing officers were in the 1980s. In fact, there was early concern about a connection being made between the acronym "CAPS" and "cap pistols," which are not "real guns." Instead of splitting the force, CAPS became the plan for the entire department. The transformation began with the patrol division, but the introduction of a managerial accountability system later forced units from all over the department to coordinate their efforts around the districts' priorities. During the fall of 1994 the remaining twenty police districts followed the experimental districts by dividing their officers into rapid response units and beat teams. Beat-team officers spent most of their time responding to calls in their assigned area, and 911 dispatching procedures were fine-tuned to ensure that they stayed there most of the time. Sergeants and midlevel managers went through several training programs, and between January and May 1995, more than nine thousand officers completed three days of problem-solving training. By then, a coordinated system for delivering city services in response to requests submitted by officers had been phased in throughout the city. Civilian administrative managers were assigned to each of the districts in order to beef up their management capability. About 250 beat meetings were held each month, creating opportunities for residents to get involved throughout the city. An average of five to seven officers attended these meetings, most of whom worked on assignments in the area. Starting in autumn 1995, community organizing and problem-solving training sessions were conducted across the city by teams of civilians and police officers, and in the end almost twelve thousand residents were trained. The Strategic Inspections Task Force was formed in November 1996 to coordinate the efforts of police and other city agencies against gang and drug houses, and negligent landlords.

During 1996 and 1997 the city expanded its staff of civilian community-outreach workers charged with turning residents out for marches and rallies, and sustaining participation in beat meetings. More staff members were brought on to support a new emphasis on housing issues and the court advocacy program, which enlisted community members to support the districts' prosecution priorities. Civilian staff members also coordinated city services in support of CAPS problem-solving projects, and as part of district efforts to target gang and drug hotspots. Beginning in 1997, the department began to tailor its rookie-training curriculum to CAPS. During 1996 and 1997 the city mounted a substantial civic education effort through the media. Television and radio programs, billboards, videos, brochures, mailings, festival booths, and district and citywide rallies were targeted at promoting awareness of CAPS and involvement in its activities. Block-club conventions, citywide and regional neighborhood assemblies, CAPS rallies, and a national conference on community policing showcased Chicago's program. At the end of the 1990s, city attorneys were assigned to selected district stations to work directly with officers on buildings in their beats with drug and gang problems, and the county prosecutor began a community-prosecutions program in three neighborhood offices. A new city department was created that consolidated many CAPS-related quality-of-life cases for administrative adjudication, moving them from the courts for quicker processing.

Overall, the pace of change was impressive. Chapter 3 described the 1998–1999 period as one in which CAPS was "dead in the water," yet during that very period, forces for change within the department were gathering to impose managerial controls that helped ensure that many aspects of CAPS became "bureaucratized," in the good meaning of that word. Earlier, the program's successes depended too much on the extraordinary efforts of its founders, the good intentions of street officers, and the attention that the mayor could give this new venture. A new generation of managers clearly defined who was responsible for what, and everyone was more thoroughly trained in their new roles. In 2000, a new unit was created within the department that was charged with revitalizing key components of the city's community-policing effort. The CAPS unit was housed in a management bureau that was created to oversee the department's effectiveness on a broad front. The internal inspections unit was also transferred there, to increase management control over CAPS-related activities. The bureau ran the department's equivalent of New York City's CompStat process, and included CAPS and community-related issues on the list of issues for which district commanders were held accountable. At its founding, CAPS was an acronym for "Chicago Alternative Policing Strategy." By 2003, it was no longer an alternative, but the way the department did business.

An unknowable that is still on the horizon is the longer-term impact of moving—as many departments have—toward centralized, data-driven management. I dubbed this "Chicago style" CompStat because the local version retained a somewhat broader and more community-policing focus that New York City's model. However, what gets measured is what matters, and the department is best at measuring crimes and arrests. Beginning about 2003, priorities at police headquarters began to shift toward tough, focused enforcement. A crime scare created by a major local newspaper (The *Chicago Tribune*) led the mayor and a new chief of police to reorganize and refocus the department on guns, gangs, and homicides. There is a risk that the focus of the department will shift away from community policing back to activities that better fit a recentralized management structure driven by recorded crime.

Challenge: Engage the Community

It was not just changing the police department that was a high-risk CAPS venture. Community involvement in community policing also could not be taken for granted. It would be hard to get the message out, and police were not accustomed to finding customers by marketing their services. There was concern that people would not turn out for beat meetings once the novelty of CAPS wore off. Participation might spike in the early months of CAPS, but attending beat meetings month in and month out is hard work, since they are held in good weather and bad, and consume a good chunk of the evenings of hard-working people. It was also feared that the *wrong* people would turn out, reflecting the middle-class bias that afflicts many voluntary programs. Police priority setting might be commandeered by articulate, well-organized people already experienced in getting what they wanted from city hall. CAPS threatened to become the domain of neighborhoods that were in good shape, where people already had a history of getting along with the police. It was also not clear that the public could be relied on to take any initiative in tackling neighborhood problems. Face-to-face meetings with the police might turn out merely to be gripe sessions, an inefficient alternative to 911. It was clear that ordinary residents would need training if they were to become effective CAPS activists, for abstractions like problem solving using the crime triangle had proved hard even for police officers to understand.

We have seen that some of these concerns were realized, but many were not. Archon Fung (2004) worried that the quality of beat meetings, the effectiveness with which they were conducted, and the attention paid to them by police would be correlated with the sophistication, affluence, and political skills of the audience. However, in the field he found that the structure and organizational resources provided by the police helped smooth out the effects of these divisions. Our systematic observations of hundreds of beat meetings found no link at all between the race or class of the area and measures of what went on there. Most people who attended were pretty ordinary, but the issues that were discussed and the information that was presented were concrete, locally oriented, and easy for them to relate to their own experiences. Because the police who were there were also answering calls in the neighborhood, everyone understood they had a concrete stake in the outcome of the meetings. There was demographic bias in meeting turnout: within neighborhoods (an important caveat), older, home-owning, long-term residents were substantially overrepresented at the meetings, and this had consequences. It tended to devalue community concern about some crime problems (notably burglary and street crime) and dissatisfaction with the police, because people who were concerned about those issues tended to be underrepresented at the meetings.

However, concern that the wrong people would turn out was unfounded in many other important ways. Those who showed up at the meetings adequately represented their neighbors on many dimensions. They accurately represented public concern about two of the most highly ranked and important issues facing the city's neighborhoods: gang violence and street drug markets. Participants also mirrored their communities' views concerning the extent of social disorder and physical decay. By and large, those who attended and those who did not still shopped at the same supermarkets, stood on the same subway platforms, and saw the same graffiti when they walked around the neighborhood. An important feature of CAPS was that the areas involved were small. The "establishment" that predominated was not some nonlocal elite faction; they lived down the street. Size mattered, in this case ensuring that everyone faced pretty much the same everyday problems.

The concern that the better off would take most advantage of the program also overlooked the issue of *why* people got involved with CAPS. The short answer is that they were propelled to attend by crime and disorder problems in their neighborhoods. Compared to their neighbors, those who came to the meetings were more concerned about almost every issue. At the beat level, the number one correlate of meeting attendance rates was violent crime. As a result, CAPS attendance was highest in the poorest, more disorganized parts of the city. Attendance rates were highest in predominantly African American beats, as was awareness of CAPS and awareness that the meetings were taking place. As chapter 4 pointed out, participation rates were also higher where other institutions were failing to deliver; meeting turnout was highest in places with the lowest school test scores and attendance rates, and in the beats where infant mortality and tuberculosis rates were highest. Beat meeting attendance was strongest in places where informal social controls were weakest, and where, in the past, residents were least confident in their ability to intervene and take charge of problems themselves. During the mid-1990s, teams of civilian and police trainers fanned out to conduct problem-solving training sessions for the public, and an analysis of turnout for training found that it was higher in poor, high-crime, African American areas as well (Skogan et al. 1999). It was bad news as well as good news that people without many other alternatives were attending beat meetings and training sessions in larger numbers, but participating they were. Another piece of good news was that the civic-action component of the program was at its best in the beats that needed it the most. We observed that efforts to use beat meetings to bring out people for action projects was more common in troubled areas, and beat-meeting participants were most likely to get involved in aggressive CAPS-sponsored problem-solving projects in high-crime beats.

Variations in the ability of residents to stick with CAPS remained a reason for concern. Surveys of meeting participants revealed the importance of the cadre of regular attenders. Regulars counted for more numerically, because over time they contributed very disproportionately to the overall attendance rate. They were also much more likely to report being involved in diverse CAPS-related activities, ranging from attending citywide forums to marching and participating in stand-ups and smoke-outs. Attendance, as well as activism, was low in beats where not very many regulars stuck it out. On the other hand, frequent participants were older than their neighbors, more likely to be retired, and they did not have children at home or in the local schools. They were more likely than their neighbors to be concerned about physical decay—a property-value related issue—and they were less concerned about crime. They were also more likely to be pro-police, another representativeness problem with beat meetings. The demography of attending conspired with language and culture to severely disadvantage Latinos, leaving them underrepresented and uninvolved.

Figure 10.1 examines the city's over-time success in involving residents. It tracks cumulative turnout at beat meetings for beats classified by their predominate race in 1990. Between 1995 and 2003, Chicagoans turned up at the meetings on about 582,000 occasions, and the figure tracks this growing number for each category of beats. It examines turnout *rates* because these groupings of beats varied considerably in population size, and it examines *adult* turnout because some Chicagoans (e.g., whites) had far fewer children, skewing population totals. Generally, turnout was highest where it was needed the most. As the figure illustrates, attendance rates were highest in predominantly African American areas, and lowest (and only about half as high) in majority-white beats. Latino areas and diverse beats (most including varying mixes of whites, Latinos, and Asians) fell between the two poles, and had almost exactly the same turnout pattern. The right panel divides the beats into four categories, based on the index of concentrated poverty. The index is based on household income, home ownership, family structure, and the rate at which residents of the area received public aid.

While there was a great deal of good news regarding the ability of CAPS to engage the community, Chicago's Latinos presented a difficult challenge. They were least likely to be aware of CAPS and opportunities to participate, and they did not turn out in expected numbers despite worsening conditions in predominantly Latino beats. Their views were underrepresented at beat meetings, and this turned out to be one of the most important factors that kept the meetings from adequately representing public concern about crime. Latinos were least likely to turn out for the problem-solving training sessions held dur-

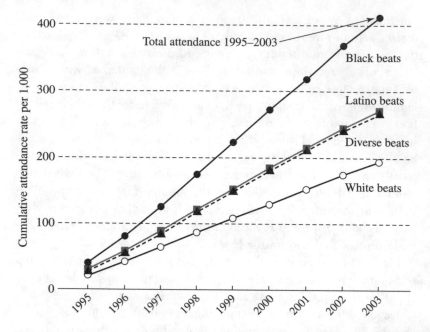

Figure 10.1. Cumulative Beat Meeting Turnout Rates by Race, 1995–2003

ing the mid-1990s, and the participation gap for Latinos was even larger when the amount of crime in their neighborhood—which should have encouraged participation—was taken into account (Skogan et al. 1999). A later section of this chapter reviews some of the reasons for this participation gap, as well as explanations for deteriorating conditions in the city's Latino neighborhoods.

Challenge: Respond Effectively to Crime and Fear

Our surveys documented that, early on, crime was the number one issue on Chicagoans' minds. CAPS itself was a political reaction to crime, for as the city scrabbled to put together a credible response to mounting violence at the end of the 1980s and early 1990s, doing something about the police department was within the mayor's power and could afford to get started in a few areas.

CAPS-related strategies for responding to crime included targeting the department's resources on a more diverse and nuanced list of priorities. There was hope that the new beat teams would be close observers of the scene and would gain more local knowledge about crime in their assigned areas. They might pick up useful information and informants at beat meetings. More important, decentralization enabled officers to have different priorities and adopt different tactics from place to place, something that did not happen easily in a top-down, command-and-control-oriented organization. Later, the department's new accountability-management system brought more pressure from downtown to respond effectively to local crime patterns. District resource allocation was to be helped along by the department's new data analysis capacity, including sophisticated computer mapping. A revised anti-loitering ordinance gave officers new powers to tackle gangs and street drug sales, and the Strategic Inspection Task Force targeted gang and drug houses.

To evaluate police effectiveness, we have to look at the priorities that are set for them. They do not have the resources to take on every problem with equal vigor, and they inevitably will do better at some things than others. Crime fighting embraces community policing at the priority-setting stage. One goal of CAPS was to involve the public in setting local priorities, enabling residents to identify the crimes that were most worrisome to them, and then to focus on responding more effectively to those. In twelve years of study, I never saw the department originate a crime-reduction goal downtown. Rather than promise to achieve some percentage decrease in crime, its strategy was to listen to the public and respond as effectively as it could to the issues concerning the residents of each neighborhood. Our evaluation of the effectiveness of CAPS in its original experimental districts followed up on this by tracking progress against the top priorities of the public in each area. We identified these priorities by conducting local surveys. We found successes vis-à-vis local priorities in every district. Police did best countering gang and drug problems, street crime, and burglary and, overall, they succeeded (compared to trends in matched comparison districts) in significantly reducing about half of the public's high-priority problems (Skogan and Hartnett 1997).

For police, judging public priorities was a not an exact science. We saw that participants at beat meetings were not at their most effective when it came to representing community concern about crimes like burglary and street crime. This was partly due to the underrepresentation of Latinos and younger adults at the meetings, because they were generally more concerned about those problems. However, the meetings did a good job mirroring community concern about gangs, drugs, and disorder. Further, surveys of both groups found that police officers who attended the meetings were in broad agreement with residents concerning the significance of the problems they were facing. This was not just because they were meeting with activists and hearing their concerns, of course. By and large, the officers attending worked in the beat and could observe conditions there firsthand. They were fielding 911 calls from the general public as well as receiving complaints voiced at the meetings. All of this helped orient them toward the priorities brought to the meetings by residents.

Figure 10.2 summarizes trends in survey measures of the extent of neighborhood crime problems and fear. As it illustrates, these varied depending on to whom we were talking. The left-hand panel examines the index of concern about burglary, auto theft, and street crime that was discussed in chapter 8. It compares 1994 and 2003 survey responses for respondents grouped by race. The figure also reports the exact percentage-point changes for each group over that ten-year period. Compared to 1994, concern among African Americans in 2003 dropped by half. Whites reported a little less concern about these problems over time (the index declines by only 2 percent), but they were not very worried about them even at the outset; in 1994, only 6 percent thought that crime was a big problem in their neighborhoods. Among Latinos, on the other hand, concern about these crimes skyrocketed. By 2003, Latinos were almost *twice* as concerned about crime as they were in 1994; their index rose from 17 to 30 percent.

The surveys also document a great deal of variation in trends in fear of crime. Overall, the percentage of Chicagoans who were afraid to walk the streets of their neighborhoods at night declined from 41 percent to 26 percent between 1994 and 2003. African Americans were initially the most fearful group, but by 2003, fear among this group had dropped by 22 percentage points. As we have seen, fear was linked to neighborhood conditions, and among African Americans the percentage dropped in tandem with the tremendous improvement in recorded crime in their neighborhoods. Fear also dropped a great deal among whites, who saw smaller but across-the-board improvements in their neighborhoods. Fear declined only a little among Latinos (5 percentage points), so by 2003 they were, as a group, substantially more fearful than were African Americans. Fear dropped the least among Spanish speakers, who were not seeing any improvement in their lives.

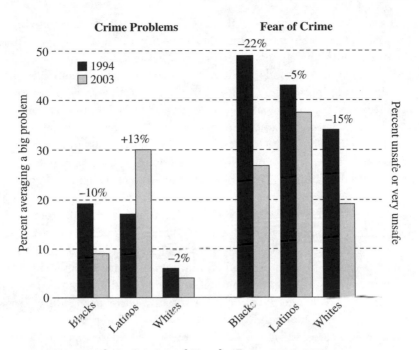

Figure 10.2. Trends in Crime and Fear by Race, 1994–2003

In short, when it came to crime and fear, Chicago saw both successes and noticeable failures. Things got a lot better for African Americans, the city's largest group. They got better for the declining number of whites. The losers were Latinos, who made up more than a quarter of the city's population by 2003.

Challenge: Fix Broken Windows

Another challenge facing the police was to succeed in tackling a broad problem-solving agenda. From the beginning CAPS focused on grime as well as crime. Police began to delve into a broad range of social-disorder and physical-decay issues that heretofore had low priority. This was one of the consequences of opening themselves up to the public, for residents did not make neat legal or bureaucratic distinctions about who was responsible for what. Observations of beat meetings found residents were often as vocal about graffiti on garage doors and people draining their car radiators at the curb as they were about burglary. Chicago was also deeply committed to the "broken windows" argument that social disorder and demoralizing physical decay can undermine the capacity of neighborhoods to defend themselves against serious victimizing crime. Police could help keep neighborhoods healthy by encouraging self-help efforts and backstopping residents when the problems they faced were too complex, demanding, or dangerous for them to tackle on their own. Finally, a focus on the city's appearance fit the mayor's vision for a postindustrial Chicago. The city had to attract tourists and convention-goers, retain white-collar and service jobs, and encourage housing construction and rehabilitation. Keeping the city clean and green as well as safe was integral to his agenda.

The CAPS strategy included mobilizing the public in its own defense. Many community-policing cities do not go this far, at most encouraging residents to call 911 quickly. Chicago planned from the outset to utilize block clubs and community organizations whenever possible, and the CAPS Implementation Office tried to organize them in communities where the civic infrastructure was weak. Public participation in problem solving proved to be widespread. Substantial numbers of beat-meeting participants were involved in marches and rallies, prayer vigils, neighborhood patrols, and "positive loitering" campaigns to reclaim the roadways from street prostitutes. They participated in weekend graffiti cleanups and attacked underage and public drinking using the city's "vote dry" procedures. A survey of participants at beat meetings found half reporting involvement in one or more CAPS-related problem-solving activities. Just as important, involvement in problem solving was heaviest in poorer, high-crime, predominately African American neighborhoods that needed this kind of help most.

Agency partnerships were another key feature of the city's initiative. In cities where community policing is the police department's program, problem solving typically addresses crime patterns identified through the personal observations of officers while driving around, rather than the broad range of problems that CAPS took on. In Chicago, community policing is the city's program, and every relevant agency made an effort to support problem solving at the beat and district levels. This was not easy to accomplish, for the bureaucracies had their own priorities and operating routines, and they initially did not realize that community policing was their program too.

In addition to harnessing existing bureaucracies, CAPS was intimately involved in the operation of problem-solving structures that were created during the course of the 1990s. A new quasi-judicial administrative process sped the processing of those cited for municipal ordinance violations. Through fines, restitution orders, license suspensions, and orders to perform community service, the hearings increased pressure on slumlords and the owners of drug houses to regain control of their buildings and quickly bring them into compliance with health and safety regulations. Aggressive administrative action was taken against troublemaking bars. An inspections task force coordinated efforts by the police and fire departments, building inspectors, and health and business-licensing departments to attack buildings prioritized by the police districts' problem-building coordinators. The city's attorney threw a small staff of lawyers into the project, assigning them to prosecute cases identified by the task force and police liaison officers in their assigned districts. They sought fines for building owners and negotiated settlements that forced them to install new security measures, repair code violations, evict problem tenants, or close and board up hopeless buildings.

Getting the police behind this agenda was the most difficult task of all. It did not fit the department's fast-response culture. It called upon officers to think through complex cause-and-effect explanations for the concentration of crimes in particular places, which was not their strong suit. After the initial push they had inadequate follow-up training, and neither their immediate supervisors nor the top brass who devised this strategy had ever actually done any formal problem solving of their own. In practice, beat officers often did not get very far past patrolling more and making more car stops when faced with a chronic, hard-to-resolve problem. The bottom-up beat planning process described in chapter 3 placed major responsibility for identifying priority problems in the hands of the city's 279 beat teams. A field study of what these teams actually did about these problems found that police frequently adopted very traditional problem-solving strategies, including high-visibility patrol, aggressive stops and field interrogations, and undercover operations.

However, nontraditional policing strategies were also employed fairly often, particularly for property crime and social disorders. These included prevention awareness efforts, working closely with beat-meeting participants, talking with residents, and using the inspections task force. Block club organizing and community marches and patrols were frequently scheduled for drug and gang sites. "Positive-loitering" campaigns by the public were one of their most frequent strategies for responding to prostitution. Overall, police identified service problems requiring help from other city agencies in

63 percent of our 2002 study beats. The coordinated involvement of other city agencies was impressive, and the CAPS Implementation Office helped keep them focused on locations that were department priorities.[1]

Figure 10.3 charts trends in survey measures of the extent of neighborhood social disorder and physical decay problems over time. As in earlier chapters, the social disorder index combines responses to questions concerning public drinking, group loitering, and school disruption. The extent of concern about physical decay is indexed by responses to questions about abandoned cars, abandoned buildings, graffiti, and vacant lots filled with trash and junk. The regression lines presented in the figure were statistically smoothed to better depict the general pattern underlying the yearly data points. Trends for white respondents are omitted since, except for graffiti, they were not very concerned about these problems even before CAPS began.

The surveys indicate again that there were both successes and disappointing failures in the city's efforts to address neighborhood decline. In 1994, African Americans and Latinos had remarkably similar views of conditions in their neighborhoods. This congruence had clearly disappeared by about 1997, when African Americans began reporting neighborhood improvements. Among African Americans,

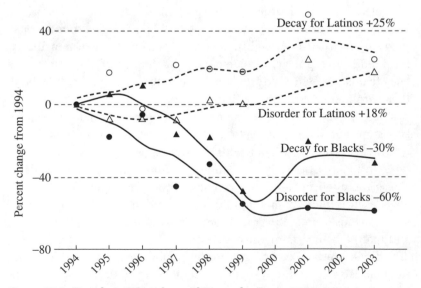

Figure 10.3. Trends in Disorder and Decay by Race, 1994–2003

the extent of social disorder dropped by almost one-third, and concern about physical decay dropped by 60 percent. The picture was the opposite among Latinos, for whom things grew worse: physical decay was up by about 25 percent and social disorder by 18 percentage points. By the early 2000s, the views of Chicago's "minorities" (by 2004 both groups were more numerous than whites) diverged considerably. Things were not going well in the city's emerging Spanish-speaking barrios.

Challenge: Heal the Breech between the Police and the Public

Near the end of *Together We Can,* the chief of police concluded that, with the adoption of community policing, "we have made a commitment to establish a relationship between the community and the police that will break down long-standing barriers, reduce community tensions, open up avenues of information, and provide constructive and meaningful opportunities for collaboration.[2] The impetus behind this turn toward the community lay partly in shifts in the city's population. These challenged real institutional imperatives in city politics and government. As noted in chapter 2, the continued decline of the city's white population meant that the mayor had to be reelected by an increasingly black and brown city, so he had to build bridges to minority communities. Our polling (and undoubtedly his) revealed that dissatisfaction with the quality of police service was widespread among both African Americans and Latinos, who otherwise were divided on important issues like access to city jobs, contracts, and elected positions. His declining white constituency was happier about the police, but just "getting tough" in response to crime problems was probably not a winning strategy if he wanted to be on the victorious side of the divide.

Similarly, the police faced a "legitimacy deficit" of major proportions, and their more sophisticated executives knew that this was undermining their effectiveness. Shootings by police and charges of brutality were commonplace in African American neighborhoods, and we saw in chapter 9 that even routine traffic stops were evaluated more negatively by African American and Spanish-speaking Latinos. Memories of the 1991 Rodney King episode in Los Angeles were still vivid when discussion took place with city hall about how to respond to the soaring crime rate.

Finally, neighborhood conditions were not good. Reported crime peaked in the early 1990s, and concern about crime and social disorder was widespread. The seeming inability of police to deal with widely known gangs and highly visible street drug markets was a divisive issue in the city's poorest communities. In *Together We Can* the chief noted that even his officers were fed up. A very important feature of policing in Chicago is that all officers are required to live in the city itself. This is not the normal big-city pattern, which is for police to live as far away as they possibly can. So despite their differences, police and residents in Chicago were largely in the same boat. The chief claimed that his new community-policing strategy "recognizes members' frustration, as both police officers and responsible community members, over the intolerable conditions that exist in many of our neighborhoods, and the Department's inability to remedy those conditions using a totally incident-driven approach to policing."[3] During the tough recession of the early 1990s there certainly was not going to be money for more police, but promising to become more effective by joining the national movement toward community policing was a route that was still open to the city.

The creation of recognizable teams of officers who responded to calls on their beats and regularly attended meetings with the public was part of the strategy to get the two together. Feedback at the meetings was supposed to make for more responsive—and perhaps even better—policing. The meetings provided a forum for networking and building a sense of community among local activists that, for the first time, included the police. Police were also included in the marches and rallies organized by the CAPS Implementation Office. All of these activities were spotlighted in the publicity campaign surrounding the program. Television appeals, print campaigns, mass flyers and mailings, and door-to-door campaigns by community organizers all focused on raising awareness of CAPS and beat meetings. The statistical analysis presented in chapter 9 indicates that the meetings and awareness of community policing played a role in increasing confidence in the police, but that improving neighborhood conditions for many, and declining recorded crime for almost everyone, accounted for most of the improvement.

Figure 10.4 summarizes trends in opinion about the police. It separately describes trends in popular views of police effectiveness, responsiveness, and demeanor. The surveys indicate that substantial progress was made on all three dimensions, but that even by 2003 there was still plenty of room for improvement. The percentage of

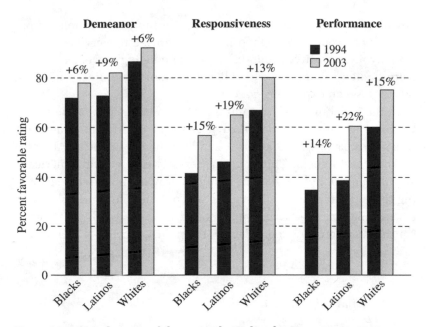

Figure 10.4. Trends in Confidence in the Police by Race, 1994–2003

Chicagoans who give the police positive marks on their effectiveness in controlling crime, maintaining order, and helping victims rose the most, from a dismal 37 percent to a bare majority of 51 percent The percentage who were satisfied with police responsiveness in dealing with local priorities and working with residents went from 44 to 56 percent. In 1994, Chicago police did best in terms of their demeanor (their perceived fairness, helpfulness, politeness, and concern), but by 2003 even their demeanor rating rose a bit, from 66 percent to 73 percent. Most of these gains were made during the 1990s, when neighborhood conditions were improving for many and official crime rates were dropping most sharply.

Another bit of good news was that confidence improved across the city, and it was up significantly among all three major racial groups. The bad news is that the gulf between the races and classes did not change much at all. Figure 10.4 compares ratings given the police in 1994 and 2004 by race. The percentage gains within each group are presented for each comparison, and they were notable. Satisfaction with police performance (at controlling crime, keeping order, and helping victims) was up the most, by 14 percent among generally skeptical African Americans and by 22 percent among Latinos. Latinos also showed the most improvement in their impressions of police responsiveness to neighborhood concerns, but everyone was noticeably more positive about this aspect of policing as well. The gains were smaller when it came to police demeanor (helpfulness, fairness, politeness, and expressing concern).

In the end, however, the contrast between the general optimism of whites and the still-widespread pessimism of African Americans was almost as large in 2003 as it had been in 1994, when CAPS was still in development. Things got better between African Americans and the police, but confidence had also grown among whites, keeping the gap just as wide. "The glass was only half full" when it came to heading the breech between police and the public, for while Chicagoans were more confident in the police, they were still deeply divided by race.

What Happened to Latinos?

What happened to the Latino community in Chicago? Although we began this evaluation prepared to observe community policing flounder in high-crime African American neighborhoods, it turned out that the city's burgeoning Latino population presented CAPS' most daunting challenges. Police struggled to build awareness of CAPS and beat meetings, only to see recognition of the program *drop* beginning in the late 1990s. Involvement in beat meetings was driven by concern about disorder and crime, but Latinos did not turn out in expected numbers. They were particularly underrepresented at beat meetings in racially diverse areas, and the Latino community lacked representation by loyal participants who kept coming back and getting involved in neighborhood projects. Their relations with the police were mixed. While they stood between whites and African Americans on most measures of attitudes concerning the police, Latinos were noticeably more critical than were the city's white residents. There was evidence that they were avoiding contact with the police, including not reporting crimes when they occurred, as well as not getting involved in CAPS.

Figure 10.5 illustrates the magnitude of this underrepresentation at two points in time. The right panel is based on data collected in 253 beats in 1998, and the left-hand panel documents what was found in a follow-up study conducted in a sample of 130 beats in 2002. During the interim, police and the CAPS Implementation Of-

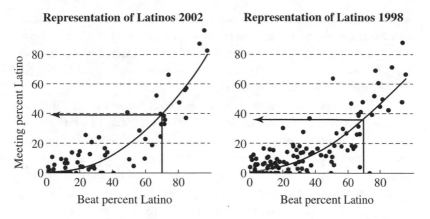

Figure 10.5. Trends in Latino Representation, 1998 and 2002

fice worked hard to increase Latino turnout. Their efforts included distributing promotional material at Catholic churches, hanging posters in business windows and apartment entrance ways, organizing marches and rallies, and offering Saturday Spanish-language meetings. However, as the arrows in figure 10.5 highlight, these efforts made little headway. In both 1998 and 2002, Latinos constituted 40 percent or less of the turnout even in beats that were about 75 percent Latino. Despite the department's efforts, the curve describing the underrepresentation of Latinos at beat meetings changed scarcely at all.

Some of the most significant barriers to CAPS involvement among Latinos were demographic. Latinos were the youngest of Chicago's large demographic groups, and young people generally did not participate in the program. Latinos also rented their homes and moved frequently, and home ownership and the length of time that people had invested in a neighborhood were also powerful predictors of CAPS involvement. Latinos were also the most likely to both be in the labor force and to have children living at home—two competing demands for their time. Most of these demographic disadvantages are redoubled among the city's Spanish-speaking Latinos, who were even more likely to be young, poor, less educated, and renters than were their English-speaking counterparts. Police and many knowledgeable community leaders attributed their limited involvement to concern about immigration issues, and to the experiences with police in their home countries that recent immigrants brought with them. Predominantly Latino beats were also distinctively likely to be on the list of places where we observed discussions of fear of retaliation from gangs and drug dealers for attending meetings and cooperating with the police. On the long list of reasons why Latino involvement should be low, many items were more or less beyond the ability of the police to do anything about.

We have seen that things did not go well for many of Chicago's Latinos, beginning in the latter half of the 1990s. Over time, the Latino community broke apart under the pressure of immigration and internal growth. Mostly, things got better for established Latinos living in racially integrated areas. However, things grew worse for Spanish-speaking immigrants concentrated in heavily Latino beats. Reports by Spanish speakers accounted for the divergent trends that were evident among Latinos. Because the number of Spanish speakers and barrio dwellers was growing fastest, Latinos as a group found themselves progressively worse off.

The effects of immigration on the composition of the Latino population could be seen in the surveys. The number of Spanish speakers grew by half over the course of our surveys. Because they arrived without much formal education—in fact, many are illiterate even in Spanish—immigration had the effect of pushing down average levels of education for Latinos as a whole. The effects of immigration in Chicago reflected the national pattern, for immigrants from Mexico and Central America have distinctively low levels of education, even in comparison to immigrants from South America or the Caribbean. Many describe the twenty-first-century urban economy as an "hourglass," bulging with good jobs at the top and unskilled, low-wage, service sector jobs at the bottom, but thin in the middle where better paying, unionized, industrial-sector jobs with health benefits used to be found. Chicago's new Latino residents had to find their place at the bottom of the economic hourglass.

Another key point about demographic change among Chicago's Latinos is that during the course of the 1990s they became more geographically concentrated. Between 1990 and 2000 most of this growth in the Latino population was concentrated in heavily Latino neighborhoods on the city's Southwest and Near North sides. In the time between the 1990 U.S. Census and the 2000 U.S. Census, the number of Latinos living in police beats that were majority Latino in 1990 rose by almost 70 percent. By contrast, the number of Latinos living in beats that were less than half Latino in 1990 grew by only two percent. By 2000, two-thirds of all Chicago's Latinos lived in predominantly Latino police beats. Statistically, language, ethnic concentration, and concentrated poverty in these emerging barrios accounted for most of the negative trends revealed in the surveys. Spanish speakers always reported more problems, but over time they began to report more divergent experiences, and one reason for this was their increasing concentration in poorer beats already heavily populated by Spanish speakers. The effects of this concentration were nonlinear, with reports of problems jumping sharply among Latinos where their neighborhoods were more than about 60 percent Latino.

The improving fortune of Chicago's African Americans was, by contrast, a relatively widespread trend. Changes for the better in reports of both decay and disorder problems ran in parallel for subgroups within the African American population. African Americans were divided by social class. The largest split was between homeowners and renters, who differed by about 10 percentage points on levels of social disorder, and 7 percentage points on physical decay. More-educated African Americans reported fewer neighborhood problems than did less-educated African Americans, and there were parallel differences by income as well. But although poor and better-off African Americans began with different *levels* of problems, trend lines for these groups dropped in unison between 1994 and 1999, then leveled off in the new century.

How Did Chicago Do?

Chicago certainly fielded the most impressive big-city community-policing program in the country. Police officials and city leaders come from around the world to observe beat meetings and the citizen-involvement components of the program. Police chiefs wonder when they hear about the support that problem solving gets from city agencies, for in their cities the service bureaucracies think that community policing is the police department's program. Chicago police officers' problem-solving efforts were halting and never really got beyond the more focused application of the tried and true, but this is pretty much the way it has gone in departments around the country. Crime went down a lot, but it did so almost everywhere. The 1993–1995 experiment in selected districts indicated that the decline in crime there was in part attributable to CAPS. The benefits of this decline were enormous for the city's African Americans, who saw tremendous improvements in the quality of their lives. The city's whites really did not need community policing in the first place. They could already get things done when needed, through strong neighborhood organizations and political channels, and they were already chummy with the police. In the end, the inability of the city to engage its large and fast-growing Latino population remained the biggest shortfall of community policing in Chicago. Police were facing challenges thrown up by demographic turmoil and the globalization of the economy in their own backyard, and they did not make much headway against them. This was important. Not just in Chicago, but around the world, immigration will be the story of the twenty-first century. Latinos are now the second largest group in the city, and along with a smaller number of Asians, they are the only group that is growing. It is quite possible that by 2012 or so Latinos will surpass African Americans and become the largest group in the city; by 2005 they outnumbered whites. As the political significance of this shift becomes apparent and their representatives gain a larger place at the table, issues of the quality of life in the Latino community and their relationship with the police almost certainly will be on it.

Notes

Chapter 2

1. Most of the housing data cited in this book were calculated from Chicago's Sanborn File, a database documenting the use of each of the city's 620,989 land parcels and the condition of the buildings in each parcel. These data were made available by the Department of Business Information.

2. In the 2000 U.S. Census, persons who checked the "some other race" box and then wrote "Lebanese," "Near Easterner," or "Arab" in the blank space provided were reclassified as white (U.S. Bureau of the Census 2000c).

3. Surveys planned for 2000 and 2002 were skipped in order to save money. It seemed more important to gather a *longer* barometer of trends rather than proceed with year-by-year surveys in lockstep fashion.

4. See Grinc (1994), 442, 437.

5. See Chicago Police Department (1993), 5.

6. Ibid., 9–10.

Chapter 3

1. A detailed description of early stages in the development of Chicago's community policing can be found in Skogan and Hartnett (1997), so this period is discussed only briefly.

2. Chicago Police Department (1993), ii.

3. Ibid., 11.

4. Chicago Police Department (1993), 7.

5. Ibid., 8.

6. Chicago Police Department (1993), 15–16.

7. Ibid., 16.

8. Ibid.

9. Details about office and resident problem-solving training can be found in a book by Skogan, et al. (1999).

10. Chicago Police Department (1993), 5.

11. Ibid., 8.

12. Ibid., 5.

13. Ibid., 6.

14. Ibid., 3.

15. Illinois Advisory Committee (1993), 34.

16. Chicago Police Department (1993), 23.

17. Ibid., 23.

18. A self-serving discussion of New York's accountability process can be found in Bratton (1998); more analytic views are presented by Silverman (1999), Karmen (2000), and McDonald (2002). But there has been no thorough analysis of CompStat because the New York City Police Department does not cooperate easily with researchers and does not release its data in the form needed for independent analysis. The best effort in analyzing data regarding the impacr ot CompStat and many related initiatives is found in Kelling and Sousa (2001).

Chapter 4

1. Chicago Police Department (1993), 9.

Chapter 5

1. The officer was referring to the Office of Professional Standards, the city's official body that investigates public complaints against police officers.

2. An earlier version of this section of chapter 5 is presented in Skogan (2003).

Chapter 6

1. Chicago Police Department (1996), 2.

2. Ibid., 12.

3. Ibid.,

4. This chronology of school security policies was gleaned from many editions of *Catalyst*, a bimonthly magazine sponsored by the Community Renewal Society that is devoted to covering educational policy in Chicago and Illinois, and from a list of school initiatives complied by its editor, Linda Lenz.

5. Fung (2004), 3.

6. Chicago Police Department (1996), 2.

Chapter 7

1. Chicago Police Department (1996), 1.
2. Ibid.
3. Thanks to John Easton, director of the Chicago School Research Consortium, for this special analysis of their student-survey data.
4. An earlier version of the statistical material presented here appeared in Skogan and Steiner (2004b).
5. This analysis excludes respondents who failed to answer questions about disorder and decay, or the demographic and neighborhood questions itemized in the table. It also drops respondents when we could not identify their beat of residence, and a few who lived in one of the city's nine primarily nonresidential beats. Together these criteria excluded about 14 percent of the Latinos who were originally interviewed between 1994 and 2003.
6. Chicago Police Department (1996), 9.
7. Ibid., 11.

Chapter 8

1. Chicago Police Department (1993), 2.
2. Ibid., 14.
3. Ibid., 7.
4. Ibid.
5. Ibid., 9.
6. Ibid., 2.
7. Chicago Police Department (2002), 8.
8. Richard Block, the city's leading expert on crime data analysis, was very generous in working with me on this project.
9. Some of the statistical material in this section appeared previously in Skogan and Steiner (1994).
10. Some material in this section appears in Skogan (forthcoming).
11. Cook and Cook (1976), 654.
12. This analysis excludes respondents who failed to answer the fear question or the demographic and neighborhood questions itemized in table 8.1. It also drops respondents when we could not identify their beat of residence, and a few who lived in one of the city's nine primarily nonresidential beats. The last were excluded because crime rate data are uninterpretable for those areas. Together these criteria excluded about 18 percent of the 20,363 individuals who were originally interviewed between 1994 and 2003.

Chapter 9

1. Chicago Police Department (1993), 9.
2. Ibid., 8.
3. Ibid., 9.
4. Ibid., 10.
5. Goldstein (1994), 2.
6. Nimocks (1994), 8.
7. Illinois Advisory Committee to the United States Commission on Civil Rights (1993), 41.
8. Ibid., 42.
9. Chicago Police Department (1993), 9.
10. Some respondents inevitably reply "don't know" to specific questions about police activity; for the questions discussed in this section, this fraction ranged from 2 to 17 percent. Those respondents are excluded from consideration on a question-by-question basis.
11. Chicago Police Department (1993), 27.
12. Cao, Frank, and Cullen (1996), 13.
13. This analysis excludes a relatively small number of respondents who were of Asian or other backgrounds, or whose race was undetermined. It also excludes respondents who failed to answer several of the police opinion questions, those for whom we could not identify a residential beat, and a few respondents who lived in one of the city's nine primarily nonresidential beats. The latter were excluded because crime rate data are uninterpretable for those areas. Together these criteria excluded about 20 percent of those interviewed.
14. These neighborhood factor scores were constructed generally following Sampson, Raudenbush, and Earls (1997). The poverty measure includes: percent of families with female heads, percent of families on public aid, percent of households in poverty, percent of households with children, and percent of population under age eighteen. I differ from Sampson, Raudenbush, and Earls in not including indicators of the racial composition of beats in the poverty factor; the effect of race is considered separately, Chicago Police Department (1993), 9.
15. Moy and Pfau (2000), 13.

Chapter 10

1. For a detailed look at police problem solving in these sample beats, see Skogan et al. 2003, 49–63.
2. Chicago Police Department (1993), 27.
3. Ibid., 2–3.

Bibliography

Bennett, Trevor. 1989. *Contact Patrols in Birmingham and London: An Evaluation of a Fear Reducing Strategy.* Cambridge: Institute of Criminology.

Beckett, Katherine. 1997. *Making Crime Pay: Law and Order in Contemporary American Politics.* New York: Oxford University Press.

Bland, Nick, Joel Miller, and Paul Quinton. 2000. *Upping the PACE? An Evaluation of the Recommendations of the Stephen Lawrence Inquiry on Stops and Searches.* Police Research Series, Paper 128. London: Home Office.

Block, Carolyn R., and Richard Block. 1993. *Street Gang Crime in Chicago.* Washington, D.C.: National Institute of Justice, U.S. Department of Justice.

Block, Carolyn R., Antigone Christakos, Ayad Jacob, and Roger Przybylski. 1996. Research Bulletin: *1996 Street Gangs and Crime, Patterns and Trends in Chicago.* Chicago: Illinois Criminal Justice Information Authority.

Block, Carolyn R., and Christine Martin. 1997. *Major Trends in Chicago Homicide: 1965–1995.* Chicago: Illinois Criminal Justice Information Authority.

Boggs, Sarah. 1971. "Formal and Informal Crime Control: An Exploratory Study of Urban, Suburban and Rural Orientations," *Sociological Quarterly* 12, 319–327.

Booz, Allen & Hamilton, Inc. 1992. "Improving Police Service: Summary of Findings To-Date." Unpublished consulting report to the City of Chicago, July 8, 1992.

Brandl, Steven G., James Frank, Robert W. Worden, and Timothy S. Bynum. 1994. "Global and Specific Attitudes toward the Police: Disentangling the Relationship," *Justice Quarterly* 11, 119–134.

Bratton, William, with Peter Knobler. 1998. *Turnaround: How America's Top Cop Reversed the Crime Epidemic.* New York: Random House.

Bryan, Frank M. 2004. *Real Democracy: The New England Town Meeting and How It Works.* Chicago: University of Chicago Press.

Bucke, Tom. 1997. *Ethnicity and Contacts with the Police: Latest Findings from the British Crime Survey.* Home Office Research Study, No. 59. London: Home Office.

Bureau of Justice Statistics. 2003. *Local Police Departments 2000.* Washington, D.C.: Bureau of Justice Statistics, U.S. Department of Justice.

Butterfield, Fox. 2004. "As Cities Struggle, Police Get By with Less." *The New York Times.* July 27.

Cao, Liqun, James Frank, and Francis T. Cullen. 1996. "Race, Community Context, and Confidence in the Police" *American Journal of Police* 15, 3–22.

Carlson, James M. 1985. *Prime Time Law Enforcement: Crime Show Viewing and Attitudes toward the Criminal Justice System.* New York: Praeger.

Carr, Patrick. 2005. *Clean Streets: Crime, Disorder and Social Control in a Chicago Neighborhood.* New York and London: New York University Press.

Chicago Police Department. 1993. *Together We Can: A Strategic Plan for Reinventing the Chicago Police Department.*

———. 1996. *Patrol Division Strategy to Address Chronic Crime and Disorder Problems: The Role of City Services in the CAPS Problem-Solving Model.*

———. 2002. Annual Report, 2001.

Chicago Tribune. 2000. "Feds Report Eight Year Decline in School Violence." October 27.

Cohen, Adam, and Elizabeth Taylor. 2000. *American Pharaoh: Mayor Richard J. Daley—His Battle for Chicago and the Nation.* Boston: Little Brown and Company.

Commission on Police Integrity. 1997. Report Presented to the City of Chicago, Richard M. Daley Mayor. Nov. 7, 1997.

Cook, Fay Lomax, and Thomas D. Cook. 1976. "Evaluating the Rhetoric of Crisis: A Case Study of Criminal Victimization of the Elderly," *Social Service Review* 50, 632–646.

Cordner, Gary, and Elizabeth Perkins Biebel. 2005. "Problem-Oriented Policing in Practice," *Criminology & Public Policy* 4, 155–180.

Dean, Debra. 1980. "Citizen Ratings of the Police: The Difference Police Contact Makes," *Law and Policy Quarterly* 2, 445–471.

Durose, Matthew R., Erica L. Schmitt, and Patrick A. Langan. 2005. *Contacts between Police and the Public: Findings from the 2002 National Survey.* Washington, D.C.: Bureau of Justice Statistics, U.S. Department of Justice.

Eck, John, and Edward Maguire. 2000. "Have Changes in Policing Reduced Violent Crime? An Assessment of the Evidence," in *The Crime Drop in America,* ed. Alfred Blumstein and Joel Wallman, 207–65. New York: Cambridge University Press.

Eck, John E., and William Spelman. 1987. *Problem Solving: Problem-Oriented Policing in Newport News.* Washington, D.C.: Police Executive Research Forum.

Eschholz, Sarah, Ted Chiricos, and Marc Gertz. 2003. "Television and Fear of Crime: Program Types, Audience Traits and the Mediating Effect of Perceived Neighborhood Racial Composition," *Social Problems 50*, 395–415.

Fattah, Ezzat, and Vincent F. Sacco. 1989. *Crime and Victimization of the Elderly.* New York: Springer-Verlag.

Finn, Peter. 1988. *Street People.* Washington, D.C.: National Institute of Justice, U.S. Department of Justice.

Flanagan, Timothy J., and Michael S. Vaughn. 1996. "Public Opinion About Police Abuse of Force," in *Police Violence,* ed. William Geller and Hans Toch, 113–128. New Haven, Conn.: Yale University Press.

Frank, James, Steven G. Brandl, Francis T. Cullen, and Amy Stichman. 1996. "Reassessing the Impact of Race on Citizen's Attitudes Toward the Police: A Research Note," *Justice Quarterly* 13, 321–334.

Fraser, Nancy. 1992. "Rethinking the Public Sphere: A Contribution to the Critique of Actually Existing Democracy," in *Habermas and the Public Sphere,* ed. Craig Calhoun, 109–142 . Cambridge, Mass.: MIT Press.

Friedman, Warren. 2001. "20 Years: Place the Blame and Move On." *Neighborhoods* (Newsletter of the Chicago Alliance for Neighborhood Safety) (November): 4, 6.

Friedman, Warren, Arthur Lurigio, Richard Greenleaf, and Stephanie Albertson. 2002. *The Social Costs of Disrespect: Young People and Police in Chicago.* Chicago: Chicago Alliance for Neighborhood Safety.

Fung, Archon. 2001. "Accountable Autonomy: Toward Empowered Deliberation in Chicago Schools and Policing," *Politics & Society* 29, 73–103.

————. 2004. *Empowered Participation: Reinventing Urban Democracy.* Princeton, N.J.: Princeton University Press.

Furstenberg, Frank F., and Charles F. Wellford. 1973. "Calling the Police: The Evaluation of Police Service," *Law & Society Review* 7, 393–406.

Garofalo, James, and McLeod, Maureen. 1988. "Improving the Use and Effectiveness of Neighborhood Watch Programs." In *Research in Action.* Washington, D.C.: National Institute of Justice, U. S. Department of Justice.

Gates, Henry Louis Jr. 1995. "Thirteen Ways of Looking at a Black Man," *New Yorker* (October), 59.

Geller, William A., and Kevin J. Karales. 1981. *Split-second Decisions: Shootings of and by Chicago Police.* Chicago: Chicago Law Enforcement Study Group.

Goldstein, Herman. 1994. "The O. W. Wilson Era," *Police Forum* 4, 2–5.

Graber, Doris. 1980. *Crime News and the Public.* New York: Praeger.

Green, Donald P., Alan S. Gerber, and David W. Nickerson. 2003. "Getting Out the Vote in Local Elections." *Journal of Politics* 65, 1083–1096.

Greenberg, Stephanie W., William M. Rohe, and Jay R. Williams. 1982. *Safe and Secure Neighborhoods: Physical Characteristics and Informal Territorial Control in High and Low Crime Neighborhoods.* Washington, D.C.: National Institute of Justice, U.S. Department of Justice.

Grinc, Randolph M. 1994. "'Angles in Marble': Problems in Stimulating Community Involvement in Community Policing," *Crime & Delinquency* 40, 437–468.

Guyot, Dorothy. 1991. *Policing as Though People Matter.* Philadelphia: Temple University Press.

Hart, Timothy C., and Callie Rennison. 2003. *Reporting Crime to the Police, 1992–2000.* Washington, D.C.: Bureau of Justice Statistics, U.S. Department of Justice.

Henig, Jeffrey R. 1978. "Coping a Cop: Neighborhood Organizations and Police Patrol Allocation," *Journal of Voluntary Action Research* 7, 75–84.

———. 1982. *Neighborhood Mobilization.* New Brunswick, N.J.: Rutgers University Press.

Hickman, Matthew J., and Brian A. Reaves. 2003. *Local Police Departments 2000.* Washington, D.C.: Bureau of Justice Statistics, U.S. Department of Justice.

Higgins, Daniel F., and James R. Coldren Jr. 2000. *Evaluating Gang and Drug House Abatement in Chicago.* Chicago: Illinois Criminal Justice Information Authority.

Homant, Robert J., Daniel B. Kennedy, and Roger M. Fleming. 1984. "The Effects of Victimization and the Police Response on Citizen Attitudes Toward Police," *Journal of Police Science and Administration* 12, 323–332.

Illinois Advisory Committee to the United States Commission on Civil Rights. 1993. *Police Protection of the African American Community in Chicago.*

———. 1999. *Police Protection of the African American Community in Chicago: An Update.*

Illinois Criminal Justice Information Authority. 1995. Major Trends in Chicago Homicide: 1965–1995.

Jacob, Herbert. 1971. "Black and White Perceptions of Justice in the City," *Law & Society Review* 6, 69–90.

Karmen, Andrew. 2000. *New York Murder Mystery: The True Story Behind the Crime Crash of the 1990s.* New York: New York University Press.

Kelling, George, Anthony M. Pate, Duanne Dieckman, and Charles E. Brown 1974. *The Kansas City Preventive Patrol Experiment: Summary Report.* Washington, D.C.: The Police Foundation.

Kelling, George, and William H. Sousa Jr. 2001. *Do Police Matter? An*

Analysis of the Impact of New York City's Police. Reforms Civic Report 22. New York: Manhattan Institute for Policy Research.

Kelling, George L., and Catherine M. Coles. 1996. *Fixing Broken Windows.* New York: Touchstone.

Kohfeld, Carol W., Barbara S. Salert, and Sandra Schoenberg. 1983. "Neighborhood Associations and Urban Crime." In *Community Crime Prevention.* St. Louis: Center for Responsive Government.

Krasno, Jonathan S., and Donald P. Green. 2005. "Do Televised Presidential Ads Increase Voter Turnout? Evidence from a Natural Experiment." Paper presented at the annual meeting of the Midwest Political Science Association, Chicago, Illinois.

Krivo, Lauren J., and Ruth D. Peterson. 1996. "Extremely Disadvantaged Neighborhoods and Urban Crime," *Social Forces* 75, 619–650.

Lane, Jodi, and James W. Meeker. 2003. "Fear of Gang Crime: A Look at Three Theoretical Models," *Law & Society Review* 37, 425–456.

Lavrakas, Paul J., and Lisa Herz. 1982. "Citizen Participation in Neighborhood Crime Prevention," *Criminology* 20, 479–98.

Leigh, Adrian, Tim Read, and Nick Tilley. 1998. *Brit Pop II: Problem-Oriented Policing in Practice.* Police Research Series, Paper 93. London: Home Office.

Maltz, Michael. 1972. *Evaluation of Crime Control Programs.* Washington, D.C.: National Institute of Law Enforcement and Criminal Justice.

Marx, Gary, and Archer, Dane. 1971. "Citizen Involvement in the Law Enforcement Process: The Case of Community Police Patrols," *American Behavioral Scientist* 15, 52–72.

Massey, Douglas S., and Nancy A. Denton. 1993. *American Apartheid: Segregation and the Making of the Underclass.* Cambridge, Mass.: Harvard University Press.

Maxfield, Michael J. 1988. "The London Metropolitan Police and Their Clients: Victim and Suspect Attitudes," *Journal of Research in Crime and Delinquency* 25, 188–206.

Maxson, Cheryl, Karen Hennigan, and David C. Sloane. 2003. *Factors That Influence Public Opinion of the Police. NIJ Research for Practice.* Washington, D.C.: National Institute of Justice, U.S. Department of Justice.

Mayhew, Pat, David Elliott, David Dowds, and Lizanne Dowds. 1989. *The 1988 British Crime Survey.* Home Office Research Study, No. 111. London: Home Office.

McDonald, Phyllis. 2002. *Managing Police Operations: Implementing the New York Crime Control Model–CompStat.* Belmont, Calif.: Wadsworth.

Meares, Tracey L. 2002. "Praying for Community Policing," *California Law Review* 90, 1593–1634.

Merry, Sally Engle. 1981. Urban Danger: Life in a Neighborhood of Strangers. Philadelphia: Temple University Press.

Miller, Joel, Robert C. Davis, Nicole J. Henderson, John Markovic, and Christopher Ortiz. 2005. "Measuring Influences on Public Opinion of the Police Using Time-Series Data: Results of a Pilot Study," *Police Quarterly* 8, 394–401.

Moy, Patricia, and Mark Pfau. 2000. *With Malice Toward All? The Media and Public Confidence in Democratic Institutions.* Westport, Conn.: Praeger.

National Commission on the Causes and Prevention of Violence. 1968. *Rights in Conflict: The Violent Confrontation of Demonstrators and Police in the Parks and Streets of Chicago During the Week of the Democratic National Convention of 1968.* A report submitted by Daniel Walker, director of the Chicago Study Team, to the National Commission on the Causes and Prevention of Violence. Washington, D.C.: U.S. Government Printing Office.

National Institute of Justice. 1997. *Measuring What Matters, Part Two: Developing Measures of What Police Do.* Washington, D.C.: Office of Justice Programs, U.S. Department of Justice.

National Paint & Coatings Association, et al. v. City of Chicago, 45 F.3d 1124 (7th Cir. 1995).

Nimocks, Rudy. 1994. "The Aftermath of O. W. Wilson," *Police Forum* 4, 5–9.

Oberwittler, Dietrich. 2004. "A Multilevel Analysis of Neighborhood Contextual Effects on Serious Juvenile Offending: The Role of Subcultural Values and Social Disorganization," *European Journal of Criminology* 1, 201–236.

Padilla, Felix M. 1984. "On the Nature of Latino Ethnicity," *Social Science Quarterly* 65, 652–664.

Pate, Antony. 1976. *Police Response Time: Its Determinants and Effects.* Washington, D.C.: Police Foundation.

Pate, Antony, Marlys McPherson, Marlys Silloway, and Glen Silloway. 1987. *The Minneapolis Community Crime Prevention Experiment.* Washington, D.C.: The Police Foundation.

Pate, Antony M. 1986. "Experimenting with Foot Patrol: The Newark Experience." In *Community Crime Prevention,* ed. Dennis Rosenbaum. Newbury Park, Calif.: Sage, 137–156.

Pate, Antony M., and Penny Shtull. 1994. "Community Policing Grows in Brooklyn: An Inside View of the New York Police Department's Model Precinct," *Crime & Delinquency* 40, 384–410.

Pate, Antony M., Mary Ann Wycoff, Wesley G. Skogan, and Lawrence Sherman. 1986. *Reducing Fear of Crime in Houston and Newark: A Summary Report.* Washington, D.C.: National Institute of Justice and The Police Foundation.

Pattillo-McCoy, Mary. 1999. *Black Picket Fences: Privilege and Peril among the Black Middle Class.* Chicago: University of Chicago Press.

Percy, Steven. 1980. "Response Time and Citizen Evaluation of Police," *Journal of Police Science and Administration* 8, 75–86.

Podolefsky, Aaron, and Fred DuBow. 1981. *Strategies for Community Crime Prevention.* Springfield, Ill.: Charles C. Thomas.

Poister, Theodore H., and James C. McDavid. 1978. "Victims' Evaluation of Police Performance," *Journal of Criminal Justice* 6, 133–149.

Putnam, Robert D. 2000. *Bowling Alone: The Collapse and Revival of American Community.* New York: Simon & Schuster.

Quinton, Paul, Nick Bland, and Joel Miller. 2000. *Police Stops: Decision-making and Practice.* Police Research Series, Paper 130. London: Home Office.

Rakove, Milton L. 1975. *Don't Make No Waves, Don't Back No Losers.* Bloomington: Indiana University Press.

Reaves, Brian A., and Matthew J. Hickman. 2002. *Police Departments in Large Cities, 1990–2000.* Washington, D.C.: Bureau of Justice Statistics, U.S. Department of Justice.

Reisig, Michael, and Andrew Giacomazzi. 1998. "Citizen Perceptions of Community Policing: Are Attitudes toward Police Important," *Policing* 21, 547–561.

Reisig, Michael, and Roger B. Parks. 2004. "Can Community Policing Help the Truly Disadvantaged?" *Crime & Delinquency* 50, 139–167.

Reisig, Michael D., and Roger B. Parks. 2000. "Experience, Quality of Life, and Neighborhood Context: A Hierarchical Analysis of Satisfaction with Police," *Justice Quarterly* 17, 607–630.

———. 2003. "Neighborhood Context, Police Behavior and Satisfaction with Police," *Justice Research and Policy* 5, 1–29.

Reiss, Albert J. Jr. 1971. *The Public and the Police.* New Haven, Conn.: Yale University Press.

———. 1985. "Policing a City's Central District: The Oakland Story." Research Paper, National Institute of Justice, U.S. Department of Justice, Washington, D.C.

Roberts, Julian V., and Loretta J. Stalans. 1997. *Public Opinion, Crime, and Criminal Justice.* Boulder, Col.: Westview.

Robinson, Jennifer B., Brian A. Lawton, Ralph B. Taylor, Ralph Perkins, and Douglas Perkins. 2003. "Multilevel Longitudinal Impacts of Incivilities: Fear of Crime, Expected Safety, and Block Satisfaction," *Journal of Quantitative Criminology* 19, 237–274.

Rosenbaum, Dennis. 1987. "The Theory and Research behind Neighborhood Watch: Is It a Sound Fear and Crime Reduction Strategy?" *Crime & Delinquency* 33, 103–134.

Rosenthal, Lawrence. 2001. "Gang Loitering and Race," *Journal of Criminal Law and Criminology* 91, 99–160.

Sadd, Susan, and Randolph Grinc. 1994. "Innovative Neighborhood Oriented Policing" An Evaluation of Community Policing Programs in Eight Cities." *The Challenge of Community Policing: Testing the Promises*, ed. Dennis P. Rosenbaum, 27–52. Newbury Park, Calif.: Sage.

Sampson, Robert J., and Dawn Jeglum-Bartusch. 1998. "Legal Cynicism and (Subcultural?) Tolerance of Deviance: The Neighborhood Context of Racial Differences," *Law and Society Review* 32, 777–804.

Sampson, Robert J., Steven Raudenbush, and Felton J. Earls. 1997. "Neighborhoods and Violent Crime," *Science* 277, 918–924.

Schneider, Anne L. 1976. "Victimization Surveys and the Criminal Justice System." In *Sample Surveys of the Victims of Crime,* ed. Wesley G. Skogan, 135–150. Cambridge, Mass.: Ballinger.

———. 1986. "Neighborhood-Based Anti-Burglary Strategies: An Analysis of Public and Private Benefits from the Portland Program." In *Community Crime Prevention: Does It Work?* ed. Dennis Rosenbaum, 68–86. Newbury Park, Calif.: Sage.

Seidman, David, and Michael Couzens. 1974. "Getting the Crime Rate Down: Political Pressure and Crime Reporting," *Law & Society Review* 8, 457–493.

Silverman, Eli. 1999. *NYPD Battles Crime: Innovative Strategies.* Boston: Northeastern University Press.

Skogan, Wesley G. 1976a. "Citizen Reporting of Crime: Some National Panel Data," *Criminology* 13, 535–549.

———. 1976b. *Chicago Since 1840: A Time-Series Data Handbook.* Urbana, Ill.: Institute of Government and Public Affairs, University of Illinois.

———. 1976c. "Crime and Crime Rates." In *Sample Surveys of the Victims of Crime,* ed. Wesley G. Skogan, 115–119. Cambridge, Mass.: Ballinger.

———. 1979. "Citizen Satisfaction with Police Services: Individual and Contextual Effects," *Policy Studies Journal* 7, 469–479.

———. 1987. "The Impact of Victimization on Fear," Crime and Delinquency, 33 (January, 1987), 135–154.

———. 1988. "Community Organizations and Crime." In *Crime and Justice,* ed. Michael Tonry and Norval Morris, 39–78. Chicago: University of Chicago Press.

———. 1989. "The Impact of Police on Victims." In *Crime and Its Victims,* ed. Emilio Viano, 71–78. Washington, D.C.: Hemisphere.

———. 1990a. *Disorder and Decline: Crime and the Spiral of Decay in American Cities.* New York: The Free Press.

———. 1990b. *The Police and Public in England and Wales.* Home Office Research Study, No. 117. London: Home Office.

———. 1993. "The Various Meanings of Fear." In *The Fear of Crime and*

Criminal Victimization, ed. Wolfgang Bilsky, Christian Pfeiffer, and Peter Wetzels, 131–140. Stuttgart: Enke.

————. 1994. *Contacts between Police and the Public: A British Crime Survey Report.* Home Office Research Study, No. 135. London: Home Office.

————. 2003. Representing the Community in Community Policing." In *Community Policing: Can It Work?* ed., Wesley G. Skogan, 57–75. Belmont, Calif.: Wadsworth.

————. 2004. "Impediments to Community Policing." In *The Future of Community Policing,* ed. Lorie Fridell and Mary Ann Wycoff. Washington, D.C.: Police Executive Research Forum.

————. 2005. "Citizen Satisfaction with Police Encounters," *Police Quarterly* 8, 298–321.

————. 2006. "Asymmetry in the Impact of Encounters with the Police." *Policing & Society* 16, 99–126.

————. forthcoming. "Trends in Crime and Fear: Lessons from Chicago, 1994–2003." In *Emotions, Crime and Justice,* ed. Suzanne Karstedt, Ian Loader, and Heather Strang. Oxford: Hart Publishing.

Skogan, Wesley G., and Andrew Gordon. 1982. "Review of Detective Division Reporting Practices." In *Crime in Illinois 1982,* 167–182. Springfield, Ill.: Illinois Department of Law Enforcement.

Skogan, Wesley G., and Susan M. Hartnett. 1997. *Community Policing, Chicago Style.* New York and London: Oxford University Press.

Skogan, Wesley G., Susan M. Hartnett, Jill DuBois, Jennifer T. Comey, Marianne Kaiser, and Justine H. Lovig. 1999. *On the Beat: Police and Community Problem Solving.* Boulder, Col.: Westview.

Skogan, Wesley G., and Michael G. Maxfield. 1981. *Coping with Crime: Individual and Neighborhood Reactions.* Beverly Hills, Calif.: Sage.

Skogan, Wesley G., Lynn Steiner, Susan M. Hartnett, Jill DuBois, Jason Bennis, Brandon Rottinghaus, So Young Kim, Kimmy Van, and Dennis P. Rosenbaum. 2003. *Community Policing in Chicago Years Eight and Nine.* Chicago: Illinois Criminal Justice Information Authority.

Skogan, Wesley G., and Lynn Steiner. 2004a. *CAPS at Ten: Community Policing in Chicago.* Chicago: Illinois Criminal Justice Information Authority.

————. 2004b. "Crime, Disorder and Decay in Chicago's Latino Community," *Journal of Ethnicity in Criminal Justice* 1–2, 7–26.

Smith, Paul E., and Richard O. Hawkins. 1973. "Victimization, Types of Citizen-Police Contacts and Attitudes toward the Police," *Law & Society Review* 8, 135–152.

Smith, Steven K., Greg W. Steadman, Todd D. Minton, and Meg Townsend. 1999. *Criminal Victimization and Perceptions of Community Safety in 12 Cities, 1998.* Washington, D.C.: Bureau of Justice Statistics, U.S. Department of Justice.

Spelman, William, and John E. Eck. 1987. "Problem-Oriented Policing," *NIJ Research in Brief*. Washington, D.C.: National Institute of Justice, U.S. Department of Justice.

Stone, Vanessa, and Nick Pettigrew. 2000. *The Views of the Public on Stops and Searches*. Police Research Series, Paper 129. London: Home Office.

Sunshine, Jason, and Tom R. Tyler. 2003. "The Role of Procedural Justice and Legitimacy in Shaping Public Support for Policing," *Law & Society Review* 37, 513–548.

Taub, Richard P., D. Garth Taylor, and Jan Dunham. 1984. *Patterns of Neighborhood Change: Race and Crime in Urban America*. Chicago: University of Chicago Press.

Taylor, Ralph B., Stephen D. Gottfredson, and Sydney Brower. 1981. "Informal Control in the Urban Residential Environment." Report to the National Institute of Justice, U.S. Department of Justice, from the Center for Metropolitan Planning and Research, Johns Hopkins University.

Tuch, Steven A., and Ronald Weitzer. 1997. "Racial Differences in Attitudes toward the Police," *Public Opinion Quarterly* 61, 642–663.

Tyler, Tom R. 1980. "The Effect of Directly and Indirectly Experienced Events: The Origin of Crime-Related Judgments and Behavior," *Journal of Personality and Social Psychology* 39, 13–28.

Tyler, Tom R., and Yuen J. Huo. 2002. *Trust in the Law*. New York: Russell Sage Foundation.

U.S. Bureau of the Census. 1999. *The Foreign Born Population in the United States. Current Population Reports P20–519*. Washington, D.C.

———. 2000a. *The Hispanic Population. Census 2000 Brief C2KBR/01–3*. Washington, D.C.

———. 2000b. *Overview of Race and Hispanic Origin. Census 2000 Brief C2KBR/01–1*. Washington, D.C.

———. 2000c. *The Foreign Born Population in the United States. Current Population Reports P20–519*. Washington, D.C.

———. 2000d. *State of Illinois STF 3 CD-ROM*. Washington, D.C.

U.S. Supreme Court Reports. 1999. *City of Chicago v. Morales*, 527 U.S. 41.

Van Dijk, Jan. 1982. "The Victim's Willingness to Report to Police: A Function of Prosecution Policy." In *The Victim in International Perspective*, ed. Hans Joachim Schneider, 327–334. Berlin: DeGruyter.

Verba, Sydney, Kay Lehman Schlozman, and Henry E. Brady. 1995. *Voice and Equality: Civic Voluntarism in American Politics*. Cambridge, Mass.: Harvard University Press.

Weisburd, David, and John E. Eck. 2004. "What Can Police Do to Reduce

Crime, Disorder and Fear?" *Annals of the American Academy of Political and Social Science* 593, 42–65.

Weitzer, Ronald. 2000. "Racialized Policing: Residents' Perception in Three Neighborhoods," *Law and Society Review* 34, 129–155.

Weitzer, Ronald, and Claris E. Kubrin. 2004. "Breaking News: How Local TV News and Real-World Conditions Affect Fear of Crime," *Justice Quarterly* 21, 497–520.

Whitaker Catherine J. 1986. *Crime Prevention Measures. Bureau of Justice Statistics Special Report*. Washington, D.C.: Bureau of Justice Statistics, U. S. Department of Justice.

Williams, Debra. 1994. "Violence in School Drops as Security Grows," *Catalyst* 6:3, 15.

Wilson, James Q., and George Kelling. 1982. "Broken Windows," *The Atlantic Monthly* (March): 29–38.

Wilson, William J. 1978. *The Declining Significance of Race: Blacks and Changing American Institutions*. Chicago: University of Chicago Press,

———. 1987. *The Truly Disadvantaged: The Inner City, the Underclass, and Public Policy*. Chicago: University of Chicago Press.

———. 1996. *When Work Disappears: The World of the New Urban Poor*. New York: Knopf.

Wintemute, Garen. 2000. "Guns and Gun Violence." In *The Crime Drop in America*, ed. Alfred Blumstein and Joel Wallman, 45–96. Cambridge: Cambridge University Press.

Xu, Yili, Mora L. Fiedler, and Karl H. Flaming. 2005. "Discovering the Impact of Community Policing: The Broken Windows Thesis, Collective Efficacy, and Citizens' Judgment," *Journal of Research in Crime and Delinquency* 42, 147–186.

Zhao, Jihong, Matthew Scheider, and Quint Thurman. 2002. "The Effect of Police Presence on Public Fear Reduction and Satisfaction: A Review of the Literature," *The Justice Professional* 15, 273–299.

Zimring, Franklin, and Gordon Hawkins. 1997. *Crime Is Not the Problem: Lethal Violence in America*. New York: Oxford University Press.

Index

abandoned building problems, 215-218

accountability, 92, 96, 99 308

administrative hearings, 185-188

agency partnerships, 76-81, 316-317, 180-196

ANOV (Administrative Notice of Violation), 186-187

Asians, 31

beat meetings, 67-70
   activity at, 127-136
   agenda setting at, 142-145
   alternatives to, 170-174
   attendance rate, 112-118
   demographic representation, 154
   effectiveness of, 165-170
   interest representation by, 154-160
   mobilizing problem solving at, 147-148
   monitoring police at, 135-136, 145-147
   participants in, 111-112, 118-127
   views of police at, 160-165

broken windows, 178-179, 315-319

Burge, John, 273-274

code enforcement, 80. 181-188

collective efficacy, 172-173

community
   definition of, 139-141
   involvement of, 7, 65-70, 72, 96-97, 204-209, 308-312, 316-317

confidence in police, 44-47
   and demographics, 283-287
   and neighborhood conditions, 287-292
   and personal experience, 292-301
   trends in, 277-283, 319-322

community policing
   and crime, 235-236
   and fear, 236-237
   definition of, 5
   implementation of, 9-10, 56-57, 64-65, 81-92, 305-308

crime
   comparison to other cities, 268-270
   measuring, 237-239
   recording by police, 34-35
   trends in, 32-36, 239-247
   trends in concern about, 250-251

decentralization, 6, 58-65

Drug and Gang House Enforcement Section, 182-185

district advisory committees, 70

drugs, 38-41, 130

drugs, trends in concern about, 248-250

evaluation methods, 13-14, 16, 31-32, 103

fear reduction, 8

fear, trends in, 255-267

gang problems, 38-41, 132-133

gangs, trends in concern, 248-250

graffiti problems, 212-215

informal social control, 171-172

Latinos
  crime reporting by, 253-255
  definition of group, 25-27
  disorder trends among, 225-232
  immigration concerns of, 153-154
  trends in community among, 322-326
  trends in concern about crime among, 251-253
liquor regulation, 188-190
loitering, 219-220

marketing CAPS, 103-111

organizational involvement, 120-122

parking and traffic problems, 131-132
physical decay problems, 41-44, 131
physical decay problems and race, 218
physical decay problems, trends in, 211-218, 318-319
planning CAPS, 84-85
police, attitudes of, 47-49
police, history of problems with, 271-275
police, resistance to change among, 4
politics, 16-17, 63, 139-141, 173-174

problem solving, 7-8, 70-80, 97-98
problem solving and resident involvement, 196-209
program development, 54-56
prostitution, 200
public awareness, 104-106, 108-110
public drinking, 197-198, 221-223

race, 11, 15, 21, 31
  and confidence in police, 45-46, 275-277, 279-282
  and crime, 36-38
  and experience with police, 294-295
  and trends in concern and fear, 312 315
  and trends in crime, 242-246

school disruption, 223-224
school safety, 190-193
service requests, 77-79
Strategic Inspections Task Force, 181-182
social disorder problems, 41-44, 134-135, 224-225
social disorder problems, trends in, 219-224, 318-319

television, effects of, 122-124
Together We Can, 55
trash and junk problems, 216-217

zero tolerance, 50-51, 179-180